Thomas Cook

# EUROPEAN
# TRAVEL
# PHRASEBOOK

Thomas
Cook

Published by Thomas Cook Publishing
The Thomas Cook Group Ltd
PO Box 227
Peterborough PE3 8BQ
United Kingdom

ISBN 0 906273 69 2

Editor: Giovanna Battiston

Translations by UPS Translations, London and Transtec, Stamford,
Lincs
Typeset by Thomas Cook Publishing using Advent 3B2
Printed in Great Britain by Bell & Bain Ltd, Glasgow

# Contents

# Editor's Introduction

This phrasebook contains a selection of vocabulary essential to English-speaking tourists travelling across Europe through countries where English is not widely spoken.

Languages of countries where English *is* widely spoken or understood (such as the northern European destinations of the Netherlands, Norway, Sweden, Denmark and Finland) are not included; however, any attempts to speak a few words in the native tongue of these countries would no doubt be greatly appreciated. French, Italian and German, which are spoken in more than one European country, are included and between them they cover a large area of central Europe. The Eastern European languages that have been selected for this phrasebook are those spoken in countries with the greatest tourist appeal.

## Comment utiliser ce recueil d'expressions

Les expressions contenues dans chaque section de langue sont numérotées pour que les personnes ne parlant pas l'anglais puissent les retrouver facilement dans d'autres langues. Par exemple, une personne parlant le français et recherchant une traduction en polonais de l'expression 57 de la section Français (Où est la boutique hors-taxe?), la trouvera au numéro 57 de la section Polonais (Gdzie jest sklep wolno-cłowy?).

## Benutzung dieses Sprachführers

Die Redewendungen sind in den einzelnen Sprachen jeweils numeriert, sodaß man auch ohne Kenntnis der englischen Sprache leicht die entsprechende Übersetzung finden kann.

# EDITOR'S INTRODUCTION

Zum Beispiel: Jemand mit deutscher Muttersprache schlägt im deutschen Teil die Redewendung Nummer 57 nach (Wo ist der zollfreie Laden?), und weiß dann, daß die Redewendung mit der Nummer 57 im polnischen Teil die genaue Übersetzung wiedergibt (Gdzie jest sklep wolno-cłowy?).

## Empleo del libro de frases

La sección correspondiente a cada idioma comprende frases numeradas que remiten al usuario a otros idiomas y facilitan el manejo del libro por parte de quienes no sepan inglés. Por ejemplo, los hispanohablantes que quieran saber el equivalente polaco de la frase numero 57 (¿Dónde está el duty free?) no tienen más que ver la frase del mismo número en la sección de ese idioma (Gdzie jest sklep wolno-cłowy?), que denota lo mismo exactamente.

## Como Usar este Livro de Frases

As frases em cada secção de idioma numeradas de modo a que leitores de língua não-inglesa possam encontrar facilmente referências cruzadas. Por exemplo, um leitor de língua Portuguesa pode procurar a frase 57 na secção portuguesa (Onde é a loja duty-free?) e sabe que a frase 57 na secção polaca (Gdzie jest wolno-clowy?) é uma tradução exacta da mesma.

## Come utilizzare questo frasario

Le frasi contenute nella sezione di ciascuna lingua sono numerate in modo che chi non parla inglese possa consultarle facilmente. Ad esempio una persona di lingua italiana può cercare la frase 57 nella sezione italiana (Dov'è il duty free?) e sapere che la frase 57 nella sezione polacca (Gdzie jest sklep wolno-cłowy?) ne è l'esatta traduzione.

Czech — Language(s) found in this book.
*English* — Most useful second language.

TURKEY — Turkish
UKRAINE
ESTONIA
LATVIA
LITHUANIA
ROMANIA — Romanian
BULGARIA — Bulgarian
GREECE — Greek
SWEDEN — *English*
POLAND — Polish
SLOVAKIA — Czech
HUNGARY — Hungarian
YUGO-SLAVIA
ALBANIA
CZECH REPUBLIC — Czech
AUSTRIA — German
BOSNIA
NORWAY — *English*
DENMARK — *English*
GERMANY — German
SLOVENIA
CROATIA
ITALY — Italian
NETHERLANDS — *English*
BELGIUM — French, *English*
LUXEMBOURG — French
SWITZERLAND — French, German, Italian
TUNISIA — French
UNITED KINGDOM
FRANCE — French
ALGERIA — French
REPUBLIC OF IRELAND
SPAIN — Spanish
PORTUGAL — Portuguese
MOROCCO — French, Spanish

# Introduction

Bulgarian is a Slavic language, and like Russian, to which it is distantly related, it uses Cyrillic script, which is a development of the Greek alphabet. Russian itself is widely understood in Bulgaria – English and German are the other two languages which may be spoken to a degree by some people in larger cities, especially in establishments catering to tourists. As with Greek, body language can be confusing if you are unaware that Bulgarians traditionally nod their heads up and down to signify no and shake them from side to side to mean yes. As Western influences increase, you can expect younger and westernised Bulgarians to begin adopting the opposite conventions, which will increase confusion.

## Addresses for travel and tourist information

**UK:** *Balkan Holidays (National Tourist Office)*, Sofia House, 19 Conduit St, London W1R 9TD; tel: (0171) 491 4499.
**USA:** *Balkan Holidays (National Tourist Office)*, 161 East 86th St, New York, NY 10028; tel: (212) 573-5530 or 722-1110.

## ESSENTIALS

### Alphabet

| | |
|---|---|
| А *ah* | Б *bah* |
| В *vah* | Г *gah* |
| Д *dah* | Е *eh* |
| Ж *zhe* | З *ze* |
| И *ee* | Й *iy* |
| К *kah* | Л *lah* |
| М *meh* | Н *neh* |
| О *o* | П *pe* |
| Р *re* | С *ce* |
| Т *te* | У *ou* |
| Ф *fa* | Х *ha* |
| Ц *tsa* | Ч *ch* |
| Ш *sh* | Щ *shch* |
| Ъ *eu* | Ь *y* |
| Ю *yu* | Я *ya* |

## Basic Words and Phrases

1. **Yes**
   Да
   *Da*

   **No**
   Не
   *Ne*

2. **Please**
   Моля
   *Molya*

   **Thank you**
   Благодаря Ви
   *Blagodarya vi*

3. **That's O.K.**
   Няма проблеми
   *Nyama problemi*

   **Perhaps**
   Може би
   *Mozhe bi*

4. **To**
   До
   *Do*

   **From**
   От
   *Ot*

5. **Here**
   Тук
   *Took*

   **There**
   Там
   *Tam*

6. **None**
   Нищо
   *Nishto*

   **Also**
   Също
   *Sushto*

7. **How**
   Как
   *Kak*

   **When**
   Кога
   *Koga*

8. **What**
   какво
   *kakvo*

   **Why**
   Защо
   *Zashto*

9. **I don't understand.**
   Не разбирам.
   *Ne razbiram.*

10. **I don't speak Bulgarian.**
    Не говоря български.
    *Ne govorya bulgarski.*

11. **Do you speak English?**
    Говорите ли английски?
    *Govorite li angliyski?*

8

12 **Can you please write it down?**
Може ли да го напишете,
моля?
*Mozhe li da go napishete, molya?*

13 **Can you please speak more slowly?**
Може ли да говорите по-
бавно, моля?
*Mozhe li da govorite po-bavno, molya?*

14 **How much does it/this cost?**
Колко струва това?
*Kolko stroova tova?*

## Days

15 **Monday**          **Tuesday**
Понеделник       Вторник
*Ponedelnik*        *Ftornik*

16 **Wednesday**       **Thursday**
Сряда            Четвъртък
*Sryada*            *Chetvurtuk*

17 **Friday**            **Saturday**
Петък            Събота
*Petuk*             *Subota*

18 **Sunday**           **Morning**
Неделя           Сутрин
*Nedelya*           *Sootrin*

19 **Afternoon**        **Evening**
Следобед         Вечер
*Sletobet*          *Vecher*

20 **Night**             **Week**
Нощ              Седмица
*Nosht*             *Sedmitsa*

21 **Yesterday**        **Tomorrow**
Вчера            Утре
*Fchera*            *Ootre*

## Numbers

22 **Zero**              **One**
Нула             Едно
*Noola*             *Edno*

23 **Two**               **Three**
Две              Три
*Dve*               *Tri*

24 **Four**              **Five**
Четири           Пет
*Chetiri*           *Pet*

25 **Six**               **Seven**
Шест             Седем
*Shest*             *Sedem*

26 **Eight**             **Nine**
Осем             Девет
*Osem*              *Devet*

27 **Ten**               **Eleven**
Десет            Единадесет
*Deset*             *Edinadeset*

28 **Twelve**            **Thirteen**
Дванадесет       Тринадесет
*Dvanadeset*        *Trinadeset*

29 **Fourteen**          **Fifteen**
Четиринадесет Петнадесет
*Chetirinadeset*    *Petnadeset*

30 **Sixteen**           **Seventeen**
Шестнадесет      Седемнадесет
*Shestnadeset*      *Sedemnadeset*

31 **Eighteen**          **Nineteen**
Осемнадесет      Деветнадесет
*Osemnadeset*       *Devetnadeset*

**32 Twenty**
Двадесет
*Dvadeset*

**Twenty-one**
Двадесет и едно
*Dvadeset i edno*

**33 Twenty-two**
Двадесет и две
*Dvadeset i dve*

**Thirty**
Тридесет
*Trideset*

**34 Forty**
Четиридесет
*Chetirideset*

**Fifty**
Петдесет
*Petdeset*

**35 Sixty**
Шестдесет
*Shestdeset*

**Seventy**
Седемдесет
*Sedemdeset*

**36 Eighty**
Осемдесет
*Osemdeset*

**Ninety**
Деветдесет
*Devetdeset*

**37 One hundred**
Сто
*Sto*

**Five hundred**
Пет стотин
*Petstotin*

**38 One thousand**
Хиляда
*Hilyada*

**One million**
Един милион
*Edin milion*

## Time

**39 9.00**
Точно девет часа
*Tochno devet chasa*

**40 9.05**
Девет часа и пет минути
*Devet chasa i pet minooti*

**41 9.10**
Девет часа и десет минути
*Devet chasa i deset minooti*

**42 9.15**
Девет часа и петнадесет минути
*Devet chasa i petnadeset minooti*

**43 9.20**
Девет часа и двадесет минути
*Devet chasa i dvadeset minooti*

**44 9.25**
Девет часа и двадесет и пет минути
*Devet chasa dvadeset i pet minooti*

**45 9.30**
Девет часа и тридесет минути
*Devet chasa i trideset minooti*

**46 9.35**
Девет часа и тридесет и пет минути
*Devet chasa i trideset i pet minooti*

**47 9.40**
Девет часа и четиридесет минути
*Devet chasa i chetirideset minooti*

**48 9.45**
Девет часа и четиридесет и пет минути
*Devet chasa i chetirideset i pet minooti*

**49 9.50**
Девет часа и петдесет минути
*Devet chasa i petdeset minooti*

**50 9.55**
Девет часа и петдесет и пет минути
*Devet chasa i petdeset i pet minooti*

**51 12.00/Midday/Midnight**

Точно дванадесет часа/
обед/полунощ
*Tochno dvanadeset chasa/Obet/
Poloonosht.*

**52** **What time is it?**
Колко е часът?
*Kolko e chasa?*

**53** **It is . . .**
Часът е . . .
*Chasa e . . .*

## ARRIVING AND DEPARTING

### Airport

**54** **Excuse me, where is the
check-in desk for . . . airline?**
Извинявайте, къде е
гишето за авиолиния . . ?
*Izvinyavayte, kude e gisheto za
avioliniya . . ?*

**55** **What is the boarding gate/
time for my flight?**
Къде е изходът за (В колко
часа е) моят полет?
*Kude e izhodut za (F kolko chasa e)
moyat polet?*

**56** **How long is the delay likely
to be?**
Колко може да продължи
закъснението?
*Kolko mozhe da produlzhi
zakusnenieto?*

**57** **Where is the duty-free shop?**
Къде е безмитният
магазин?
*Kude e bezmitniyat magazin?*

**58** **Which way is the baggage
reclaim?**
Къде се получава багажът?
*Kude se poloochava bagazhut?*

**59** **Where can I get the bus to
the city centre?**
Къде мога да взема
автобус до центъра на
града?
*Kude moga da vzema aftoboos do
tsentura na grada?*

### Train Station

**60** **Where is the ticket office/
information desk?**
Къде е касата/
информацията?
*Kude e kasata/informatsiyata?*

**61** **Which platform does the
train to . . . depart from?**
От кой перон тръгва
влакът за . . ?
*Ot koy peron trugva vlaka za . . ?*

**62** **Where is platform . . ?**
Къде е . . . перон?
*Kude e . . . peron?*

**63** **When is the next train to . . ?**
Кога е следващият
влак за . . ?
*Koga e sledvashtiya vlak za . . ?*

**64** **Is there a later train to . . ?**
Има ли по-късен влак
за . . ?
*Ima li po-kusen vlak za . . ?*

B
U
L
G
A
R
I
A
N

52
↕
64

**B U L G A R I A N**

65
↕
84

## Port

65 **How do I get to the port?**
Как да стигна до
пристанището?
*Kak da stigna do pristanishteto?*

66 **When is the next sailing to . . ?**
Кога е следващият рейс
за . . ?
*Koga e sledvashtiya reys za . . ?*

67 **Can I catch an earlier ferry
with this ticket?**
Мога ли да се кача на по-
ранен ферибот с този
билет?
*Moga li da se kacha na po-ranen
feribot s tozi bilet?*

## Notices and Signs

68 **Вагон-ресторант**
*Vagon-restorant*
Buffet (Dining) Car

69 **Автобус**
*Aftoboos*
Bus

70 **Питейна/непитейна вода**
*Piteyna/Nepiteyna voda*
Drinking/Non-drinking water

71 **Вход**
*Vhot*
Entrance

72 **Изход**
*Ishot*
Exit

73 **Информация**
*Informatsiya*

Information

74 **Гардероб за багаж**
*Garderop za bagash*
Left Luggage (Baggage Claim)

75 **Сейфове за багаж**
*Seyfove za bagash*
Luggage Lockers

76 **Поща**
*Poshta*
Post Office

77 **Перон**
*Peron*
Platform

78 **Железопътна гара**
*Zhelezoputna gara*
Railway (Railroad) Station

79 **Аерогара/Летище**
*Aerogara/Letishte*
Airport

80 **Пристанище**
*Pristanishte*
Port

81 **Ресторант**
*Restorant*
Restaurant

82 **Пушачи/непушачи**
*Pooshachi/Nepooshachi*
Smoking/Non-smoking

83 **Телефон**
*Telefon*
Telephone

84 **Билетна каса**
*Biletna kasa*
Ticket Office

85 **Гише за регистриране за полета/Чек-ин**
*Gishe za registrirane za poleta/ Check-in*
Check-in Desk

86 **Разписание**
*Raspisanie*
Timetable (Schedule)

87 **Тоалетна**
*Toaletna*
Toilets (Restrooms)

88 **Мъже**
*Muzhe*
Gentlemen

89 **Жени**
*Zheni*
Ladies'

90 **Трамвай**
*Tramvay*
Tram (Streetcar)

91 **Метро**
*Metro*
Underground (Subway)

92 **Чакалня**
*Chakalnya*
Waiting Room

## Buying a ticket

93 **I would like a first-class/ second-class single (one-way)/return (round-trip) ticket to . . .**
Искам билет първа/втора класа/ведна посока за отиване и връщане ндо . . .
*Iskam bilet purva/ftora clasa/*

*fedna posoka za otivane i vrushtane ndo . . .*

94 **Is my rail pass valid on this train/ferry/bus?**
Картата ми за пътуване с влак важи ли за този влак/ ферибот/автобус?
*Kartata mi za putoovane s vlak vazhi li za tozi vlak/feribot/ aftoboos?*

95 **I would like an aisle/window seat.**
Искам място от вътрешната страна/до прозореца.
*Iskam myasto ot vutreshnata strana/do prozoretsa.*

96 **No smoking/smoking, please.**
Не пушете/пушете, моля.
*Ne pooshete/pooshete, molya.*

97 **We would like to sit together.**
Искаме да седим заедно.
*Iskame da sedim zaedno.*

98 **I would like to make a seat reservation.**
Искам да запазя място.
*Iskam zapazeno myasto.*

99 **I would like to reserve a couchette/sleeper for one person/two people/my family.**
Искам място в кушет/ спален вагон за един/ двама/за семейството ми.
*Iskam myasto f kooshet/spalen vagon za edin/dvama/za semeystvoto mi.*

**100** I would like to reserve a cabin.
Искам да ре ервирам кабина/каюта.
*Iskam da rezerviram kabina/kayoota.*

## Timetables (Schedules)

**101** Пристига
*Pristiga*
Arrive

**102** Спира На
*Spira na*
Calls (Stops) at

**103** Хранене
*Hranene*
Catering Service

**104** Прехвърляне
*Prehvurlyane na*
Change at

**105** Връзка
*Vruska*
Connection

**106** Дневно
*Dnevno*
Daily

**107** На всеки четиридесет минути
*Na vseki chetirideset minooti*
Every 40 Minutes

**108** Първа класа
*Purva clasa*
First-class

**109** Всеки час
*Vseki chas*
Hourly

**110** Препоръчват се запазени места
*Preporuchvat se zapazeni mesta*
Seat reservations are recommended

**111** Втора класа
*Ftora clasa*
Second-class

**112** Допълнително заплащане
*Dopulnitelno zaplashtane*
Supplement Payable

**113** През
*Pres*
Via

## Luggage

**114** How much will it cost to send (ship) my luggage in advance?
Колко струва да изпратя багажа си предварително?
*Kolko stroova da ispratya bagazha si predvaritelno?*

**115** Where is the left luggage (baggage claim) office?
Къде е гардеробът за багаж?
*Kude e garderoba za bagash?*

**116** What time do you open/close?
Кога отваряте/затваряте?
*Koga otvaryate/zatvaryate?*

**117** Where are the luggage trolleys (carts)?
Къде са количките за багаж?
*Kude sa kolichkite za bagash?*

**B
U
L
G
A
R
I
A
N**

**118
↕
130**

### [118] Where are the lockers?
Къде са сейфовете за багаж?
*Kude sa seyfovete za bagash?*

### [119] I have lost my locker key.
Загубих ключа за сейфа.
*Zagoobih klyoocha za seyfa.*

## On Board

### [120] Is this seat free?
Свободно ли е това място?
*Svobodno li e tova myasto?*

### [121] Excuse me, you are sitting in my reserved seat.
Извинете, седите на моето запазено място.
*Izinete, sedite na moeto zapazeno myasto.*

### [122] Which station is this?
Коя е тази гара?
*Koya e tazi gara?*

### [123] What time is this train/bus/ferry/flight due to arrive/depart?
Кога трябва да пристигне/замине този влак/автобус/ферибот/полет?
*Koga tryabva da pristigne/zamine tozi vlak/aftoboos/feribot/polet?*

### [124] Will you wake me just before we arrive?
Можете ли да ме събудите малко преди да пристигнем?
*Mozhete li da me suboodite malko predi da pristignem?*

## Customs and Passports

### [125] Passports, please!
Паспортите, моля!
*Pasportite, molya.*

### [126] I have nothing/wine/spirits (alcohol)/tobacco to declare.
Нямам нищо/вино/концентрати/цигари да декларирам.
*Nyamam nishto/vino/kontsentrati/tsigari da deklariram.*

### [127] I shall be staying for . . . days/weeks/months.
Ще пребивавам . . .дни/седмици/месеци.
*Shte prebivavam . . . dni/sedmitsi/mesetsi.*

## AT THE TOURIST OFFICE

### [128] Do you have a map of the town/area?
Имате ли карта на града/областта?
*Imate li karta na grada/oblasta?*

### [129] Can I reserve accommodation here?
Мога ли да резервирам стая тук?
*Moga li da rezerviram staya took?*

### [130] Do you have a list of accommodation?
Имате ли списък на местата за нощуване?
*Imate li spisuk na mestata za noshtoovane?*

15

# ACCOMMODATION

## ACCOMMODATION

### Hotels

**131** I have a reservation in the name of . . .
Имам резервация на името на . . .
*Imam rezervatsiya na imeto na . . .*

**132** I wrote to/faxed/telephoned you last month/last week in . . .
Аз ви писах/телефонирах/изпратих факс миналия месец/миналата седмица в . . .
*Az vi pissah/telefonirah/izpratih faks minaliya mesets/minalata sedmitsa f . . .*

**133** Do you have any rooms free?
Имате ли свободни стаи?
*Imate li svobodni stayi?*

**134** I would like to reserve a single/double room with/without bath/shower.
Искам да резервирам единична/двойна стая с/без баня/душ.
*Iskam da rezerviram edinichna/dvoyna staya s/bes banya/doosh.*

**135** I would like bed and breakfast/(room and) half board/(room and) full board.
Искам стая със закуска/половин пансион/пълен пасион.

*Iskam staya sus zakooska/polovin pansion/pulen pansion.*

**136** How much is it per night?
Колко е за една нощ?
*Kolko e za edna nosht?*

**137** Is breakfast included?
Включва ли се закуска?
*Vklyoochva li se zakooska?*

**138** May I see the room?
Може ли да видя стаята?
*Mozhe li da vidya stayata?*

**139** Do you have any cheaper rooms?
Имате ли по-евтини стаи?
*Imate li po-eftini stai?*

**140** I would like to take the room.
Искам да наема стаята.
*Iskam da naema stayata.*

**141** I would like to stay for . . . nights.
Искам да пребивавам . . . дни.
*Iskam da prebivavam . . . dni.*

**142** The shower/light/tap doesn't work.
Душът/осветлението/кранът не работи.
*Dooshut/osvetlenieto/kranut ne raboti.*

**143** At what time/where is breakfast served?
Кога/къде сервирате закуска?
*Koga/kude servirate zakooska?*

16

**144** What time do I have to check-out?

Кога трябва да се отпиша?

*Koga tryabva da se otpisha?*

**145** Can I have the key to room no . . ?

Може ли да ми дадете ключа за стая номер . . ?

*Mozhe li da mi dadete klyucha za staya nomer . . ?*

**146** My room number is . . .

Номерът на стаята ми е . . .

*Nomera na stayata mi e . . .*

**147** Do you accept travellers' cheques/Eurocheques/credit cards?

Приемате ли туристически чекове/еврочекове/ кредитни карти?

*Priemate li tooristicheski chekove/ evrochekove/krediíni karti?*

**148** May I have the bill, please?

Може ли сметката, моля?

*Mozhe li smetkata, molya?*

**149** Excuse me, I think there is a mistake in this bill.

Извинявайте, мисля, че в сметката ми има грешка.

*Izvinyavaite, mislya, che f smetkata mi ima greshka.*

## Youth Hostels

**150** How much is a dormitory bed per night?

Колко е легло в обща стая?

*Kolko e leglo f opshta staya?*

**151** I am/am not an HI member.

Аз съм/не съм IУHA член.

*As cum/ne sum IYHA chlen.*

**152** May I use my own sleeping bag?

Мога ли да ползвам спалния си чувал?

*Moga li da polzvam spalniya si chooval?*

**153** What time do you lock the doors at night?

Кога заключвате през ноща?

*Koga zaklyoochvate pres noshta?*

## Camping

**154** May I camp here for the night/two nights?

Мога ли да прекарам нощa/две нощи?

*Moga li da prekaram noshta/dve noshti?*

**155** Where can I pitch my tent?

Къде да сложа палатката си?

*Kude da slozha palatkata si?*

**156** How much does it cost for one night/one week?

Колко струва за една нощ/ една седмица?

*Kolko srtoova za edna nosht/edna sedmitsa?*

**157** Where can we park our caravan?

Къде може да паркираме караваната си?

*Kude mozhe da parkirame karavanata si?*

**158** Where are the washing facilities?

Къде е умивалнята?

*Kude e oomivalnyata?*

**159** Is there a restaurant/ supermarket/swimming pool on site/nearby?

Има ли ресторант/ супермаркет/басейн тук/ наоколо?

*Ima li restorant/supermarket/ baseyn took/naokolo?*

**160** Do you have a safety deposit box?

Имате ли сейф?

*Imate li seyf?*

## EATING AND DRINKING

### Cafés and Bars

**161** I would like a cup of/two cups of/another coffee/tea.

Искам чаша/две чаши/ още едно кафе/чай.

*Iskam chaha/dve chashi/oshte edno kafe/chay.*

**162** With/without milk/sugar.

С/без мляко/захар.

*S/bes mlyako/zahar.*

**163** I would like a bottle/glass/ two glasses of mineral water/ red wine/white wine, please

Искам бутилка/чаша/две чаши минерална вода/ червено вино/бяло вино, моля.

*Iskam bootilka/chasha/dve chashi mineralna voda/cherveno vino/ byalo vino, molya.*

**164** I would like a beer/two beers, please.

Искам една бира/две бири, моля.

*Iskam edna bira/dve biri, molya.*

**165** May I have some ice?

Ли малко лед?

*Li malko led?*

**166** Do you have any matches/ cigarettes/cigars?

Имате ли кибрит/цигари/ пури?

*Imate li kibrit/tsigari/poori?*

### Restaurants

**167** Can you recommend a good/ inexpensive restaurant in this area?

Препоръчайте ми добър/ евтин ресторант наоколо?

*Preporuchayte mi dobur/eftin restorant naokolo?*

**168** I would like a table for . . . people.

Искам маса за . . . човека.

*Iskam masa za . . . choveka.*

169 Do you have a non-smoking area?
Имате ли място за непушачи?
*Imate li myasto za nepooshachi?*

170 Waiter/Waitress!
Келнер!
*Kelner!*

171 Do you have a set menu/children's menu/wine list?
Имате ли меню за деня/детско меню/листа за вината?
*Imate li menyoo za denya/detsko menyoo/lista za vinata?*

172 Do you have any vegetarian dishes, please?
Имате ли нещо вегетарианско, моля?
*Imate li neshto vegetariyansko, molya?*

173 Are there any local specialities?
Има ли някакви местни специалитети?
*Ima li nyakakvi mestni spetsialiteti?*

174 Are vegetables included?
Това включва ли гарнитура/зеленчуци?
*Tova fklyuchva li garnitoora/zelenchootsi?*

175 Could I have it well-cooked/medium/rare please?
Искам го добре сготвено/средно/ал англе, моля

*Iskam go dobre sgotveno/sredno/al angle, molya.*

176 What does this dish consist of?
Какво има в яденето?
*Kakvo ima f yadeneto?*

177 I would like the set menu, please.
Искам менюто за деня, моля.
*Iskam menyooto za denya, molya.*

178 We have not been served yet.
Още не са ни сервирали.
*Oshte ne sa ni servirali.*

179 Excuse me, this is not what I ordered.
Извинявайте, аз не поръчах това.
*Izvinyavayte, az ne poruchah tova.*

180 May I have some/some more bread/water/coffe/tea?
Може ли да ми дадете/още хляб/вода/кафе/чай?
*Mozhe li da mi dadete/oshte hlyap/voda/kafe/chay?*

181 May I have the bill, please?
Може ли сметката, моля?
*Mozhe li smetkata, molya?*

182 Does this bill include service?
Обслужването включва ли се в сметката?
*Opsloozhvaneto fklyoochva li se f smetkata?*

183 Do you accept travellers'
cheques (travelers' checks)/
Eurocheques/MasterCard/US
dollars?
Приемате ли туристически
чекове/еврочекове/мастер
кард/долари?
*Priemate li tooristicheski chekove/
Evrochekove/MasterCard/dolari?*

184 Can I have a receipt, please?
Може ли да ми дадете
разписка/фактура, моля?
*Mozhe li da mi dadete razpiska/
faktoora, molya?*

185 Where is the toilet
(restroom), please?
Извинете, къде е
тоалетната?
*Izvinete, kude e toaletnata?*

## On the Menu

186 First courses
Предястия
*Predyastiya*

187 Soups
Супи
*Soopi*

188 Main courses
Главни/втори ястия
*Glavni/ftori yastiya*

189 Fish dishes
Рибни ястия
*Ribni yastiya*

190 Meat dishes
Месни ястия
*Mesni yastiya*

191 Vegetarian dishes
Вегетариански ястия
*Vegetarianski yastiya*

192 Cheese
Сирене
*Sirene*

193 Desserts
Десерти
*Deserti*

194 Specialities
Специалитети
*Spetsialiteti*

## GETTING AROUND

### Public Transport

195 Where is the bus stop/coach
station/nearest metro
(subway) station?
Къде е автобусната
спирка/автогарата/най-
близката гара на метрото?
*Kude e aftoboosnata spirka/
aftogarata/nay-bliskata gara na
metroto?*

196 When is the next/last bus
to . . ?
Кога е следващият/
последният автобус за . . ?
*Koga e sledvashtiya/posledniya
aftoboos za . . ?*

197 How much is the fare to the
city centre (downtown)/
railway (railroad) station/
airport?

Колко е билетът до
центъра/гарата/летището?
*Kolko e bileta do tsentura/garata/
letishteto?*

[198] Will you tell me when to get
off?
Бихте ли ми казали кога
да сляза?
*Bihte li mi kazali koga da slyaza?*

[199] Does this bus go to . . ?
Този автобус отива ли
до . . ?
*Tozi aftoboos otiva li do . . ?*

[200] Which number bus goes to . . ?
Кой номер автобус отива
до?
*Koy nomer aftoboos otiva do . . ?*

[201] May I have a single (one
way)/return (round trip)/day
ticket/book of tickets?
Искам билет за един
посока/билет за отиване и
връщане/дневна карта/
кочан билети.
*Iskam bilet f edna posoka/bilet za
otivane i vrushtane/dnevna karta/
kochan bileti?*

## Taxis

[202] I would like to go to . . . How
much will it cost?
Искам да отида до . . . Колко
ще струва?
*Iskam da otida do . . . Kolko shte
stroova?*

[203] Please stop here.
Спрете тук, моля.
*Sprete took, molya.*

[204] I would like to order a taxi
today/tomorrow at 2pm to
go from . . . to . . .
Искам да поръчам такси
за днес/утре в 14 часа
от . . . до . . .
*Iskam da porucham taksi za dnes/
ootre f 14 chasa ot . . . do . . .*

## Asking the Way

[205] Excuse me, do you speak
English?
Извинете, говорите ли
английски?
*Izvinete, govorite li angliyski?*

[206] Excuse me, is this the right
way to . . ?
Извинявайте, това ли е
пътят за . . ?
*Izvinyavayte, tova li e putyat za . . .*

[207] . . . the cathedral/the tourist
information office/the castle/
the old town
. . . катедралата/
туристическата
информация/замъкът/
старият град?
*. . . katedralata/tooristicheskata
informatsiya/zamukut/stariyat
grat?*

21

**208** Can you tell me the way to the railway (railroad) station/bus station/taxi rank (stand)/city centre (downtown)/beach?
Можете ли да ми кажете къде е гарата/автогарата/колонката за такситa/центъра/плажа?
*Mozhete li da mi kazhete kude e garata/aftogarata/kolonkata za taksita/tsentura/plazha?*

**209** First/second/left/right/straight ahead.
Първата/втората/наляво/надясно/направо.
*Purvata/ftorata/nalyavo/nadyasno/napravo.*

**210** Where is the nearest police station/post office?
Къде е най-близкият полицейски участък/най-близката поща?
*Kude e nay-bliskiya politseyski oochastuk/nay-bliskata poshta?*

**211** Is it far?
Далече ли е?
*Dalache li e?*

**212** Do I need to take a taxi/catch a bus?
Трябва ли да взема такси/автобус?
*Tryabva li da vzema taksi/aftobus?*

**213** Can you point to it on my map?
Покажете ми го на картата, моля?
*Pokazhete mi go na kartata, molya?*

**214** Thank you for your help.
Благодаря Ви за помощта.
*Blagodarya vi za pomoshta.*

## SIGHTSEEING

**215** Where is the Tourist Information Office?
Къде е туристическата информация?
*Kude e tooristicheskata informatsiya?*

**216** Where is the cathedral/church/museum?
Къде е катедралата/църквата/музеят?
*Kude e katedralata/tsurkvata/moozeya?*

**217** How much is the entrance (admission) charge?
Колко е входът?
*Kolko e fhoda?*

**218** Is there a discount for children/students/senior citizens?
Има ли намаление за деца/студенти/пенсионери?
*Ima li namalenie za detsa/stoodenti/pensioneri?*

**219** What time does the next guided tour start?
Кога е следващата обиколка с екскурзовод?
*Koga e sledvashtata obikolka s ekskoorzovod?*

**220** One/two adults/children, please.
Един/двама възрастни/деца, моля.
*Edin/dvama vuztrastni/detsa, molya.*

**221** May I take photographs here?
Мога ли да правя снимки тук?
*Moga li da pravya snimki took?*

## ENTERTAINMENT

**222** Can you recommend a good bar/nightclub?
Препоръчайте ми добър бар/нощен клуб?
*Preporuchayte mi dobur bar/noshten cloop?*

**223** Do you know what is on at the cinema (playing at the movies)/theatre at the moment?
Знаете ли какво дават в киното/театъра в момента?
*Znaete li kakvo davat f kinoto/teatura f momenta?*

**224** I would like to book (purchase) . . . tickets for the matinée/evening performance on Monday.
Искам да запазя (купя). . . билети за сутрешното/вечерното представление в понеделник.
*Iskam da zapazya koopya . . . bileti za sootreshnoto/vechernoto predstavlenie f ponedelnik.*

**225** What time does the film/performance start?
Кога започва филмът/представлението?
*Koga zapochva filma/predstavlenieto?*

## MEETING PEOPLE

**226** Hello/Goodbye.
Здравейте/Довиждане.
*Zdraveyte/Dovizhdane.*

**227** Good morning/good afternoon/good evening/goodnight.
Добро утро/добър ден/добър вечер/лека нощ.
*Dobro ootro/dubur den/dobur vecher/leka nosht.*

**228** Pleased to meet you.
Радвам се да се запозная с вас.
*Radvam se da se zapoznaya s vas.*

**229** How are you?
Как сте?
*Kak ste?*

230 Fine, thank you. And you?
Благодаря, добре. А Вие?
*Blagodarya, dobre. A Vie?*

231 My name is . . .
Аз се казвам . . .
*Az se kazvam . . .*

232 This is my friend/boyfriend/
girlfriend/husband/wife/
brother/sister.
Това е приятелят ми/
приятелката ми/съпругът
ми/съпругата ми/брат ми/
сестра ми.
*Tova e priyatelya mi/priyatelkata
mi/suprooga mi/suproogata mi/
brat mi/sestra mi.*

233 Where are you travelling to?
За къде пътувате?
*Za kude putoovate?*

234 I am/we are going to . . .
Аз/ние отивам/е до . . .
*As/nie otivam/e do . . .*

235 How long are you travelling
for?
За колко дълго пътувате.?
*Za kolko dulgo putoovate?*

236 Where do you come from?
От къде сте?
*Ot kude ste?*

237 I am/we are from . . .
Аз/ ние съм/сме от . . .
*As/nie sum/sme ot . . .*

238 We're on holiday.
Ние сме на почивка.
*Nie sme na pochifka.*

239 This is our first visit here.
За първи път сме тук.
*Za purvi put sme took.*

240 Would you like/May I have a
cigarette?
Искате ли/може ли
цигара?
*Iskate li/Mozhe li tsigara?*

241 I am sorry, but I do not
understand.
Извинете, не разбирам.
*Izvinete, ne razbiram.*

242 Please speak slowly.
Моля, говорете бавно.
*Molya, govorete bavno.*

243 Do you mind if I smoke?
Мога ли да пуша?
*Moga li da poosha?*

244 Do you have a light?
Имате ли огънче?
*Imate li ogunche?*

245 I am waiting for my husband/
wife/boyfriend/girlfriend.
Чакам мъжа/жена/
приятеля/приятелката си.
*Chakam muzhu/zhena/
priyatelya/priyatelkata si.*

## TRAVELLING WITH CHILDREN

246 Do you have a high chair/
baby-sitting service/cot?
Имате ли детски стол/
детски гледачки/детско
легло?
*Imate li detski stol/detski
gledachki/detsko leglo?*

**247** Where is the nursery/
playroom?
Къде е занималнята/
детската стая?
*Kude e zanimalnyata/detskata
staya?*

**248** Where can I warm the baby's
bottle?
Къде мога да стопля
бебешката бутилка?
*Kude moga da stoplya bebeshkata
bootilka?*

## COMMUNICATIONS

### Post

**249** How much will it cost to send
a letter/postcard/this
package to Britain/Ireland/
America/Canada/Australia/
New Zealand?
Колко струва да изпратя
писмо/картичка/този
колет до Англия/
Ирландия/Америка/
Канада/Австралия/Нова
Зеландия?
*Kolko stroova da ispratya pismo/
kartichka/tozi kolet do Angliya/
Irlandiya/Amerika/Kanada/
Afstraliya/Nova Zelandiya?*

**250** I would like one stamp/two
stamps.
Искам една марка/две
марки.
*Iskam edna marka/dve marki.*

**251** I'd like . . . stamps for
postcards to send abroad,
please.
Искам . . . марки за
изпращане на картички в
чужбина, моля.
*Iskam . . . marki za izprashtane na
kartichki f choozhbina, molya.*

## Phones

**252** I would like to make a
telephone call/reverse the
charges to (make a collect call
to) . . .
Искам да се обадя/за
тяхна сметка до . . .
*Iskam da se obadya/za tyahna
smetka do . . .*

**253** Which coins do I need for the
telephone?
Какви монети ми трябват
за телефон?
*Kakvi moneti mi tryabvat za
telefon?*

**254** The line is engaged (busy).
Линията е заета.
*Liniyata e zaeta.*

**255** The number is . . .
Номерът е . . .
*Nomera e . . .*

**256** Hello, this is . . .
Ало, обажда се . . .
*Allo, obazhda se . . .*

**257** May I speak to . . ?
Мога ли да говоря с . . ?
*Moga li da govorya s . . ?*

25

**B
U
L
G
A
R
I
A
N**

**258
↕
273**

²⁵⁸ He/She is not in at the moment. Can you call back?
Той/тя не е тук в момента. Може ли да се обадите пак?
*Toy/tya ne e took f momenta. Mozhe li da se obadite pak?*

## MONEY

²⁵⁹ I would like to change these travellers' cheques (travelers' checks)/this currency/this Eurocheque.
Искам да обменя тези туристически чекове/тази валута/този Еврочек.
*Iskam da obmenya tezi tooristicheski chekove/tazi valuta/tozi Evrochek.*

²⁶⁰ How much commission do you charge? (What is the service charge?)
Колко е комисионната?
*Kolko e komisionnata?*

²⁶¹ Can I obtain money with my MasterCard?
Мога ли да използвам мастер кард?
*Moga li da ispolzvam MasterCard?*

## SHOPPING

### Names of Shops and Departments

²⁶² Книжарница/Книжарски стоки
*Knizharnitsa/Knizharski stoki*
Bookshop/Stationery

²⁶³ Бижутерия/Подаръци
*Bizhooteriya/Podarutsi*
Jeweller's/Gifts

²⁶⁴ Обувки
*Oboofki*
Shoes

²⁶⁵ Железария
*Zhelezariya*
Hardware

²⁶⁶ Антики
*Antiki*
Antiques

²⁶⁷ Фризьорски/бръснарски салон
*Frizyorski/Brusnarski salon*
Hairdressers (men's)/(women's

²⁶⁸ Будка/щанд за цигари
*Bootka/Shtant za tsigari*
Tobacconist

²⁶⁹ Хлебарница
*Hlebarnitsa*
Baker's

²⁷⁰ Супермаркет
*Soopermarket*
Supermarket

²⁷¹ Фотомагазин
*Fotomagazin*
Photoshop

²⁷² Играчки
*Igrachki*
Toys

²⁷³ Туристическа агенция
*Tooristicheska agentsiya*
Travel Agent

²⁷⁴ **Парфюмерия/Тоалетни принадлежности**
*Parfyumeriya/Toaletni prinadlezhnosti*
Toiletries

²⁷⁵ **Грамофонни плочи**
*Gramofonni plochi*
Records

## In the Shop

²⁷⁶ **What time do the shops open/close?**
Кога отварят/затварят магазините?
*Koga otvaryat/zatvaryat magazinite?*

²⁷⁷ **Where is the nearest market?**
Къде е най-близкият пазар?
*Kude e nay-bliskiyat pazar?*

²⁷⁸ **Can you show me the one in the window/this one?**
Може ли да ми покажете онова от витрината/това.
*Mozhe li da mi pokazhete onova ot vitrinata/tova?*

²⁷⁹ **Can I try this on?**
Може ли да пробвам това?
*Mozhe li da probvam tova?*

²⁸⁰ **What size is this?**
Какъв размер е това?
*Kakuf razmer e tova?*

²⁸¹ **This is too large/too small/too expensive.**
Това е твърде голямо/малко/скъпо.

*Tova e tvurde golyamo/malko/skupo.*

²⁸² **Do you have any others?**
Имате ли и други?
*Imate li i droogi?*

²⁸³ **My size is . . .**
Моят размер е . . .
*Moyat razmer e . . .*

²⁸⁴ **Where is the changing room/childrens'/cosmetic/ladieswear/menswear/food department?**
Къде е пробната/детският щанд/козметиката/дамското облекло/мъжкото облекло/щандът за храна?
*Kude e probnata/detskiya shtand/kozmetikata/damskoto obleklo/muzhkoto obleklo/shtanda za hrana?*

²⁸⁵ **I would like . . .**
Искам . . .
*Iskam . . .*

²⁸⁶ **I would like a quarter of a kilo/half a kilo/a kilo of bread/butter/cheese/ham/tomatoes.**
Искам четвърт/половин/един килограм хляб/масло/сирене/шунка/домати.
*Iskam chetvurt/polovin/edin kilogram hlyap/maslo/sirene/shoonka/domati.*

**B U L G A R I A N**

287
↑
298

**287** How much is this?
Колко струва Това?
*Kolko stroova Tova?*

**288** I'll take this one, thank you.
Ще взема това, благодаря.
*Shte vzema tova, blagodarya.*

**289** Do you have a carrier (shopping) bag?
Имате ли торба?
*Imate li torba?*

**290** Do you have anything cheaper/larger/smaller/of better quality?
Имате ли нещо по-евтино/по-голямо/по-малко/по-качествено?
*Imate li neshto po-eftino/po-golyamo/po-malko/po-kachestveno?*

**291** I would like a film for this camera.
Искам филм за този фотоапарат.
*Iskam film za tozi fotoaparat.*

**292** I would like some batteries, the same size as this old one.
Искам батерии, същият размер като тази старата.
*Isakm baterii, sushtiya razmer kato tazi starata.*

**293** Would you mind wrapping this for me, please?
Може ли да ми опаковате това, моля?

Може ли да ми опаковате това, моля?

**294** Sorry, but you seem to have given me the wrong change.
Извинете, но ми връщате неточно ресто.
*Izvinete, no mi vrushtate netochno resto.*

## MOTORING

### Car Hire (Rental)

**295** I have ordered (rented) a car in the name of . . .
Поръчах наех кола на името на . . .
*Poru hah naeh kola na imeto na . . .*

**296** How much does it cost to hire (rent) a car for one day/two days/one week?
Колко струва да наема кола за един ден/два дни/седмица?
*Kolko stroova da naema kola za edin den/dva dni/sedmitsa?*

**297** Is the tank already full of petrol (gas)?
Пълен ли е резервоарът с бензин?
*Pulen li e rezervoara s benzin?*

**298** Is insurance and tax included? How much is the deposit?
Включени ли са застраховката и данък?
Колко е депозитът?

*F klyoocheni li sa zastrahofkata i danuk? Kolko e depozita?*

**299** **By what time must I return the car?**
Кога трябва да върна колата?
*Koga tryabva da vurna kolata?*

**300** **I would like a small/family car with a radio/cassette player.**
Искам малка/голяма кола с радио/касетофон.
*Iskam malka/golyama kola s radio/kasetofon.*

## Asking the Way

**301** **Excuse me, can you help me please?**
Извинявайте, може ли да ми помогнете, моля?
*Izvinyavayte, mozhe li da mi pomognete, molya?*

**302** **How do I reach the motorway/main road?**
Как да стигна до автомагистралата/главния път?
*Kak da stigna do aftomagistralata/glavniya put?*

**303** **I think I have taken the wrong turning.**
Мисля, че завих неправилно.
*Mislya, che zavih nepravilno.*

**304** **I am looking for this address.**
Търся този адрес.

*Tursya tozi adres.*

**305** **I am looking for the . . . hotel.**
Търся хотел . . .
*Tursya hotel . . .*

**306** **How far is it to . . . from here?**
Колко е от тук до . . .
*Kolko e ot took do . . .*

**307** **Carry straight on for . . . kilometres.**
Продължете направо около . . . километра.
*Produlzhete napravo okolo . . . kilometra.*

**308** **Take the next turning on the right/left.**
Завийте на следващата пресечка на дясно/ляво.
*Zaviyte na sledvashtata presechka na dyasno/lyavo.*

**309** **Turn right/left at the next crossroads/traffic lights.**
Завийте надясно/наляво на следващото кръстовище/следващия светофар.
*Zaviyte nadyasno/nalyavo na sledvashtoto krustovishte/sledvashtiya svetofar.*

**310** **You are going in the wrong direction.**
Вие се движите в грешната посока.
*Vie se dvizhite f greshnata posoka.*

# MOTORING

## Parking

**311** How long can I park here?
За колко време мога да паркирам тук?
*Za kolko vreme moga da parkiram took?*

**312** Is there a car park near here?
Има ли паркинг наблизо?
*Ima li parking nablizo?*

**313** At what time does this car park close?
Кога затварят този паркинг?
*Koga zatvaryat tozi parking?*

## Signs and Notices

**314** Еднопосочна улица
*Ednoposochna oolitsa*
One way

**315** Влизането забранено
*Vlizaneto zabraneno*
No entry

**316** Паркирането забранено
*Parkiraneto zabraneno*
No parking

**317** Отклонение.
*Otklonenie*
Detour (diversion

**318** Спри/Стоп
*Spri/Stop*
Stop

**319** Дай път
*Dai put*
Give way (yield)

**320** Хлъзгав път
*Hluzgaf put*
Slippery road.

**321** Изпреварването забранено
*Isprevarvaneto zabraneno*
No overtaking

## At the Filling Station

**322** Unleaded (lead-free)/ Standard/Premium
Бензин без олово/ обикновен/супер
*Benzin bes olovo/obiknoven/ sooper.*

**323** Fill the tank please.
Напълнете резервоара, моля
*Napulnete rezervoara, molya*

**324** Do you have a road map of this area?
Имате ли пътна карта на този район?
*Imate li putna karta na tozi rayon?*

**325** How much is the car-wash?
Колко струва измиването на кола?
*Kolko stroova izmivaneto na kola?*

## Breakdowns

**326** I've had a breakdown at . . .
Колата ми се повреди в . . .
*Kolata mi se povredi f . . .*

**327** I am on the road from . . . to . . .

**B U L G A R I A N**

Аз съм на пътя от . . .
за . . .
*Az sum na putya ot . . .*
*za . . .*

**328** I can't move the car. Can you send a tow-truck?
Не мога да подкарам колата. Може ли да изпратите камион за теглене?
*Ne moga da potkaram kolata. Mozhe li da ispratite kamiyon za teglene?*

**329** I have a flat tyre.
Спуках гума.
*Spookah gooma.*

**330** The windscreen (windshield) has smashed/cracked.
Предното стъкло е счупено/спукано.
*Prednoto stuklo e schupeno/ spookano.*

**331** There is something wrong with the engine/brakes/ lights/steering/gearbox/ clutch/exhaust.
Двигателят/спирачките/ светлините/кормилото/ скоростната кутия/ амбреажът/ауспухът ми не е/са в ред.
*Dvigatelyat/spirachkite/svetlinite/ kormiloto/skorostnata kootiya/ ambreazhut/aspoohut mi ne e/ sa f ret.*

**332** It's overheating.
Прегрява.
*Pregryava.*

**333** It won't start.
Не иска да пали.
*Ne iska da pali.*

**334** Where can I get it repaired?
Къде могат да я поправят?
*Kude mogat da ya popravyat?*

**335** Can you take me there?
Може ли да ме заведете там?
*Mozhe li da me zavedete tam?*

**336** Will it take long to fix?
Много ли време трябва, за да се поправи?
*Mnogo li vreme tryabva, za da se popravi?*

**337** How much will it cost?
Колко ще струва?
*Kolko shte stroova?*

## Accidents

**338** Can you help me? There has been an accident.
Може ли да ми помогнете? Стана катастрофа.
*Mozhe li da mi pomognete? Stana katastrofa.*

**339** Please call the police/an ambulance.
Моля, повикайте полиция/ линейка.
*Molya, povikayte politsiya/ lineyka.*

328
↑
339

**B
U
L
G
A
R
I
A
N**

**340
↕
351**

### 340 Is anyone hurt?
Има ли ранени?
*Ima li raneni?*

## Traffic Offences

### 341 I'm sorry, I didn't see the sign.
Съжалявам. Не видях знака.
*Suzhalyavam, ne vidiyah znaka.*

### 342 Must I pay a fine? How much?
Трябва ли да платя глоба? Колко?
*Tryabva li da platya globa? Kolko?*

### 343 Show me your documents.
Покажете ми документите си.
*Pokazhete mi dokoomentite si.*

## HEALTH

### Pharmacy

### 344 Do you have anything for a stomachache/headache/sore throat/toothache?
Имате ли нещо за стомах/ глава/гърло/зъби?
*Imate li neshto za stomah/glava/ gurlo/zubi?*

### 345 I need something for diarrhoea (diarrhea)/ constipation/a cold/a cough/ insect bites/sunburn/travel (motion) sickness.

Трябва ми нещо за разстройство/запек/ настинка/кашлица / ухапване от насекоми/ слънчево изгаряне/гадене при пътуване.
*Tryabva mi neshto za rastroystvo/ zapek/nastinka/kashlitsa/ oohapvane ot nasekomi/slunchevo izgaryane/gadene pri putoovane.*

### 346 How much/how many do I take?
Колко се взема?
*Kolko se vzema?*

### 347 How often do I take it/them?
Колко често се взема?
*Kolko chesto se vzema?*

### 348 How much does it cost?
Колко струва?
*Kolko stroova?*

### 349 Can you recommend a good doctor/dentist?
Можете ли да ми препоръчате добър доктор/зъболекар?
*Mozhete li da mi preporuchate dobur doktor/zubolekar?*

### 350 Is it suitable for children?
Подходящо ли е за деца?
*Pothodyashto li e za detsa?*

## Doctor

### 351 I have a pain here/in my arm/ leg/chest/stomach.
Боли ме тук/ръката/ крака/гърдите/стомахът.

*Boli me took/rukata/kraka/
gurdite/stomaha.*

352 **Please call a doctor, this is an
emergency.**
Извикайте лекар, това е
спешен случай.
*Izvikayte lekar, tova e speshen
sloochay.*

353 **I would like to make an
appointment to see a doctor.**
Искам час за преглед.
*Iskam chas za pregled.*

354 **I am diabetic/pregnant.**
Аз съм диабетик/
бременна.
*As sum diabetik/bremenna.*

355 **I need a prescription for . . .**
Искам рецепта за . . .
*Iskam retsepta za . . .*

356 **Can you give me something
to ease the pain?**
Можете ли да ми дадете
болкоуспокояващо?
*Mozhete li da mi dadete
bolkooospokoyavashto?*

357 **I am/he is/she is allergic to
penicillin.**
Имам/има алергия към
пеницилин
*Imam/ima alergiya kum penitsilin.*

358 **Does this hurt?**
Боли ли?
*Boli li?*

359 **You must/he must/she must
go to hospital.**

Вие/той/тя трябва да
отиде/те в болница.
*Vie/toy/tya tryabva da otide/te f
bolnitsa.*

360 **Take these once/twice /three
times a day.**
Вземайте от тези веднъж/
два/три пъти на ден.
*Vzemayte ot tezi vednuzh/dva/tri/
puti na den.*

361 **I am/he is/she is taking this
medication.**
Аз вземам / той/тя взема
това лекарство.
*Az vzemam/ toy/tya vzema tova
lekarstvo.*

362 **I have medical insurance.**
Имам медицинска/
здравна застра овка.
*Imam meditsinska/zdravna
zastrahovka.*

## Dentist

363 **I have toothache.**
Боли ме зъб.
*Boli me zup.*

364 **My filling has come out.**
Падна ми пломба.
*Padna mi plomba.*

365 **I do/do not want to have an
injection first.**
Искам/не искам първо
инжекция.
*Iskam/ne iskam purvo inzhektsya.*

## EMERGENCIES

**366** Help!
Помощ!
*Pomosht!*

**367** Call an ambulance/a doctor/
the police!
Извикайте линейка/
доктор/полицията!
*Izvikayte lineyka/doktor/
politsiyata!*

**368** I have had my travellers'
cheques (travelers' checks)/
credit cards/purse/handbag/
rucksack (knapsack)/
luggage/wallet stolen.
Откраднаха ми
туристическите чекове/
кредит картите/
портмонето/чантата/
раницата/багажа
портфейла.
*Orkradnaha mi tooristicheskite
chekove/kredit kartite/
portmoneto/chantata/ranitsata/
bagazha portfeyla.*

**369** Can you help me, I have lost
my daughter/son?

Може ли да ми помогнете,
загубих дъщеря/сина си?
*Mozhe li da mi pomognete,
zagoobih dushterya si/sina si?*

**370** Please, go away/leave me
alone.
Оставете ме на мира.
*Ostavete me na mira.*

**371** Fire!
Пожар!
*Pozhar!*

**372** I want to contact the British/
American/Canadian/Irish/
Australian/New Zealand/
South African consulate.
Искам да се свържа с
британското/
американското/
канадското/ирландското/
австралийското/
новозеландското/
южноафриканското
консулство.
*Iskam da se svurzha s britanskoto/
amerikanskoto/kanatskoto/
irlandskoto/afstraliyskoto/
novozelandskoto/
yuzhnoafrikanskoto konsulstvo.*

# Introduction

Czech is the official language of the Czech Republic. The language spoken in neighbouring Slovakia is Slovak, but the two are so closely related that speakers of one can easily understand the other. Both belong to the Slavic family of languages that includes Russian and Polish. In larger cities, particularly in the Czech Republic, English is spoken, and German is often a second language for many Czechs. Russian is also widely understood, but not popular.

## Addresses for travel and tourist information

The following addresses are the tourist authorities for both the Czech Republic and for Slovakia.

**UK:** *Cedok*, 49 Southwark St, London SE1 1RU; tel: (0171) 378 6009.

**USA:** *Cedok*, 10 East 40th St, New York, NY 10016; tel: (212) 689-9720.

**C Z E C H**

**01 ↕ 11**

### Alphabet

| | |
|---|---|
| A *ah* | B *bey* |
| C *tsey* | D *dey* |
| E *ey* | F *ef* |
| G *gey* | H *hah* |
| CH *khah* | I *ee* |
| J *yeh* | K *kah* |
| L *el* | M *em* |
| N *en* | O *oh* |
| P *pey* | Q *koo* |
| R *yer* | S *es* |
| T *tey* | U *oo* |
| V *veh* | W *dvoyiteh veh* |
| X *iks* | Y *oopsi-lon* |
| Z *tset* | |

### Basic Words and Phrases

1  **Yes**
Ano
*Unnoh*

**No**
Ne
*neh*

2  **Please**
Prosím
*Prosseem*

**Thank you**
Děkuji
*Dyekoo-yi*

3  **That's o.k.**
Prima
*Preemmah*

**Perhaps**
Možná
*Mozhnah*

4  **To**
Do
*Doh*

**From**
Od
*odd*

5  **Here**
Zde
*Zdhe*

**There**
Tam
*Tahm*

6  **None**
Žádný
*Zhadnee*

**Also**
Také
*Tukeh*

7  **How**
Jak
*Yuck*

**When**
Kdy
*Gdy*

8  **What**
Co
*Tsoh*

**Why**
Proč
*Prroch*

9  **I don't understand.**
Nerozumím.
*Nerohzuhmeem.*

10  **I don't speak Czech.**
Nemluvím česky.
*Nemluhveem chesky.*

11  **Do you speak English?**
Mluvíte anglicky?
*Mluhveete ahnglitsky?*

**C**
**Z**
**E**
**C**
**H**

12 **Can you please write it down?**
Můžete to, prosím, napsat?
*Moozheteh toh, prohseem, nahpsaht?*

13 **Can you please speak more slowly?**
Můžete, prosím, mluvit pomaleji?
*Moozheteh, prohseem, mluhvit pohmahlayi?*

14 **How much does it/this cost?**
Kolik to/tohle stojí?
*Kollick toh/toh-hleh stoyee?*

## Days

15 **Monday**       **Tuesday**
pondělí       úterý
*Pondyellee*   *Ooteree*

16 **Wednesday**   **Thursday**
středa       čtvrtek
*Stzheddah*   *Shtvertek*

17 **Friday**       **Saturday**
pátek       sobota
*Pahtek*     *Sobbottah*

18 **Sunday**       **Morning**
neděle       ráno
*Neddyelleh*   *Rahnoh*

19 **Afternoon**   **Evening**
odpoledne     večer
*Odpoledneh*   *Vesherr*

20 **Night**       **Week**
noc       týden
*Nots*     *Teeden*

21 **Yesterday**   **Tomorrow**
včera       zítra
*Fcherah*     *Zeetrah*

## Numbers

22 **Zero**       **One**
nula       jedna
*Noola*     *Yednah*

23 **Two**       **Three**
dvě       tři
*Dvyeh*     *Tzhee*

24 **Four**       **Five**
čtyři       pět
*Shteezhee*   *Pyet*

25 **Six**       **Seven**
šest       sedm
*Shest*     *Seddoom*

26 **Eight**       **Nine**
osm       devět
*Ossoom*     *Devyet*

27 **Ten**       **Eleven**
deset       jedenáct
*Desset*     *Yeddenahtst*

28 **Twelve**       **Thirteen**
dvanáct       třináct
*Dvunnahtst*   *Tzheenahtst*

29 **Fourteen**   **Fifteen**
čtrnáct       patnáct
*Shternahtst*   *Puttnahtst*

30 **Sixteen**       **Seventeen**
šestnáct       sedmnáct
*Shestnahtst*   *Seddoomnahtst*

31 **Eighteen**   **Nineteen**
osmnáct       devatenáct
*Ossoomnahtst*   *Devvuttehnahtst*

12
↑
31

37

**C Z E C H**

**32 ↕ 53**

**32 Twenty**
dvacet
*Dvutset*

**Twenty-one**
dvacet jeden
*Dvutset yedden*

**33 Twenty-two**
dvacet dva
*Dvutset dvah*

**Thirty**
třicet
*Tzhitset*

**34 Forty**
čtyřicet
*Shteezhitset*

**Fifty**
padesát
*Puddessaht*

**35 Sixty**
šedesát
*Sheddessaht*

**Seventy**
sedmdesát
*Seddoomdessaht*

**36 Eighty**
osmdesát
*Ossoodessaht*

**Ninety**
devadesát
*Devvuddessaht*

**37 One hundred**
sto
*Stoh*

**Five hundred**
pět set
*Pyet set*

**38 One thousand**
tisíc
*Tyisseets*

**One million**
milión
*Meeleeon*

## Time

**39 9.00**
devět hodin
*Devvyet hoddyinn*

**40 9.05**
devět pět
*Devvyet pyet*

**41 9.10**
devět deset
*Devvyet desset*

**42 9.15**
čtvrt na deset
*Shtvert naa desset*

**43 9.20**
devět dvacet
*Devvyet dvutset*

**44 9.25**
devět dvacet pět
*Devvyet dvutset pyet*

**45 9.30**
půl desáté
*Pool dessahte*

**46 9.35**
devět třicet pět
*Devvyet tzhitset pyet*

**47 9.40**
devět čtyřicet
*Devvyet shteezhitset*

**48 9.45**
třičtvrtě na deset
*Tzheeshtvertye naa desset*

**49 9.50**
za deset minut deset
*Zaa desset minnoot desset*

**50 9.55**
za pět minut deset
*Zaa pyet minnoot desset*

**51 12.00/Midday/Midnight**
dvanáct/poledne/půlnoc
*Dvunnahtst/poledne/poolnots*

**52 What time is it?**
Kolik je hodin
*Kollick yeh hoddin*

**53 It is . . .**
Je . . .
*Yeh . . .*

## ARRIVING AND DEPARTING

## Airport

**54** Excuse me, where is the check-in desk for . . . airline?
Promiňte, kde se odbavuje letecká společnost . . .?
*Prohminyete, gde sse ohdbahvuhyeh letetskar spohletchnost . . ?*

**55** What is the boarding gate/time for my flight?
Kterou branou/V kolik hodin se nastupuje na můj let?
*Kteroe brahnoe/Fkollick hodyin sse nahstuhpuhyeh nah mooy let?*

**56** How long is the delay likely to be?
Jak velké asi bude to zpoždění?
*Yuck velkeh ahssee buhdeh toh zpohzhdyenyee?*

**57** Where is the duty-free shop?
Kde je bezcelní obchod?
*Gdeh yeh beztselnee ophod?*

**58** Which way is the baggage reclaim?
Kde je výdej zavazadel?
*Gdeh yeh veedey zahvahzahdel?*

**59** Where can I get the bus to the city centre?
Odkud jede autobus do centra města?
*Otkuhd yede aootobuhs dotsentrah mnyesta?*

## Train Station

**60** Where is the ticket office/information desk?
Kde je výdejna jízdenek/Kde jsou informace?
*Gdeh yeh veedeynah yeezdenek/gdeh sow informatse?*

**61** Which platform does the train to . . . depart from?
Z kterého nástupiště odjíždí vlak do . . ?
*Z ktehraihoh nahstoopishtyeh odyeezhdee vluck doh . . ?*

**62** Where is platform . . ?
Kde je . . . nástupiště?
*Gdeh yeh . . . nahstoopishtyeh?*

**63** When is the next train to . . ?
Kdy jede další vlak do . . ?
*Gdy yeddeh daalshee vluck do . . ?*

**64** Is there a later train to . . ?
Jede později vlak do . . ?
*Yeddeh pozdyeyee vluck doh . . ?*

## Port

**65** How do I get to the port?
Jak se dostanu do přístavu . . ?
*Yuck seh dostahnoo doh pzheestavoo . . ?*

**66** When is the next sailing to . . ?
Kdy jede příští loď?
*Gdy yedeh pzheeshtee lodye?*

**C Z E C H**

**67 ↕ 88**

**67** Can I catch an earlier ferry
with this ticket?
Mohu jet na tenhle lístek
dřívější lodí?
*Mohuh yet nah tenhleh leestek
drzheevyeyshee lodyee?*

## Notices and Signs

**68** **Bufetový vůz**
*Boofetovee vooz*
Buffet (Dining) Car

**69** **Autobus**
*Aootohbooss*
Bus

**70** **Pitná voda/nepitná voda**
*Peetnah voddah*
Drinking/Non-drinking water

**71** **Vchod**
*Vkhod*
Entrance

**72** **Východ**
*Veekhod*
Exit

**73** **Informace**
*Informatseh*
Information

**74** **Úschovna zavazadel**
*Ooskhovnah zuvvahzuddel*
Left Luggage (Baggage Claim)

**75** **Skříňky na zavazadla**
*Skzheenkee nah zuvvahzuddlah*
Luggage Lockers

**76** **Pošta**
*Poshtah*
Post Office

**77** **Nástupiště**
*Nahstoopishtyeh*
Platform

**78** **Železniční nádraží**
*Zheleznechnee nahdrahzhee*
Railway (Railroad) Station

**79** **Letiště**
*Letyishtye*
Airport

**80** **Přístav**
*Przheestahf*
Port

**81** **Restaurace**
*Restauratse*
Restaurant

**82** **Kuřáci/nekuřáci**
*Koozhahtsi/nehkoozhatsi*
Smoking/Non-smoking

**83** **Telefon**
*Tellefohn*
Telephone

**84** **Pokladna**
*Pokludnah*
Ticket Office

**85** **Odbavovací přepážka**
*Ohdbahvohvahtsee przhepashka*
Check-in Desk

**86** **Jízdní řád**
*Yeezdnyee zhaht*
Timetable (Schedule)

**87** **Záchod**
*Zahkhot*
Toilets (Restrooms)

**88** **Páni**

*Pahni*
Gentlemen

89 **Dámy**
*Dahmy*
Ladies'

90 **Tramvaj**
*Trumvahay*
Tram (Streetcar)

91 **Podzemní dráha**
*Podzemnee draahah*
Underground (Subway)

92 **Čekárna**
*Chekaarnah*
Waiting Room

## Buying a Ticket

93 **I would like a first-class/
second-class single (one-
way)/return (round-trip)
ticket to . . .**
Prosím jízdenku první/druhé
třídy/zpáteční do . . .
*Prosseem yeezdenkooh pervnee
tzheedy/droohe tzheedy/
zpaatechnee doh . . .*

94 **Is my rail pass valid on this
train/ferry/bus?**
Platí moje sí ťová železniční
jízdenka na tento vlak/na tuto
loď/na tento autobus?
*Plahtyee moye seetyovar
zhelezniychnyee yeezdenkah nah
tentoh vluck/nah tuhtoh lodye/
nah tentoh aootohbuhs?*

95 **I would like an aisle/
window seat.**

Přeji si místo u chodbičky/u
okna.
*Pzheye ssi meestoh oo
khodbichky/oo ocknah.*

96 **No smoking/smoking,
please.**
Nekuřáci/kuřáci, prosím.
*Nehckuzhaatsi/kuzhaatsi,
prosseem.*

97 **We would like to sit
together.**
Chceme sedět spolu.
*Khtsemeh ssedyet spohloo.*

98 **I would like to make a seat
reservation.**
Rád(a) bych si rezervoval(a)
místenku.
*Rahd(ah) bikh sih
rezerrvoval(ah) meestenkuh.*

99 **I would like to reserve a
couchette/sleeper for one
person/two people/for my
family.**
Rád bych rezervoval lehátko/
lůžko pro jednu osobu/dvě
osoby/pro rodinu.
*Rahd bykh rezervohvahl
lehhahtkoh/loozhkoh proh
yednoo osohboo/dvyeh osohby/
proh rodyeenoo.*

100 **I would like to reserve a
cabin.**
Rád(a) bych si rezervoval(a)
kabinu.
*Rahd(ah) bikh sih
rezerrvooval(ah) kahbinuh.*

C
Z
E
C
H

89
↑
100

CZECH

101
↕
118

## Timetables (Schedules)

**101 Přijede**
*Pzhiyeddeh*
Arrive

**102 Zastavuje . . .**
*Zustahvooye . . .*
Calls (Stops) at . . .

**103 Dodávky jídla**
*Dohdaafkee yeedlah*
Catering Service

**104 Přestupte . . .**
*Pzhestoopteh . . .*
Change at . . .

**105 Spojení**
*Spoyenee*
Connection

**106 Denně**
*Denye*
Daily

**107 Každých čtyřicet minut**
*Kazhdeekh shteezhitset minnoot*
Every 40 minutes

**108 První třída**
*Peronee tzheedah*
First-class

**109 Každou hodinu**
*Kahzhdoow hoddyinoo*
Hourly

**110 Doporučují se místenky**
*Dohporuchoyee seh meestenky*
Seat reservations are recommended

**111 Druhá třída**
*Droohah tzheedah*

Second-class

**112 Platí se příplatek**
*Plahtee seh pzheeplahtek*
Supplement Payable

**113 Přes**
*Pzhez*
Via

## Luggage

**114 How much will it cost to send (ship) my luggage in advance?**
Kolik stojí poslat zavazadlo dopředu?
*Kohlick stohyee poslaht zuvvahzuddlah dohpzhedoo?*

**115 Where is the left luggage (baggage claim) office?**
Kde je úschovna?
*Gde yeh ooskhohvnah?*

**116 What time do you open/ close?**
Kdy otvíráte/zavíráte?
*Gdy ohtveerahteh/zuvveerahteh?*

**117 Where are the luggage trolleys (carts)?**
Kde jsou vozíky na zavazadla?
*Gde ysow vohzeeky nah zuvvazuddlahd?*

**118 Where are the lockers?**
Kde jsou skříňky na zavazadla?
*Gdeh soe skrzheenyeki nahzahvahzahddah?*

**119** I have lost my locker key.
Ztratil jsem klíč od skříňky.
*Ztrahtil sehm kleech odh skzheenky.*

## On Board

**120** Is this seat taken?
Je toto místo volné?
*Yeh tohotoh meestoh vohlneeh?*

**121** Excuse me, you are sitting in my reserved seat.
Promiňte, to je moje rezervované místo.
*Prohminyteh, toh yeh mohye rezervohvahneeh meestoh.*

**122** Which station is this?
Která je to stanice?
*Ktehraah yeh toh stanitseh?*

**123** What time is this train/bus/ferry/flight due to arrive/depart?
V kolik hodin tenhle vlak/tenhle autobus/tahle loď/tohle letadlo přijíždí/odjíždí?
*Fkollick hodyin tenhleh vluck/tenhleh aootohbuhs/tahhleh lodye/tohhleh lehtadloh przhiyeezhdyee/odyeezhdyee?*

**124** Will you wake me just before we arrive?
Probudíte mě než zastavíme?
*Prohbudyteh mnye nezh zahstahveemeh?*

## Customs and Passports

**125** Prosím pasy!

*Prosseem passy!*
Passports, please!

**126** I have nothing/wine/spirits (alcohol)/tobacco to declare.
Nemám nic/Mám víno/alkohol/tabák k proclení.
*Nemaahm nits/Maahm veenoh/alckohol/tabaack kh protslenee.*

**127** I shall be staying for . . . days/weeks/months.
Budu zde . . . dní/týdnů/měsíců.
*Boodoo zdeh . . . dnee/teednoo/mnyesseetsoo.*

## AT THE TOURIST OFFICE

**128** Do you have a map of the town/area?
Máte mapu města/okolí?
*Mahteh mahpoo mnyestah/ohkohlee?*

**129** Can I reserve accommodation here?
Mohu si zde rezervovat ubytování?
*Mohhooseezdeh rezervohvaht oobytovaanyee?*

**130** Do you have a list of accommodation?
Máte seznam možností ubytování?
*Mahteh seznam mozhnostyee ubitohvahnyee?*

C
Z
E
C
H

119
↕
130

## ACCOMMODATION

### Hotels

**131** I have a reservation in the name of . . .
Mám rezervaci na jméno . . .
*Mahm rezervatsi nah mehnnoh . . .*

**132** I wrote to/faxed/telephoned you last month/last week in . . .
Psa (a)/faxoval(a)/telefonoval(a) jsem vám minulý měsíc/minulý týden v . . .
*Psal(ah)/fahksoval(ah)/ telefohnoval(ah) sem vahm minuhlee mnyesseets/minuhlee teeden v . . .*

**133** Do you have any rooms free?
Máte nějaké volné pokoje?
*Mahte nyeyakeh volneh pockoyeh?*

**134** I would like to reserve a single/double room with/ without bath/shower.
Rád bych rezervoval jednolůžkový/dvojlůžkový pokoj s koupelnou/bez koupelny/se sprchou.
*Rahd bykh rezervohvahl pockoy ss kowpelnow/bess kowpelny/ seh sperkhow.*

**135** I would like bed and breakfast/(room and) half board/(room and) full board.
Rád bych pokoj se snídaní/

polopenzí/plnou penzí.
*Rahd bykh pockoy seh sneedanee/pohlohpenzee/plnow penzi.*

**136** How much is it per night?
Kolik to stojí za jednu noc?
*Kollick toh stoyee zah yednoo nots?*

**137** Is breakfast included?
Je to se snídaní?
*Ye toh seh sneedahnee?*

**138** May I see the room?
Smím se na pokoj podívat?
*Smeem seh nah pokoy podeevaht?*

**139** Do you have any cheaper rooms?
Máte lacinější pokoje?
*Mahte latsinyeyshee pockoyeh?*

**140** I would like to take the room.
Vezmu si tento pokoj.
*Vezmoo si tento pockoy.*

**141** I would like to stay for . . . nights.
Rád bych zůstal . . . nocí.
*Rahd bykh zoostahl . . . notsee.*

**142** The shower/light/tap doesn't work.
Sprcha/světlo/kohoutek nefunguje.
*Sprhah/svyetloh/kohoetek nefunguyeh.*

**143** At what time/where is breakfast served?

Kdy a kde se podává snídaně?
*Gdy a gde se pohdahvah sneedahnye?*

### 144 What time do I have to check-out?
Kdy musím uvolnit pokoj?
*Gdy moozem oovolniht pockoy?*

### 145 Can I have the key to room no . . ?
Můžu dostat klíč od pokoje číslo . . ?
*Moozhuh dohstaht kleech ot pockohyeh cheesloh . . ?*

### 146 My room number is . . .
Číslo mého pokoje je . . .
*Cheesloh mehoh pockoyeh yeh . . .*

### 147 Do you accept travellers' cheques/Eurocheques/ credit cards?
Přijímáte cestovní šeky/ Eurošeky/kreditní karty?
*Prziyeemahteh tsestovnyee sheki/ eoorosheki/kreditnyee karti?*

### 148 May I have the bill please?
Účet, prosím?
*Oochet, prosseem?*

### 149 Excuse me, I think there is a mistake in this bill.
Promiňte, myslím, že v tomto účtu je chyba.
*Prominyete, misleem zhe ftomtoh oochtuh yeh hibah.*

## Youth Hostels

### 150 How much is a dormitory bed per night?

Kolik stojí lůžko v noclehárně?
*Kollick stoyee loozhkoh v notslehahrnye?*

### 151 I am/am not an HI member.
Jsem/nejsem členem HI.
*Sem/neysem chlehnehm ee, oopsi-lon, hah, ah.*

### 152 May I use my own sleeping bag?
Můžu používat vlastní spacák?
*Moozhoo powsheevath vlastnee spatsahck?*

### 153 What time do you lock the doors at night?
Kdy v noci zamykáte?
*Gdy v notsi zahmykahteh?*

## Camping

### 154 May I camp here for the night/two nights?
Můžu zde stanovat jednu noc/dvě noci?
*Moozhoo zdeh stahnovaht jehdnoo nots/dvye notsi?*

### 155 Where can I pitch my tent?
Kde můžu postavit stan?
*Gde moozhoo postahvit stahn?*

### 156 How much does it cost for one night/one week?
Kolik stojí jedna noc/jeden týden?
*Kollick stoyee yednah nots/yeden tyhdehn?*

**157** Where can we park our caravan?
Kam můžeme zaparkovat náš obytný přívěs?
*Kam moozhemeh zaparrkohvat nahsh obitnee przheevyes?*

**158** Where are the washing facilities?
Kde jsou umývárny?
*Gde sow oomyhvahrny?*

**159** Is there a restaurant/ supermarket/swimming pool on site/nearby?
Je tady/blízko restaurce/ supermarket/plovárna?
*Yeh tahdyh/bleezkoh restauratseh/supermarkeht/ plohvahrnah?*

**160** Do you have a safety deposit box?
Máte trezor?
*Mahteh trehzohr?*

## EATING AND DRINKING

### Cafés and Bars

**161** I would like a cup of/two cups of/another coffee/tea.
Prosím šálek/dva šálky kávy/ ještě kávu/čaje.
*Prosseem shahleck/dvah shahlkyh/yeshtye kahvoo/chaye.*

**162** With/without milk/sugar.
S mlékem/cukrem. Bez mléka/ cukru.
*Ss mlaikehm/tsookrehm. Behz mlaikah/tsookroo.*

**163** I would like a bottle/glass/ two glasses of mineral water/red wine/white wine, please.
Prosím láhev/sklenku/dvě sklenky minerální vody/ červeného vína/bílého vína.
*Prosseem lahhehv/sklehnku/ dvye sklehnkyh minehrahlnee voddy/chervehnehoh veenah/ beelehhoh veenah.*

**164** I would like a beer/two beers, please.
Prosím pivo/dvě piva.
*Prosseem pivoh/dvye pivah.*

**165** May I have some ice?
Led, prosím.
*Lehd, prosseem.*

**166** Do you have any matches/ cigarettes/cigars?
Máte zápalky/cigarety/ doutníky?
*Mahte zahpalkyh/tsigartyh/ dowtneekyh?*

### Restaurants

**167** Can you recommend a good/inexpensive restaurant in this area?
Můžete doporučit dobrou/ lacinou restauraci v okolí?
*Moozheteh dohporuhchit dohbrow latsinow restauratsi vh ohkohlee?*

**168** I would like a table for . . . people.
Přeji si stůl pro . . . osoby.

46

*Pzheyee sih stool proh . . .*
*ohsohby.*

**169 Do you have a non-smoking area?**
Máte nekuřáckou část?
*Mahteh nehkuhrzhahtskoe chahst?*

**170 Waiter/Waitress!**
Číšníku/číšnice!
*Cheeshneekoo/cheeshnitse!*

**171 Do you have a set menu/children's menu/wine list?**
Máte sestavené menu? dětské menu/ceník nápojů?
*Mahteh sehstahveneh menuh?*
*dyetskeh menuh/tseneek nahpojoo?*

**172 Do you have any vegetarian dishes, please?**
Máte, prosím, vegetariánská jídla?
*Mahteh, prosseem, veghetahriahnskeh yeedlah?*

**173 Are there any local specialities?**
Máte nějaké místní speciality?
*Mahte nyeyakeh meestnyee spetsialiti?*

**174 Are vegetables included?**
Je v tom také zelenina?
*Yeh ftom tahkeh zelenyinah?*

**175 Could I have it well-cooked/medium/rare please?**
Mohl(a) bych to dostat dobře/středně/jen lehce propečené, prosím?

*Mohl(ah) bikh toh dostat dobrzhe/strzhednye/yen lehtse propetcheneh, prosseem?*

**176 I would like the set menu, please.**
Sestavené menu, prosím.
*(Sestahveneh menuh, prosseem.)*

**177 I would like the set menu, please.**
Sestavené menu, prosím.
*Sestahveneh menuh, prosseem.*

**178 We have not been served yet.**
Ještě jsme nebyli obslouženi.
*Yeshtye smeh nehbyhli obslowzhenih.*

**179 Excuse me, this is not what I ordered.**
Promiňte, ale tohle jsem si neobjednal(a).
*Prohminyete, ahle toh-hle sem si ne-ohbyednal(ah).*

**180 May I have some/some more bread/water/coffee/tea?**
Přeji si/více chleba/vody/kávy/čaje.
*Pzheyi sih/veetse khbleba/voddy/chaye.*

**181 May I have the bill, please?**
Účet, prosím?
*Oochet, prosseem?*

**182 Does this bill include service?**
Zahrnuje účet obsluhu?
*Zahrnooye oochet obsloohoo?*

**CZECH**

**183** Do you accept travellers' cheques (travelers' checks)/ Eurocheques/MasterCard/ US dollars?
Berete cestovní šeky/ Eurošeky/MasterCard/ americké dolary?
*Bereteh tsestovnee shehkyh/ Euroshekyh/Masterkard/ ahmehritskeh dohlaryh?*

**184** Can I have a receipt, please?
Můžete mi vystavit účtenku, prosím?
*Moozhetemi vistahvit oochtenkuh, prosseem?*

**185** Where is the toilet (restroom), please?
Prosím, kde jsou toalety?
*Prosseem, gde sow toaletyh?*

## On the Menu

**186** First courses
Předkrmy
*Przhetkrmi*

**187** Soups
Polévky
*Polehvki*

**188** Main courses
Hlavní jídla
*Hlavnyee yeedlah*

**189** Fish dishes
Rybí pokrmy
*Ribee pohkrmi*

**190** Meat dishes
Masitá jídla
*Mahssitah yeedlah*

**191** Vegetarian dishes
Vegetariánská/Bezmasá jídla
*Vehgehtahrianskah/Bezmahssah yeedlah*

**192** Cheese
Sýry
*Seerri*

**193** Desserts
Moučníky/Zákusky
*Moechnyeeki/Zahkooski*

**194** Specialities
Speciality
*Spetsialiti*

## GETTING AROUND

### Public Transport

**195** Where is the bus stop/ coach station/nearest metro (subway) station?
Kde je autobusová zastávka/ autokarová stanice/nejbližší metro zastávka?
*Gde yeh aoothoboosovah zahstahvkah/ auuthokahrovah stanitseh/neyblizhshee metroh zahstahvkah?*

**196** When is the next/last bus to . . ?
Kdy jede další/poslední autobus do . . ?
*Gdy yedeh dalshee/poslednee aoothobos doh . . ?*

**197** How much is the fare to the city centre (downtown)/ railway (railroad) station/ airport?

48

Kolik stojí jízdenka do středu
města/na železniční nádraží/
na letiště?
*Kollick stoyee yeezdehnkah doh
stzhedoo mystah/nah
zheleznichnee nahdrazhee/nah
lehtishtye?*

**198** Will you ell me when to
get off?
Řekněte mi kde vystoupit?
*Zheknyeteh mee gdeh
vyhstowpith?*

**199** Does this bus go to . . ?
Jede tento autobus do . . ?
*Yedeh tentoh aoothoboos
doh . . ?*

**200** Which number bus goes
to . . ?
Které číslo autobusu jede do . . ?
*Ktehreh cheesloh aoothoboosoo
yedeh doh . . ?*

**201** May I have a single (one-
way)/return (round-trip)/
day ticket/book of tickets?
Prosím jízdenku/zpáteční/
denní lístek/svazek lístků.
*Prosseem yeezdehnkoo/
zpahtechnee/dehnee leesteck/
svahzeck leestkoo.*

## Taxis

**202** I would like to go to . . .
How much will it cost?
Jedu do . . . Kolik to stojí?
*Yedoo doh . . . Kollick toh
stoyee?*

**203** Please stop here.
Zastavte zde, prosím.
*Zahstahvteh zdeh, prosseem.*

**204** I would like to order a taxi
today/tomorrow/at 2pm to
go from . . . to . . .
Rád bych objednal taxi na
dnešek/zítra/ve čtrnáct hodin
od . . . do . . .
*Rahd bykh ohbyednahl taxi nah
dnehsheck/zeetrah/ve shternahtst
hoddinh od . . .doh . . .*

## Asking the Way

**205** Excuse me, do you speak
English?
Promiňte, mluvíte anglicky?
*Prohmihnyete, mlooveeteh
ahnlitskyh?*

**206** Excuse me, is this the
right way to . . ?
Promiňte, jdu tudy
správně . . .
*Prohminyete, jduh toodi
sprahvnye . . .*

**207** . . . the cathedral/the
tourist information office/
the castle/the old town
. . . ke katedrále/k turistické
informační kanceláři/ke
hradu/ke starému městu
*ke kahtedrahleh/ktooristitskeh
informmachnyee kahntselahrzhi/
ke hradoo/ke stahrehmuh
mnyestuh.*

**208** Can you tell me the way to the railway station/bus station/taxi rank (stand)/ city centre (downtown)/ beach?
Jak se dostanu na nádraží/ autobusové nádraží/ stanoviště autotaxi/střed města/pláž?
*Yuck seh dostahnoo nah nahdrazhee/aootohboosoveh nahdrahzhee/stahnovishtye aoototaxi/stzhed mnyestah/ plazh?*

**209** First/second/left/right/ straight ahead.
První/druhá/nalevo/napravo/ rovně.
*Pervnee/droohah/nahlevoh/ naprahvoh/rovnye.*

**210** Where is the nearest police station/post office?
Kde je nejbližší policejní stanice/pošta?
*Gde yeh neyblizhshee politseynee stanitseh/poshtah?*

**211** Is it far?
Je to daleko?
*Yeh toh dahlekoh?*

**212** Do I need to take a taxi/ catch a bus?
Musím jet taxíkem/autobusem?
*Mooseem yeht taxeekehm/ aoothoboosehm?*

**213** Can you point to it on my map?

Ukažte to na mapě.
*Ookazhte toh nah mahpye.*

**214** Thank you for your help.
Děkuji za Vaši pomoc.
*Dyekooyi zah vashi pohmots.*

## SIGHTSEEING

**215** Where is the Tourist Information office?
Kde jsou turistické informace?
*Gde sow tooristitskeh informatseh?*

**216** Where is the cathedral/ church/museum?
Kde je katedrála/kostel/ muzeum?
*Gde ye kahtehdrahlah/kohstehl/ moozeoom?*

**217** How much is the entrance (admission) charge?
Kolik je vstupné?
*Kollick yeh vstoopneh?*

**218** Is there a reduction for children/students/senior citizens?
Je sleva pro děti/studenty/ důchodce?
*Yeh slehvah proh dyetee/ stoodehnty/dookhodtseh?*

**219** What time does the next guided tour start?
Kdy jde další skupina s průvodcem?
*Gdy ydeh dahlshee skoopinah ss proovohdtsehm?*

**220** One/two adults/children, please.
Jeden/dva dospělí/děti, prosím.
*Yedehn/dvah dohspyelee/dyetee, prosseem.*

**221** May I take photographs here?
Smím tady fotografovat?
*Smeem tahdi fotografohvaht?*

## ENTERTAINMENT

**222** Can you recommend a good bar/nightclub?
Doporučíte dobrý bar/noční podnik?
*Dohpohrucheeteh dohbree bahr/nochnee pohdnick?*

**223** Do you know what is on at the cinema (playing at the movies)/theatre at the moment?
Co dávají v kině/v divadle?
*Tsoh dahvahyee vh kihnye/vh divahdleh?*

**224** I would like to book (purchase) . . . tickets for the matinée/evening performance on Monday.
Rád bych zamluvil . . . vstupenek na pondělní odpolední/večerní představení.
*Rahd bykh zahmloovil . . . vstoopehnehck nah pohndyelnee ohdpohlehdnee/vecherrnee pzhedstahvehnee.*

**225** What time does the film/performance start?
Kdy začíná film/představení?

Gdy zacheenah film/pzhedstahvehnee?

## MEETING PEOPLE

**226** Hello/Goodbye
Nazdar/Na shledanou
*Nahzdahr/Nah-skhleddunnow*

**227** Good morning/good afternoon/good evening/goodnight.
Dobré jitro/dobrý den/dobrý večer/dobrou noc.
*Dohbreh yitroh/dohbree den/dohbree vecherr/dohbroe nots.*

**228** Pleased to meet you.
Těší mě.
*Tyehshee mnye.*

**229** How are you?
Jak se daří?
*Yuck seh dazhee?*

**230** Fine, thank you. And you?
Dobře, děkuji. A vy?
*Dobrzhe, dyekuhyi. A vi?*

**231** My name is . . .
Jmenuji se . . .
*Menooyi seh . . .*

**232** This is my friend/boyfriend/girlfriend/husband/wife/brother/sister.
To je můj přítel/chlapec/dívka/manžel/manželk ?/bratr/sestra.
*Toh jeh mooy pzheetehl/khlahpets/dyeefkah/mahnzhel/mahnzhelkah/brahtr/sehstrah.*

51

**C Z E C H**

**233** Where are you travelling to?
Kam jedete?
*Kahm yehdehteh?*

**234** I am/we are going to . . .
Jedu/jedeme do . . .
*Yehdoo/yehdehmeh doh . . .*

**235** How long are you
travelling for?
Jak dlouho cestujete?
*Yuck dlowhoh tsehstooyeteh?*

**236** Where do you come from?
Odkud jste?
*Odkood steh?*

**237** I am/we are from . . .
Jsem/jsme z . . .
*Sem/sme z . . .*

**238** We're on holiday.
Jsme tu na dovolené.
*Smeh tuh nahdohvohleneh.*

**239** This is our first visit here.
Jsme tady na návštěvě
poprvé.
*Smeh tahdi nah nahfshtyevye
pohpreveh.*

**240** Would you like/May I have
a cigarette?
Přejete si/Můžu si vzít
cigaretu?
*Pzheyeteh sih/Moozhuu sih
vzeet tsigahrehtoo?*

**241** I am sorry, but I do not
understand.
Promiňte, nerozumím Vám.
*Prohminyteh, nehrozoomeem
vahm.*

**242** Please speak slowly.
Mluvte, prosím, pomalu.
*Mloofteh, prosseem, pohmahloo.*

**243** Do you mind if I smoke.
Smím si zapálit?
*Smeem sih zahpahlit?*

**244** Do you have a light?
Můžu si připálit?
*Moozhoo sih pzhipahlit?*

**245** I am waiting for my
husband/wife/boyfriend/
girlfriend.
Čekám na svého manžela/
svou ženu/svého přítele/svou
přítelkyni.
*Chekahm na svehhoh
mahnzhela/svoe zhenuh/
svehhoh przheeteleh/svoe
przheetelkynyi*

## TRAVELLING WITH CHILDREN

**246** Do you have a high chair/
baby-sitting service/cot?
Máte dětskou židli/
opatrovatelskou službu/
postýlku?
*Mahteh dyetskow zhidli/
ohpahtrohvahtelskow sloozhboo/
posteelkoo?*

**247** Where is the nursery/
playroom?
Kde jsou jesle/dětský pokoj?
*Gde sow yesleh/dyetskee pockoy?*

**248** Where can I warm the
baby's bottle?
Kde můžu ohřát lahvičku?

*Gde moozhoo ohzhaht lahvichkoo?*

## COMMUNICATIONS

### Post

²⁴⁹ How much will it cost to send a letter/postcard/this package to Britain/Ireland/America/Canada/Australia/New Zealand?
Kolik stojí dopis/pohlednice/tento balík do Británie/Irska/Ameriky/Kanady/Australie/na Nový Zéland?
*Kollick stoyee dohpis/pohlehdnitseh/tehntoh bahleeck doh Britahnie/Irskah/Ahmehrickyh/Kahnahdy/Aoostrahliah/nah nohvee zehlahnd?*

²⁵⁰ I would like one stamp/two stamps.
Prosím známku/dvě známky.
*Prosseem znahmkoo/dvye znahmky.*

²⁵¹ I'd like . . . stamps for postcards to send abroad, please.
Potřebuji . . . poštovní známky na pohlednice do ciziny, prosím.
*Potrzhebuhyi . . . pohshtovnyee znahmki nahpohhlednyitse do tsizini, prosseem.*

## Phones

²⁵² I would like to make a telephone call/reverse the charges to (make a collect call to) . . .
Rád bych zatelefonoval/na účet volaného do . . .
*Rahd bykh zahtelephonohvahl/nah oochet vohlahnehoo doh . . .*

²⁵³ Which coins do I need for the telephone?
Jaké mince potřebuji pro telefon?
*Yuckeh mintseh pohtzhebooyee proh telephohn?*

²⁵⁴ The line is engaged (busy).
Linka je obsazena.
*Linkah yeh obsazhenah.*

²⁵⁵ The number is . . .
Číslo je . . .
*Cheesloh yeh . . .*

²⁵⁶ Hello, this is . . .
Haló, tady je . . .
*Hulloh, tahdiye . . .*

²⁵⁷ May I speak to . . ?
Mohu mluvit s . . ?
*Mohu mluhvit s . . ?*

²⁵⁸ He/She is not in at the moment. Can you call back?
Momentálně tady není.
Můžete zavolat později?
*Mohmentahlnyeh tahdi nenyee. Moozheteh zahvolat pohzdyeyi?*

**CZECH**

**259
↕
274**

## MONEY

**259** I would like to change these travellers' cheques (travelers' checks)/this currency/this Eurocheque.
Rád bych vyměnil tyto cestovní šeky/tuto měnu/ tento Eurošek.
*Rahd bykh vymnyenil tytoh tsehstovnee shecky/tootoh mnyenoo/tehntoh Ehurohsheck.*

**260** How much commission do you charge? (What is the service charge?)
Kolik účtujete provize?
*Kollick oochtooyeteh prohvizeh?*

**261** Can I obtain money with my MasterCard?
Můžu vybrat peníze s MasterCard?
*Moozhoo vybraht pehneezeh ss MasterCard?*

## SHOPPING

### Names of Shops and Departments

**262** Knihkupectví/ Papírnictví
*Knyihkoopetstvee/ Pahpeernyictvee*
Bookshop/Stationery

**263** Klenotnictví/Dárky
*Klehnotnyitstvee/Dahrrki*
Jeweller's/Gifts

**264** Obuv

*Ohbuhf*
Shoes

**265** Železářství
*Zhelezahrzhstvee*
Hardware

**266** Starožitnosti
*Starrozhitnohstyi*
Antiques

**267** Holič/Kadeřník
*Holich/Kahdehrzhnyeek*
Hairdressers (men's)/ (women's)

**268** Tabák
*Tahbahk*
Tobacconist

**269** Pekárna
*Pehkahrrnah*
Baker's

**270** Samoobsluha
*Sahmoh-opsloohah*
Supermarket

**271** Fotografické potřeby
*Fotografitskeh pohtrzhebi*
Photoshop

**272** Hračky
*Hrachki*
Toys

**273** Cestovní kancelář
*Tsestovnyee kahntselahrzh*
Travel Agent

**274** Drogerie/Parfumerie
*Drohgueriyeh/Parrfuhmehriye*
Toiletries

**275 Desky**
*Dahski*
Records

## In the Shop

**276 What time do the shops open/close?**
Kdy jsou obchody otevřené/zavřené?
*Gdy sow obkhody ohtevzheneh/zavzheneh?*

**277 Where is the nearest market?**
Kde je nejbližší trh?
*Gdeye neyblizhshee treh?*

**278 Can you show me the one in the window/this one?**
Můžete mi ukázat to ve výloze/tady to?
*Moozhetemi uhkahzat toh veveelozeh/tahdi toh?*

**279 Can I try this on?**
Můžu to vyzkoušet?
*Moozhoo toh vyzkowshet?*

**280 What size is this?**
Jaká je to velikost?
*Yuckah yeh toh vehlikohst?*

**281 This is too large/too small/too expensive.**
Je to příliš velké/příliš malé/příliš drahé.
*Yeto przheelish velkeh/przheelish mahleh/przheelish drah-heh.*

**282 Do you have any others?**
Máte nějaké jiné?

*Mahte nyeyakeh yineh?*

**283 My size is . . .**
Moje velikost je . . .
*Moyeh velikohst ye . . .*

**284 Where is the changing room/childrens'/cosmetic/ladieswear/menswear/food department?**
Kde jsou tady převlékárny/dětské oddělení/kosmetika/dámské/pánské oddělení/potraviny?
*Gde sow tahdy pzhevlehkahrny/dyetskeh otdyelehnee/kohsmehtickah/dahmskeh/pahnskeh otdyelehne/potrahviny?*

**285 I would like . . .**
Rád(a) bych . . .
*Rahd(ah) bikh . . .*

**286 I would like a quarter of a kilo/half a kilo/a kilo of bread/butter/cheese/ham/tomatoes.**
Prosím čtvrt kila/půl kila/kilo chleba/másla/sýra/šunky/rajčat.
*Prosseem chtvert kilah/pool kilah/kiloh khlebbah/mahslah/seerah/shoonky/rahychat.*

**287 How much is this?**
Kolik to stojí?
*Kollick toh stoyee?*

**288 I'll take this one, thank you.**
Vezmu si tuhle, děkuji.
*Vezmoossi toohle, dyekuyi.*

C
Z
E
C
H

275
↕
288

# SHOPPING/MOTORING

C
Z
E
C
H

289
↕
300

**289** Do you have a carrier (shopping) bag?
Máte sáček?
*Mahteh sahcheck?*

**290** Do you have anything cheaper/larger/smaller/of better quality?
Máte něco lacinější/větší/menší/kvalitnější?
*Mahteh nyetsoh latsinyejshee/vyetshee/menshee/kvahlitnyeyshee?*

**291** I would like a film for this camera.
Rád bych film pro tento aparát.
*Rahd bykh film proh tentoh aparaht.*

**292** I would like some batteries, the same size as this old one.
Rád bych baterie, stejné velikosti jako tato stará.
*Rahd bykh bahtehrieh, stehyneh vehlikohsti yuckoh ttahtoh stharah.*

**293** Would you mind wrapping this for me, please?
Zabalte mi to, prosím.
*Zahbahlteh mee toh, prosseem.*

**294** Sorry, but you seem to have given me the wrong change.
Promiňte, vrátil jste mi peníze špatně.
*Prohminyteh, vrahtil steh mee pehneezeh shpatnye.*

## MOTORING

### Car hire (Rental)

**295** I have ordered (rented) a car in the name of . . .
Zamluvil jsem auto pod jménem . . .
*Zahmloovil sehm aootoh pohd mehnehm . . .*

**296** How much does it cost to hire (rent) a car for one day/two days/one week?
Kolik stojí vypůjčení auta na den/dva dny/na týden?
*Kollick stoyee vypoojchenee aootah nah den/dvah dnyh/nah teeden?*

**297** Is the tank already full of petrol (gas)?
Je nádrž plná benzínu?
*Yeh nahdrsh plnah behnzeenoo?*

**298** Is insurance and tax included? How much is the deposit?
Zahrnuje to pojištění a daně? Kolik je záloha?
*Zahrnooye toh poyeeshtyenee ah dahneh? Kollick ye zahlohah?*

**299** By what time must I return the car?
Do kdy musím vrátit auto?
*Doh gdyh moosseem vrahtit aootoh?*

**300** I would like a small/family car with a radio/cassette player.

56

Přeji si malé/rodinné auto s radiem/kazetou.
*Pzheyee sih mahleh/roddineh aootoh ss rahdiehm/kazetow.*

## Asking the Way

301 **Excuse me, can you help me please?**
Promiňte, můžete mi, pomoci, prosím?
*Prohminyeteh, moozhetemi pohmohtsi, prohsseem?*

302 **How do I reach the motorway/main road?**
Jak se dostanu na dálnici/na hlavní silnici?
*Yakseh dohstahnuh nadahlnyitsi/nahlavnyee silnyitsi?*

303 **I think I have taken the wrong turning.**
Myslím, že jsem špatně odbočil.
*Misleem zhessem shpatnyeh odbohchil.*

304 **I am looking for this address.**
Hledám tuto adresu.
*Hlehdahm tuhtoh adrehsuh.*

305 **I am looking for the . . . hotel.**
Hledám hotel . . .
*Hlehdahm hotel . . . .*

306 **How far is it to . . . from here?**
Jak daleko je odsud do . . ?

*Yak dahlekoh yeh odsuhd doh . . ?*

307 **Carry straight on for . . . kilometres.**
Jeďte pořád rovně asi . . . kilometrů.
*Yedye-teh porzhahd rovnyeh ahsee . . . kilohmehtroo.*

308 **Take the next turning on the right/left.**
Na příští odbočce zahněte doprava/doleva.
*Na przheeshtyee odboch-tse zahnyehteh doprahvah/ dohlehvah.*

309 **Turn right/left at the next crossroads/traffic lights.**
Odbočíte doprava/doleva na nejbližší křižovatce/u nejbližšího semaforu.
*Odbohcheeteh dohprahvah/ dohlehvah nah neyblish-shee krzhizhovaht-tse/uh neyblish-sheehoh sehmahforuh.*

310 **You are going in the wrong direction.**
Jedete špatným směrem.
*Yedyete shpahtneem smnyerem.*

## Parking

311 **How long can I park here?**
Jak dlouho tady můžu parkovat?
*Yak dloehoh tahdi moozhu parrkohvaht?*

**312**
↕
**327**

**312** Is there a car park near here?
Je tady někde blízko parkoviště?
*Yeh tahdi nyegdeh bleeskoh parrkohveeshtye?*

**313** At what time does this car park close?
V kolik hodin se tohle parkoviště zavírá?
*Fkollick hohdyin se toh-hle parrkohveeshtye zaveerah?*

## Signs and Notices

**314** Jednosměrný provoz.
*Yednohsmnyernee prohvohs.*
One way.

**315** Zákaz vjezdu.
*Zahkaz vyezduh.*
No entry.

**316** Parkování zakázáno.
*Parrkohvahnyee zahkahzahnoh.*
No parking.

**317** Objížďka
*Obyeezhdyekah*
Detour (diversion)

**318** Stůj/Stop.
*Stooy/Stop.*
Stop.

**319** Dej přednost v jízdě.
*Dey przhednost vyeezdyeh.*
Give way (yield).

**320** Kluzká vozovka/
Nebezpečí smyku.
*Kluhzkah vohzovkah/*

*Nebespechee smikuh.*
Slippery road.

**321** Zákaz předjíždění.
*Zahkaz przhedyeezhdyenyee.*
No overtaking.

## At the Filling Station

**322** Unleaded (lead-free)/
Standard/Premium
Bezolovnatý/Normál/Super
*Besolovnahtee/Norrmahl/ Suhperr*

**323** Fill the tank please.
Plnou nádrž, prosím.
*Pulnoe nahdrzh, prohseem.*

**324** Do you have a road map of this area?
Máte silniční mapu této oblasti?
*Mahteh silnyichnyee mahpuh tehtoh oblahstyi?*

**325** How much is the car-wash?
Kolik stojí umytí auta?
*Kolik stoyee uhmytyee owtah?*

## Breakdowns

**326** I've had a breakdown at . . .
Porouchalo se mi auto u . . .
*Poroekhahloh seh mi outoh uh . . .*

**327** I am on the road from . . . to . . .
Jsem na silnici z . . . do . . .
*Sehm na silneetsi z . . . doh . . .*

**328** I can't move the car. Can you send a tow-truck?
Nemohu s autem odjet. Můžete poslat havarijní odtahovou službu?
*Nehmohhu soutehm odyeht. Moozhete pohslat hahvahriynyee ohdtahhovoe sluhzhbuh?*

**329** I have a flat tyre.
Píchl(a) jsem pneumatiku.
*Peekhl(a) sehm pneuhmahtikuh.*

**330** The windscreen (windshield) has smashed/cracked.
Mám rozbité/prasklé přední sklo.
*Mahm rozbihteh/prahskleh przhednyee skloh.*

**331** There is something wrong with the engine/brakes/lights/steering/gearbox/clutch/exhaust.
Něco není v pořádku s motorem/s brzdami/se světly/s převodovkou/se spojkou/s výfukem.
*Nyetso nehnyee v pohrzhahdkuh smohtohrem/s br-zdahmee/sesvyetly/sprzehvohdohvkoe/se spoykoe/sveefookem*

**332** It's overheating.
Přehřívá se to.
*Przhehrzheevahsseh toh.*

**333** It won't start.
Nechce to nastartovat.

*Nekhtse toh nahstahrtohvat.*

**334** Where can I get it repaired?
Kde si to můžu nechat opravit?
*Gdehsi toh moozhu nekhaht ohprahvit?*

**335** Can you take me there?
Můžete mě tam zavézt?
*Moozhete mnye tahm zahvehst?*

**336** Will it take long to fix?
Bude oprava trvat dlouho?
*Buhde ohprahva turvaht dloehoh?*

**337** How much will it cost?
Kolik to bude stát?
*Kollick toh boodeh staht?*

## Accidents

**338** Can you help me? There has been an accident.
Můžete mi pomoct? Stala se nehoda.
*Moozheteh me pomotst? Stahlah seh nahodah.*

**339** Please call the police/an ambulance.
Zavolejte, prosím, policii/záchranku.
*Zahvohlehtyeh, prohseem, pohlitssiyi/zahhrankooh.*

**340** Is anyone hurt?
Je někdo zraněný?
*Jeh nyekdoh zranyehnee?*

C
Z
E
C
H

341
↑
352

## Traffic Offences

**341** I'm sorry, I didn't see the sign.

Moc mě to mrzí, neviděl jsem tu značku.

*Mohts mnye toh mrrzeeh, nevidyel sem to znachkooh.*

**342** Must I pay a fine? How much?

Musím zaplatit pokutu? Kolik?

*Muhseem zahplahtyit pohkuhtuh? Kolik?*

**343** Show me your documents.

Ukažte mi své doklady.

*Ookazhte me sveh dohklahdi.*

## HEALTH

## Pharmacy

**344** Do you have anything for a stomachache/headache/sore throat/toothache?

Máte něco proti bolení břicha/hlavy/v krku/zubu?

*Mahteh nyetso prohti bohlehnee bzhikha/vh krckoo/zooboo?*

**345** I need something for diarrhoea (diarrhea)/constipation/a cold/a cough/insect bites/sunburn/travel (motion) sickness.

Potřebuji něco proti průjmu/zácpě/rýmě/kašli/poštípání hmyzem/spálení sluncem/cestovní nevolnosti.

*Pohtzhehbooyi nyetsoh prohti prooymoo/zahtzpye/reemnye/kashli/poshteenahnee hmyzehm/spahlehnee slontsehm/tsehstovnee nehvohlnohsti.*

**346** How much/how many do I take?

Kolik toho mám vzít?

*Kollick tooho mahm vzeet?*

**347** How often do I take it/them?

Jak často to mám brát?

*Yuck chashstoh toh mah braht?*

**348** How much does it cost?

Kolik to stojí?

*Kollick toh stoyee?*

**349** Can you recommend a good doctor/dentist?

Můžete doporučit dobrého lékaře/zubaře?

*Moozheteh dopohroochit dohbrehoh lehkazhe/zoobazhe?*

**350** Is it suitable for children?

Je to vhodné pro děti?

*Yeh toh vhohdneh pro dyeti?*

## Doctor

**351** I have a pain here/in my arm/leg/chest/stomach.

Bolí mě tady/v paži/v noze/hrudi/žaludku.

*Bohlee mnye tahdy/vh pahzhi/vh nohzeh/hroodi/zhahloodkoo.*

**352** Please call a doctor, this is an emergency.

Prosím zavolejte doktora, je

to náhlá příhoda.
*Prosseem zahvohleyteh
dohktohrah, yeh toh nahlah
pzheehodah.*

**353** I would like to make an
appointment to see a
doctor.
Rád bych se objednal u
doktora.
*Rahd bykh seh ohbyednahl oo
dohktohrah.*

**354** I am diabetic/pregnant.
Mám cukrovku/jsem v jiném
stavu.
*Mahm tsookrovkoo/sem vh
yeenehm stahvoo.*

**355** I need a prescription for
. . .
Potřebuji předpis na . . .
*Pohtzhehbooyi pzhehdpiss
nah . . .*

**356** Can you give me
something to ease the
pain?
Můžete mi dát něco na
ulehčení bolesti?
*Moozhehteh mee daht nyetso
nah oolehchenee bohlehstee?*

**357** I am/he is/she is allergic
to penicillin.
Mám alergii/Má alergii/Má
alergii na penicilin.
*Mahm ahlehrguiyi/Mah
ahlehrguiyi/Mah ahlehrguiyi
nah pehnitsileen.*

**358** Does this hurt?
Bolí to?
*Bohlee toh?*

**359** You must/he must/she
must go to hospital.
Musíte/On musí/Ona musí
do nemocnice.
*Muhsseeteh/On muhsee/Onah
muhsee dohnehmohtsnyitseh.*

**360** Take these once/twice /
three times a day.
Užívejte je jednou/dvakrát/
třikrát denně.
*Oozheeveyteh yeh yednoe/
dvahkraht/trzhikraht denye.*

**361** I am/he is/she is taking
this medication.
Užívám/On užívá/Ona užívá
tyhle léky.
*Oozheevahm/On oozheevar/
Onah oozheevar teehleh lahky.*

**362** I have medical insurance.
Mám lékařské pojištění.
*Mahm lehkahrzhskeh
poyishtyenyee.*

## Dentist

**363** I have toothache.
Bolí mě zub.
*Bohlee mnye zoob.*

**364** My filling has come out.
Vypadla mně plomba.
*Vypahdlah mnye plohmbah.*

**365** I do/do not want to have an injection first.
Přeji si/nepřeji si nejdříve injekci.
*Pzheyee ssi/nehpzheyee ssi neydzheeveh inyeksti.*

## EMERGENCIES

**366** Help!
Pomoc!
*Pohmots!*

**367** Call an ambulance/a doctor/the police.
Zavolejte sanitku/doktora/ policii!
*Zahvohleyteh sahnitkoo/ docktorah/pohlitsiyee!*

**368** I have had my travellers' cheques (travelers' checks)/ credit cards/purse/handbag/ rucksack (knapsack)/ luggage/wallet stolen.
Byly mi ukradeny cestovní šeky/kreditní karty/ peněženka/kabelka/ruksak/ zavazadlo/náprsní taška.
*Byly mee ookrahdehny tsehstohvnee shecky/krehditnih kahrty/pennyehzhenkah/ kubbelkah/rooksack/ zuvvahzuddloh/nahprsnee tashkah.*

**369** Can you help me, I have lost my daughter/son?
Pomozte mi, ztratil jsem dceru/syna.
*Pohmohsteh mee, ztrahtil sem tseroo/seenah.*

**370** Please go away/leave me alone.
Běžte pryč/nechte mě být.
*Byezhteh prych/nekhteh mnye byt.*

**371** Fire!
Hoří!
*Hohrzhee!*

**372** I want to contact the British/ American/Canadian/Irish/ Australian/New Zealand/ South African consulate.
Rád(a) bych se spojil(a) s britským/americkým/ kanadským/irským/ australským/ novozélandským/ jihoafrickým konzulátem.
*Rahd(ah) byh seh spohyilah s britskeem/ahmehritskeem/ kahnahtskeem/irskeem/ aoostralskeem/nohvoh zehlahntskeem/yihoh- ahfritskeem konsuhlahtem.*

# Introduction

French is spoken as a first language not only in France but also in Monaco, in the French-speaking areas of Belgium (the south and west, and Brussels) and in western Switzerland (including the cities of Geneva and Lausanne), and it is widely spoken in Luxembourg. In all of these regions there will be quite a few people who can understand or speak some English, particularly in the more tourist-frequented localities, but it will pay dividends to at least attempt to speak some French, particularly in France itself.

F
R
E
N
C
H

## Addresses for travel and tourist information

**UK:** *Maison de la France*, 178 Piccadilly, London W1V 0AL; tel: 0891 244123. *Belgian National Tourist Office*, Premier House, 2 Gayton Rd, Harrow, Middlesex HA1 2XU; tel: (0181) 861 3300. *Swiss National Tourist Office*, Swiss Centre, London W1V 8EE; tel: (0171) 734 1921.

**USA:** *French Government Tourist Office*, 610 Fifth Avenue, New York, NY 10020-2452; tel: (212) 757-1125. *Belgian National Tourist Office*, 745 Fifth Avenue (Suite 714), New York, NY 10151; tel: (212) 758-8130. *Swiss National Tourist Office*, Swiss Center, 608 Fifth Avenue, New York, NY 10020; tel: (212) 757-5944.

**FRENCH**

**01 ↕ 12**

## ESSENTIALS

### Alphabet

| | |
|---|---|
| A *ah* | B *beh* |
| C *seh* | D *de* |
| E *eur* | F *eff* |
| G *ge* | H *ash* |
| I *ee* | J *ji* |
| K *ka* | L *elle* |
| M *emme* | N *enne* |
| O *o* | P *pe* |
| Q *ku* | R *erre* |
| S *esse* | T *te* |
| U *u* | V *ve* |
| W *dooble ve* | X *iks* |
| Y *ee grec* | Z *zede* |

### Basic Words and Phrases

**1** Yes
Oui
*Wee*

No
Non
*nawng*

**2** Please
S'il vous plaît
*Seel voo pleh*

Thank you
Merci
*Mehrsee*

**3** That's O.K.
Ça va
*Sahr vahr*

Perhaps
Peut-être
*Purtehtr*

**4** To
à
*ah*

From
De
*der*

**5** Here
Ici
*Eesee*

There
Là
*lah*

**6** None
Aucun
*Okang*

Also
Aussi
*Ossee*

**7** How
Comment
*Kommahng*

When
Quand
*kahng*

**8** What
Quel
*kehl*

Why
Pourquoi
*poorkwah*

**9** I don't understand.
Je ne comprends pas.
*Zher ner kawngprahng pah.*

**10** I don't speak French.
Je ne parle pas français.
*Zher ner pahrl pah frahngsay.*

**11** Do you speak English?
Vous parlez anglais?
*Voopahrlay ahnglay?*

**12** Can you please write it down?
Pouvez-vous l'écrire s'il vous plaît?
*Poovehvoo laycreer seelvooplay?*

13 **Can you please speak more slowly?**
Pouvez-vous parler plus lentement s'il vous plaît?
*Poovehvoo pahrlay plew lahntermahng seelvooplay?*

14 **How much does it/this cost?**
Quel est le prix?
*Kehl eh ler pree?*

## Days

15 **Monday** | **Tuesday**
Lundi | Mardi
*Langdee* | *Mahrdee*

16 **Wednesday** | **Thursday**
Mercredi | Jeudi
*Mehrkrerdee* | *Zhurdee*

17 **Friday** | **Saturday**
Vendredi | Samedi
*Vahndrerdee* | *Sahmdee*

18 **Sunday** | **Morning**
Dimanche | Le matin
*Deemahngsh* | *Ler mahtang*

19 **Afternoon** | **Evening**
L'après-midi | Le soir
*Lahpreh meedee* | *Ler swahr*

20 **Night** | **Week**
La nuit | La semaine
*Lah nwee* | *Lah sermehn*

21 **Yesterday** | **Tomorrow**
Hier | Demain
*Yehr* | *Dermang*

## Numbers

22 **Zero** | **One**
Zéro | Un

Zayroa | Ang

23 **Two** | **Three**
Deux | Trois
*Dur* | *Trwah*

24 **Four** | **Five**
Quatre | Cinq
*Kahtr* | *Sangk*

25 **Six** | **Seven**
six | Sept
*Seess* | *Seht*

26 **Eight** | **Nine**
Huit | Neuf
*Weet* | *Nurf*

27 **Ten** | **Eleven**
Dix | Onze
*Deess* | *Awngz*

28 **Twelve** | **Thirteen**
Douze | Treize
*Dooz* | *Trehz*

29 **Fourteen** | **Fifteen**
Quatorze | Quinze
*Kahtorz* | *Kangz*

30 **Sixteen** | **Seventeen**
Seize | Dix-sept
*Sehz* | *Deess seht*

31 **Eighteen** | **Nineteen**
Dix-huit | Dix-neuf
*Deez weet* | *Deez nurf*

32 **Twenty** | **Twenty-one**
Vingt | Vingt et un
*Vang* | *Vang tay ang*

33 **Twenty-two** | **Thirty**
Vingt-deux | Trente
*Vangt dur* | *Trahngt*

F
R
E
N
C
H

13
↑
33

**34** **Forty** **Fifty**
Quarante Cinquante
*Kahrahngt* *Sangkahnt*

**35** **Sixty** **Seventy**
Soixante Soixante-dix
*Swahssahngt* *Swassahngt deess*

**36** **Eighty** **Ninety**
Quatre-vingts Quatre-vingt-dix
*Kahtrer vang* *Kahtrer vang deess*

**37** **One hundred Five hundred**
Cent Cinq cents
*Sahng* *Sang sahng*

**38** **One thousand One million**
Mille Un million
*Meel* *Ang meelyawng*

## Time

**39** **9.00**
Neuf heures
*Nuro urr*

**40** **9.05**
Neuf heures cinq
*Nuro urr sangk*

**41** **9.10**
Neuf heures dix
*Nuro urr deess*

**42** **9.15**
Neuf heures et quart
*Nuro urr eh kahr*

**43** **9.20**
Neuf heures vingt
*Nuro urr vang*

**44** **9.25**
Neuf heures vingt-cinq
*Nuro urr vang sangk*

**45** **9.30**
Neuf heures et demie
*Nuro urr eh dermee*

**46** **9.35**
Dix heures moins vingt-cinq
*Dee zurr mwang vang sangk*

**47** **9.40**
Dix heures moins vingt
*Dee zurr mwang vang*

**48** **9.45**
Dix heures moins le quart
*Dee zurr mwang le kahr*

**49** **9.50**
Dix heures moins dix
*Dee zurr mwang deess*

**50** **9.55**
Dix heures moins cinq
*Dee zurr mwang sangk*

**51** **12.00/Midday/Midnight**
Douze heures/Midi/Minuit
*Doowz urr/meedee/meenurhee*

**52** **What time is it?**
Quelle heure est-il?
*Kel urr ehteel?*

**53** **It is . . .**
Il est. . .
*Eel eh . . .*

## ARRIVING AND DEPARTING

## Airport

**54** **Excuse me, where is the
check-in desk for . . . airline?**
Excusez-moi, où est le comptoir
d'enregistrement de . . ?
*Ekskewsehmwah, oo eh ler*

kongtwahr
dahngrehzheestrehmahng der . . ?

**55** **What is the boarding gate/
time for my flight?**
Quelle est la porte
d'embarquement/l'heure
d'embarquement de mon vol?
*Kehl eh lah pohrt
dahngbahrkehmahng/lurr
dahngbahrkehmahng der mawng
vohl?*

**56** **How long is the delay likely
to be?**
Le retard est de combien?
*Ler rurtahr eh der kawngbyang?*

**57** **Where is the duty-free shop?**
Où est la boutique hors-taxe?
*Oo eh lah bootik ohrtahks?*

**58** **Which way is the baggage
reclaim?**
Où se trouve l'aire de réception
des bagages?
*Oo ser troov lair der
rehssehpsseeawng deh bahgahzh?*

**59** **Where can I get the bus to
the city centre?**
Où puis-je prendre le bus pour
le centre-ville?
*Oo pweezh prahngdr ler bews poor
ler sahngtr veel?*

## Train Station

**60** **Where is the ticket office/
information desk?**
Où se trouve le guichet/le
bureau de renseignements?
*Oo ser troov ler geesheh/ler*

bewroa der rahngsehniehmahng?

**61** **Which platform does the
train to . . . depart from?**
De quel quai part le train
pour . . ?
*Der kehl kay pahr ler trang poor . . ?*

**62** **Where is platform . . ?**
Où se trouve le quai . . ?
*Oo ser troov ler kay . . ?*

**63** **When is the next train to . . ?**
Quand est le prochain train
pour . . ?
*Kahng eh ler proshang trang poor . . ?*

**64** **Is there a later train to . . ?**
Y-a-t-il un train plus tard pour
. . ?
*Ee ahteel ang trang plew tahr
poor . . ?*

## Port

**65** **How do I get to the port?**
Pour aller au port, s'il vous
plaît?
*Poor ahleh oh por, seelvooplay?*

**66** **When is the next sailing
to . . ?**
Quand est le prochain départ
pour . . ?
*Kahng eh ler proshang dehpahr
poor . . ?*

**67** **Can I catch an earlier ferry
with this ticket?**
Puis-je prendre un ferry plus tôt
avec ce billet?
*Pweezh prahngdrer ang ferry plew
tow ahvehk ser beeyeh?*

F
R
E
N
C
H

55
↑
67

## Notices and Signs

**68 Voiture-restaurant**
*Vwature restorahn*
Buffet (Dining) Car

**69 Autobus**
*Otoebewss*
Bus

**70 Eau potable/Eau non potable**
*Oa poatahbl/Oa nawng poatahbl*
Drinking/Non-drinking water

**71 Entrée**
*Ahngtray*
Entrance

**72 Sortie**
*Soartee*
Exit

**73 Renseignements**
*Rahngsehnyermahng*
Information

**74 Consigne**
*Kawngsseeñ*
Left Luggage (Baggage Claim)

**75 Consigne automatique**
*Kawngsseeñ oatomahtick*
Luggage Lockers

**76 Poste**
*Peost*
Post Office

**77 Quai**
*Kay*
Platform

**78 Gare**
*Gahr*
Railway (Railroad) Station

**79 Aéroport**
*Ahehrohpohr*
Airport

**80 Port**
*Pohr*
Port

**81 Restaurant**
*Rehstoarahng*
Restaurant

**82 Fumeurs/non fumeurs**
*Fewmurh/nawng fewmurh*
Smoking/Non-Smoking

**83 Téléphone**
*Taylayphone*
Telephone

**84 Guichet**
*Gueechay*
Ticket Office

**85 Enregistrement des bagages**
*Ahngrehzheestrehmahng day bahgahzh*
Check-in Desk

**86 Horaires**
*Oarayrh*
Timetables (Schedules)

**87 Toilettes**
*Twahlayt*
Toilets (Restrooms)

**88 Hommes**
*Ommh*
Gentlemen

**89 Femmes**
*Dahm*
Ladies'

**90 Tramway**

F
R
E
N
C
H

68
↕
90

*Trahmway*
Tram (Streetcar)

**91 Métro**
*Maytroa*
Underground (Subway)

**92 Salle d'attente**
*Sahldahtahngth*
Waiting-Room

## Buying a Ticket

**93 I would like a first-class/
second-class single (one-
way)/return (round-trip)
ticket to . . .**
Je voudrais un billet de première
classe/deuxième classe aller/
aller-retour pour . . .
*Zher voodray ang beeyeh
prermyehr/durzyehm klahss
ahlay/ahlay rertoor poor . . .*

**94 Is my rail pass valid on this
train/ferry/bus?**
Est-ce que ma carte ferroviaire
est valable pour ce train/ce
ferry/ce bus?
*Ehss ker mah kahrt fehrohveeair
eh vahlahblh dahng ser trang/ser
ferry/ser bewss?*

**95 I would like an aisle/window
seat.**
Je voudrais être près de l'allée/la
fenêtre.
*Zher voodray aytr pray der
lahlaeh/lah fernaytr.*

**96 No smoking/smoking, please.**
Non fumeur/fumeur.
*Nawng fewmur/fewmur.*

**97 We would like to sit
together.**
Nous aimerions être assis
ensemble.
*Noo aymerreeawng ehtr ahssee
ahngsahngbl.*

**98 I would like to make a seat
reservation.**
Je voudrais réserver une place.
*Zher voodray rehzehrveh ewn
plahss.*

**99 I would like to reserve a
couchette/sleeper for one
person/two people/for my
family.**
J'aimerais réserver une
couchette/place de voiture-lit
pour une personne/deux
personnes/pour ma famille.
*Zhaymerray rehzehrveh ewn
kooshayt/plahss der vwature-lee
poor ewn pehrson/dur perhson/
poor mah fahmeeye.*

**100 I would like to reserve a
cabin.**
Je voudrais réserver une cabine.
*Zher voodray rehzehrveh ewn
kahbeen.*

## Timetables (Schedules)

**101 Arrive**
*Ahrivh*
Arrive

**102 S'arrête à**
*Sahrayth ah*
Calls (Stops) at

F
R
E
N
C
H

91
↑
102

69

[103] **Restauration**
*Restoarahsseeawng*
Catering Service

[104] **Changez à**
*Chahngzay ah . . .*
Change at . . .

[105] **Correspondance**
*Koarespawngdahngss*
Connection

[106] **Tous les jours**
*Too ley joorh*
Daily

[107] **Toutes les quarante minutes**
*Tooth lay kahrahngt menewt*
Every 40 Minutes

[108] **Première classe**
*Prermeeayrh class*
First-Class

[109] **Toutes les heures**
*Toot lay zur*
Hourly

[110] **Il est recommandé de réserver sa place**
*Eel eh rekomahngday der rayzayrvay sa plahs*
Seat reservations are recommended

[111] **Deuxième classe**
*Dersieme class*
Second-class

[112] **Supplément à payer**
*Sewplaymahng ah payay*
Supplement Payable

[113] **Par**
*Pah*
Via

## Luggage

[114] **How much will it cost to send (ship) my luggage in advance?**
Quel est le prix pour envoyer mes bagages en avance?
*Kehl eh ler pree poor ahngwahllay meh bahgahz ahng ahvahngss?*

[115] **Where is the left luggage (baggage claim) office?**
Où se trouve la consigne?
*Oo ser troov lah kawngseen?*

[116] **What time do you open/close?**
A quelle heure ouvrez-vous/fermez-vous?
*Ah kehl ur oovrayvoo/fairmehvoo?*

[117] **Where are the luggage trolleys (carts)?**
Où se trouve les chariots à bagages?
*Oo ser troov leh shahryo ah bahgahzh?*

[118] **Where are the lockers?**
Où se trouve la consigne automatique?
*Oo ser troov lah kawngseen awtoematique?*

[119] **I have lost my locker key.**
J'ai perdu la clé de mon casier.
*Zhay payrdew lah kleh der mawng kahzeeay.*

## On Board

**120 Is this seat taken?**
Est-ce que cette place est libre?
*Ehsker sayt plahss eh leebr?*

**121 Excuse me, you are sitting in my reserved seat.**
Excusez-moi, vous occupez la place que j'ai réservée.
*Ehskewzaymwah voo okewpeh lah plahss ker zay rehzehrveh.*

**122 Which station is this?**
Quelle est cette gare?
*Kehl eh sayt gahr?*

**123 What time is this train/bus/ferry/flight due to arrive/depart?**
A quelle heure arrive/part le train/le bus/le ferry?
*Ah kehlur ahrivh/pahr ler trang/ler bewss/ler ferry?*

**124 Will you wake me just before we arrive?**
Pouvez-vous me réveiller avant l'arrivée?
*Poovay voo mer rehvehlleh ahvahng lahreeveh?*

## Customs and Passports

**125 Les passeports, s'il vous plaît!**
*Leh pahsspor, seelvooplay!*
Passports, please!

**126 I have nothing/wine/spirits (alcohol)/tobacco to declare.**
Je n'ai rien à déclarer/J'ai du vin/de l'acool/du tabac à déclarer.
*Zher neh reeang ah dehklahreh/zhay dew vang/der lahlkol/dew tahbah ah dehklahreh.*

**127 I shall be staying for . . . days/weeks/months.**
Je vais rester . . . jours/semaines/mois.
*Zhe veh resteh . . . zoor/sermehn/mwah.*

## AT THE TOURIST OFFICE

**128 Do you have a map of the town/area?**
Avez-vous une carte de la ville/région?
*Ahveh-voo ewn cart der lah veel/rehjyawong?*

**129 Can I reserve accommodation here?**
Puis-je réserver un logement ici?
*Peweezh rehzehrveh ang lozhmahng eesee?*

**130 Do you have a list of accommodation?**
Vous avez une liste d'hôtels?
*Voozahveh ewn leesst dohtehl?*

## ACCOMMODATION

### Hotels

**131 I have a reservation in the name of . . .**
J'ai fait une réservation au nom de . . .
*Zheh feh ewn rehsehrvahssyawong o nawng der . . .*

**132** I wrote to/faxed/telephoned you last month/last week in . . .
Je vous ai écrit/faxé/téléphoné le mois dernier/la semaine dernière.
*Zher voozeh ehkree/faxeh/ tehlehfoneh ler mwah dehrnyeh/ lah sermayn dehrnyair.*

**133** Do you have any rooms free?
Vous avez des chambres disponibles?
*Voozahveh deh shahngbr deesspohneebl?*

**134** I would like to reserve a single/double room with/without bath/shower.
Je voudrais réserver une chambre pour une personne/pour deux personnes avec/sans salle de bain/douche.
*Zhe voodray rehsehrveh ewn shahngbr poor ewn pehrson/poor dur pehrson avek/sawns sal der banne/doosh.*

**135** I would like bed and breakfast/(room and) half board/(room and) full board.
Je voudrais le petit-déjeuner/la demi-pension/la pension complète.
*Zher voodray ler pewtee-dehjewneh/ lah dermee-pahngsyawng/lah pahngsyawng kawngplait.*

**136** How much is it per night?
Quel est le prix pour une nuit?
*Khel eh ler pree poor ewn nuwy?*

**137** Is breakfast included?

Est-ce que le petit-déjeuner est compris?
*Ehsker ler pertee dehjerneh eh kawngpree?*

**138** May I see the room?
Puis-je voir la chambre?
*Pweezh vwahr lah shahngbr?*

**139** Do you have any cheaper rooms?
Avez-vous des chambres moins chères?
*Ahvehvoo deh shahngbr mooang shayr?*

**140** I would like to take the room.
Je prends la chambre.
*Zhe prahng lah shangbr.*

**141** I would like to stay for . . . nights.
Je voudrais rester . . . nuits.
*Zhe voodray resteh . . . newyh.*

**142** The shower/light/tap doesn't work.
La douche/la lumière/le robinet ne marche pas.
*Lah doosh/lah luhmiair/ler rohbeenay ner marsh pah.*

**143** At what time/where is breakfast served?
A quelle heure/où servez-vous le petit-déjeuner?
*Ah khel ur/ooh serveh-voo ler perteedehjerneh?*

**144** What time do I have to check-out?
A quelle heure dois-je laisser la chambre?
*Ah khel ur dwahz lehseh lah shahngbr?*

<sup>145</sup> Can I have the key to room no
. . ?
Je voudrais la clé de la chambre . . .
*Zher voodray lah klay der lah
shahngbr . . .*

<sup>146</sup> My room number is . . .
Le numéro de ma chambre
est . . .
*ler newmehro der mah shahngbr
eh . . .*

<sup>147</sup> Do you accept travellers'
cheques/Eurocheques/credit
cards?
Vous acceptez les chèques de
voyage/les Eurochèques/les
cartes de crédit?
*Voos aksepteh leh sheck der
vwoyazh/laze eurosheck/leh kart
der krehdee?*

<sup>148</sup> May I have the bill please?
Pouvez-vous me donner la note,
s'il vous plaît?
*Poovehvoo mer doneh lah nott
seelvooplay?*

<sup>149</sup> Excuse me, I think there is a
mistake in this bill.
Excusez-moi, mais je crois qu'il
ya a une erreur dans la note.
*Ehskewzaymwah, zhe kwaw ke eel
ee ah oon erer don la not.*

## Youth Hostels

<sup>150</sup> How much is a dormitory bed
per night?
Quel est le prix d'un lit en
dortoir par nuit?
*Kehl eh ler pree dang lee ahng*

dortwarr pahr newy?

<sup>151</sup> I am/am not an HI member.
Je suis/Je ne suis pas membre
d'une Auberge de Jeunesse.
*Zhe sewy/zhe ner sewy pah
mahngbr dewn obehrz der
jurnehss.*

<sup>152</sup> May I use my own sleeping
bag?
Est-ce que je peux me servir de
mon propre sac de couchage?
*Ehsker zhe pur mer sairvyr der
mawng proprer sahk der
kooshahz?*

<sup>153</sup> What time do you lock the
doors at night?
A quelle heure fermez-vous la
porte le soir?
*Ah kehlur fehrmehvoo lah port ler
swahr?*

## Camping

<sup>154</sup> May I camp here for the
night/two nights?
Puis-je camper ici pour la nuit/
deux nuits?
*Pweehze kahngpeh ysee poor lah
newy/dur newy?*

<sup>155</sup> Where can I pitch my tent?
Où puis-je dresser ma tente?
*Oo pweehze dresseh mah tahngt?*

<sup>156</sup> How much does it cost for
one night/week?
Quel est le prix par nuit/par
semaine?
*Kehl eh ler pree pahr newy/pahr
sermayn?*

F
R
E
N
C
H

145
↑
156

73

**157** Where can we park our caravan?

Où ouvons-nous garer notre caravane?

*Oo poovong noo gahreh nohtr kahrahvahn?*

**158** Where are the washing facilities?

Où se trouve le bloc sanitaire?

*Oo ser troov ler block sanitaire?*

**159** Is there a restaurant/supermarket/swimming pool on site/nearby?

Y-a-t-il un restaurant/supermarché/piscine sur place/près d'ici?

*Yahteel ang restorahng/supermahrsheh/peassinn sewr plahss/pray deessee?*

**160** Do you have a safety deposit box?

Avez-vous un coffre-fort?

*Ahvehvoo ang koffr-for?*

## EATING AND DRINKING

### Cafés and Bars

**161** I would like a cup of/two cups of/another coffee/tea.

Je voudrais une tasse de/deux tasses de/encore une tasse de café/thé.

*Zher voodray ewn tahss der/der tahss der/oncaw ewn tahss der kafeh/teh.*

**162** With/without milk/sugar.

Avec/sans lait/sucre.

*Ahvek/sahng lay/sewkr.*

**163** I would like a bottle/glass/two glasses of mineral water/red wine/white wine, please.

Je voudrais une bouteille/un verre/deux verres d'eau minérale/de vin rouge/de vin blanc, s'il vous plaît.

*Zhe voodray ewn bootayy/ang vair/der vair doa mynehral/der vang roozh/der vang blahng, sylvooplay.*

**164** I would like a beer/two beers, please.

Je voudrais une bière/deux bières, s'il vous plaît.

*Zhe voodray ewn byair/der byair, sylvooplay.*

**165** May I have some ice?

Puis-je avoir de la glace?

*Pweezh ahvoar der lah glass?*

**166** Do you have any matches/cigarettes/cigars?

Avez-vous des allumettes/des cigarettes/ des cigares?

*Ahveh-voo dehzahlewmaitt/deh cigaraytt/deh ssigar?*

### Restaurants

**167** Can you recommend a good/inexpensive restaurant in this area?

Pouvez-vous recommander un bon restaurant/un restaurant bon marché dans les environs?

*Pooveh-voo rekomahngdeh ewn bawng restorahng/ewn restorahng bawng mahrcheh dahng lehzahngvyrawng?*

**168** I would like a table for . . . people.

Je voudrais une table pour . . . personnes.

*Zher voodray ewn tabl poor . . . pehrson.*

**169** Do you have a non-smoking area?

Vous avez une zone non-fumeurs?

*Voozahvah ewn zohn nong fewmur?*

**170** Waiter/Waitress!

Garçon/Mademoiselle, s'il vous plaît!

*Garssawng, madmwahzel, sylvooplay!*

**171** Do you have a set menu/children's menu/wine list?

Avez-vous un table d'hôte/un menu pour enfants/la carte des vins?

*Ahvehvoo ewn tabler d'ot/ewn menew poor ahngfahng/lah list deh vang?*

**172** Do you have any vegetarian dishes, please?

Avez-vous des plats végétariens, s'il vous plaît?

*ahvehvoo der plah vehgehtahryang, sylvooplay?*

**173** Are there any local specialities?

Il y a des spécialités locales?

*Eel ee a deh sawng leh spayseeahleeteh locahl?*

**174** Are vegetables included?

Est-ce que les légumes sont compris?

*Essker leh lehgewm sawng kohngpree?*

**175** Could I have it well-cooked/medium/rare please?

Je le voudrais bien cuit/ à point/ saignant.

*Zher ler voodray beeang kwee/ah pwang/saynyang.*

**176** What does this dish consist of?

En quoi consiste ce plat?

*Ahng koah kawngsist ser plah?*

**177** I would like the set menu, please.

Je voudrais la carte, s'il vous plaît.

*Zher voodray lah cart, sylvooplay.*

**178** We have not been served yet.

Nous n'avons pas été encore servis.

*Noo nahvawng pahzehteh ahngkor sehrvee.*

**179** Excuse me, this is not what I ordered.

Excusez-moi, ce n'est pas ce que j'ai commandé.

*Ekskewzaymwah, ser nay pah ser ker zheh komandeh.*

**180** May I have some/some more bread/water/coffee/tea?

Puis-je avoir du pain/encore du pain/de l'eau/du café/du thé?

*Pweezh ahvoar dew pang/ahngkor dew pang/der lo/dew kafeh/dew teh?*

75

**F
R
E
N
C
H**

**181
↕
195**

<sup>181</sup>**May I have the bill, please?**
L'addition, s'il vous plaît!
*Laddyssyawng, sylvooplay!*

<sup>182</sup>**Does this bill include service?**
Est-ce que le service est compris?
*Ehsk ler sehrveess eh kawngpree?*

<sup>183</sup>**Do you accept travellers' cheques (travelers' checks)/ Eurocheques/MasterCard/US dollars?**
Prenez-vous les chèques de voyage/les eurochèques/la Mastercard/les dollars américains?
*Prernehvoo leh cheque der vwahahzh/leh eurocheque/lah Mastercard/leh dolar ahmehrykang?*

<sup>184</sup>**Can I have a receipt, please?**
Je pourrais avoir un reçu sil vous plaît?
*Zher pooray avwahr ahng rerssew seelvooplay?*

<sup>185</sup>**Where is the toilet (restroom), please?**
Où sont les toilettes, s'il vous plaît?
*Oo sawng leh twahlaitt, sylvooplay?*

## On the Menu

<sup>186</sup>**First courses**
Entrées
*Ahngtray.*

<sup>187</sup>**Soups**
Soupes
*Soup*

<sup>188</sup>**Main courses**
Plats principaux
*Plah prangseepo.*

<sup>189</sup>**Fish dishes**
Poissons
*Pooahsong*

<sup>190</sup>**Meat dishes**
Viandes
*Veeanhd*

<sup>191</sup>**Vegetarian dishes**
Plats végétariens
*Plah vehzhehtahryang*

<sup>192</sup>**Cheese**
Fromages
*Frohmahzh*

<sup>193</sup>**Desserts**
Desserts
*Dehser*

<sup>194</sup>**Specialities**
Spécialités
*Spehsseeahleeteh*

## GETTING AROUND

## Public Transport

<sup>195</sup>**Where is the bus stop/coach station/nearest metro (subway) station?**
Où se trouve l'arrêt d'autobus le plus proche/la gare routière/la station de métro la plus proche?
*Oo ser troov lahreh dotobewss la plew prosh/lah gahr rootyair/lah stassion der mehtro lah plew prosh?*

**196** When is the next/last bus to . . ?

A quelle heure est le prochain/dernier autobus pour . . ?

*Ahkehlur eh ler prochang/dehrneeyeh otobewss poor . . ?*

**197** How much is the fare to the city centre (downtown)/railway (railroad) station/airport?

Quel est le prix du billet pour le centre-ville/la gare/l'aéroport?

*Kehl eh ler pree dew beeyeh poor ler sahngtr-veel/lah gahr/lahehropor?*

**198** Will you tell me when to get off?

Pouvez-vous me le dire quand je devrai descendre?

*Poovehvoo mer deer kahng zher deuvreh dehssahngdr?*

**199** Does this bus go to . . ?

Est-ce que cet autobus va à . . ?

*Ehsk sayt otobewss vah ah . . ?*

**200** Which number bus goes to . . ?

Quel est le numéro de l'autobus qui va à . . ?

*Khel eh ler newmehro de lotobewss kee vah ah . . ?*

**201** May I have a single (one-way)/return (round-trip)/day ticket/book of tickets?

Puis-je avoir un aller/un aller-retour/un ticket pour la journée/un carnet de tickets?

*Pweezh ahvwahr ewn ahleh/ewn ahleh-retoor/ewn tickeh poor lah joorneh/ewn kahrneh der tickeh?*

## Taxis

**202** I would like to go to . . . How much will it cost?

Je voudrais aller à . . . Quel est le prix?

*Zhe voodray ahleh ah . . . kehl eh ler pree?*

**203** Please stop here.

Arrêtez ici, s'il vous plaît.

*Ahrehteh yssy, sylvooplay.*

**204** I would like to order a taxi today/tomorrow/at 2pm to go from . . . to . . .

Je voudrais réserver un taxi aujourd'hui/demain/à deux heures pour aller de . . . à . . .

*Zher voodray rehzehrveh ewn taxi ojoordewee/dermang/ah derzur poor ahleh der . . . ah . . .*

## Asking the Way

**205** Excuse me, do you speak English?

Excusez-moi, parlez-vous anglais?

*Ekskewsehmwah, pahrlehvoo ahnglay?*

**206** Excuse me, is this the right way to . . ?

Excusez-moi, c'est la bonne direction pour . . ?

*Ekskewzaymwah, seh lah bon deerekseeawng poor . . ?*

**207** . . . the cathedral/the tourist information office/the castle/the old town.

. . . la cathédrale/l'office de tourisme/le château/la vieille ville.

*. . . lah kahtehdrahl/lohfeece de tooreezm/ler chateau/lah veeay veel*

**208** Can you tell me the way to the railway (railroad) station/bus station/taxi rank (stand)/city centre (downtown)/beach?

Pour aller à la gare/gare routière/station de taxis/au centre ville/à la plage, s'il vous plaît?

*Poor ahleh ah lah gahr/gahr rootyair/stahssion der taxi/oh sahngtr veel/ah lah plahzh, sylvooplay?*

**209** First/second left/right/straight ahead.

Première/deuxième à gauche/à droite/tout droit.

*Prermeyair/derzeaim ah goash/ah drwaht/too drwah.*

**210** Where is the nearest police station/post office?

Où se trouve le poste de police/le bureau de poste le plus près?

*Oo ser troov ler post der poliss/ler bewro der post ler plew pray?*

**211** Is it far?

C'est loin?

*seh looang?*

**212** Do I need to take a taxi/catch a bus?

Faut-il prendre un taxi/un autobus?

*Foteel prahngdr ewn taxi/ewn otobewss?*

**213** Can you point to it on my map?

Pouvez-vous me le montrer sur la carte?

*Poovehvoo mer ler mawngtreh sewr lah kart?*

**214** Thank you for your help.

Merci pour votre aide.

*Mehrsee poor votrayd.*

## SIGHTSEEING

**215** Where is the Tourist Information office?

Où se trouve l'office de tourisme?

*Oo ser troov loffyss de toorism?*

**216** Where is the cathedral/church/museum?

Où se trouve la Cathédrale/l'Église/le Musée?

*Oo ser troov lah katehdral/lehglyz/ler mewzeh?*

**217** How much is the entrance (admission) charge?

Quel est le prix d'entrée?

*Khel eh ler pree delahngtreh?*

**218** Is there a reduction for children/students/senior citizens?

Y-a-til une réduction pour les enfants/les étudiants/les

personnes du troisième âge?
*Eeahteel ewn rehdewkssyawong
poor lehzahngfahng/
lehzehtewdyahng/leh pehrson dew
trwahzyehm ahzh?*

219 **What time does the next
guided tour start?**
A quelle heure commence la
prochaine visite guidée?
*Ah kehlur komahngs lah proshain
vysyt gueedeh?*

220 **One/two adults/children,
please.**
Un/deux adulte(s /enfant(s), s'il
vous plaît.
*Ewn/durzahdewlt/ahngfahng, seel
voo play.*

221 **May I take photographs here?**
Je peux prendre des photos ici?
*Zher per prangdr deh phowtoh
eessee?*

## ENTERTAINMENT

222 **Can you recommend a good
bar/nightclub?**
Pouvez-vous me recommander
un bar/une boîte de nuit?
*Poovehvoo mer rerkomahngdeh
ang bahr/ewn boaht der newee?*

223 **Do you know what is on at
the cinema (playing at the
movies)/theatre at the
moment?**
Savez-vous ce qu'il y a au
cinéma/théâtre en ce moment?
*Sahvehvoo ser keelyah o cinema/
tehahtr ahng ser momahng?*

224 **I would like to book
(purchase) . . . tickets for the
matinée/evening
performance on Monday.**
Je voudrais réserver . . . places
pour la séance en matinée/
soirée lundi.
*Zher voodray rehzehrveh . . . plass
poor lah sehahngss ahng
mahteeneh/swoiray lerndi.*

225 **What time does the film/
performance start?**
A quelle heure commence la
séance/la représentation?
*Ah kehlur komahngss lah
sehahngs/lah
rerprehzahngtahssyawong?*

## MEETING PEOPLE

226 **Hello/Goodbye.**
Bonjour/Au revoir.
*Bawngzhoor/oa revwahr.*

227 **Good morning/good
afternoon/good evening/
goodnight.**
Bonjour/bonjour/bonsoir/
bonne nuit.
*Bawngzhoor/bawngzhoor/
bawngswahr/bun nwee.*

228 **Pleased to meet you.**
Enchanté de faire votre
connaissance.
*Ahngsahngteh der fair votr
konehssahngss.*

229 **How are you?**
Comment allez-vous?
*Komahng ahlehvoo?*

**230** Fine, thank you. And you?
Bien merci. Et vous?
*Beeang mehrsee. Eh voo?*

**231** My name is . . .
Je m'appelle. . .
*Zher mahpehl . . .*

**232** This is my friend/boyfriend/
girlfriend/husband/wife/
brother/sister.
C'est un ami/c'est mon ami/
mon amie/mon mari/ma
femme/mon frère/ma soeur.
*Saytangnahmee/say
mawngnahmee/mawngnahmee/
mawong mahree/mah fahm/
mawong frayr/mah surr.*

**233** Where are you travelling to?
Où partez-vous en voyage?
*Oo pahrtehvoo ahng vwahahzh?*

**234** I am/we are going to . . .
Je vais/nous allons à . . .
*Zher vay/noozahlawng ah . . .*

**235** How long are you travelling
for?
Combien de temps partez-vous?
*Kawngbeeang der tahng
pahrtehvoo?*

**236** Where do you come from?
D'où venez-vous?
*Doo vernehvoo?*

**237** I am/we are from . . .
Je suis/nous sommes de . . .
*Zher sewea/noo soam der . . .*

**238** We're on holiday.
Nous sommes en vacances.
*Noo som ahng vahkahngss.*

**239** This is our first visit here.
C'est la première fois que nous
venons ici.
*Seh lah prermiair fwah ker noo
vernon eeesee.*

**240** Would you like/May I have a
cigarette?
Voulez-vous/Puis-je avoir une
cigarette?
*Voolehvoo/pweezhahvwahr ewn
seegahrett?*

**241** I am sorry but I do not
understand.
Je suis désolé(e) mais je ne
comprends pas.
*Zher sewee dehzoleh meh zher ner
kawngprahng pah.*

**242** Please speak slowly.
Veuillez parler lentement.
*Vuryeh pahrleh lahngtmahng.*

**243** Do you mind if I smoke?
Est-ce que cela vous ennuie si je
fume?
*Ehsker cerlah voo ahngnewee ssi
zher fewm?*

**244** Do you have a light?
Avez-vous du feu?
*Ahveh-voo dew fur?*

**245** I am waiting for my husband/
wife/boyfriend/girlfriend.
J'attends mon mari/ma femme/
mon ami/mon amie.
*Zhatahng mawng mahree/mah
fahm/mawongnahmee/
mawongnahmee.*

## TRAVELLING WITH CHILDREN

**246** Do you have a high chair/
baby-sitting service/cot?
Avez-vous une chaise pour
bébé/un service de garde pour
enfants/un berceau?
*Ahvehvoo ewn shehz poor behbeh/
ang sehrvees der gahrd poor
ahngfahng/ang behrso?*

**247** Where is the nursery/
playroom?
Où se trouve la chambre
d'enfants/la salle de jeux?
*Ooser troov lah shahngbr
dahngfahng/lah sall der zur?*

**248** Where can I warm the baby's
bottle?
Où puis-je faire réchauffer le
biberon?
*Oo pweezh fair rehshoffeh ler
beebrawng?*

## COMMUNICATIONS

### Post

**249** How much will it cost to send
a letter/postcard/this
package to Britain/Ireland/
America/Australia/
New Zealand/Canada?
Quel est le tarif pour envoyer
une lettre/carte postale/ce
paquet en Grande-Bretagne/
Irlande/Amérique/Australie/
Nouvelle-Zélande/au Canada?
*Kehl eh ler tariff poor
ahngvwahyeh ewn lettr/kahrt
postahl/ser pahkeh ahng grahngd-
brertahnya/irland/amehrick/
ostrahlee/noovel-zehland/oh
kahnahdah?*

**250** I would like one stamp/two
stamps.
Je voudrais un timbre/deux
timbres.
*Zher voodray ang tangbr/der
tangbr.*

**251** I'd like . . . , stamps for
postcards to send abroad,
please.
Je voudrais . . . timbres pour
envoyer des cartes postales à
l'étranger sil vous plaît.
*Zher voodray . . . tangbr poor
ahngvwahyeh deh kahrt postahl
ah lehtrahngzhai seelvooplay*

### Phones

**252** I would like to make a
telephone call/reverse the
charges to (make a collect
call to) . . .
Je voudrais téléphoner/
téléphoner en PCV à . . .
*Zher voodray telephoneh/telephoneh
ahng PehCehVeh ah . . .*

**253** Which coins do I need for the
telephone?
Quelles pièces me faut-il pour
téléphoner?
*Kehl peaehss mer foteel poor
tehlehphoneh?*

**F R E N C H**

**254 ↑ 270**

254 The line is engaged (busy).
La ligne est occupée.
*Lah lyñ eh okewopeh.*

255 The number is . . .
Le numéro est . . .
*Ler newmehro eh . . .*

256 Hello, this is . . .
Bonjour, c'est . . . à lapparel.
*Bawngzhoor, seh . . . ahlahparay.*

257 May I speak to . . ?
Je voudrais parler à . . .
*Zher voodray pahrlay ah . . .*

258 He/She is not in at the
moment. Can you call back?
Il/elle n'est pas là. Pouvez-vous
rappeler?
*Eel/ehl nay pah lah. Voo poovay
rahperlay?*

## MONEY

259 I would like to change these
travellers' cheques (travelers'
checks)/this currency/this
Eurocheque.
J'aimerais changer ces chèques
de voyage/ces devises/cet
Eurochèque.
*Zhaymray shahngzheh seh cheque
der vwahahzh/seh derveez/seht
eurocheque.*

260 How much commission do
you charge? (What is the
service charge?)
Quelle commission prenez-vous?
*Kehl komyssyawng prernehvoo?*

261 Can I obtain money with my

MasterCard?
Puis-je avoir de l'argent avec
ma MasterCard?
*Pweezh ahvwahr der largaang
ahvek mah mastercard?*

## SHOPPING

### Names of Shops and Departments

262 Librairie/Papeterie
*Leebrayree/pahpaytehree*
Bookshop/Stationery

263 Bijoutier/Cadeaux
*Beezhootehree/Kahdow*
Jeweller's/Gifts

264 Chaussures
*Showsewor*
Shoes

265 Quincaillerie
*Kahngkahyeree*
Hardware

266 Antiquaire
*Ahnteekair*
Antiques

267 Coiffeur (hommes)/(femmes)
*Cwafferr*
Hairdressers (men's)/(women's)

268 Bureau de tabac
*Bewrow der tahbah*
Tobacconist

269 Boulangerie
*Boolahngzheree*
Baker's

270 Supermarché
*Sewpermahrshay*

Supermarket

**271 Photographe**
*Phohtowgraf*
Photoshop

**272 Jouets**
*Zhooay*
Toys

**273 Bureau de voyages**
*Bureoh der vwoyazh*
Travel Agency

**274 Articles de toilette**
*Ahrteekl der twahleht*
Toiletries

**275 Disques**
*Deesk*
Records

## In the Shop

**276 What time do the shops open/close?**
A quelle heure ouvrent/ferment les magasins?
*Ah kehlur oovr/fehrm leh mahgazhang?*

**277 Where is the nearest market?**
Où est le marché le plus proche?
*Oo eh ler mahrshay ler plew prosh?*

**278 Can you show me the one in the window/this one?**
Pouvez-vous me montrer celui/celle dans la vitrine/celui-ci/celle-ci?
*Poovayvoo mer mohntray serlwee/sel dahng lah veetreen/serlweesi/selsi?*

**279 Can I try this on?**

Puis-je essayer ceci?
*Pweezh ehssayeh cerssee?*

**280 What size is this?**
Quelle est cette taille?
*Kehleh saytt tahye?*

**281 This is too large/too small/too expensive.**
C'est trop grand/trop petit/trop cher.
*Say trohw grahng/trohw pertee/trohw share.*

**282 Do you have any others?**
Vous en avez d'autres?
*Voozahngnahvay doatr?*

**283 My size is . . .**
Ma taille (clothes)/ma pointure (shoes) est . . .
*Mah tie (clothes)/mah pooahngtewr ay . . .*

**284 Where is the changing room/childrens/cosmetic/ladieswear/menswear/food department?**
Où se trouve le salon d'essayage/le rayon enfants/le rayon produits de beauté/le rayon femmes/le rayon hommes /l'alimentation?
*Oo ser troov ler sahlawng dehsayahzh/ler rehyawng ahngfahng/ler rehyawng prodewee der boteh/ler rehyawng fahm/ler rehyawng ohm/lahleemahngtahsyawng?*

**285 I would like . . .**
Je voudrais . . .
*Zher voodray . . .*

**F R E N C H**

271 ↑ 285

83

**286** I would like a quarter of a kilo/half a kilo/a kilo of bread/butter/cheese/ham/tomatoes.

e voudrais deux cent cinquante grammes (250g)/un demi-kilo/un kilo de pain/beurre/fromage/jambon/tomates.

*Zher voodray dur sahng sangkahngt gram/ahng dermeekilo/ang kilo der pang/burr/frohmahzh/zhahngbawng/tomaht.*

**287** How much is this?

C'est combien?

*Cey combeean?*

**288** I'll take this one, thank you.

Je prends celui-ci/celle-ci merci.

*Zher prahng serlweesi/sehlsee mehrsee.*

**289** Do you have a carrier (shopping) bag?

Avez-vous un sac?

*Ahvehvoo ang sahk?*

**290** Do you have anything cheaper/larger/smaller/of better quality?

Avez-vous quelque chose de moins cher/plus petit/plus grand/de meilleure qualité?

*Ahvehvoo kehlkershos der moang shehr/plew pertee/plew grohnd/der mehyur kaleeteh?*

**291** I would like a film for this camera.

Je voudrais une pellicule pour cet appareil photo.

*Zher voodray ewn pehleekewl poor sayt ahpahrehye foto*

**292** I would like some batteries, the same size as this old one.

Je voudrais des piles, comme celle-ci.

*Zher voodray deh peel, kom cehlsee.*

**293** Would you mind wrapping this for me, please?

Pourriez-vous m'envelopper ceci, s'il vous plaît?

*Pooreeehvoo mahngverloppeh cersee, seelvooplay?*

**294** Sorry, but you seem to have given me the wrong change.

Excusez-moi, mais je crois que vous ne m'avez pas rendu le compte.

*Excewsehmwah meh zher krwah ker voo ner mahveh pah rahngdew ler kawngt.*

## MOTORING

### Car Hire (Rental)

**295** I have ordered (rented) a car in the name of . . .

J'ai réservé une voiture au nom de . . .

*Zhay rehzehrveh ewn vwahtewr o nawng der . . .*

**296** How much does it cost to hire (rent) a car for one day/two days/one week?

Quel est le prix de location d'une voiture pour un jour/deux jours/une semaine?

*Kehl eh ler pree der lokahsyawng
d'ewn vwahtewr poor ang zoor/
der zoor/ewn sermen?*

**297** **Is the tank already full of
petrol (gas)?**
Le plein est-il fait?
*Ler plang ehtylfeh?*

**298** **Is insurance and tax
included? How much is the
deposit?**
Est-ce que l'assurance et les
taxes sont comprises? Combien
faut-il donner de caution?
*Ehss ker lahsewrahngss eh leh tax
sawng kawngpreezh? Kawngbyabg
foteel doneh der kossyawng?*

**299** **By what time must I return
the car?**
A quelle heure dois-je ramener
la voiture?
*Ah kehlur dwahzh rahmerneh lah
vwahtewr?*

**300** **I would like a small/family
car with a radio/cassette
player.**
Je voudrais une petite voiture/
une grosse voiture avec radio/
lecteur de cassettes.
*Zher voodray ewn perteet
vwahtewr/ewn gross vwahtewr
ahvehk rahdio/lecturr der kassaytt.*

## Asking the Way

**301** **Excuse me, can you help me
please?**
Excusez-moi, vous pouvez
m'aider s'il vous plaît?

*Ekskewzaymwah, voo poovay
mahyday seelvooplay*

**302** **How do I reach the
motorway/main road?**
Pour aller jusqu'à l'autoroute/la
route principale?
*Poor ahleh zhewskah lowtohroot/
lah root prahngsipahl?*

**303** **I think I have taken the
wrong turning.**
Je crois que je me suis trompé
de chemin.
*Zher krawh ker zhay mer trompay
der sheman.*

**304** **I am looking for this address.**
Je cherche cette adresse.
*Zher shaersh set adress.*

**305** **I am looking for the . . .
hotel.**
Je cherche l'hôtel . . .
*Zher shaersh lohtel . . .*

**306** **How far is it to . . .
from here?**
. . . c'est loin d'ici?
*. . . say looahng deesee?*

**307** **Carry straight on for . . .
kilometres.**
Continuez tout droit pendant . .
. kilomètres.
*Kohnteeneway too drooah
pahngdahng . . . kilomehtr.*

**308** **Take the next turning on the
right/left.**
Prenez la prochaine rue/route à
droite/à gauche.
*Prenay lah proshen rew/root ah
drwaht/ah goash.*

**F R E N C H**

**297 ↑ 308**

**FRENCH**

**309**
↕
**325**

**309** Turn right/left at the next crossroads/traffic lights.
Tournez à droite/à gauche au prochain croisement/aux feux.
*Toornay ah drwaht/ah goash oh prohshahng krowzmahng/oh phyer.*

**310** You are going in the wrong direction.
Vous allez dans la mauvaise direction.
*Vooz ahleh dahng lah mowvehz deerekseeawng.*

## Parking

**311** How long can I park here?
Combien de temps est-ce que je peux rester garé ici?
*Kawngbeeang der tahng essker zher per restay gahray eessee?*

**312** Is there a car park near here?
Y a-t-il un parking près d'ici?
*Eeyahteel ahng parking preh deessee?*

**313** At what time does this car park close?
A quelle heure est-ce que le parking ferme?
*Ah kehl urr essker ler parking fehrm?*

## Signs and Notices

**314** Sens unique
*Sahns uhneek*
One way

**315** Sens interdit
*Sahns ahngterdee*
No entry

**316** Stationnement interdit
*Stassionmahng ahngterdee*
No parking

**317** Déviation
*Dehveeasseeawng*
Detour (diversion)

**318** Stop
*Stop*
Stop

**319** Cédez la
*Preeohreetay*
Give way (yield)

**320** Chaussée glissante
*Showsay gleesahnt*
Slippery road

**321** Dépassement interdit
*Daypassmahng ahngterdee*
No overtaking

## At the Filling Station

**322** Unleaded (lead-free)/ Standard/Premium
Sans plomb/normal/super
*Sahng plong/normall/sewpehr*

**323** Fill the tank please.
Le plein s'il vous plaît.
*Ler plahng seelvooplay.*

**324** Do you have a road map of this area?
Vous avez une carte de la région?
*Voozahvay ewn kahrt der lah rehzheeawng?*

**325** How much is the car-wash?

Le lavage automatique coûte combien?
*Ler lahvahzh automateek koot kawngbeeang?*

## Breakdowns

### 326 I've had a breakdown at . . .
Je suis tombé(e) en panne à . . .
*Zher sewee tombay ahng pan ah . . .*

### 327 I am on the road from . . . to . . .
Je suis sur la route de . . . à . . .
*Zher sewee sewr lah root der . . . ah . . .*

### 328 I can't move the car. Can you send a tow-truck?
Je ne peux pas déplacer la voiture. Vous pouvez envoyer une dépanneuse?
*Zher ner purr pah dehplahsay lah vwahtewr. Voo poovay ahngvwahyeh ewn daypahnurze?*

### 329 I have a flat tyre.
J'ai un pneu crevé.
*Zhai ang punerr krervay.*

### 330 The windscreen (windshield) has smashed/cracked.
Le pare-brise est cassé/fendu.
*Ler pahrbreez ay kahseh/ fahngdew.*

### 331 There is something wrong with the engine/brakes/ lights/steering/gearbox/ clutch/exhaust.
Il y a un problème avec le moteur/les freins/les feux/la direction/la boîte à vitesses/ l'embrayage/le pot d'échappement.
*Eeleeyah ang problairm ahvek ler mowturr/leh frahng/leh fur/lah deerehkseeawng/lah bwahtahveetess/lahngbrayyazh/ ler poh dehshahpmahng.*

### 332 It's overheating.
Le moteur chauffe.
*Ler mohturr showf.*

### 333 It won't start.
La voiture ne démarre pas.
*Lah vwahtewr ner dehmahr pah.*

### 334 Where can I get it repaired?
Où est-ce que je peux le/la faire réparer?
*Oo essker zher purr ler/lah fair rehpahray?*

### 335 Can you take me there?
Vous pouvez m'y emmener?
*Voo poovay mee ahngmernay?*

### 336 Will it take long to fix?
La réparation prendra longtemps?
*Lah rehpahrasseeawng prahngdrah lohngtahng?*

### 337 How much will it cost?
Ça coûtera combien?
*Sah kootrah kawngbeeang?*

## Accidents

### 338 Can you help me? There has been an accident.
Vous pouvez m'aider? Il y a eu un accident.
*Voo poovay mayday? Eelyaew ang akseedahng.*

**F R E N C H**

³³⁹ Please call the police/an
ambulance.
Vous pouvez appeler la police/
une ambulance s'il vous plaît.
*Voo poovay ahperleh lah poleess/
ewn ahngbewlahngss seelvooplay.*

³⁴⁰ Is anyone hurt?
Y a-t-il des blessés?
*Eeahteel deh blaysay?*

## Traffic Offences

³⁴¹ I'm sorry, I didn't see the
sign.
Je suis désolé(e), je n'ai pas vu le
panneau.
*Zher sewee dehzoleh, zher nay pah
vew ler panow.*

³⁴² Must I pay a fine? How
much?
Est-ce que je dois payer une
amende? Combien?
*Ehsker zher dwah payeh ewn
amahnd? Kawngbeeang?*

³⁴³ Show me your documents.
Vos papiers s'il vous plaît.
*Vow pahpyeh seelvooplay.*

## HEALTH

### Pharmacy

³⁴⁴ Do you have anything for a
stomachache/headache/sore
throat/toothache?
Avez-vous quelque chose
contre le mal à l'estomac/les
maux de tête/le mal de gorge/le
mal de dents?

*Ahveh-voo kelhkshoz kawngtr ler
mal ah lestoma/leh mo der teht/ler
mal der gorzh/ler mal der dahng?*

³⁴⁵ I need something for
diarrhoea (diarrhea)/
constipation/a cold/a cough/
insect bites/sunburn/travel
(motion) sickness.
J'ai besoin de quelque chose
contre la diarrhée/la
constipation/un rhume/la toux/
les piqûres d'insectes/les
brûlures de soleil/le mal de la
route (car)/de l'air (plane)/de
mer (boat).
*Zhai berzwoang der kehlkshoz
kawngtr lah diarrhae/ang rhoom/
ewn tou/lers peakewr dangsect/leh
koo der soleye/ler mal der lah
root/der l'air/der mair.*

³⁴⁶ How much/how many do I
take?
Combien dois-je en prendre?
*Kawngbeeang dwahzh ahng
prahngdr?*

³⁴⁷ How often do I take it/them?
Combien de fois dois-je en
prendre?
*Kawngbeeang der fwah dwahzh
ahng prahngdr?*

³⁴⁸ How much does it cost?
Quel est le prix?
*Khel eh ler pree?*

³⁴⁹ Can you recommend a good
doctor/dentist?
Pouvez-vous me recommander
un bon médecin/dentiste?

*Pooveh-voo mer rerkomahngdeh*
*ang bawng doctur/dahngtist?*

**350** Is it suitable for children?
Est-ce qu'on peut le donner aux
enfants?
*Esskawng pew ler doneh*
*ozahnfahn?*

## Doctor

**351** I have a pain here/in my arm/
leg/chest/stomach.
J'ai mal ici/au ras/à la jambe/à
la poitrine/à l'estomac.
*Zhai mal eessee/o brah/ah lah*
*zhahngb/ah lah pwahtryn/ah*
*lestomah.*

**352** Please call a doctor, this is an
emergency.
Appelez un médecin, s'il vous
plaît, c'est urgent.
*Ahperleh ewn doctur, seel voo*
*play, sehteworzhahng.*

**353** I would like to make an
appointment to see a doctor.
Je voudrais prendre rendez-
vous chez le médecin.
*Zher voodray prahngdr*
*rahngdehvoo sheh ler doctur.*

**354** I am diabetic/pregnant.
Je suis diabétique/enceinte.
*Zher sewee diabetic/ahngsang.*

**355** I need a prescription for . . .
J'ai besoin d'une ordonnance
pour . . .
*Zhai berzooang dewnordonahngss*
*poor . . .*

**356** Can you give me something
to ease the pain?
Pouvez-vous me donner
quelque chose contre la
douleur?
*Poovayvoo mer doneh kehlkshoz*
*kawngtr lah doolur?*

**357** I am/he is/she is allergic to
penicillin.
Je suis/il est/elle est allergique à
la pénicilline.
*Zher sewee/eel ay/ehl ay*
*allerzheek ah lah pehneeseeleen.*

**358** Does this hurt?
Ça fait mal?
*Sah fay mahl?*

**359** You must/he must/she must
go to hospital.
Vous devez/il doit/elle doit
aller à l'hôpital.
*Voo dervay/eel dwah/ehl dwah*
*ahleh ah lopeetahl.*

**360** Take these once/twice/three
times a day.
Prenez ces médicaments une
fois/deux fois/trois fois par
jour.
*Prernay say medeekahmahng ewn*
*fwah/dur fwah/trwah fwah pahr*
*zhoor.*

**361** I am/he is/she is taking this
medication.
Je prends/il prend/elle prend
ces médicaments.
*Zher prahng/eel prahng/ehl*
*prahng say medeekahmahng.*

**F**
**R**
**E**
**N**
**C**
**H**

**350**
**↑**
**361**

**362** I have medical insurance.
J'ai une assurance médicale.
*Zhay ewn assurans mehdeekahl.*

## Dentist

**363** I have toothache.
J'ai mal aux dents.
*Zhai mahl o dahng.*

**364** My filling has come out.
Mon plombage est tombé.
*Mawng plawngbahz eh tawngbeh.*

**365** I do/do not want to have an injection first.
Je veux/je ne veux pas qu'on me donne une piqûre avant.
*Zher vur/zher nur vur pah ke orn mer don oon peakewr ahvehn.*

## EMERGENCIES

**366** Help!
Au secours!
*Ossercoor!*

**367** Call an ambulance/a doctor/the police!
Appelez une ambulance/un docteur/la police!
*Ahperleh ewnahngbewlahngss/ang doctur/lah poleess!*

**368** I have had my travellers' cheques (travelers' checks)/credit cards/purse/handbag/rucksack (knapsack)/luggage/wallet stolen.
On m'a volé mes chèques de voyage/mes cartes de crédits/mon porte-monnaie/mon sac à main/mon sac à dos/mes bagages/mon porte-feuille.
*Awng mah voleh meh cheque der vwahahzh/meh carte der crehdite/mawng portemonneh/mawng sackamahn/mawng sackadoe/meh bahgagzh/mawng portfur-ye.*

**369** Can you help me, I have lost my daughter/son?
Pouvez-vous m'aider, j'ai perdu ma fille/mon fils?
*Poovehvoo mehdeh, jeh pehrdew mah feeye/mawng feess?*

**370** Please go away/leave me alone.
Allez-vous en/Laissez-moi tranquille.
*Ahlehvoozahng/lehssehmwah trahngkeel.*

**371** Fire!
Au feu!
*Oh fur!*

**372** I want to contact the British/American/Canadian/Irish/Australian/New Zealand/South African consulate.
Je veux contacter le Consulat britannique/américain/canadien/irlandais/australien/néo-zélandais/sud-africain.
*Zher vurr kontaktay ler kohnsewlah breetahneek/ahmehreekahng/kahnahdyahng/eerlahnday/austrahleeahng/nayozaylahngday/sewdafreekahng.*

# Introduction

German is the official language of Germany and Austria, and is spoken in the northern and eastern regions of Switzerland, as well as in the East Cantons area of Belgium, near the German border; some areas of northern Italy near Austria have a German-speaking population. German is also spoken in Luxembourg, and is often used as a second language in Central European countries, such as Hungary and the Czech Republic. Considering the wide geographical extent of the language, it is not surprising that considerable regional variation exists in accent and vocabulary (and sometimes spelling).

## Addresses for travel and tourist information

**UK:** *German National Tourist Office*, 65 Curzon St, London W1Y 7PE; tel: (0171) 495 3990. *Austrian National Tourist Office*, 30 St George St, London W1R 0AL; tel: (0171) 629 0461. *Swiss National Tourist Office*, Swiss Centre, London W1V 8EE; tel: (0171) 734 1921.

**USA:** *German National Tourist Office*, Chanin Building, 122 East 42nd St (52nd Floor), New York, NY 10168-0072; tel: (212) 308-3300. *Austrian National Tourist Office*, 500 Fifth Ave (Suite 2009–2022), New York, NY 10110; tel: (212) 944-6880. *Swiss National Tourist Office*, Swiss Center, 608 Fifth Avenue, New York, NY 10020; tel: (212) 757-5944.

## ESSENTIALS

**G
E
R
M
A
N**

**01
↑
11**

### Alphabet

| | |
|---|---|
| A | Ä |
| *ah* | *ah oomlowt* |
| B | C |
| *bey* | *tsey* |
| D | E |
| *dey* | *ey* |
| F | G |
| *ef* | *gey* |
| H | I |
| *hah* | *ee* |
| J | K |
| *yot* | *kah* |
| L | M |
| *el* | *em* |
| N | O |
| *en* | *oh* |
| Ö | P |
| *oh oomlowt* | *pey* |
| Q | R |
| *koo* | *eyr* |
| S | ß ( = double S) |
| *es* | *ess-tsett* |
| T | U |
| *tey* | *oo* |
| Ü | V |
| *oo oomlowt* | *fow* |
| W | X |
| *vey* | *iks* |
| Y | Z |
| *oopsilon* | *tset* |

## Basic Words and Phrases

**1** Yes — No
Ja — Nein
*Yah* — *nine*

**2** Please — Thank you
Bitte — Danke
*Bitter* — *Danke*

**3** That's O.K. — Perhaps
Das stimmt — Vielleicht
*Das shtimt* — *Feellykht*

**4** To — From
Nach — Von
*Nakh* — *fon*

**5** Here — There
Hier — dort
*Here* — *dort*

**6** None — Also
Kein — Auch
*Kinee* — *Aukh*

**7** How — When
Wie — Wann
*Vee* — *Ven*

**8** What — Why
Was — Warum
*Vas* — *Varum*

**9** I don't understand.
Ich verstehe Sie nicht.
*Ikh ferhstayher zee nikht.*

**10** I don't speak German.
Ich spreche kein Deutsch.
*Ikh shprekker kine doitsh.*

**11** Do you speak English?
Sprechen Sie Englisch?
*Shprekhen zee english?*

12 **Can you please write it down?**
Könnten Sie das bitte aufschreiben?
*Kernten zee das bitter owfshryben?*

13 **Can you please speak more slowly?**
Könnten Sie bitte langsamer sprechen?
*Kernten zee bitter langzamer shprekhen?*

14 **How much does it/this cost?**
Was kostet es/das?
*Vas kostet es/das?*

## Days

15 **Monday** **Tuesday**
Montag Dienstag
*Mohntagh* *Deenstagh*

16 **Wednesday** **Thursday**
Mittwoch Donnerstag
*Mitvokh* *Donnerstagh*

17 **Friday** **Saturday**
Freitag Samstag
*Frytagh* *Samstagh*

18 **Sunday** **Morning**
Sonntag Morgen
*Sontagh* *Morgen*

19 **Afternoon** **Evening**
Nachmittag Abend
*Naakhmittag* *Aabend*

20 **Night** **Week**
Nacht Woche
*Naakht* *Wokhe*

21 **Yesterday** **Tomorrow**
Gestern Morgen
*Gess-tern* *Morgen*

## Numbers

22 **Zero** **One**
Null Eins
*Nool* *Ines*

23 **Two** **Three**
Zwei Drei
*Tsvy* *Dry*

24 **Four** **Five**
Vier Fünf
*Feer* *Foonf*

25 **Six** **Seven**
Sechs Sieben
*Zex* *Zeeben*

26 **Eight** **Nine**
Acht Neun
*Akht* *Noyn*

27 **Ten** **Eleven**
Zehn Elf
*Tseyn* *Elf*

28 **Twelve** **Thirteen**
Zwölf Dreizehn
*Tsverlf* *Drytseyn*

29 **Fourteen** **Fifteen**
Vierzehn Fünfzehn
*Feertseyn* *Foonftseyn*

30 **Sixteen** **Seventeen**
Sechzehn Siebzehn
*Zekhtseyn* *Zeeptseyn*

31 **Eighteen** **Nineteen**
Achtzehn Neunzehn
*Akhttseyn* *Noinetseyn*

G E R M A N

12 ↑ 31

G
E
R
M
A
N

32 **Twenty**
Zwanzig
*Tvantsig*

**Twenty-one**
Einundzwanzig
*Ine-oont-tsvantsikh*

33 **Twenty-two**
Zweiundzwanzig
*Zvioonttvantsikh*

**Thirty**
Dreißig
*Drysikh*

34 **Forty**
Vierzig
*Feertsikh*

**Fifty**
Fünfzig
*Foonftsikh*

35 **Sixty**
Sechzig
*Zekhtsikh*

**Seventy**
Siebzig
*Zeebtsikh*

36 **Eighty**
Achtzig
*Akhtsikh*

**Ninety**
Neunzig
*Noyntsikh*

37 **One hundred**
Hundert
*Hoondert*

**Five hundred**
Fünfhundert
*Foonfhoondert*

38 **One thousand**
Ein tausend
*Ine towsend*

**One million**
Eine Million
*Iner millyohn*

## Time

39 **9.00**
Neun Uhr
*Noyn oor*

40 **9.05**
Neun Uhr fünf
*Noyn oor foonf*

41 **9.10**
Neun Uhr zehn
*Noyn oor tseyn*

42 **9.15**
Neun Uhr fünfzehn

43 **9.20**
Neun Uhr zwanzig
*Noyn oor tvantsikh*

44 **9.25**
Neun Uhr fünfundzwanzig
*Noyn oor foonf-oont-tsvantsig*

45 **9.30**
Neun Uhr drei ig
*Noyn oor drytsig*

46 **9.35**
Neun Uhr fünfunddreißig
*Noyn oor foonf-oont-drysikh*

47 **9.40**
Neun Uhr vierzig
*Noyn oor feertsikh*

48 **9.45**
Neun Uhr fünfunvierzig
*Noyn oor foonf-oont-feertsikh*

49 **9.50**
Neun Uhr fünfzig
*Noyn oor foonftsikh*

50 **9.55**
Neun Uhr fünfundfünfzig
*Noyn oor foonf-oont-foonftsikh*

51 **12.00/Midday/Midnight**
Mittag/Mitternacht
*Mittagh/mitternakht*

52 **What time is it?**
Wie spät ist es?
*Vee shpeyt is es?*

53 **It is . . .**
Es ist . . .
*Es ist . . .*

## Airport

**54** Excuse me, where is the
check-in desk for . . . airline?
Entschuldigung, wo ist der
Abfertigungsschalter für . . ?
*Entshuldeegen, vo ist dair
abfairtigoongs-shalter foor . . ?*

**55** What is the boarding gate/
time for my flight?
Von welchem Flugsteig geht
mein Flug ab?/Wann muß ich
einsteigen?
*Fon velchem floogstyge geyht mine
floog ab?/Vann moos ikh
eynstygen?*

**56** How long is the delay likely
to be?
Wieviel Verspätung hat mein
Flug?
*Veefeel fershpeytung hat mine floog?*

**57** Where is the duty-free shop?
Wo ist der zollfreie Laden?
*Vo ist dair tsollfryer larden?*

**58** Which way is the baggage
reclaim?
Wo ist die Gepäckausgabe?
*Vo ist dee gepekowsgarber?*

**59** Where can I get the bus to
the city centre?
Wo fährt der Bus ins
Stadtzentrum ab?
*Vo fairt dair boos ins shtat-
tsentrum ab?*

## Train Station

**60** Where is the ticket office/
information desk?
Wo ist der Fahrkartenschalter/
das Informationszentrum?
*Voh ist der faarkartenshalter/das
informatsion tsentroom?*

**61** Which platform does the
train to . . . depart from?
Von welchem Bahnsteig fährt
der Zug nach . . . ab?
*Fon velkhen baanshtykh fairt der
tsook nakh . . . ab?*

**62** Where is platform . . ?
Wo ist Bahnsteig . . ?
*Voh ist baanshtykh . . ?*

**63** When is the next train to . . ?
Wann fährt der nächste Zug
nach . . ?
*Vann fairt der nexter tsook
nakh . . ?*

**64** Is there a later train to . . ?
Gibt es einen späteren Zug
nach . . ?
*Geebt es inen shpaeteren tsook
nakh . . ?*

## Port

**65** How do I get to the port?
Wie komme ich zum Hafen?
*Vee kommer ikh zoom haafen?*

**66** When is the next sailing to
. . ?
Wann fährt die nächste Fähre
nach . . ?
*Van fairt dee nexter fairer nakh . . ?*

GERMAN

54
↕
66

95

67 **Can I catch an earlier ferry with this ticket?**
Kann ich mit diesem Ticket eine frühere Fähre nehmen?
*Can ikh mit deesem ticket iner froohere fairer neymen?*

## Notices and Signs

68 **Speisewagen**
*shpyzevaagen*
Buffet (Dining) Car

69 **Bus**
*Bus*
Bus

70 **Trinkwasser/kein Trinkwasser**
*treenkvasser/kine treenkvasser*
Drinking/Non-drinking water

71 **Eingang**
*Ine-gang*
Entrance

72 **Ausgang**
*Ows-gang*
Exit

73 **Information**
*Eenformatsion*
Information

74 **Gepäckaufbewahrung**
*gepeckowfbevaarung*
Left Luggage (Baggage Claim)

75 **Schließfächer**
*schleessfekher*
Luggage Lockers

76 **Postamt**
*postamt*
Post Office

77 **Bahnsteig**
*baanshtykh*
Platform

78 **Bahnhof**
*baanhof*
Railway (Railroad) Station

79 **Flughafen**
*Floogharfen*
Airport

80 **Hafen**
*Harfen*
Port

81 **Restaurant**
*restohrong*
Restaurant

82 **Raucher/Nichtraucher**
*raukher/nikhtraukher*
Smoking/Non-smoking

83 **Telefon**
*taylefohn*
Telephone

84 **Fahrkartenschalter**
*faarkartenshalter*
Ticket Office

85 **Abfertigungsschalter**
*Abfairtigoongs-shalter*
Check-in Desk

86 **Fahrplan**
*faarplaan*
Timetable (Schedule)

87 **Toiletten**
*toletten*
Toilets (Restrooms)

**88 Herren**
*Herren*
Gentlemen

**89 Damen**
*Daamen*
Ladies'

**90 Straßenbahn**
*Shtraasenbaan*
Tram (Streetcar)

**91 Die U-Bahn**
*Dee Oo-baan*
Underground (Subway)

**92 Warteraum**
*Varterowm*
Waiting Room

## Buying a Ticket

**93 I would like a first-class/
second-class/single (one-
way)/return (round-trip)
ticket to . . .**
Ich möchte bitte eine (einfache
Fahrkarte)/Rückfahrkarte
(Rundfahrkarte) erster Klasse/
zweiter Klasse nach . . .
*Eek merkhter bitter iner inefakhe
faarkaarte/rookfaarkaarte airster
classer/tsvyter classer nakh . . .*

**94 Is my rail pass valid on this
train/ferry/bus?**
Gilt mein Rail Pass für diesen
Zug/diese Fähre/diesen Bus?
*Guilt mine rail pass foor deesen
tsug/deese fairer/deesen boos?*

**95 I would like an aisle/window
seat.**

Bitte einen Sitzplatz am
Fenster/Durchgang.
*Bitter inen plaats am fenster/
doorkhgang.*

**96 No smoking/smoking, please.**
Raucher/Nichtraucher.
*Raukher/nikhtraukher.*

**97 We would like to sit
together.**
Wir möchten gerne zusammen
sitzen.
*Veer merkhten gairner
tsoozammen zitsen.*

**98 I would like to make a seat
reservation.**
Ich möchte gern einen Platz
reservieren.
*Ikh merkhter gairn inen plats
resairveeren.*

**99 I would like to reserve a
couchette/sleeper for one
person/two people/for my
family.**
Ich möchte eine Schlafwagen-/
Liegewagenreservierung für
eine Person/zwei Personen/
meine Familie.
*Ikh merkhter ine shlaafvaagen-/
leegevaagen-reserveerung foor iner
pairzohn/tsvy pairzohnen/miner
fameelyer.*

**100 I would like to reserve a
cabin.**
Ich möchte gern eine Kabine
reservieren.
*Ikh merkhther gairn iner cabeener
resairveeren.*

G
E
R
M
A
N

88
↑
100

97

**GERMAN**

## Timetables (Schedules)

**101 Ankunft**
*Ankunft*
Arrive

**102 Hält in . . . an**
*Helt in . . . an*
Calls (Stops) at

**103 Mini bar**
*Minibar*
Catering Service

**104 In . . . umsteigen**
*In . . . oomshtygen*
Change at . . .

**105 Anschluß**
*Aanshluss*
Connection

**106 Täglich**
*Tayglikh*
Daily

**107 Alle . . . Minuten**
*Aller . . . minooten*
Every 40 Minutes

**108 Erste Klasse**
*Airster classer*
First-class

**109 Stündlich**
*Shtundlikh*
Hourly

**110 Sitzplatzreservierung empfohlen**
*Zitsplats-reserveerung empvoolen*
Seat reservations are recommended

**111 Zweite Klasse**
*Tsvyte classe*
Second class

**112 Zuschlagspflichtig**
*tsooshlaags-pfleechteeg*
Supplement Payable

**113 über**
*Oober*
Via

## Luggage

**114 How much will it cost to send (ship) my luggage in advance?**
Wieviel kostet es mein Gepäck vorauszuschicken?
*Veefeel kostet es mine gepeck forowss-tsoosheeken?*

**115 Where is the left luggage (baggage claim) office?**
Wo ist die Gepäckaufbewahrung?
*Voo ist dee gepeck-owfbevaarung?*

**116 What time do you open/close?**
Um wieviel Uhr machen Sie auf/zu?
*Oom veefeel oor makhen zee owf/tsoo?*

**117 Where are the luggage trolleys (carts)?**
Wo finde ich die Gepäckwagen?
*Voo feende ikh dee gepeckvaagen?*

**118 Where are the lockers?**
Wo sind die Schließfächer?
*Vo seent dee shlees-fekher?*

101
↕
118

98

**119** I have lost my locker key.
Ich habe den Schlüssel für mein Schließfach verloren.
*Ikh haaber den shloossel foor mine shleesfakh ferlooren.*

## On Board

**120** Is this seat taken?
Ist dieser Platz besetzt?
*Ist deezer plats bezetst?*

**121** Excuse me, you are sitting in my reserved seat.
Entschuldigen Sie bitte, aber Sie sitzen auf meinem reservierten Platz.
*Entshuldigen zee bitter, aber zee zitsen owf minem rezerveerten plats.*

**122** Which station is this?
Wie heißt dieser Bahnhof?
*Vee hysst deezer baanhof?*

**123** What time is this train/bus/ferry/flight due to arrive/depart?
Wann kommt dieser Zug/dieser Bus/diese Fähre/dieser Flug an?/Wann geht dieser Zug/dieser Bus/diese Fähre/dieser Flug?
*Van kommt deeser tsug/deeser boos/deeser fairer/deeser floog an?/Van geyt deeser tsug/deeser boos/deeser fairer/deeser floog?*

**124** Will you wake me just before we arrive?
Bitte wecken Sie mich kurz bevor wir ankommen.
*Bitter vekken zee meekh koorts before veer ankommen.*

## Customs and Passports

**125** Ihren Reisepass bitte!
Passports, please!
*Eeren ryzerpass, bitter!*

**126** I have nothing/wine/spirits (alcohol)/tobacco to declare.
Ich habe nichts/keinen Wein/keinen Schnaps/keinen Tabak zu verzollen.
*Ikh haabe neekhst/kinen vine/kinen shnapps/kinen tabak tsoo fertsollen.*

**127** I shall be staying for . . . days/weeks/months.
Ich werde für . . . Tage/Wochen/Monate bleiben.
*Ikh verder foor . . . taager/wokhen/mohnate blyben.*

## AT THE TOURIST OFFICE

**128** Do you have a map of the town/area?
Haben Sie eine Stadtkarte/Landkarte?
*Haaben zee iner shtatkaarter/landkaarter?*

**129** Can I reserve accommodation here?
Kann ich hier eine Unterkunft reservieren?
*Can ikh here iner oonterkoonft reserveeren?*

**G E R M A N**

**130 ↑ 142**

**130** Do you have a list of accommodation?
Haben Sie ein Unterkunftsverzeichnis?
*Haben see ine unterkunfts-fertsychnis?*

## ACCOMMODATION

### Hotels

**131** I have a reservation in the name of . . .
Ich habe eine Reservierung foor . . .
*Ikh haabe iner reserveerung foor . . .*

**132** I wrote to/faxed/telephoned you last month/last week in . . .
Ich habe Ihnen letzten Monat/die letzte Woche im . . . geschrieben/ein Fax geschickt/angerufen
*Ikh haber eenen letsten mohnat/dee letste wokhe im . . . geshreeben/ine fax gesheekt/angeroofen*

**133** Do you have any rooms free?
Haben Sie Zimmer frei?
*Haben zee tsimmer fry?*

**134** I would like to reserve a single/double room with/without bath/shower.
Ich möchte ein Einzelzimmer/Doppelzimmer mit/ohne Bad/Dusche reservieren.
*Ikh merkhter ine inetsel-tsimmer/doppel-tsimmer meet/oohner baad/doosher reserveeren.*

**135** I would like bed and breakfast/(room and) half board/(room and) full board.
Ich möchte Übernachtung mit Frühstück/Halbpension/Vollpension.
*Ikh merkter oobernakhtung meet frooshtook/halbpensiohn/follpensiohn.*

**136** How much is it per night?
Wieviel kostet das pro Nacht?
*Veefeel kostet das pro nakht?*

**137** Is breakfast included?
Einschließlich Frühstück?
*Ineshleesslykh frooshtook?*

**138** May I see the room?
Kann ich das Zimmer bitte sehen?
*Can ikh das tsimmer bitter sehen?*

**139** Do you have any cheaper rooms?
Haben Sie billigere Zimmer?
*Haaben see beeligerer tsimmer?*

**140** I would like to take the room
Ich nehme das Zimmer, bitte.
*Ikh nehmer das tsimmer, bitter.*

**141** I would like to stay for . . . nights.
Ich möchte für . . . Nächte bleiben.
*Ikh merkhter foor . . . nekhte blyben*

**142** The shower/light/tap doesn't work.
Die Dusche/das Licht/der Wasserhahn funktioniert nicht.
*Dee doosher/das licht/dair vasserharn foonktsioneert nikht.*

**100**

**143** At what time/where is
breakfast served?
Um wieviel Uhr/wo wird
Frühstück serviert?
*Omm veefeel oor/vo veerd
frooshtook serveert?*

**144** What time do I have to check
out?
Um wieviel Uhr müssen wir das
Zimmer verlassen?
*Oom veefeel oor moossen veer das
tsimmer ferlassen?*

**145** Can I have the key to room
no . . ?
Könnten Sie mir bitte den
Schlüssel für Zimmer Nummer .
. . geben?
*Kernten zee mere bitter dayn
shloosel foor tsimmer noomer . . .
geyben?*

**146** My room number is . . .
Meine Zimmernummer ist . . .
*Miner tsimmer-noomer ist . . .*

**147** Do you accept travellers'
cheques/Eurocheques/credit
cards?
Nehmen Sie Reiseschecks/
Euroschecks/Kreditkarten an?
*Neymen zee ryzersheks/oirosheks/
credeetcarten an?*

**148** May I have the bill please?
Die Rechnung, bitte?
*Dee rekhnung, bitter?*

**149** Excuse me, I think there is a
mistake in this bill.
Entschuldigung, ich glaube auf
dieser Rechnung ist ein Fehler.

*Entshuldeegen, ikh glowbe owf
deeser rekhnoong ist ine feyler.*

## Youth Hostels

**150** How much is a dormitory bed
per night?
Wieviel kostet ein Bett im
Schlafsaal pro Nacht, bitte?
*Veefeel kostet ine bet eem
shlaafzaal pro nakht, bitter?*

**151** I am/am not an HI member.
Ich bin ein/kein Mitglied des
internationaler
Jugendherbergsverbands.
*Ikh been ine/kine meetgleed des
internatsionaaler yoogent-
hairbairgs-ferbands.*

**152** May I use my own sleeping bag?
Kann ich meinen eigenen
Schlafsack benutzen?
*Can ikh minen ygenen shlaafzack
benootsen?*

**153** What time do you lock the
doors at night?
Um wieviel Uhr wird abends
abgeschlossen?
*Oom veefeel oor weerd abends
abgeshlossen?*

## Camping

**154** May I camp here for the
night/two nights?
Kann ich für eine Nacht/zwei
Nächte hier campen?
*Can ikh foor ine/tsvy nekhte here
campen?*

**G
E
R
M
A
N**

**155
↕
166**

**155** Where can I pitch my tent?
Wo kann ich mein Zelt
aufstellen?
*Voo can ikh mine tselt owfshtellen?*

**156** How much does it cost for
one night/week?
Wieviel kostet es für eine
Nacht/Woche?
*Veefeel kostet es foor iner nakht/
wokhe?*

**157** Where can we park our
caravan?
Wo können wir unseren
Wohnwagen parken?
*Vo kernen veer oonseren
vohnvargen parken?*

**158** Where are the washing
facilities?
Wo sind die Waschraüme?
*Voo seent dee vashroyme?*

**159** Is there a restaurant/
supermarket/swimming pool
on site/nearby?
Gibt ein Restaurant/einen
Supermarkt/ein Schwimmbad in
der Nähe dieses
Campingplatzes?
*Geebt es ine restohrong/inen
zoopermarkt/ine shvimmbad in
der neyher deezes campingplatses?*

**160** Do you have a safety deposit
box?
Haben Sie eine
Sicherheitsverwahrung?
*Haaben see iner zeekherhytes-
fervaarung?*

## EATING AND DRINKING

### Cafés and Bars

**161** I would like a cup of/two
cups of/another coffee/tea.
Eine Tasse/Zwei Tassen/noch
eine Tasse Kaffee/Tee, bitte.
*Ikh merkhter iner tasser/tsvy
tassen kafey/tey, bitter.*

**162** With/without milk/sugar
Mit/ohne Milch/Zucker.
*Meet/ohner milkh/tsukker.*

**163** I would like a bottle/glass/
two glasses of mineral water/
red wine/white wine, please
Ich möchte eine Flasche/ein
Glas/zwei Gläser
Mineralwasser/Rotwein/
Weißwein, bitte.
*Ikh merkhter iner flasher/ine glas/
tsvy glayzer mineraalvasser/
rohtvine/vice-vine, bitter.*

**164** I would like a beer/two
beers, please.
Ein Bier/Zwei Biere, bitte.
*Ine beer/tsvy beerer, bitter.*

**165** May I have some ice?
Kannich etwas Eis haben?
*Can ikh etvas ice haaben?*

**166** Do you have any matches/
cigarettes/cigars?
Haben Sie Streichhölzer/
Zigaretten/Zigarren?
*Haaben see shtrykhherltser/
tseegaretten/tseegarren?*

## Restaurants

**167** Can you recommend a good/
inexpensive restaurant in this
area?
Können Sie ein gutes/nicht zu
teueres Restaurant in dieser
Gegend empfehlen?
*Kernen zee ine gootes/nikht tsoo
toyeress restohrong in deezer
geygent empfeylen?*

**168** I would like a table for . . .
people.
Ein Tisch für . . . Personen, bitte.
*Ine teesh foor . . . perzohnen, bitter.*

**169** Do you have a non-smoking
area?
Haben Sie einen Bereich für
Nichtraucher?
*Haben zee inen berykh foor
nikhtrowkher?*

**170** Waiter/Waitress!
Herr Ober/Fräulein, bitte!
*Hair ohber/froyline, bitter!*

**171** Do you have a set menu/
children's menu/wine list?
Haben Sie eine Tageskarte/
Kinderspeisekarte/Weinkarte?
*Haaben zee iner tahgeskaarter/
keender-shpyzekaarter/
vinekaarter?*

**172** Do you have any vegetarian
dishes, please?
Gibt es bei Ihnen vegetarische
Gerichte, bitte?
*Geebt es by eehnen vegetareesher
gereekhter, bitter?*

**173** Are there any local
specialities?
Gibt es örtliche Spezialitäten?
*Geebt es ortlikhe specialitayten?*

**174** Are vegetables included?
Ist Gemüse dabei?
*Ist gemoose darbye?*

**175** Could I have it well-cooked/
medium/rare please?
Ich möchte es bitte durch/halb
durch/englisch gebraten.
*Ikh merkhter es bitter doorkh/halb
doorkh/english gebrarten.*

**176** What does this dish consist of?
Was für ein Gericht ist es?
*Vas foor ine gereekht ist es?*

**177** I would like the set menu,
please.
Das Tageskarte, bitte.
*Das tahgeskaarte, bitter.*

**178** We have not been served yet.
Wir warten noch auf
Bedienung.
*Veer varten nokh owf bedeenung.*

**179** Excuse me, this is not what I
ordered.
Entschuldigung, das habe ich
nicht bestellt.
*Entshuldeegen, das haber ikh nikht
beshtelt.*

**180** May I have some/some more
bread/water/coffee/tea?
Kann ich noch etwas Brot,
Wasser/Kaffee/Tee haben?
*Can ikh etvas/nokh etvas broht/
vasser/kaffey/tey haaben?*

**G
E
R
M
A
N**

**181
↑
195**

181 **May I have the bill, please?**
Die Rechnung, bitte?
*Dee rekhnung, bitter?*

182 **Does this bill include service?**
Ist diese Rechnung einschließlich Bedienung?
*Ist deeze rekhnung ine-shleessleekh bedeenung?*

183 **Do you accept travellers' cheques (travelers' checks)/ Eurocheques/MasterCard/ US dollars?**
Nehmen sie Reiseschecks/ uroschecks/MasterCard/US Dollars?
*Naymen zee Ryzersheks/ Eurosheks/MasterCard/US Dollars?*

184 **Can I have a receipt, please?**
Könnte ich bitte eine Quittung haben?
*Kernter ikh bitter ine kwitoong harben?*

185 **Where is the toilet (restroom), please?**
Wo sind die Toiletten, bitte?
*Voo zeent dee toletten, bitter?*

## On the Menu

186 **First courses**
Vorspeisen
*Fore-shpysen*

187 **Soups**
Suppen
*Sooppen*

188 **Main courses**
Hauptgerichte
*Howpt-gerikhte*

189 **Fish dishes**
Fischgerichte
*Fish-gerikhte*

190 **Meat dishes**
Fleischgerichte
*Flyesh-gerikhte*

191 **Vegetarian dishes**
Vegetarische Gerichte
*Vegetairishe gerikhte*

192 **Cheese**
Käse
*Keyse*

193 **Desserts**
Desserts
*Desayrs*

194 **Specialities**
Spezialitäten
*Specialitayten*

## GETTING AROUND

### Public Transport

195 **Where is the bus stop/coach station/nearest metro (subway) station?**
Wo ist die nächste Bushaltestelle/der nächste Busbahnhof/die U-Bahnhaltestelle, bitte?
*Voo ist die nexter bushaltersteller/ der nexter busbaanhof/dee nexter Oo-baahn-halter-shteller?*

**196** When is the next/last bus
to . . ?
Wann fährt der nächste/letzte
Bus nach . . ?
*Vann fairt der nexter/letster bus
nakh . . ?*

**197** How much is the fare to the
city centre (downtown)/
railway (railroad) station/
airport?
Wieviel kostet es zur
Stadtmitte/zum Bahnhof/
Flughafen?
*Veefeel kostet es tsoor shtatmitte/
tsoom baanhof/flooghaafen?*

**198** Will you tell me when to
get off?
Sagen Sie mir bitte wann ich
aussteigen muß?
*Zaagen zee meer bitter vann ikh
owsstygen moos?*

**199** Does this bus go to . . ?
Fährt dieser Bus nach . . ?
*Fairt deezer bus nakh . . ?*

**200** Which number bus goes to
. . ?
Welcher Bus fährt nach . . ?
*Velkher bus fairt nakh . . ?*

**201** May I have a single (one-
way)/return (round-trip)/
day ticket/book of tickets?
Ich möchte eine einfache
Fahrkarte/Rückfahrkarte/
Rundfahrkarte/Tageskarte/ein
Fahrkartenheft?
*Ikh merkhter iner inefakher
faarkaarter/ruekfaarkaarter/*

*tagheskaarter/iner
faarkaartenheft?*

## Taxis

**202** I would like to go to . . .
How much will it cost?
Ich möchte nach . . . fahren,
wieviel kostet das?
*Ikh merkhter nakh . . . faaren,
veefeel kostet das?*

**203** Please stop here.
Bitte anhalten.
*Bitter anhalten.*

**204** I would like to order a taxi
today/tomorrow/at 2pm to
go from . . . to . . .
Ich möchte gerne ein Taxi für
heute/morgen/zwei Uhr
bestellen um von . . . nach . . . zu
fahren.
*Ikh merkhter gairner ine Taxi foor
hoyter morgen/tsvy oor bestellen
oom fon . . . nakh . . . zu faaren.*

## Asking the Way

**205** Excuse me, do you speak
English?
Entschuldigen Sie, sprechen Sie
Englisch?
*Entshuldigen zee, shprekhen zee
english?*

**206** Excuse me, is this the right
way to . . ?
Entschuldigung, bin ich hier
richtig für . . ?
*Entshuldeegen, bin ikh here rikhtig
foor . . ?*

207 ... the cathedral/the tourist information office/the castle/the old town
... den Dom/die Touristeninformation/das Schloß/die Altstadt?
*... den dorm, dee touristen-informatsion/das shloss/dee altshtat?*

208 Can you tell me the way to the railway station/bus station/taxi rank (stand)/city centre (downtown)/beach?
Können sie mir bitte sagen wie ich zum Bahnhof/zum Busbahnhof/zum TaxiRank/zur Stadtmitte/zum Strand komme?
*Kernen zee meer bitter zaagen, vee ikh tsoom baanhof/tsoom busbaanhof/tsoom taxirank/tsoor shtatmitter/tsoom shtrant kommer?*

209 First/second left/right/straight ahead.
Die erste Straße links/rechts/geradeaus.
*Dee airste shtraasser leenks/rekhts/geraader-ows.*

210 Where is the nearest police station/post office?
Wo ist die nächste Polizeiwache/das nächste Postamt?
*Voo ist dee nexter politsywakhe/das nexter postamt?*

211 Is it far?
Ist es weit?
*Ist es vyte?*

212 Do I need to take a taxi/a bus?
Muß ich eine Taxi/einen Bus nehmen?
*Moos ikh iner taxi/inen bus nayhmen?*

213 Can you point to it on my map?
Können Sie es mir bitte auf der Karte zeigen?
*Kernen see es meer bitter owf der kaarte tsygen?*

214 Thank you for your help.
Vielen Dank für Ihre Hilfe.
*Feelen dank foor eehrer heelfe.*

## SIGHTSEEING

215 Where is the Tourist Information office?
Wo ist das TouristenInformationsbüro?
*Voo ist das touristen-informatisons-booro?*

216 Where is the cathedral/church/museum?
Wo ist der Dom/die Kirche/das Museum?
*Voh ist der dohm/dee keerkhe/das moozeyum?*

217 How much is the entrance (admission) charge?
Was kostet der Eintritt?
*Vas kostet der inetreet?*

218 Is there a reduction for children/students/senior citizens?
Gibt es eine Ermäßigung für Kinder/Studenten/Rentner?

*Geebt es iner ermeyssigung foor kinder/shtudenten/rentner?*

**219** **What time does the next guided tour start?**
Um wieviel Uhr ist die nächste Führung?
*Oom veefeel oor ist dee nexter foohrung?*

**220** **One/two adults/children, please.**
Ein Erwachsener/zwei Erwachsene/Kinder, bitte.
*Ine ervaxener/tsvy ervaxener/kinder, bitter.*

**221** **May I take photographs here?**
Darf man hier fotografieren?
*Darf man here fotografeeren?*

## ENTERTAINMENT

**222** **Can you recommend a good bar/nightclub?**
Können Sie eine gute Bar/einen guten Nachtklub empfehlen?
*Kernen zee iner gooter bar/inen gooten nakhtklub empfehlen?*

**223** **Do you know what is on at the cinema (playing at the movies)/theatre at the moment?**
Was spielt im Augenblick im Kino/Theater?
*Vass shpeelt im augenbleek im keeno/teyaater?*

**224** **I would like to book (purchase) . . . tickets for the matinée/evening**

**performance on Monday.**
Ich möchte gerne Eintrittskarten für die Frühvorstellung am Montag bestellen.
*Ikh merkhter gairner inetreetskaarten foor dee frooforshtellung am mohntagh beshtellen.*

**225** **What time does the film/performance start?**
Um wieviel Uhr fängt der Film/die Vorstellung an?
*Oom veefeel oor fengt der film/dee forshtellung an?*

## MEETING PEOPLE

**226** **Hello/Goodbye.**
Hallo/Auf Wiedersehen.
*Hallo/Owf Veederzeyhen.*

**227** **Good morning/good afternoon/good evening/goodnight.**
Guten Morgen/guten Tag/guten Abend/gute Nacht.
*Gooten morgen/gooten targ/gooten arbent/goote nakht.*

**228** **Pleased to meet you.**
Es freut mich Sie kennenzulernen.
*Es froyt mikh zee kennen-tsoo-lernen.*

**229** **How are you?**
Wie geht es Ihnen?
*Vee gayht es eehnen?*

**230** **Fine, thank you. And you?**
Gut danke, und Ihnen?
*Goot, danker, oond eenen?*

**231** My name is . . .
Mein Name ist . . .
*Mine naamer ist . . .*

**232** This is my friend/boyfriend/
girlfriend/husband/wife/
brother/sister.
Dies ist mein Freund/mein
Freund/meine Freundin/mein
Mann/meine Frau/mein Bruder/
meine Schwester.
*Dees ist mine froynd/mine froynd/
miner froindeen/mine man/miner
frow/mine brooder/miner shvester.*

**233** Where are you travelling to?
Wohin reisen Sie?
*Voheen ryzen zee?*

**234** I am/we are going to . . .
Ich fahre/wir fahren nach . . .
*Ikh faare/weer faaren nakh . . .*

**235** How long are you travelling
for?
Wie lange reisen Sie?
*Vee lange ryzen zee?*

**236** Where do you come from?
Woher kommen Sie?
*Vohair kommen zee?*

**237** I am/we are from . . .
Ich komme/wir kommen aus . . .
*Ikh kommer/veer kommen aus . . .*

**238** We're on holiday.
Wir machen Urlaub.
*Veer makhen oorlowb.*

**239** This is our first visit here.
Wir sind zum ersten Mal hier.
*Veer sind tsum airsten marl here.*

**240** Would you like a ciagrette?/
May I have a cigarette?
Möchten Sie eine Zigarette/
Kann ich bitte eine Zigarette
haben?
*Merkhten zee iner tsigaretter/Can
ikh bitter iner tsigaretter haaben?*

**241** I am sorry but I do not
understand.
Es tut mir leid, aber ich verstehe
es nicht.
*Es toot meer lite, aaber ikh
ferstayher es nikht.*

**242** Please speak slowly.
Sprechen Sie bitte langsam.
*Sprekhen zee bitter langzam.*

**243** Do you mind if I smoke?
Darf ich rauchen?
*Darf ikh raukhen?*

**244** Do you have a light?
Haben Sie Feuer bitte?
*Haaben see foyer bitter?*

**245** I am waiting for my husband/
wife/boyfriend/girlfriend.
Ich warte auf meinen Mann/
meine Frau/meinen Freund/
meine Freundin.
*Ikh varter owf minen mann/miner
frow/minen froind/miner froindin.*

## TRAVELLING WITH CHILDREN

**246** Do you have a high chair/
babysitting service/cot?
Haben Sie einen Kinderstuhl/
Babysitter/ein Kinderbett?
*Haaben zee inen kindershtool/
Babysittier/ine kinderbet?*

**247** Where is the nursery/
playroom?
Wo ist das Kinderzimmer/
pielzimmer?
*Voh ist das kindertsimmer/
speeltsimmer?*

**248** Where can I warm the baby's
bottle?
Wo kann ich die Milchflasche
für das Baby aufwärmen?
*Voh can ikh die Milkflasher foor
das Baby owf-vairmen?*

## COMMUNICATIONS

### Post

**249** How much will it cost to
send a letter/postcard/this
package to Britain/Ireland/
America/Canada/Australia/
New Zealand?
Wieviel kostet ein Brief/eine
Postkarte/dieses Paket nach
England/Irland/Amerika/
Kanada/Australien/Neuseeland?
*Veefeel kostet ine breef/iner
postkaarter/deezes pakayt nakh
England/Eerland/America/
Canada/Owstralee-en/
Noyzeyland.*

**250** I would like one stamp/two
stamps.
Ich möchte eine/zwei
Briefmarke(n).
*Ikh merkhter iner/tsvy
breefmarke(n).*

**251** I'd like . . . stamps for
postcards to send abroad,
please.
Ich möchte . . . Briefmarken
für Postkarten ins Ausland
bitte.
*Ikh merkhter . . . breefmarken
foor postkarten ins owslund bitter.*

### Phones

**252** I would like to make a
telephone call/reverse the
charges to (make a collect
call to) . . .
Ich möchte einen Anruf/ein
RGespräch nakh . . . machen
*Ikh merkhter inen aanroof/ine eyr-
geshprekh nakh . . . makhen*

**253** Which coins do I need for
the telephone?
Welche Münzen brauche ich
für dieses Telefon?
*Velkhe moontsen browkhe ikh
foor deezes teylefohn?*

**254** The line is engaged (busy).
Die Nummer ist besetzt.
*Dee noommer ist bezetst.*

**255** The number is . . .
Die Nummer ist . . .
*Dee noommer ist . . .*

**256** Hello, this is . . .
Hallo, hier spricht . . .
*Hallo, here shprikht . . .*

G
E
R
M
A
N

247
↕
256

**GERMAN**

²⁵⁷ May I speak to . . ?
Kann ich bitte mit . . .
sprechen?
*Can ikh bitter mit . . .
shprekhen?*

²⁵⁸ He/She is not in at the
moment. Can you call back?
Er/Sie ist im Moment nicht da.
Könnten Sie später noch einmal
anrufen?
*Air/Zee ist im morment nikht dar.
Kernten zee shpeter nokh inemarl
anroofen?*

## MONEY

²⁵⁹ I would like to change these
travellers' cheques (travelers'
checks)/this currency/this
Eurocheque.
Ich möchte gerne diese
Reiseschecks/dieses Geld/
diesen Euroscheck wechseln.
*Ikh merkhter gairner deezer
ryzersheks/deezes gelt/deezen
Euroshek vexseln.*

²⁶⁰ How much commission do
you charge (What is the
service charge)?
Wie hoch ist Ihre Provision?
*Vee hokh ist eere provizion?*

²⁶¹ Can I obtain money with my
MasterCard?
Kann ich mit meiner
MasterCard Geld bekommen?
*Can ikh meet miner MasterCard
gelt bekommen?*

²⁵⁷
↕
²⁷¹

## SHOPPING

### Names of Shops and Departments

²⁶² Buchgeschäft/Schreibwaren
*Bookhgesheft/Shribevahren*
Bookshop/Stationery

²⁶³ Schmuckgeschäft/Geschenke
*Shmookgesheft/Geshenker*
Jeweller's/Gifts

²⁶⁴ Schuhe
*Shooher*
Shoes

²⁶⁵ Eisenwaren
*Eyesenvahren*
Hardware

²⁶⁶ Antiquitäten
*Anteekweeteyten*
Antiques

²⁶⁷ Friseur (Herren)/(Damen)
*Freesoor (hairren)/(darmen)*
Hairdressers (men's)/(women's)

²⁶⁸ Tabakwarengeschäft
*Tabakvahrengesheft*
Tobacconist

²⁶⁹ Bäckerei
*Bekkereye*
Baker's

²⁷⁰ Supermarkt
*Soopermarkt*
Supermarket

²⁷¹ Fotogeschäft
*Fotogesheft*
Photoshop

**272** Spielwaren
*Speelvahren*
Toys

**273** Reisebüro
*Ryesebooro*
Travel Agent

**274** Toilettenartikel
*Toiletenarteekel*
Toiletries

**275** Schallplatten
*Shallplatten*
Records

## In the Shop

**276** What time do the shops open/close?
Um wieviel Uhr öffnen/ schließen die Geschäfte?
*Oom veefeel oor erffnen/shleessen dee gesherfter?*

**277** Where is the nearest market?
Wo ist der nächste Markt?
*Vo ist dair nekster markt?*

**278** Can you show me the one in the window/this one?
Zeigen Sie mir bitte den im Fenster/diesen da?
*Tsyegen zee mere bitter den im fenster/deezen dar?*

**279** Can I try this on?
Kann ich das anprobieren?
*Can ikh das anprobeeren?*

**280** What size is this?
Welche Größe ist dieses Stück?
*Velkhe grersser ist deezes shtook?*

**281** This is too large/too small/ too expensive.
Es ist zu groß/zu klein/zu teuer.
*Es ist tsu gross/tsu kline/tsu toyer.*

**282** Do you have any others?
Haben Sie noch andere?
*Haben zee nokh anderer?*

**283** My size is . . .
Ich habe Größe . . .
*Ikh haber grerser . . .*

**284** Where is the changing room/ children's/cosmetic/ ladieswear/menswear/food department?
Wo ist der Umkleideraum/ Kinder- /Damen- / Herrenkleidungs- / Lebensmittel-abteilung?
*Voh ist der oomklyderowm/dee kinder/daamen/herenklydungs/ leybensmittel abtlung?*

**285** I would like . . .
Ich hätte gern . . .
*Ikh hetter gairn . . .*

**286** I would like a quarter of a kilo/half a kilo/a kilo of bread/butter/cheese/ham/ tomatoes.
Ich möchte gerne ein viertel Kilo/halbes Kilo/ein Kilo Brot/ Butter/Käse/Schinken/ Tomaten.
*Ikh merkhter gairner ine feertel keelo/halbes keelo/ine keelo broht/ bootter/kayzer/sheenken/tomaten.*

**G**
**E**
**R**
**M**
**A**
**N**

287 **How much is this?**
Wieviel kostet das?
*Veefeel kostet das?*

288 **I'll take this one, thank you.**
Ich nehme das, dankeschön.
*Ikh neymer das, dankershern.*

289 **Do you have a carrier (shopping) bag?**
Haben Sie eine Tragetasche?
*Haaben zee iner traager-tasher?*

290 **Do you have anything cheaper/larger/smaller/of better quality?**
Haben Sie etwas billigeres/größeres/kleineres/Haben Sie eine bessere Qualität?
*Haaben zee etvas billigeress/grersseress/klineress/Haaben zee iner bessere qualitaet?*

291 **I would like a film for my camera.**
Ich möchte einen Film für meinen Fotoapparat.
*Ikh merkhter inen film foor minen fotoaparat.*

292 **I would like some batteries, the same size as this old one.**
Ich möchte einige Batterien, die gleiche Größe wie die alten.
*Ikh merkhter iyniger batteree-en, dee glykhe grersser vee dee alten.*

293 **Would you mind wrapping this for me, please?**
Können Sie es bitte einpacken?
*Kernen zee es bitter ine-pakken?*

294 **Sorry, but you seem to have given me the wrong change.**
Entschuldigung, aber Sie scheinen einen Fehler mit dem Wechselgeld gemacht zu haben.
*Entshuldigung, aber zee shinern inen fayler mit dem vekhselgeld gemahkt tsoo haaben.*

## MOTORING

### Car Hire (Rental)

295 **I have ordered (rented) a car in the name of . .**
Ich habe einen Wagen für . . . bestellt.
*Ikh haaber inen vaagen foor . . . beshtellt.*

296 **How much does it cost to hire (rent) a car for one day/two days/one week?**
Was kostet es einen Wagen für einen Tag/zwei Tage/eine Woche zu mieten?
*Vas kostet es inen vaagen foor inen taagh/tsvy taager/iner wokher tsoo meeten?*

297 **Is the tank already full of petrol (gas)?**
Ist der Tank voll?
*Ist der tank foll?*

298 **Is insurance and tax included? How much is the deposit?**
Ist die Versicherung und Steuer inbegriffen? Wieviel muß man anzahlen?
*Ist dee ferzeekherung oont shtoyer inbegreeffen? Veefeel moos man aantsahlen?*

299 **By what time must I return the car?**
Um wieviel Uhr muß ich den Wagen zurückbringen?
*Oom veefeel oor moos ikh den vaagen tsoo-rookh bringen?*

300 **I would like a small/family car with a radio/cassette player.**
Ich möchte einen kleinen/ Familienwagen mit Radio und Kassettenspieler.
*Ikh merkhte inen klinen/fameelien vaagen mit radio oont cassettenshpeeler.*

## Asking the Way

301 **Excuse me, can you help me please?**
Entschuldigung, könnten Sie mir bitte helfen?
*Entshuldeegen, kernten zee mere bitter helfen?*

302 **How do I reach the motorway/main road?**
Wie komme ich zur Autobahn/ zur Hauptstraße?
*Vee kommer ikh tsur owtobarn/ tsur howpt-shtrarser?*

303 **I think I have taken the wrong turning.**
Ich glaube, ich bin falsch abgebogen.
*Ikh glowber, ikh bin falsh abgeborgen.*

304 **I am looking for this address.**
Ich suche diese Adresse.
*Ikh sookher deeser ardresse.*

305 **I am looking for the ... hotel.**
Ich suche das ... Hotel.
*Ikh sookher das ... hotel.*

306 **How far is it to ... from here?**
Wie weit ist es bis ... von hier?
*Vee vite ist es bees ... fon here?*

307 **Carry straight on for ... kilometres.**
Fahren Sie ... Kilometer geradeaus.
*Faren zee ... keelometer gerarde ows.*

308 **Take the next turning on the right/left.**
Biegen Sie die nächste Straße rechts/links ab.
*Beegen zee dee nekste shtrarser rekhts/links ab.*

309 **Turn right/left at the next crossroads/traffic lights.**
Biegen Sie an der nächsten Kreuzung/Ampel rechts/links ab.
*Beegen zee un dair neksten kroitsung/ampel rekhts/links ab.*

310 **You are going in the wrong direction.**
Sie fahren in die falsche Richtung.
*Zee faren in dee falser richtung.*

113

## Parking

**311** How long can I park here?
Wie la ge darf man hier parken?
*Vee langer darf man here parken?*

**312** Is there a car park near here?
Gibt es einen Parkplatz in der Nähe?
*Geebt es inen parkplats in dair neher?*

**313** At what time does this car park close?
Wann schließt dieser Parkplatz?
*Van shleest deeser parkplats?*

## Signs and Notices

**314** Einbahnstraße.
*Ine-barn-shtraser.*
One way.

**315** Zutritt/Einfahrt verboten.
*Tsutreet/Inefart ferbohten.*
No entry.

**316** Parkverbot.
*Park-ferboht.*
No parking.

**317** Umweg (Umleitung)
*Oomweyg (oomlytung)*
Detour (diversion)

**318** Halt.
*Halt.*
Stop.

**319** Vorfahrt beachten.
*Forfart beakhten.*
Give way (yield).

**320** Straßenglätte.
*Shtrasen-gletter.*
Slippery road.

**321** Überholen verboten.
*Ooberhohlen ferbohten.*
No overtaking.

## At the Filling Station

**322** Unleaded (lead-free)/Standard/Premium
Bleifrei/Normal/Super
*Blye-frye/normahl/super*

**323** Fill the tank please.
Volltanken, bitte.
*Foll-tanken, bitter.*

**324** Do you have a road map of this area?
Haben Sie eine Straßenkarte für diese Gegend?
*Haben zee iner shtrasen-karte foor deeser gegent?*

**325** How much is the car-wash?
Was kostet die Autowäsche?
*Vas kostet dee owtowesher?*

## Breakdowns

**326** I've had a breakdown at . . .
Ich habe eine Panne bei . . .
*Ikh haber ine panner bye . . .*

**327** I am on the road from . . . to . . .
Ich bin auf der Straße von . . . nach . . .
*Ikh bin owf dair shtrase fon . . . nakh . . .*

**328** I can't move the car. Can you send a tow-truck?
Mein Auto ist kaputt. Können Sie einen Abschleppwagen schicken?
*Mine owto ist kapoot. Kernen zee inen Abshlep-vagen shiken?*

**329** I have a flat tyre.
Mein Reifen ist platt.
*Mine ryefen ist platt.*

**330** The windscreen (windshield) has smashed/cracked.
Die Windschutzscheibe ist kaputt/gesprungen.
*Dee vindshoots-shyeber ist kapoot/geshprungen.*

**331** There is something wrong with the engine/brakes/lights/steering/gearbox/clutch/exhaust.
Ich habe Probleme mit dem Motor/der Bremse/dem Licht/der Steuerung/dem Getriebe/der Kupplung/dem Auspuff.
*Ikh haber probleyme mit dem motor/dair bremser/dem licht/dair shtoyerung/dem getreeber/dair koopploong/dem owspooff.*

**332** It's overheating.
Der Motor ist überhitzt.
*Dair motor ist ooberhitst.*

**333** It won't start.
Es springt nicht an.
*Es shpringt nikht an.*

**334** Where can I get it repaired?
Wo kann ich es reparieren lassen?
*Vo can ikh es repareeren lassen?*

**335** Can you take me there?
Können Sie mich dort hinbringen?
*Kernen zee mikh dort hinbringen?*

**336** Will it take long to fix?
Dauert die Reparatur lange?
*Dowert dee reparatoor languer?*

**337** How much will it cost?
Was wird es kosten?
*Vas veerd es kosten?*

## Accidents

**338** Can you help me? There has been an accident.
Können Sie mir helfen? Es ist ein Unfall passiert.
*Kernen zee mere helfen? Es ist ine oonfal paseert.*

**339** Please call the police/an ambulance.
Bitte rufen Sie die Polizei/einen Krankenwagen.
*Bitter roofen zee dee politsye/inen krankenvagen.*

**340** Is anyone hurt?
Ist jemand verletzt?
*Ist yemant fairletst?*

## Traffic Offences

**341** I'm sorry, I didn't see the sign.
Tut mir leid, ich habe das Schild nicht gesehen.
*Toot mere lyed, ikh haber das shilt nikht gesayhen.*

G
E
R
M
A
N

328
↑
341

**G E R M A N**

**342**
↑
**352**

**342** Must I pay a fine? How much?
Gibt das einen Strafzettel? Wieviel?
*Geebt das inen shtraf-tsettel? Veefeel?*

**343** Show me your documents.
Zeigen Sie mir Ihre Papiere.
*Tsyegen zee mere eere papeerer.*

## HEALTH

### Pharmacy

**344** Do you have anything for a stomachache/headache/sore throat/toothache?
Haben Sie etwas für Magen-schmerzen/Kopfschmerzen/Halsschmerzen/Zahn-schmerzen?
*Haaben zee etvas foor maagenshmertsen/kopfshmertsen/hals-shmertsen/tsahnschmertsen?*

**345** I need something for diarrhoea (diarrhea)/constipation/a cold/a cough/insect bites/sunburn/travel (motion) sickness.
Ich benötige etwas für Durchfall/Verstopfung/eine Erkältung/einen Husten/Insektenstiche/Sonnenbrand/Reisekrankheit.
*Ikh benertiger etvas foor doorkhfall/fershtopfung/iner erkeltung/inen hoosten/insektenshteekhe/zonnenbrand/ryzerkrankhite.*

**346** How much/how many do I take?
Wieviel/wieviele soll ich nehmen?
*Veefeel/veefeeler soll ikh neymen?*

**347** How often do I take it/them?
Wie oft soll ich es/sie nehmen?
*Vee oft soll ikh es/zee neymen?*

**348** How much does it cost?
Wieviel kostet das?
*Veefeel kostet das?*

**349** Can you recommend a good doctor/dentist?
Können Sie einen guten Arzt/Zahnarzt empfehlen?
*Kernen see meer inen gooten artst/tsaanartst empfehlen?*

**350** Is it suitable for children?
Ist es gut mit Kindern?
*Ist es goot mit kindern?*

### Doctor

**351** I have a pain here/in my arm/leg/chest/stomach.
Ich habe hier Schmerzen/an meinem Arm/Bein/an meiner Brust/an meinem Magen.
*Ikh haaber shmertsen here/an minem arm/bine/an miner broost/an minem maagen.*

**352** Please call a doctor, this is an emergency.
Rufen Sie bitte einen Arzt, es ist ein Notfall.
*Roofen zee bitter inen artst, es ist ine nohtfall.*

**353** I would like to make an appointment to see a doctor.
Ich möchte einen Arzttermin vereinbaren.
*Ikh merkhter inen artst-termeen ferinebaaren.*

**354** I am diabetic/pregnant.
Ich bin ein Diabetiker/ich bin schwanger.
*Ikh been ine deeabetiker/ikh been shvanger.*

**355** I need a prescription for . . .
Ich benötige ein Rezept foor . . .
*Ikh benertiger ine retsept foor . . .*

**356** Can you give me something to ease the pain?
Können Sie mir etwas gegen die Schmerzen geben?
*Kernen zee meer etvas geygen dee shmertsen geyben?*

**357** I am/he is/she is allergic to penicillin.
Ich bin/er ist/sie ist allergisch auf Penizillin.
*Ikh bin/air ist/zee ist allergish owf penitsileen.*

**358** Does this hurt?
Tut das weh?
*Toot das way?*

**359** You must/he must/she must go to hospital.
Sie müssen/er muß/sie muß ins Krankenhaus.
*Zee moossen/air mousse/zee mous ins krankenhouse.*

**360** Take these once/twice /three times a day.

Nehmen Sie diese einmal/ zweimal/dreimal täglich.
*Naymen zee deeser inemal/ tsvyemal/drymal teyglikh.*

**361** I am/he is/she is taking this medication.
Ich nehme/er nimmt/sie nimmt diese Medikamente.
*Ikh naymer/air nimmt/zee nimmt deeser medikamenter.*

**362** I have medical insurance.
Ich habe eine Krankenversicherung.
*Ikh haber ine kranken-fersikheroong.*

## Dentist

**363** I have toothache.
Ich habe Zahnschmerzen.
*Ikh haabe tsahn-shmertsen.*

**364** My filling has come out.
Eine Füllung ist herausgefallen.
*Iner fooloong ist herowsgefallen.*

**365** I do/do not want to have an injection first.
Ich will eine/keine Spritze haben.
*Ikh vill iner/kiner shpreetse haaben.*

## EMERGENCIES

**366** Help!
Hilfe!
*Heelfe!*

**367** Call an ambulance/a doctor/
the police!
Rufen Sie bitte einen
Krankenwagen/einen Arzt/die
Polizei!
*Roofen zee bitter inen
krankenvaagen/inen artst/dee
politsye!*

**368** I have had my travellers'
cheques (travelers' checks)/
credit cards/purse/handbag/
rucksack (knapsack)/
luggage/wallet stolen.
Man hat mir meine
Reiseschecks/Kreditkarten/
meinen Geldbeutel/meine
Handtasche/meinen Rucksack/
mein Gepäck/meine Brieftasche
gestolen.
*Man hat meer miner ryzersheks/
creditkaarten/minen geldboytel/
miner handtasher/minen
ruckzack/mine gepeck/miner
breeftasher geshtohlen.*

**369** Can you help me, I have lost
my daughter/son?
Können Sie mir bitte helfen, ich
habe meine Tochter/meinen

Sohn verloren?
*Kernen zee meer bitter helfen, ikh
haabe miner tokhter/minen zohn
ferloren?*

**370** Please go away/leave me
alone.
Lassen Sie mich bitte in Ruhe!
*Lassen see meekh bitter in roohe!*

**371** Fire!
Feuer!
*Foyer!*

**372** I want to contact the British/
American/Canadian/Irish/
Australian/New Zealand/
South African consulate.
Ich möchte mich mit dem
britischen/amerikanischen/
kanadischen/irischen/
australischen/neuseeländischen/
südafrikanischen Konsulat in
Verbindung setzen.
*Ikh merkhter mikh mit dem
britishen/amerikanishen/
karnardishen/eereeshen/
owstralishen/noysaylendishen/
soodafrikanishen konsoolat in
ferbeendoong setsen.*

# Introduction

Greek is a language with a 3000-year history, and modern written Greek would be readable, and probably to a large degree comprehensible, by an ancient Athenian. The non-roman script is the most difficult aspect of the language for the visitor, although many street signs and notices have both the Greek characters and a transliteration into the roman alphabet. This is in itself a source of potential confusion, however, as there is no one accepted way of writing a Greek word in roman script, so any Greek text can have a variety of spellings in the roman alphabet.

The spoken language has fewer pitfalls, although beware that the word for 'yes' sounds like English 'nay', whereas a Greek who nods his head up and down is probably saying 'no', this being the equivalent of shaking the head. English is widely spoken in tourist areas, and French is an official second language, but be prepared to speak Greek when off the beaten track.

## Addresses for travel and tourist information

**UK:** *National Tourist Organisation of Greece*, 4 Conduit St, London W1R 0DJ; tel: (0171) 734 5997.

**USA:** *National Tourist Organisation of Greece*, Olympic Tower, 645 Fifth Ave (5th Floor), New York, NY 10022; tel: (212) 421-5777.

# ESSENTIALS

## ESSENTIALS

### Alphabet

| | |
|---|---|
| Α, α *alpha* | Β, β *vita* |
| Γ, γ *gamma* | Δ, δ *delta* |
| Ε, ε *epsilon* | Ζ, ζ *zeeta* |
| Η, η *eeta* | Θ, θ *theeta* |
| Ι, ι *iota* | Κ, κ *kappa* |
| Λ, λ *lamda* | Μ, μ *mi* |
| Ν, ν *ni* | Ξ, ξ *xi* |
| Ο, ο *omikron* | Π, π *pi* |
| Ρ, ρ *ro* | Σ, σ *sigma* |
| Τ, τ *taf* | Υ, υ *ipsilon* |
| Φ, φ *fi* | Χ, χ *hi* |
| Ψ, ψ *psi* | Ω, ω *omega* |

### Basic Words and Phrases

1 **Yes**
Ναι
*Ne*

**No**
Οχι
*Ohi*

2 **Please**
Παρακαλώ

**Thank you**
Ευχαριστώ

*Parakalo*

*Efharisto*

3 **That's O.K.**
Εντάξει
*Entaxi*

**Perhaps**
Ισως
*Isos*

4 **To**
Προς
*Pros*

**From**
Από
*Apo*

5 **Here**
Εδώ
*Edo*

**There**
Εκεί
*Eki*

6 **None**
Τίποτα
*Tipota*

**Also**
Επίσης
*Episis*

7 **How**
Πώς
*Pos*

**When**
Πότε
*Pote*

8 **What**
Τι
*Ti*

**Why**
Πού;
*Pu?*

9 **I don't understand.**
Δεν καταλαβαίνω.
*Den katalaveno*

10 **I don't speak Greek.**
Δεν μιλώ Ελληνικά.
*Den milo Ellinika*

11 **Do you speak English?**
Μιλάτε Αγγλικά;
*Milate Anglika?*

12 **Can you please write it down?**
Μπορείτε σας παρακαλώ να το γράψετε;
*Borite sas parakalo na to grapsete?*

13 **Can you please speak more slowly?**

Μπορείτε σας παρακαλώ να
μιλάτε πιο αργά;
*Borite sas parakalo na milate pio
arga?*

**14** **How much does it/this cost?**
Πόσο κοστίζει αυτό;
*Poso kostizi afto?*

## Days

**15** **Monday** **Tuesday**
Δευτέρα Τρίτη
*Deftera* *Triti*

**16** **Wednesday** **Thursday**
Τετάρτη Πέμπτη
*Tetarti* *Pembti*

**17** **Friday** **Saturday**
Παρασκευή Σάββατο
*Paraskevi* *Savvato*

**18** **Sunday** **Morning**
Κυριακή Πρωί
*Kiriaki* *Proi*

**19** **Afternoon** **Evening**
Απόγευμα Βράδυ
*Apoyevma* *Vradi*

**20** **Night** **Week**
Νύχτα Εβδομάδα
*Nihta* *Evdomada*

**21** **Yesterday** **Tomorrow**
Χτες Αύριο
*Htes* *Avrio*

## Numbers

**22** **Zero** **One**
Μηδέν Ένα
*Miden* *Ena*

**23** **Two** **Three**
Δύο Τρία
*Dio* *Tria*

**24** **Four** **Five**
Τέσσερα Πέντε
*Tessera* *Pente*

**25** **Six** **Seven**
Έξι Επτά
*Exi* *Epta*

**26** **Eight** **Nine**
Οκτώ Εννέα
*Okto* *Ennea*

**27** **Ten** **Eleven**
Δέκα Έντεκα
*Deka* *Endeka*

**28** **Twelve** **Thirteen**
Δώδεκα Δεκατρία
*Dodeka* *Dekatria*

**29** **Fourteen** **Fifteen**
Δεκατέσσερα Δεκαπέντε
*Dekatessera* *Dekapente*

**30** **Sixteen** **Seventeen**
Δεκαέξι Δεκαεπτά
*Dekaexi* *Dekaepta*

**31** **Eighteen** **Nineteen**
Δεκαοχτώ Δεκαεννέα
*Dekaokto* *Dekaennea*

**32** **Twenty** **Twenty-one**
Είκοσι Είκοσι ένα
*Ikosi* *Ikosi ena*

**33** **Twenty-two** **Thirty**
Είκοσι δύο Τριάντα
*Ikosi dio* *Trianta*

G
R
E
E
K

14
↑
33

121

**GREEK**

**34 ↑ 54**

34 **Forty** **Fifty**
Σαράντα Πενήντα
*Saranta* *Peninta*

35 **Sixty** **Seventy**
Εξήντα Εβδομήντα
*Exinta* *Evdominta*

36 **Eighty** **Ninety**
Ογδόντα Ενενήντα
*Ogdonta* *Eneninta*

37 **One hundred** **Five hundred**
Εκατό Πεντακόσια
*Ekato* *Pentakosia*

38 **One thousand** **One million**
Χίλια Ένα εκατομμύριο
*Hilia* *Ena ekatommirio*

## Time

39 **9.00**
Εννέα
*Ennea*

40 **9.05**
Εννέα και πέντε
*Ennea ke pente*

41 **9.10**
Εννέα και δέκα
*Ennea ke deka*

42 **9.15**
Εννέα και τέταρτο
*Ennea ke tetarto*

43 **9.20**
Εννέα και είκοσι
*Ennea ke ikosi*

44 **9.25**
Εννέα και είκοσι πέντε
*Ennea ke ikosi pente*

45 **9.30**
Εννέα και μισή
*Ennea ke misi*

46 **9.35**
Δέκα πάρα είκοσι πέντε
*Deka para ikosi pente*

47 **9.40**
Δέκα πάρα είκοσι
*Deka para ikosi*

48 **9.45**
Δέκα πάρα τέταρτο
*Deka para tetarto*

49 **9.50**
Δέκα πάρα δέκα
*Deka para deka*

50 **9.55**
Δέκα πάρα πέντε
*Deka para pente*

51 **12.00/Midday/Midnight**
Δώδεκα/Μεσημέρι/
Μεσάνυχτα
*Dodeka/Mesimeri/Mesanihta*

52 **What time is it?**
Τί ώρα είναι;
*Ti ora ine?*

53 **It is . . .**
Είναι . . .
*Ine . . .*

## ARRIVING AND DEPARTING

### Airport

54 **Excuse me, where is the check-in desk for . . . airline?**
Με συγχωρείτε, πού είναι ο έλεγχος αποσκευών και

# ARRIVING AND DEPARTING

εισιτηρίων για την
αερογραμμή . . ;
*Me sinhorite, pu ine o elenhos
aposkevon kai isitirion ya tin
aerogrammi . . ?*

**55** **What is the boarding gate/
time for my flight?**
Ποια είναι η θύρα/ώρα
επιβίβασης για την πτήση μου;
*Pia ine i thira/ora epivivasis ya tin
ptisi mu?*

**56** **How long is the delay likely
to be?**
Πόσο προβλέπεται να
διαρκέσει η καθυστέρηση;
*Poso provlepete na diarkesi i
kathisterisi?*

**57** **Where is the duty-free shop?**
Πού είναι το κατάστημα
αφορολόγητων;
*Pu ine to katastima aforoloyiton?*

**58** **Which way is the baggage
reclaim?**
Πού είναι η αίθουσα
αποσκευών;
*Pu ine i ethusa aposkevon?*

**59** **Where can I get the bus to
the city centre?**
Από πού μπορώ να πάρω το
λεωφορείο για το κέντρο
της πόλης;
*Apo pu boro na paro to leoforio ya
to kentro tis polis?*

## Train Station

**60** **Where is the ticket office/
information desk?**

Πού είναι το γραφείο
εισιτηρίων/το γραφείο
πληροφοριών;
*Pu ine to grafio isitirion/to grafio
pliroforion?*

**61** **Which platform does the
train to . . . depart from?**
Από ποια πλατφόρμα
αναχωρεί το τραίνο για
την . . ;
*Apo pia platforma anahori to
treno ya tin . . ?*

**62** **Where is platform . . ?**
Πού είναι η πλατφόρμα . . ;
*Pu ine i platforma . . ?*

**63** **When is the next train to . . ?**
Πότε είναι το επόμενο
τραίνο για την . . ;
*Pote ine to epomeno treno ya tin . . ?*

**64** **Is there a later train to . . ?**
Υπάρχει αργότερα τραίνο
για την . . ;
*Iparhi argotera treno ya tin . . ?*

## Port

**65** **How do I get to the port?**
Πώς μπορώ να πάω στο
λιμάνι;
*Pos boro na pao sto limani?*

**66** **When is the next sailing
to . . ?**
Ποια είναι η επόμενη
πλεύση για την . . ;
*Pia ine i epomeni plefsi ya tin . . ?*

**GREEK**

55
↕
66

123

**67 Can I catch an earlier ferry with this ticket?**
Με αυτό το εισιτήριο μπορώ να επιβιβαστώ σε φέρρυ που φεύγει νωρίτερα;
*Me avto to isitirio boro na epivivasto se ferry pu fevyi noritera?*

## Notices and Signs

**68 Αμαξοστοιχία με μπουφέ**
*Amaxostihia me Buffet*
Buffet (Dining) Car

**69 Λεωφορείο**
*Leoforio*
Bus

**70 Πόσιμο/μη πόσιμο νερό**
*Posimo/mi posimo nero*
Drinking/Non-drinking water

**71 Είσοδος**
*Isodos*
Entrance

**72 Εξοδος**
*Exodos*
Exit

**73 Πληροφορίες**
*Plirofories*
Information

**74 Χώρος Αποσκευών**
*Horos Aposkevon*
Left Luggage

**75 Θυρίδες Αποσκευών**
*Thirides Aposkevon*
Luggage Lockers

**76 Ταχυδρομείο**
*Tahidromio*

Post Office

**77 Πλατφόρμα/Εξέδρα**
*Platforma/Exedra*
Platform

**78 Σιδηροδρομικός Σταθμός**
*Sidirodromikos Stathmos*
Railway (Railroad) Station

**79 Αεροδρόμιο**
*Aerodromio*
Airport

**80 Λιμάνι**
*Limani*
Port

**81 Εστιατόριο**
*Estiatorio*
Restaurant

**82 Για Καπνιστές/Για μη καπνιστές**
*Ya kapnistes/ya mi kapnistes*
Smoking/Non-smoking

**83 Τηλέφωνο**
*Tilephono*
Telephone

**84 Γραφείο Εισιτηρίων**
*Grafio Isitirion*
Ticket Office

**85 Ελεγχος Αποσκευών & Εισιτηρίων**
*Elenhos Aposkevon ke Isitirion*
Check-in Desk

**86 Δρομολόγιο**
*Dromologio*
Timetable (Schedule)

**87 Αποχωρητήρια**
*Apohoritiria*

G
R
E
E
K

67
↕
87

Toilets (Restrooms)

**88** **Ανδρών**
*Andron*
Gentlemen

**89** **Γυναικών**
*inekon*
Ladies'

**90** **Τραμ**
*Tram*
Tram (Streetcar)

**91** **Υπόγειος Σιδηρόδρομος**
*Ipoyios Sidirodromos*
Underground (Subway)

**92** **Αίθουσα Αναμονής**
*Ethusa Anamonis*
Waiting Room

## Buying a Ticket

**93** I would like a first-class/
second-class single (one-
way)/return (round-trip)
ticket to . . .
Θα ήθελα πρώτης θέσεως/
δευτέρας θέσεως απλό/μετ'
επιστροφής εισιτήριο για
την . . .
*Tha ithela protis theseos/defteras
theseos/aplo/met epistrofis isitirio
ya tin . . .*

**94** Is my rail pass valid on this
train/ferry/bus?
Το σιδηροδρομικό
εισιτήριο που έχω ισχύει
για αυτό το τραίνο/φέρρυ/
λεωφορείο;

*To sidirodromiko isitirio pu eho
ishii ya afto to treno/ferry/
leoforio?*

**95** I would like an aisle/window
seat.
Θα ήθελα μια θέση δίπλα
στο διάδρομο/παράθυρο.
*Tha ithela mia thesi dipla sto
diadromo/parathiro.*

**96** No smoking/smoking, please.
Απαγορεύεται το
κάπνισμα/επιτρέπεται το
κάπνισμα, παρακαλώ.
*Apagorevete to kapnisma/
epitrepete to kapnisma, parakalo.*

**97** We would like to sit
together.
Θα θέλαμε να καθίσουμε
μαζί.
*Tha thelame na kathisoume mazi.*

**98** I would like to make a seat
reservation.
Θα ήθελα να κρατήσω μία
θέση.
*Tha ithela na kratiso mia thesi.*

**99** I would like to reserve a
couchette/sleeper for one
person/two people/my
family.
Θα ήθελα να κρατήσω
κουκέτα/κλινάμαξα για ένα
άτομο/δύο άτομα/την
οικογένειά μου.
*Tha ithela na kratiso kuketa/
klinamaxa ya ena atomo/dio
atoma/tin ikoyenia mu.*

GREEK

88
↑
99

125

100 I would like to reserve a cabin.
Θα ήθελα να κρατήσω μία
καμπίνα.
*Tha ithela na kratiso mia kabina.*

## Timetables (Schedules)

101 Αφίξεις
*Afixis*
Arrive

102 Σταματά στο
*Stamata sto*
Calls (Stops) at

103 Υπηρεσία Εστίασης
*Ipiresia estiasis*
Catering Service

104 Αλλάζει στο
*Allazi sto*
Change at

105 Σύνδεση
*Sindesi*
Connection

106 Καθημερινά
*Kathimerina*
Daily

107 Κάθε σαράντα (40) λεπτά
*Kathe saranta (40) lepta*
Every 40 minutes

108 Πρώτης θέσεως
*Protis Theseos*
First-class

109 Κάθε ώρα
*Kathe ora*
Hourly

110 Συστήνονται κρατήσεις
θέσεων

*Sistinonte kratisis theseon*
Seat reservations are
recommended

111 Δευτέρας Θέσεως
*Defteras Theseos*
Second-class

112 Συμπληρωματικό Ποσό
*Simpliromatiko Poso*
Supplement Payable

113 Μέσω
*Meso*
Via

## Luggage

114 How much will it cost to send
(ship) my luggage in
advance?
Πόσο θα μου στοιχίσει να
στείλω εκ των προτέρων τις
αποσκευές μου;
*Poso tha mu stihisi na stilo ek ton
proteron tis aposkeves mu?*

115 Where is the left luggage
(baggage claim) office?
Πού είναι το γραφείο
αποσκευών;
*Pu ine to grafio aposkevon?*

116 What time do you open/
close?
Τί ώρα ανοίγετε/κλείνετε;
*Ti ora aniyete/klinete?*

117 Where are the luggage
trolleys (carts)?
Πού είναι τα τρόλλεϋ των
αποσκευών;
*Pu ine ta trolley ton aposkevon?*

**118** Where are the lockers?
Πού είναι οι θυρίδες;
*Pu ine i thirides?*

**119** I have lost my locker key.
Εχασα το κλειδί της
θυρίδας μου.
*Ehasa to klidi tis thiridas mu.*

## On Board

**120** Is this seat taken?
Μήπως αυτή η θέση είναι
ελεύθερη;
*Mipos afti i thesi ine eleftheri?*

**121** Excuse me, you are sitting in
my reserved seat.
Με συγχωρείτε, αλλά
κάθεστε στην κρατημένη
μου θέση.
*Me sinhorite, alla katheste stin
kratimeni mu thesi.*

**122** Which station is this?
Ποιος σταθμός είναι αυτός;
*Pios stathmos ine aftos?*

**123** What time is this train/bus/
ferry/flight due to arrive/
depart?
Τι ώρα αναμένεται να
φθάσει/αναχωρήσει το
τραίνο/λεωφορείο/φέρρυ/
πτήση;
*Ti ora anamenete na fthasi/
anahorisi to treno/leoforio/ferry/
ptisi?*

**124** Will you wake me just before
we arrive?
Μπορείτε να με ξυπνήσετε
προτού φτάσουμε;
*Borite na me xipnisete protu
ftasume?*

## Customs and Passports

**125** Τα διαβατήριά σας,
παρακαλώ!
*Ta diavatiria sas, parakalo!*
Passports, please!

**126** I have nothing/wine/spirits
(alcohol)/tobacco to declare.
Δεν έχω τίποτα να δηλώσω/
κρασί/οινοπνευματώδη/
καπνό.
*Den eho tipota na diloso/krasi/
inopnevmatodi/kapno.*

**127** I shall be staying for . . .
days/weeks/months.
Θα μείνω για . . . ημέρες/
εβδομάδες/μήνες.
*Tha mino ya . . . imeres/
evdomades/mines.*

## AT THE TOURIST OFFICE

**128** Do you have a map of the
town/area?
Μήπως έχετε χάρτη της
πόλης/περιοχής;
*Mipos ehete harti tis polis/
periohis?*

**129** Can I reserve accommodation
here?
Μπορώ να κρατήσω
δωμάτια εδώ;
*Boro na kratiso domatia edo?*

G
R
E
E
K

118
↑
129

130 Do you have a list of accommodation?
Εχετε κάποια λίστα δωματίων που νοικιάζονται;
*Ehete kapia lista domation pu nikiazonte?*

## ACCOMMODATION

### Hotels

131 I have a reservation in the name of . . .
Εχω κράτηση στο όνομα . . .
*Eho kratisi sto onoma . . .*

132 I wrote to/faxed/telephoned you last month/last week in . . .
Σας έγραψα/έστειλα φαξ/ τηλεφώνησα τον/την περασμένο(η) μήνα/ εβδομάδα . . .
*Sas egrapsa/estila fax/tilephonisa ton/ tin perasmeno(i) mina/evdomada . . .*

133 Do you have any rooms free?
Εχετε ελεύθερα δωμάτια;
*Ehete elefthera domatia?*

134 I would like to reserve a single/double room with/ without bath/shower.
Θα ήθελα να κρατήσω ένα μονό/διπλό δωμάτιο με/ χωρίς μπάνιο/ντους.
*Tha ithela na kratiso ena mono/ diplo domatio me/horis banio/ dush.*

135 I would like bed and breakfast/(room and) half

board/(room and) full board.
Θα ήθελα δωμάτιο με πρόγευμα/δωμάτιο με δύο φαγητά/δωμάτιο με φαγητά.
*Tha ithela domatio me proyema/ domatio me dio fayita/domatio me fayita.*

136 How much is it per night?
Πόσο στοιχίζει τη νύχτα;
*Poso stihizi ti nihta?*

137 Is breakfast included?
Περιλαμβάνει και πρόγευμα;
*Perilamvani ke proyevma?*

138 May I see the room?
Μπορώ να δω το δωμάτιο;
*Boro na do to domatio?*

139 Do you have any cheaper rooms?
Μήπως έχετε φτηνότερα δωμάτια;
*Mipos ehete ftinotera domatia?*

140 I would like to take the room.
Θα ήθελα να πάρω αυτό το δωμάτιο.
*Tha ithela na paro afto to domatio.*

141 I would like to stay for . . . nights.
Θα ήθελα να μείνω για . . . νύχτες.
*Tha ithela na mino ya . . . nihtes.*

142 The shower/light/tap doesn't work.
Το ντους/ηλεκτρικό/βρύση δεν λειτουργεί.
*To dush/ilektriko/vrisi den lituryi.*

128

143 At what time/where is
breakfast served?
Τι ώρα/πού σερβίρεται το
πρόγευμα;
*Ti ora/pu servirete to proyevma?*

144 What time do I have to
check-out?
Τι ώρα πρέπει να αδειάσω
το δωμάτιο;
*Ti ora prepi na adiaso to domatio?*

145 Can I have the key to room
no . . ?
Μπορείτε να μου δώσετε το
κλειδί για το δωμάτιο αριθ.
. . ;
*Borite na mu dosete to klidi ya to
domatio arithmos . . ?*

146 My room number is . . .
Ο αριθμός του δωματίου
μου είναι . . .
*O arithmos tu domatiu mu ine . . .*

147 Do you accept travellers'
cheques/Eurocheques/credit
cards?
Δέχεστε ταξιδιωτικές
επιταγές/Ευρωεπιταγές/
πιστωτικές κάρτες;
*Deheste taxidiotikes epitayes/
Evroepitayes/pistotikes kartes?*

148 May I have the bill, please?
Μπορώ να έχω το
λογαριασμό, παρακαλώ;
*Boro na eho to logariasmo,
parakalo?*

149 Excuse me, I think there is a
mistake in this bill.
Με συγχωρείτε, νομίζω πως

υπάρχει κάποιο λάθος στο
λογαριασμό.
*Me sinhorite, nomizo pos iparhi
kapio lathos sto logariasmo.*

## Youth Hostels

150 How much is a dormitory bed
per night?
Πόσο κάνει ένα κρεβάτι
κοιτώνα τη νύχτα;
*Poso kani ena krevati kitona ti
nihta?*

151 I am/am not an HI member.
Είμαι/δεν είμαι μέλος της
HI.
*Ime/den ime melos tis HI.*

152 May I use my own sleeping
bag?
Μπορώ να χρησιμοποιήσω
το δικό μου σλήπινγκ μπαγκ;
*Boro na hrisimopiiso to diko mu
sleeping bag?*

153 What time do you lock the
doors at night?
Τί ώρα κλείνετε τις πόρτες
τα βράδια;
*Ti ora klinete tis portes ta vradia?*

## Camping

154 May I camp here for the
night/two nights?
Μπορώ να κάνω κάμπινγκ
εδώ για τη νύχτα/δύο
νύχτες;
*Boro na kano camping edo ya ti
nihta/dio nihtes?*

**155** Where can I pitch my tent?
Πού μπορώ να στήσω την
τέντα μου;
*Pu boro na stiso tin tenta mu?*

**156** How much does it cost for
one night/one week?
Πόσο στοιχίζει για μία
νύχτα/μία εβδομάδα;
*Poso stihizi ya mia nihta/mia
evdomada?*

**157** Where can we park our
caravan?
Πού μπορούμε να
παρκάρουμε το τροχόσπιτό
μας;
*Pu borume na parkarume to
trochospito mas?*

**158** Where are the washing
facilities?
Πού είναι οι ευκολίες
πλυσίματος;
*Pu ine i efkolies plisimatos?*

**159** Is there a restaurant/
supermarket/swimming pool
on site/nearby?
Υπάρχει μήπως
εστιατόριο/υπεραγορά/
πισίνα εδώ/εδώ κοντά;
*Iparhi mipos estiatorio/iperagora/
pisina edo/edo konta?*

**160** Do you have a safety deposit
box?
Μήπως έχετε θυρίδα
ασφαλείας αντικειμένων;
*Mipos ehete thirida asfalias
antikimenon?*

## EATING AND DRINKING

### Cafés and Bars

**161** I would like a cup of/two
cups of/another coffee/tea.
Θα ήθελα ένα φλιτζάνι/δύο
φλιτζάνια/ακόμη ένα καφέ/
τσάι.
*Tha ithela ena flitzani/dio
flitzania/akomi ena kafe/tsai.*

**162** With/without milk/sugar.
Με/χωρίς γάλα/ζάχαρη.
*Me/horis gala/zahari.*

**163** I would like a bottle/glass/
two glasses of mineral water/
red wine/white wine, please.
Θα ήθελα ένα μπουκάλι/
ποτήρι/δύο ποτήρια
μεταλλικό νερό/κόκκινο
κρασί/άσπρο κρασί,
παρακαλώ.
*Tha ithela ena bukali/potiri/dio
potiria metalliko nero/kokkino
krasi/aspro krasi, parakalo.*

**164** I would like a beer/two
beers, please.
Θα ήθελα μια μπύρα/δύο
μπύρες, παρακαλώ.
*Tha ithela mia bira/dio bires,
parakalo.*

**165** May I have some ice?
Μπορώ να έχω λίγο πάγο;
*Boro na eho ligo pago?*

**166** Do you have any matches/
cigarettes/cigars?
Μήπως έχετε σπίρτα/
τσιγάρα/πούρα;

*Mipos ehete spirta/tsigara/pura?*

## Restaurants

**167** Can you recommend a good/ inexpensive restaurant in this area?
Μπορείτε να μου συστήσετε ένα καλό/φτηνό εστιατόριο σε αυτή την περιοχή;
*Borite na mu sistisete ena kalo/ ftino estiatorio se afti tin periohi?*

**168** I would like a table for . . . people.
Θα ήθελα ένα τραπεζάκι για . . . άτομα.
*Tha ithela ena trapezaki gia . . . atoma.*

**169** Do you have a non-smoking area?
Εχετε ορισμένη περιοχή για αυτούς που δεν καπνίζουν;
*Ehete orismeni periohi ya aftus pu den kapnizun?*

**170** Waiter/Waitress!
Γκαρσόν/Σερβιτόρα!
*Garson/Servitora!*

**171** Do you have a set menu/ children's menu/wine list?
Εχετε σετ μενού/παιδικό μενού/κατάλογο κρασιών;
*Ehete set menu/pediko menu/ katalogo krasion?*

**172** Do you have any vegetarian dishes, please?
Μήπως έχετε πιάτα για χορτοφάγους, παρακαλώ;
*Mipos ehete piata ya hortofagous, parakalo?*

**173** Are there any local specialities?
Εχετε κάτι το ειδικό που συνηθίζεται τοπικά;
*Ehete kati to idiko pu sinithizete topika?*

**174** Are vegetables included?
Χορταρικά και λαχανικά συμπεριλαμβάνονται;
*Hortarika ke lahanika simperilamvanonte?*

**175** Could I have it well-cooked/ medium/rare please?
Μπορώ να το έχω καλά/ μέτρια/ελάχιστα ψημένο, παρακαλώ;
*Boro na to eho kala/metria/ elahista psimeno, parakalo?*

**176** What does this dish consist of?
Από τι αποτελείται αυτό το πιάτο;
*Apo ti apotelite afto to piato?*

**177** I would like the set menu, please.
Θα ήθελα το σετ μενού, παρακαλώ.
*Tha ithela to set menu, parakalo.*

**178** We have not been served yet.
Δεν σερβιριστήκαμε ακόμη.
*Den serviristikame akomi.*

G
R
E
E
K

167
↕
178

179 **Excuse me, this is not what I ordered.**
Με συγχωρείτε, δεν είναι αυτό που παράγγειλα.
*Me sinhorite, den ine afto pu paragila.*

180 **May I have some/some more bread/water/coffee/tea?**
Μπορώ να έχω λίγο/ακόμη λίγο ψωμί/νερό/καφέ/τσάι;
*Boro na eho ligo/akomi ligo psomi/nero/kafe/tsai?*

181 **May I have the bill, please?**
Μπορώ να έχω το λογαριασμό, παρακαλώ;
*Boro na eho to logariasmo, parakalo?*

182 **Does this bill include service?**
Ο λογαριασμός περιλαμβάνει και σέρβις;
*O logariasmos perilamvani ke service?*

183 **Do you accept travellers' cheques (travelers' checks)/ Eurocheques/MasterCard/US dollars?**
Μήπως παίρνετε ταξιδιωτικές επιταγές/ Ευρωεπιταγές/Μάστερ Καρτς/Αμερικανικά Δολλάρια;
*Mipos pernete taxidiotikes epitayes/ Evroepitayes/MasterCard/ Amerikanika dollaria?*

184 **Can I have a receipt, please?**
Μπορώ να έχω την απόδειξη, παρακαλώ;
*Boro na eho tin apodixi, parakalo?*

185 **Where is the toilet (restroom), please?**
Πού είναι η τουαλέτα, παρακαλώ;
*Pu ine i tualeta, parakalo?*

## On the Menu

186 **First courses**
Πρώτα φαγητά
*Prota fayita*

187 **Soups**
Σούπες
*Supes*

188 **Main courses**
Κύρια φαγητά
*Kiria fayita*

189 **Fish dishes**
Φαγητά με ψάρι
*Fayita me psari*

190 **Meat dishes**
Φαγητά με κρέας
*Fayita me kreas*

191 **Vegetarian dishes**
Είδη χορτοφαγίας
*Idi hortofayias*

192 **Cheese**
Τυριά
*Tiria*

193 **Desserts**
Επιδόρπιο
*Epidorpio*

194 **Specialities**
Πιάτο της ημέρας
*Piato tis imeras*

## GETTING AROUND

### Public Transport

**195** Where is the bus stop/coach station/nearest metro (subway) station?
Πού είναι η στάση λεωφορείων/ο σταθμός των πούλμαν/το πλησιέστερο μετρό;
*Pu ine i stasi leoforion/o stathmos ton pullman/to plisiestero metro?*

**196** When is the next/last bus to . . ?
Πότε είναι το επόμενο/ τελευταίο λεωφορείο για την . . ;
*Pote ine to epomeno/telefteo leoforio ya tin . . ?*

**197** How much is the fare to the city centre (downtown)/ railway (railroad) station/ airport?
Πόσο κάνει το εισιτήριο για το κέντρο της πόλης/το σιδηροδρομικό σταθμό/το αεροδρόμιο;
*Poso kani to isitirio ya to kentro tis polis/to sidirodromiko stathmo/to aerodromio?*

**198** Will you tell me when to get off?
Μου λέτε πού να κατέβω;
*Mu lete pu na katevo?*

**199** Does this bus go to . . ?
Αυτό το λεωφορείο πάει στο . . ;

*Afto to leoforio pai sto . . ?*

**200** Which number bus goes to . . ?
Ποιο λεωφορείο πηγαίνει στο . . ;
*Pio leoforio piyeni sto . . ?*

**201** May I have a single (one-way)/return (round-trip)/day ticket/book of tickets?
Μπορώ να έχω μονό/μετ' επιστροφής/ημερήσιο εισιτήριο/βιβλίο εισιτηρίων;
*Boro na eho mono/met epistrofis/ imerisio isitirio/vivlio isitirion?*

### Taxis

**202** I would like to go to . . . How much will it cost?
Θα ήθελα να πάω στο . . ., πόσο θα μου στοιχίσει;
*Tha ithela na pao sto . . ., poso tha mu stihisi?*

**203** Please stop here.
Παρακαλώ σταματάτε εδώ.
*Parakalo stamatate edo.*

**204** I would like to order a taxi today/tomorrow/at 2pm to go from . . . to . . .
Θα ήθελα να παραγγείλω ταξί σήμερα/αύριο/στις 2 μ.μ. να με πάρει από το . . . στο . . .
*Tha ithela na parangilo taxi simera/avrio/stis 2 to apoyevma na me pari apo to . . . sto . . .*

## Asking the Way

**205** Excuse me, do you speak English?
Με συγχωρείτε, μήπως μιλάτε Αγγλικά;
*Me sinhorite, mipos milate Anglika?*

**206** Excuse me, is this the right way to . . ?
Με συγχωρείτε, μπορείτε να μου πείτε πώς θα πάω στο/στη . . ;
*Me sinhorite, borite na mu pite pos tha pao sto/sti . . ?*

**207** . . . the cathedral/the tourist information office/the castle/the old town
. . . καθεδρικό ναό/ τουριστικό γραφείο πληροφοριών/κάστρο/ παλιά πόλη
*. . . kathedriko nao/turistiko grafio pliroforion/kastro/palia poli*

**208** Can you tell me the way to the railway (railroad) station/bus station/taxi rank (stand)/city centre (downtown)/beach?
Μπορείτε να μου πείτε το δρόμο προς τον σιδηροδρομικό σταθμό/ σταθμό λεωφορείων/στάση ταξί/το κέντρο της πόλεως/ την πλαζ;
*Borite na mu pite ton dromo pros ton sidirodromiko stathmo/ stathmo leoforion/stasi taxi/to kentro tis poleos/tin plaz?*

**209** First/second/left/right/straight ahead.
Πρώτη/δεύτερη στροφή/ αριστερά/δεξιά/ευθεία.
*Proti/defteri strofi/aristera/dexia/efthia.*

**210** Where is the nearest police station/post office?
Πού είναι ο πλησιέστερος αστυνομικός σταθμός/το ταχυδρομείο;
*Pu ine o plisiesteros astinomikos stathmos/to tahidromio?*

**211** Is it far?
Είναι μακριά;
*Ine makria?*

**212** Do I need to take a taxi/catch a bus?
Χρειάζομαι να πάρω ταξί/ λεωφορείο;
*Hriazome na paro taxi/leoforio?*

**213** Can you point to it on my map?
Μπορείτε να μου το υποδείξετε στο χάρτη;
*Borite na mu to ipodixete sto harti?*

**214** Thank you for your help.
Σας ευχαριστώ για τη βοήθειά σας.
*Sas efharisto ya ti voithia sas.*

## SIGHTSEEING

**215** Where is the Tourist Information office?
Πού είναι το Γραφείο Τουρισμού;
*Pu ine to grafio Turismu?*

**216** Where is the cathedral/
church/museum?
Πού είναι η Μητρόπολη/
Εκκλησία/το Μουσείο;
*Pu ine i mitropoli/ekklisia/to
musio?*

**217** How much is the entrance
(admission) charge?
Πόσο κάνει η είσο ος;
*Poso kani i isodos?*

**218** Is there a reduction for
children/students/senior
citizens?
Μήπως υπάρχει έκπτωση
για παιδιά/φοιτητές/
ηλικιωμένους;
*Mipos iparhi ekptosi ya pedia/
fitites/ilikiomenus?*

**219** What time does the next
guided tour start?
Τί ώρα αρχίζει η επόμενη
περιοδεία με ξεναγό;
*Ti ora arhizi i epomeni periodia me
xenago?*

**220** One/two adults/children,
please.
Ενα/δυό ενήλικες/παιδιά,
παρακαλώ.
*Ena/dio enilikes/pedia, parakalo.*

**221** May I take photographs
here?
Επιτρέπεται η λήψη
φωτογραφιών εδώ;
*Epitrepete i lipsi photographion
edo?*

## ENTERTAINMENT

**222** Can you recommend a good
bar/nightclub?
Μπορείτε να μου
συστήσετε ένα καλό μπαρ/
νυχτερινό κέντρο;
*Borite na mu sistisete ena kalo
bar/nihterino kentro?*

**223** Do you know what is on at
the cinema (playing at the
movies)/theatre at the
moment?
Ξέρετε τι παίζεται τώρα στο
σινεμά/στο θέατρο;
*Xerete ti pezete tora sto cinema/sto
theatro?*

**224** I would like to book
(purchase) . . . tickets for the
matinée/evening
performance on Monday.
Θα ήθελα να κρατήσω . . .
εισιτήρια για
απογευματινή/βραδινή
παράσταση τη Δευτέρα.
*Tha ithela na kratiso . . . isitiria ya
apoyevmatini/vradini parastasi ti
Deftera.*

**225** What time does the film/
performance start?
Τί ώρα αρχίζει το φιλμ/η
παράσταση;
*Ti ora arhizi to film/i parastasi?*

## MEETING PEOPLE

**226** Hello/Goodbye.
Γειά σας/Χαίρετε.
*Ya sas/Herete.*

GREEK

216
↑
226

135

**227** Good morning/good afternoon/good evening/goodnight.
Καλημέρα/χαίρετε/καλησπέρα/καληνύχτα.
*Kalimera/herete/kalispera/kalinihta.*

**228** Pleased to meet you.
Χαίρω πολύ.
*Hero poli.*

**229** How are you?
Τι κάνετε;
*Ti kanete?*

**230** Fine, thank you. And you?
Πολύ καλά, ευχαριστώ. Κι εσείς;
*Poli kala, efharisto. Ki esis?*

**231** My name is . . .
Ονομάζομαι . . .
*Onomazome . . .*

**232** This is my friend/boyfriend/girlfriend/husband/wife/brother/sister.
Σας συστήνω το φίλο μου/το φίλο μου/τη φίλη μου/το σύζυγό μου/τη σύζυγό μου/τον αδελφό μου/την αδελφή μου.
*Sas sistino to filo mu/to filo mu/ti fili mu/to sizigo mu/ti sizigo mu/ton adelfo mu/tin adelfi mu.*

**233** Where are you travelling to?
Για πού ταξιδεύετε;
*Ya pu taxidevete?*

**234** I am/we are going to . . .
Πάω/πάμε στο . . .
*Pao/pame sto . . .*

**235** How long are you travelling for?
Για πόσο καιρό θα ταξιδέψετε;
*Ya poso kero tha taxidepsete?*

**236** Where do you come from?
Από πού είστε;
*Apo pu iste?*

**237** I am/we are from . . .
Είμαι/είμαστε από την . . .
*Ime/imaste apo tin . . .*

**238** We're on holiday.
Είμαστε σε διακοπές.
*Imaste se diakopes.*

**239** This is our first visit here.
Είναι η πρώτη μας επίσκεψη εδώ.
*Ine i proti mas episkepsi edo.*

**240** Would you like/May I have a cigarette?
Θα θέλατε/Μπορώ να έχω ένα τσιγάρο;
*Tha thelate/Boro na eho ena tsigaro?*

**241** I am sorry, but I do not understand.
Λυπάμαι, μα δεν καταλαβαίνω.
*Lipame, ma den katalaveno.*

**242** Please speak slowly.
Παρακαλώ, μιλάτε αργά.
*Parakalo, milate arga.*

**243** Do you mind if I smoke?
Θα σας πείραζε αν κάπνιζα;
*Tha sas piraze an kapniza?*

**244** Do you have a light?
Μήπως έχετε φωτιά;
*Mipos ehete fotia?*

G
R
E
E
K

227
↕
244

**245** I am waiting for my husband/
wife/boyfriend/girlfriend.
Περιμένω τον/την/το/τη
άντρα/γυναίκα/φίλο/φίλη
μου.
*Perimeno ton/tin/to/ti/antra/
gineka/filo/fili mu.*

## TRAVELLING WITH CHILDREN

**246** Do you have a high chair/
baby-sitting service/cot?
Μήπως έχετε καρέκλα
μωρού/υπηρεσία μπέιμπυ
σίττιγκ/παιδικό κρεβάτι;
*Mipos ehete karekla moru/ipiresia
baby-sitting/pediko krevati?*

**247** Where is the nursery/
playroom?
Πού είναι το νηπιαγωγείο/
η αίθουσα παιχνιδιών;
*Pu ine to nipiagoyio/i ethusa
pehnidion?*

**248** Where can I warm the baby's
bottle?
Πού μπορώ να ζεστάνω το
μπουκάλι του μωρού;
*Pu boro na zestano to bukali tu
moru?*

## COMMUNICATIONS

### Post

**249** How much will it cost to send
a letter/postcard/this
package to Britain/Ireland/
America/Canada/Australia/
New Zealand?

Πόσο θα στοιχίσει να
στείλω μια επιστολή/καρτ
ποστάλ/αυτό το πακέτο στη
Βρετανία/Ιρλανδία/
Αμερική/Καναδά/Νέα
Ζηλανδία;
*Poso tha stihisi na stilo mia
epistoli/card postale/afto to paketo
sti Vretania/Irlandia/Ameriki/
Canada/Nea Zilandia?*

**250** I would like one stamp/two
stamps.
Θα ήθελα ένα
γραμματόσημο/δύο
γραμματόσημα.
*Tha ithela ena grammatosimo/dio
grammatosima.*

**251** I'd like . . . stamps for
postcards to send abroad,
please.
Θα ήθελα . . .
γραμματόσημα για
καρτποστάλ να τις στείλω
στο εξωτερικό, παρακαλώ.
*Tha ithela . . . gramatosima ya
card postale na tis stilo sto
exoteriko, parakalo.*

### Phones

**252** I would like to make a
telephone call/reverse the
charges to (make a collect call
to) . . .
Θα ήθελα να τηλεφωνήσω/
να αντιστρέψω το κόστος
στο . . .
*Tha ithela na tilefoniso/na
antistrepso to kostos . . .*

GREEK

245
↕
252

# COMMUNICATIONS/MONEY/SHOPPING

253
↕
266**GREEK**

²⁵³ Which coins do I need for the telephone?
Ποια κέρματα χρειάζομαι για το τηλέφωνο;
*Pia kermata hriazome ya to tilefono?*

²⁵⁴ The line is engaged (busy).
Η γραμμή είναι κατειλημμένη.
*I grami ine katilimeni.*

²⁵⁵ The number is . . .
Ο αριθμός είναι . . .
*O arithmos ine . . .*

²⁵⁶ Hello, this is . . .
Εμπρός, είμαι . . .
*Empros, ime . . .*

²⁵⁷ May I speak to . . ?
Μπορώ να μιλήσω στον/στην . . ;
*Boro na miliso ston/stin . . ?*

²⁵⁸ He/She is not in at the moment. Can you call back?
Δεν είναι εδώ αυτή τη στιγμή. Μπορείτε να ξανακαλέσετε;
*Den ine edo avti ti stigmi. Borite na xanakalesete?*

## MONEY

²⁵⁹ I would like to change these travellers' cheques (travelers' checks)/this currency/this Eurocheque.
Θα ήθελα να εξαργυρώσω αυτές τις ταξιδιωτικές επιταγές/αυτό το συνάλλαγμα/αυτή την Ευρωεπιταγή.
*Tha ithela na exaryiroso aftes tis taxidiotikes epitayes/afto to sinallagma/afti tin Evroepitayi.*

²⁶⁰ How much commission do you charge? (What is the service charge?)
Τί προμήθεια επιβάλλετε;
*Ti promithia epivallete?*

²⁶¹ Can I obtain money with my MasterCard?
Μπορώ να τραβήξω λεφτά με την Μάστερκαρτ μου;
*Boro na travixo lefta me tin MasterCard mu?*

## SHOPPING

## Names of Shops and Departments

²⁶² Βιβλιοπωλείο/Χαρτοπωλείο
*Vivliopolio/Hartopolio*
Bookshop/Stationery

²⁶³ Κατάστημα Κοσμημάτων/Δώρων
*Katastima Kosmimaton/Thoron*
Jeweller's/Gifts

²⁶⁴ Υποδήματα
*Ipodimata*
Shoes

²⁶⁵ Είδη Κιγκαλερίας
*Idi Kingalerias*
Hardware

²⁶⁶ Αντίκες
*Antikes*
Antiques

138

267 **Κομμωτήριο (ανδρών)/**
**(γυναικών)**
*Komotirio (andron)/(ginekon)*
Hairdressers (men's)/(women's)

268 **Καπνοπωλείο**
*Kapnopolio*
Tobacconist

269 **Αρτοποιείο**
*Artopiio*
Baker's

270 **Σουπερμάρκετ**
*Supermaket*
Supermarket

271 **Φωτογραφείο**
*Photographio*
Photoshop

272 **Παιχνίδια**
*Pehnidia*
Toys

273 **Ταξιδιωτικός Πράκτορας**
*Taxidiotikos Praktoras*
Travel Agent

274 **Είδη Τουαλέτας**
*Idi Tualetas*
Toiletries

275 **Δίσκοι**
*Diski*
Records

## In the Shop

276 **What time do the shops**
**open/close?**
Τι ώρα ανοίγουν/κλείνουν
τα καταστήματα;
*Ti ora anigun/klinun ta*
*katastimata?*

277 **Where is the nearest**
**market?**
Πού είναι η κοντινότερη
αγορά;
*Pu ine i kontinoteri agora?*

278 **Can you show me the one**
**in the window/this one?**
Μπορείτε να μου δείξετε
κάτι που είδα στη βιτρίνα/
αυτό εδώ;
*Borite na mu dixete kati pu ida*
*sti vitrina/afto edo?*

279 **Can I try this on?**
Μπορώ να το
δοκιμάσω;
*Boro na to dokimaso?*

280 **What size is this?**
Τι μέγεθος είναι;
*Ti meyethos ine?*

281 **This is too large/too small/**
**too expensive.**
Είναι πολύ μεγάλο/μικρό/
ακριβό.
*Ine poli megalo/mikro/*
*akrivo.*

282 **Do you have any others?**
Έχετε άλλα;
*Ehete ala?*

283 **My size is . . .**
Το νούμερό μου
είναι . . .
*To numero mu ine . . .*

**284** Where is the changing room/childrens'/cosmetic/ladieswear/menswear/food department?

Πού είναι το δοκιμαστήριο/το παιδικό τμήμα/το τμήμα καλλυντικών/γυναικείων/ανδρικών/τροφίμων.

*Pu ine to dokimastirio/to pediko tmima/to tmima kalintikon/ginekion/andrikon/trofimon?*

**285** I would like . . .

Θα ήθελα . . .

*Tha ithela . . .*

**286** I would like a quarter of a kilo/half a kilo/a kilo of bread/butter/cheese/ham/tomatoes.

Θα ήθελα ένα τέταρτο κιλό/μισό κιλό/ένα κιλό ψωμί/βούτυρο/τυρί/ζαμπόν/τομάτες.

*Tha ithela ena tetarto kilo/miso kilo/ena kilo psomi/vutiro/tiri/zambon/tomates.*

**287** How much is this?

Πόσο κάνει αυτό;

*Poso kani afto?*

**288** I'll take this one, thank you.

Θα πάρω αυτό εδώ, ευχαριστώ.

*Tha paro afto edo, efharisto.*

**289** Do you have a carrier (shopping) bag?

Εχετε μία σακούλα;

*Ehete mia sakula?*

**290** Do you have anything cheaper/larger/smaller/of better quality?

Εχετε τίποτα φτηνότερο/μεγαλύτερο/μικρότερο/καλύτερης ποιότητας;

*Ehete tipota ftinotero/megalitero/mikrotero/kaliteris piotitas?*

**291** I would like a film for this camera.

Θα ήθελα ένα φιλμ για αυτή την φωτογραφική μηχανή.

*Tha ithela ena film ya afti tin fotografiki mihani.*

**292** I would like some batteries, the same size as this old one.

Θα ήθελα μερικές μπαταρίες, του ίδιου μεγέθους, όπως αυτή η παλιά.

*Tha ithela merikes bataries, tu idiu meyethus, opos afti i palia.*

**293** Would you mind wrapping this for me, please?

Θα μπορούσατε να μου το τυλίξετε, παρακαλώ;

*Tha borusate na mu to tilixete, parakalo?*

**294** Sorry, but you seem to have given me the wrong change.

Συγνώμη, αλλά φαίνεται ότι μου δώσατε λάθος ρέστα.

*Signomi, alla fenete oti mu dosate lathos resta.*

G
R
E
E
K

**284**
↑
**294**

## MOTORING

### Car Hire (Rental)

295 I have ordered (rented) a car in the name of . . .
Παράγγειλα αυτοκίνητο στο όνομα . . .
*Parangila aftokinito sto onoma . . .*

296 How much does it cost to hire (rent) a car for one day/ two days/one week?
Πόσο στοιχίζει να ενοικιάσω αυτοκίνητο για ία μέρα/δύο μέρες/μία εβδομάδα;
*Poso stihizi na enikiaso aftokinito ya mia mera/dio meres/mia evdomada?*

297 Is the tank already full of petrol (gas)?
Μήπως το ντεπόζιτο είναι ήδη γεμάτο με βενζίνη;
*Mipos to deposito ine idi yemato me venzini?*

298 Is insurance and tax included? How much is the deposit?
Περιλαμβάνει ασφάλεια και φόρο; Πόσα είναι η προκαταβολή;
*Perilamvani asfalia ke foro? Posa ine prokatavoli?*

299 By what time must I return the car?
Μέχρι πότε πρέπει να επιστρέψω το αυτοκίνητο;
*Mehri pote prepi na epistrepso to aftokinito?*

300 I would like a small/family car with a radio/cassette player.
Θα ήθελα ένα μικρό/ οικογενειακό αυτοκίνητο με ράδιο/κασετόφωνο.
*Tha ithela ena mikro/ikoyeniako aftokinito me radio/kassetofono.*

### Asking the Way

301 Excuse me, can you help me please?
Με συγχωρείτε, μπορείτε σας παρακαλώ να με βοηθήσετε;
*Me sinchorite, borite sas parakalo na me voithisete?*

302 How do I reach the motorway/main road?
Από πού μπορώ να πάω στον αυτοκινητόδρομο/ κύριο δρόμο;
*Apo pu boro na pao ston aftokinitodromo/kirio dromo?*

303 I think I have taken the wrong turning.
Νομίζω πως πήρα λάθος στροφή.
*Nomizo pos pira lathos strofi.*

304 I am looking for this address.
Ψάχνω για αυτή τη διεύθυνση.
*Psachno ya afti ti diefthinsi.*

305 I am looking for the . . . hotel.
Ψάχνω για το ξενοδοχείο . . .
*Psachno ya to xenodohio . . .*

**306** How far is it to . . . from here?
Πόσο μακριά είναι από εδώ
το . . .
*Poso makria ine apo edo to . . .*

**307** Carry straight on for . . .
kilometres.
Προχωρήστε κατευθείαν
για . . . χιλιόμετρα.
*Prohoriste katefthia ya . . .
hiliometra.*

**308** Take the next turning on the
right/left.
Στρίψετε στην επόμενη
στροφή δεξιά/αριστερά.
*Stripsete stin epomeni strofi dexia/
aristera.*

**309** Turn right/left at the next
crossroads/traffic lights.
Στρίψετε δεξιά/αριστερά
στο(α) επόμενο(α)
σταυροδρόμι/φανάρια
κυκλοφορίας.
*Stripsete dexia/aristera sto(a)
epomeno(a) stavrodromi/fanaria
kikloforias.*

**310** You are going in the wrong
direction.
Εχετε πάρει την αντίθετη
κατεύθυνση.
*Ehete pari tin antitheti katefthinsi.*

## Parking

**311** How long can I park here?
Για πόσο διάστημα μπορώ
να παρκάρω εδώ;
*Ya poso diastima boro na parkaro
edo?*

**312** Is there a car park near here?
Υπάρχει χώρος
σταθμεύσεως κάπου εδώ;
*Iparhi horos stathmefseos kapu
edo?*

**313** At what time does this car
park close?
Τι ώρα κλείνει ο χώρος
σταθμεύσεως;
*Ti ora klini o horos stathmefseos?*

## Signs and Notices

**314** Μονόδρομος
*Monodromos*
One way

**315** Απαγορεύεται η είσοδος
*Apagorevete i isodos*
No entry

**316** Απαγορεύεται η
στάθμευση
*Apagorevete i stathmefsi*
No parking

**317** Παρακαμπτήριος
*Parakamptirios*
Detour (diversion)

**318** Σταμάτημα/Stop
*Stamatima/Stop*
Stop

**319** Δώσε προτεραιότητα
*Dose protereotita*
Give way (yield)

**320** Ολισθηρός δρόμος
*Olisthiros dromos*
Slippery road

**321** Απαγορεύεται η
υπέρβαση

*Apagorevete i ipervasi*
No overtaking

## At the Filling Station

**322** **Unleaded (lead-free)/**
**Standard/Premium**
Αμόλυβδη/Απλή (Regular)/
Σούπερ (Super).
*Amolivdi/Apli/Super.*

**323** **Fill the tank please.**
Γεμίστε το ντεπόζιτο
παρακαλώ.
*Gemiste to depozito parakalo.*

**324** **Do you have a road map of**
**this area?**
Εχετε χάρτη οδικού δικτύου
αυτής της περιοχής;
*Ehete harti odiku diktiu aftis tis*
*periohis?*

**325** **How much is the car-wash?**
Πόσο κοστίζει το πλύσιμο
αυτοκινήτου;
*Poso kostizi to plisimo aftokinitu?*

## Breakdowns

**326** **I've had a breakdown at . . .**
Το αυτοκίνητο χάλασε
στη . . .
*To aftokinito halase sti . . .*

**327** **I am on the road from . . . to . . .**
Είμαι στο δρόμο από . . .
στο/στη . . .
*Ime sto dromo apo . . . sto/sti . . .*

**328** **I can't move the car. Can you**
**send a tow-truck?**
Δεν μπορώ να κινήσω το

αυτοκίνητο. Μπορείτε να
στείλετε ρυμουλκό;
*Den boro na kiniso to aftokinito.*
*Borite na stilete rimulko?*

**329** **I have a flat tyre.**
Εχω ξεφουσκωμένο
λάστιχο.
*Eho xefuskomeno lastiho.*

**330** **The windscreen (windshield)**
**has smashed/cracked.**
Το παρμπρίζ έσπασε/
ράγισε.
*To parbriz espase/ragise.*

**331** **There is something wrong**
**with the engine/brakes/**
**lights/steering/gearbox/**
**clutch/exhaust.**
Κάτι δεν πάει καλά με τη/
τα μηχανή/φρένα/φώτα/
τιμόνι/ταχύτητες/
συμπλέκτη/εξάτμιση.
*Kati den pai kala me ti/ta mihani/*
*frena/fota/timoni/tahitites/*
*siblekti/exatmisi.*

**332** **It's overheating.**
Υπερθερμαίνεται.
*Iperthermenete.*

**333** **It won't start.**
Δεν ξεκινά.
*Den xekina.*

**334** **Where can I get it repaired?**
Πού μπορώ να το
επισκευάσω;
*Pu boro na to episkevaso?*

**335** **Can you take me there?**
Μπορείτε να με πάτε εκεί;
*Borite na me pate eki?*

G
R
E
E
K

322
↑
335

**336** Will it take long to fix?
Πόση ώρα θα κάνετε να το
επισκευάσετε;
*Posi ora tha kanete na to
episkevasete?*

**337** How much will it cost?
Πόσο θα κοστίσει;
*Poso tha kostisi?*

## Accidents

**338** Can you help me? There has
been an accident.
Μπορείτε να με βοηθήσετε;
Εχει συμβεί κάποιο ατύχημα.
*Borite na me voithisete? Ehi simvi
kapio atihima.*

**339** Please call the police/an
ambulance.
Παρακαλώ καλέσετε την
αστυνομία/ασθενοφόρο.
*Parakalo kalesete tin astinomia/
asthenoforo.*

**340** Is anyone hurt?
Εχει τραυματιστεί κανείς;
*Ehi travmatisti kanis?*

## Traffic Offences

**341** I'm sorry, I didn't see the
sign.
Συγγνώμη, δεν πρόσεξα την
πινακίδα.
*Signomi, den prosexa tin pinakida.*

**342** Must I pay a fine? How
much?
Πρέπει να πληρώσω
πρόστιμο; Πόσα;
*Prepi na pliroso prostimo? Posa?*

**343** Show me your documents.
Δείξτε μου τα χαρτιά σας.
*Dixte mu ta hartia sas.*

## HEALTH

### Pharmacy

**344** Do you have anything for a
stomachache/headache/sore
throat/toothache?
Εχετε κάτι για
στομαχόπονο/πονοκέφαλο/
ερεθισμένο λαιμό/
πονόδοντο;
*Ehete kati ya stomahopono/
ponokefalo/erethismeno lemo/
ponodonto?*

**345** I need something for
diarrhoea (diarrhea)/
constipation/a cold/a cough/
insect bites/sunburn/travel
(motion) sickness.
Χρειάζομαι κάτι για τη
διάρροια/δυσκοιλιότητα/
κρύο/βήχα/δαγκώματα
εντόμων/ηλιοκαύματα/
ναυτία.
*Hriazome kati ya ti diarria/
dispepsia/krio/vinha/dangomata
entomon/iliokavmata/naftia.*

**346** How much/how many do I
take?
Πόσο/Πόσα να παίρνω;
*Poso/posa na perno?*

**347** How often do I take it/them?
Κάθε πόση ώρα να το/τα
παίρνω;
*Kathe posi ora na to/ta perno?*

**348** How much does it cost?
Πόσο κοστίζει;
*Poso kostizi?*

**349** Can you recommend a good
doctor/dentist?
Μπορείτε να μου
συστήσετε ένα καλό
γιατρό/οδοντογιατρό;
*Borite na mu sistisete ena kalo
yatro/odontoyatro?*

**350** Is it suitable for children?
Είναι κατάλληλο για
παιδιά;
*Ine katallilo ya pedia?*

## Doctor

**351** I have a pain here/in my arm/
leg/chest/stomach.
Πονάω εδώ/στο βραχιονά
μου/στη γάμπα/στο
στήθος/στο στομάχι.
*Ponao edo/sto vrahiona mu/sti
gamba/sto stithos/sto stomahi.*

**352** Please call a doctor, this is an
emergency.
Παρακαλώ τηλεφωνήστε
ένα γιατρό, είναι επείγουσα
κατάσταση.
*Parakalo tilefoniste ena yatro, ine
epigusa katastasi.*

**353** I would like to make an
appointment to see a doctor.
Θα ήθελα να κλείσω
ραντεβού για να δω τον
γιατρό.
*Tha ithela na kliso rantevu ya na
tho ton yatro.*

**354** I am diabetic/pregnant.
Είμαι διαβητικός/έγκυος.
*Ime diavitikos/engios.*

**355** I need a prescription for . . .
Θέλω συνταγή για . . .
*Thelo sintayi ya . . .*

**356** Can you give me something
to ease the pain?
Μπορείτε να μου δώσετε
κάτι για να καταπραΰνει
τον πόνο;
*Borite na mu dosete kati gia na
katapraini ton pono?*

**357** I am/he is/she is allergic to
penicillin.
Είμαι/είναι/αλλεργικός(ή)
στην πενικιλίνη.
*Ime/ine/alergikos(i) stin penicilini.*

**358** Does this hurt?
Πονάει;
*Ponai?*

**359** You must/he must/she must
go to hospital.
Πρέπει να πάτε/πάει στο
νοσοκομείο.
*Prepi na pate/pai sto nosokomio.*

**360** Take these once/twice /three
times a day.
Παίρνετε αυτά μία φορά/
δύο/τρεις φορές την ημέρα.
*Pernete afta mia fora/dio/tris fores
tin imera.*

**361** I am/he is/she is taking this
medication.
Παίρνω/παίρνει αυτό το
φάρμακο.
*Perno/perni afto to pharmako.*

G
R
E
E
K

348
↑
361

145

**362** I have medical insurance.
Εχω ασφάλεια
νοσοκομειακής
περίθαλψης.
*Echo asfalia nosokomiakis
perithalpsis.*

## Dentist

**363** I have toothache.
Νοιώθω πονόδοντο.
*Niotho ponodonto.*

**364** My filling has come out.
Βγήκε το σφράγισμα.
*Vgike to sfrayisma.*

**365** I do/do not want to have an
injection first.
Θέλω/δεν θέλω να έχω
πρώτα ένεση.
*Thelo/den thelo na eho prota enesi.*

## EMERGENCIES

**366** Help!
Βοήθεια!
*Voithia!*

**367** Call an ambulance/a doctor/
the police!
Τηλεφωνήστε για
ασθενοφόρο/γιατρό/
αστυνομία !
*Tilefoniste yia asthenoforo/yatro/
astinomia!*

**368** I have had my travellers'
cheques (travelers' checks)/
credit cards/purse/handbag/
rucksack (knapsack)/
luggage/wallet stolen.
Μου κλέψανε τις

ταχυδρομικές μου επιταγές/τις
πιστωτικές μου κάρτες/το
τσαντάκι μου/τη τσάντα μου/
τον εκδρομικό σάκο/τις
αποσκευές/το πορτοφόλι μου.
*Mu klepsane tis tahidromikes mu
epitayes/tis pistotikes mu kartes/to
portofoli mu/tin tsanta mu/ton
ekdromiko sako/tis aposkeves/to
portofoli mu.*

**369** Can you help me, I have lost
my daughter/son?
Μπορείτε να με βοηθήσετε,
έχασα τη θυγατέρα μου/τον
γιο μου;
*Borite na me voithisete, ehasa ti
thigatera mu/ton yo mu?*

**370** Please go away/leave me
alone.
Παρακαλώ φύγετε/αφήστε
με μόνη.
*Parakalo fiyete/afiste me moni.*

**371** Fire!
Πυρκαγιά!
*Pirkaya!*

**372** I want to contact the British/
American/Canadian/Irish/
Australian/New Zealand/
South African consulate.
Θέλω να επικοινωνήσω με το
Βρετανικό/Αμερικανικό/
Καναδικό/Ιρλανδικό/
Αυστραλιανό/Νέας Ζηλανδίας/
Νοτίου Αφρικής Προξενείο.
*Thelo na epikinoniso me to
Vretaniko/Amerikaniko/Kanadiko/
Irlandiko/Avstraliano/Neas
Zilandias/Notiu Afrikis Proxenio.*

146

# Introduction

Hungarian, or Magyar, is distantly related to Finnish and
Estonian, but is utterly unlike the languages of the other main
linguistic groups of Europe. English is spoken to a fair degree,
at least in tourist areas. German is even more widespread as a
second language. Hungarian is undoubtedly a difficult
language to master, and Hungarians are well aware of this,
but you should nevertheless try to learn a few greetings, as
silence when entering a shop, for instance, is considered rude.

In Hungarian, prepositions are replaced by suffixes. Each
suffix has two forms, choose one that sounds harmonious with
the noun/place name.

There is no specific gender in the Hungarian language,
therefore there is no difference in the words for 'he/she/it'.

## Addresses for travel and tourist information

**UK:** IBUSZ *(Hungarian National Tourist Office)*, c/o Danube
Travel, 6 conduit St, London W1R 9TG; tel: (0171) 493 0263.
**USA:** IBUSZ *(Hungarian Travel North American Division)*, 1
Parker Plaza, Suite 1104, Fort Lee, NJ 07024; tel: (201) 592-
8585.

# ESSENTIALS

## ESSENTIALS

## Letters

| | |
|---|---|
| A | Á |
| *O* | *ah* |
| B | C |
| *bay* | *tsay* |
| CS | D |
| *chay* | *day* |
| E | É |
| *eh* | *ay* |
| F | G |
| *eff* | *gay* |
| GY | H |
| *dj* | *hah* |
| I | J |
| *ee* | *yay* |
| K | L |
| *kah* | *el* |
| LY | M |
| *yeu* | *em* |
| N | NY |
| *en* | *nee-uh* |
| O | Ó |
| *o* | *aw* |
| Ö | Ő |
| *uh* | *ur* |
| P | Q |
| *pay* | *q* |
| R | S |
| *air* | *esh* |
| SZ | T |
| *ess* | *tay* |
| TY | U |

| | |
|---|---|
| *tch* | *oo* |
| Ú | Ü |
| *ooh* | *ew* |
| Ű | V |
| *eew* | *vay* |
| W | X |
| *doop-lo vay* | *ex* |
| Y | Z |
| *eep-see-lon* | *zat* |
| ZS | |
| *zhay* | |

## Basic Words and Phrases

1. **Yes**
   Igen
   *igen*
   **No**
   Nem
   *nem*

2. **Please**
   Kérem szépen
   *kay-rem say-pan*
   **Thank you**
   Köszönöm
   *kuh-suh-nuhn*

3. **That's O.K.**
   Rendben van.
   *rhend-ben von*
   **Perhaps**
   Esetleg
   *eh-shet-leg*

4. **To**
   Fele
   *fah-lah*
   **From**
   Onnan
   *on-non*

5. **Here**
   Itt
   *it*
   **There**
   Ott
   *ot*

6. **None**
   Semelyik
   *sheh-may-yeek*
   **Also**
   Szintén
   *seen-tayn*

7. **How**
   Hogyan
   *ho-djon*
   **When**
   Mikor
   *mee-kor*

8. **What**
   **Why**

Mit          Miért
*mit*        *mee-ayrt*

**9  I don't understand.**
Nem értem.
*nem ayr-tehm.*

**10  I don't speak Hungarian.**
Nem tudok magyarul.
*nem too-dok mo-djo-rool.*

**11  Do you speak English?**
Beszél angolul?
*beh-sayl on-go-lool*

**12  Can you please write it down?**
Kérem le tudná ezt írni?
*kay-rehm leh tood-nay ehz eeyr-ni*

**13  Can you please speak more slowly?**
Kérem beszéljen lassabban?
*kay-rehm beh-sayl-yen losh-shob-bon*

**14  How much does it/this cost?**
Ez mennyibe kerül?
*ehz mehnn-yee-beh keh-rewl*

## Days

**15  Monday          Tuesday**
Hétfő               Kedd
*heyt-fur*          *kehdd*

**16  Wednesday       Thursday**
Szerda              Csütörtök
*sehr-dah*          *chew-tohr-tuhk*

**17  Friday          Saturday**
Péntek              Szombat
*payn-tehk*         *soom-bot*

**18  Sunday          Morning**
Vasárnap            Délelőtt

*vo-shahr-nop*      *dayl-eh-lurtt*

**19  Afternoon       Evening**
Délután             Este
*dayl-oo-tahn*      *esh-teh*

**20  Night           Week**
Éjjel               Hét
*eey-yehl*          *hayt*

**21  Yesterday       Tomorrow**
Tegnap              Holnap
*tehg-nop*          *hol-nop*

## Numbers

**22  Zero            One**
Nulla               Egy
*nool-lo*           *edj*

**23  Two             Three**
Kettő               Három
*keht-tur*          *hah-rom*

**24  Four            Five**
Négy                Öt
*naydj*             *uht*

**25  Six             Seven**
Hat                 Hét
*hot*               *hayt*

**26  Eight           Nine**
Nyolc               Kilenc
*nn-yolts*          *kee-lehnts*

**27  Ten             Eleven**
Tíz                 Tizenegy
*teez*              *tee-zehn-edj*

**28  Twelve          Thirteen**
Tizenkettő          Tizenhárom
*tee-zehn-keht-tur*  *tee-zehn-hah-rom*

**29  Fourteen        Fifteen**
Tizennégy           Tizenöt
*tee-zehn-naydj*    *tee-zehn-uht*

H
U
N
G
A
R
I
A
N

09
↕
29

30 **Sixteen** **Seventeen**
Tizenhat Tizenhét
*tee-zehn-hot* *tee-zehn-hayt*

31 **Eighteen** **Nineteen**
Tizennyolc Tizenkilenc
*tee-zehn-n-yolts* *tee-zehn-kee-lehnts*

32 **Twenty** **Twenty-one**
Húsz Huszonegy
*hoos* *hoo-son-edj*

33 **Twenty-two** **Thirty**
Huszonkettő Harminc
*hoo-son-keht-tur* *hor-mints*

34 **Forty** **Fifty**
Negyven Ötven
*nehdj-vehn* *uht-vehn*

35 **Sixty** **Seventy**
Hatvan Hetven
*hot-von* *heht-vehn*

36 **Eighty** **Ninety**
Nyolcvan Kilencven
*n-yolts-von* *kee-lehnts-vehn*

37 **One hundred** **Five hundred**
Egyszáz Ötszáz
*edj-sahz* *oht-sahz*

38 **One thousand** **One million**
Egyezer Egy millió
*edj-eh-zehr* *edj meel-li-aw*

## Time

39 9.00
Kilenc óra
*kee-lehnts aw-ro*

40 9.05
Kilenc óra öt perc
*kee-lehnts aw-ro uht pertz*

41 9.10

Kilenc óra tíz perc
*kee-lehnts aw-ro teez pertz*

42 9.15
Negyed tíz
*neh-djehd teez*

43 9.20
Kilenc óra húsz perc
*kee-lehntz aw-ro hoos pertz*

44 9.25
Kilenc óra huszonöt perc
*kee-lehntz aw-ro hoo-son-uht pertz*

45 9.30
Fél tíz
*fayl teez*

46 9.35
Kilenc óra harmincöt perc
*kee-lehntz aw-ro hor-mints-uht pertz*

47 9.40
Kilenc óra negyven perc
*kee-lehntz aw-ro nehdj-vehn pertz*

48 9.45
Háromnegyed tíz
*hah-rom-neh-djehd teez*

49 9.50
Kilenc óra ötven perc
*kee-lehntz aw-ro uht-ven pertz*

50 9.55
Kilenc óra ötvenöt perc
*kee-lehntz aw-ro uht-vehn-uht pertz*

51 12.00/Midday/Midnight
Tizenkét óra/Dél/Éjfél
*tee-zen-kayt aw-ro/dayl/ay-fayl*

52 **What time is it?**
Hány óra van?

*hahnn-y aw-ro von*

**53** It is . . .

. . . óra van.

. . . *aw-ro von*

## ARRIVING AND DEPARTING

### Airport

**54** Excuse me, where is the check-in desk for . . . airline?
Bocsánat, hol találom a . . . légitársaság utaskezelő pultját?
*bo-chah-not, hol to-lah-lom o . . . lay-gee-tahr-sho-shahg oo-tosh-keh-zeh-lur poolt-yaht*

**55** What is the boarding gate/time for my flight?
Melyik az én gépem beszálló kapuja?/Mikor indul a gépem?
*meh-yeek oz ayn gay-pehm beh-sahl-law ko-poo-ya?/mee-kor in-dool o gay-pehm?*

**56** How long is the delay likely to be?
Mennyi a várható késés?
*mehnn-y-ee o vahr-ho-taw kay-shaysh?*

**57** Where is the duty-free shop?
Hol van a Duty-Free üzlet?
*hol von o duty-free ewz-leht?*

**58** Which way is the baggage reclaim?
Merre van a poggyász kiváltó?
*mehr-rheh von o podj-djahs ki-vahl-taw*

**59** Where can I get the bus to the city centre?

Honnan indul a busz a városközpontba?
*hon-non in-dool o bus o vah-rosh-kuhz-pont-bo*

## Train Station

**60** Where is the ticket office/information desk?
Hol van a jegypénztár/információ?
*hol von o yedj-pehnz-tahr/in-for-mah-tsi-aw*

**61** Which platform does the train to . . . depart from?
Melyik vágányról indul a vonat . . . -ba/-be?
*meh-yeek vah-gahn-yrawl in-dool o vo-not . . . -bo/-beh*

**62** Where is platform . . . ?
Hol van a . . . . -os/es vágány?
*hol von o . . . . -osh/ash vah-gahn*

**63** When is the next train to . . ?
Mikor indul a következő vonat . . . -ba/-be?
*mee-kor in-dool o kuh-veht-keh-zur vo-not . . . -bo/-beh*

**64** Is there a later train to . . ?
Van egy későbbi vonat is . . . -ba/-be?
*von edj kay-shurb-bi vo-not eesh . . . -bo/-beh*

## Port

**65** How do I get to the port?
Hogy jutok el a kikötőbe?
*hodj yoo-tok ehl o kee-kuh-tur-beh*

**66** When is the next sailing to . . ?
Mikor indul a következő hajó . .
. -ba/-be?
*mee-kor in-dool o kuh-veht-keh-
zur ho-yaw . . . -bo/-beh*

**67** Can I catch an earlier ferry
with this ticket?
Ezzel a jeggyel egy korábbi
kompra is felszállhatok?
*ehz-zehl o yehdj-ehl edj ko-rahb-
bee komp-ro ish fehl-sahl-ho-tok*

## Notices and Signs

**68** Büfé
*buh-fay*
Buffet (Dining Car)

**69** Autóbusz
*o-oo-taw-boos*
Bus

**70** Ivóvíz/Nem ivóvíz
*ee-vaw-veez/nem ee-vaw-veez*
Drinking/Non-drinking water

**71** Bejárat
*beh-yah-rot*
Entrance

**72** Kijárat
*kee-yah-rot*
Exit

**73** Információ
*in-for-mah-tsee-aw*
Information

**74** Poggyász Kiváltó
*podj-djahs kee-vahl-taw*
Left Luggage (Baggage Claim)

**75** Kulcsra zárható
csomagmegőrző szekrény
*koolch-ro zahr-ho-taw cho-mog-*

*mehg-ur-zur sehk-raynn-y*
Luggage Lockers

**76** Posta/Postahivatal
*posh-to/posh-to-hee-vo-tol*
Post Office

**77** Peron/Vágány
*peh-ron/vah-gahn-y*
Platform

**78** Vasútállomás/Vonatállomás
*vo-shoot-ahl-lo-mahsh/vo-not-ahl-
lo-mahsh*
Railway (Railroad Station)

**79** Repülőtér
*re-pew-lur-tayr*
Airport

**80** Hajókikötő/Hajóállomás
*ho-yaw-kee-kuh-tur/ho-yaw-ahl-
lo-mahsh*
Port

**81** Étterem/Vendéglő
*ayt-teh-rehm/vehn-dayg-lur*
Restaurant

**82** Dohányzó/Nem-Dohányzó
*do-hahnn-yzaw/nem do-hahnn-
yzaw*
Smoking/Non-Smoking

**83** Telefon
*teh-leh-fon*
Telephone

**84** Jegypénztár
*yedj-paynz-tahr*
Ticket Office

**85** Utaskezelő Pult
*oo-tosh-keh-zeh-lur poolt*
Check-in Desk

86 **Menetrend**
*meh-neht-rehnd*
Timetable (Schedule)

87 **WC**
*vay-tsay*
Toilets (Restrooms)

88 **Férfiak**
*fayr-fee-ok*
Gentlemen

89 **Nők**
*nurk*
Ladies'

90 **Villamos**
*veel-lo-mosh*
Tram (Streetcar)

91 **Metro**
*meht-raw*
Underground (Subway)

92 **Váróterem**
*vah-raw-teh-rehm*
Waiting-Room

## Buying a Ticket

93 **I would like a first-class/
second-class single (one-
way)/return (round-trip)
ticket to . . .**
Kérek egy elsőosztályú/
másodosztályú egyszeri
utazásra szóló/retúr jegyet . . . -
ba/-be.
*kay-rehk edj ehl-shur-os-tah-yooh/
mah-shod-os-tah-yooh edj-seh-ree
oo-to-zahsh-ro saw-law/reh-toohr
yeh-djeht . . . -bo/-beh*

94 **Is my rail pass valid on this
train/ferry/bus?**

A jegyem erre a vonatra/
kompra/buszra is érvényes?
*o yeh-djehm er-reh o vo-not-ro/
komp-ro/boos-ro eesh ayr-vayn-
yehsh*

95 **I would like an aisle/window
seat.**
A közlekedő folyosó/ablak
melletti ülést kérném.
*o kuhz-leh-keh-dur fo-yo-shaw/
oblok mehl-leht-tee ew-laysht
kehr-nehm*

96 **No smoking/smoking, please.**
Kérem ne dohányozzanak/
Dohányozni szabad.
*kay-rehm neh do-hahnn-yoz-zo-
nok/do-hahnn-yoz-ni so-bod.*

97 **We would like to sit
together.**
Szeretnénk egymás mellett ülni.
*seh-reht-naynk edj-mahsh mehl-
lehtt ewl-ni.*

98 **I would like to make a seat
reservation.**
Szeretnék ülőhelyet foglalni.
*seh-reht-nayk ew-lur-heh-yeht fog-
lol-ni.*

99 **I would like to reserve a
couchette/sleeper for one
person/two people/for my
family.**
Szeretnék egy couchettet/
hálókocsit foglalni egy személyre/
két személyre/a családnak.
*seh-reht-nayk edj coo-shehtt-eht/
hah-law-ko-cheet fog-lol-ni edj
seh-may-reh/kayt seh-may-reh/o
cho-lah-dom-nok.*

**H
U
N
G
A
R
I
A
N**

**86
↕
99**

# ARRIVING AND DEPARTING

**100** I would like to reserve a cabin.

Egy kabint szeretnék foglalni.

*edj co-beent seh-reht-nayk fog-lolni.*

## Timetables (Schedules)

**101** Érkezés

*ayr-keh-zaysh*

Arrive

**102** Megáll . . . -ban/-ben

*mehg-ahll . . . -bon/-behn*

Calls (Stops at . . . )

**103** Étkezési Lehetőség

*ayt-keh-zay-shee le-heh-tur-shayg*

Catering Service

**104** Átszállás . . . -ban/-ben

*aht-sahl-lahsh . . . -bon/-behn*

Change at . . .

**105** Csatlakozás

*chot-lo-ko-zahsh*

Connection

**106** Napi

*no-pee*

Daily

**107** Negyven percenként

*nehdj-vehn pert-zehn-kaynt*

Every 40 Minutes

**108** Első-osztály

*el-shur os-tahy*

First-Class

**109** óránként

*aw-rahn-kaynt*

Hourly

**110** Ajánlott a helyfoglalás

*o-yahn-lott o hehy-fog-lo-lahsh*

Seat reservations are recommended

**111** Másodosztály

*mah-shod-os-tahy*

Second-class

**112** Fizetendő Pótdíj

*fee-zeh-tehn-dur pawt-deey*

Supplement Payable

**113** útvonalon

*ooht-vo-no-lon*

Via

## Luggage

**114** How much will it cost to send (ship) my luggage in advance?

Mennyibe kerül előreküldeni a poggyászomat?

*mehnn-yee-beh keh-rewl eh-lur-re-kewl-deh-nee o podj-djah-so-mot*

**115** Where is the left luggage (baggage claim) office?

Merre van a talált csomagok irodája?

*mehr-reh von o to-lahlt cho-mo-gok eero-dah-yah*

**116** What time do you open/close?

Mikor nyitnak/zárnak?

*mee-kor nn-yeet-nok/zahr-nok*

**117** Where are the luggage trolleys (carts?)

Hol találom a poggyász trolikat?

*hol to-lah-lom o podj-djahs tro-lee-kot*

**118** Where are the lockers?

Hol találom a kulcsra zárható

H
U
N
G
A
R
I
A
N

100
↕
118

154

csomagmegőrző szekrényeket?
*hol to-lah-lom o koolch-ro zahr-ho-taw cho-mog-mehg-ur-zur sehk-raynn-yeh-keht*

119 I have lost my locker key.
Elvesztettem a csomagmegőrző kulcsát.
*el-vehs-teht-tehm o cho-mog-mehg-ur-zur kool-chaht*

## On Board

120 Is this seat taken?
Foglalt ez a hely?
*fog-lolt ehz o hehy*

121 Excuse me, you are sitting in my reserved seat.
Bocsánatot kérek, de ön az én foglalt helyemen ül.
*bo-chah-no-tot kay-rehk, deh uhn oz ayn fog-lolt heh-yeh-mehn ewl*

122 Which station is this?
Ez melyik állomás?
*ehz meh-yeek ahl-lo-mahsh*

123 What time is this train/bus/ferry/flight due to arrive/depart?
Ez a vonat/busz/komp/repülő mikor érkezik/indul ?
*ehz o vonot/boos/komp/reh-pew-lur mee-kor ayr-keh-zeek/in-dool*

124 Will you wake me just before we arrive?
Felébresztene közvetlenül a megérkezésünk előtt?
*fehl-ayb-rehs-teh-neh kuhz-veht-leh-newl o mehg-ayr-keh-zay-shewnk eh-lurtt*

## Customs and Passports

125 Passports, please!
Kérjük az útleveleket!
*kayr-yewk oz ooht-leh-veh-leh-keht*

126 I have nothing to declare. I have wine/spirits (alcohol)/tobacco to declare.
Semmi elvámolni valóm sincs.
Bor/szesz/dohányárú elvámolni valóm van.
*shehm-mee ehl-vah-mol-ni vo-lawm sheench. bor/sehs/do-hahnn-y-ah-rooh ehl-vah-mol-ni vo-lawm von*

127 I shall be staying for . . . days/weeks/months.
. . . napig/hétig/hónapig maradok.
*. . . no-pig/hay-tig/haw-nopig morodok*

## AT THE TOURIST OFFICE

128 Do you have a map of the town/area?
Van egy városi/helyi térképe?
*von edj vah-ro-shee/heh-yee tayr-kay-peh*

129 Can I reserve accommodation here?
Lehet itt szállást foglalni?
*leh-heht itt sahl-lahsht fog-lol-ni*

130 Do you have a list of accommodation?
Van önnek egy szállás listája?
*von uhn-nehk edj sahl-lahsh lish-tah-yo*

HUNGARIAN

119
↑
130

155

## ACCOMMODATION

### Hotels

**131** I have a reservation in the name of . . .
Szobát foglaltam . . . néven.
*so-baht fog-lol-tom . . . nay-vehn*

**132** I wrote to/faxed/telephoned you last month/last week in . . .
Irtam/faxot küldtem/telefonáltam önnek a múlt hónapban/héten . . . -án/-én
*eer-tom/fox-ot kewld-tehm/teh-leh-fo-nahl-tom uhn-nehk o moolt haw-nop-bon/hay-tehn . . . ahn/ehn*

**133** Do you have any rooms free?
Van szabad szobájuk?
*von so-bod so-bah-yook*

**134** I would like to reserve a single/double room with/without bath/with/without shower.
Szeretnék foglalni egy egyágyas/kétágyas szobát fürdőszobával/fürdőszoba nélkül/zuhanyozóval/zuhanyozó nélkül.
*seh-reht-naynk fog-lolni edj edj-ah-djos/kayt-ahd-jos so-baht fewr-dur-so-bahvol/fewr-dur-so-bah nayl-kewl/zoo-honn-yozaw-vol/zoo-honn-yozaw nayl-kewl.*

**135** I would like bed and breakfast/room and half board/room and full board.
Szeretnék egy szobát reggelivel/Szeretnék egy szobát reggelivel és vacsorával/

Szeretnék egy szobát teljes ellátással.
*seh-reht-nayk edj so-baht rehg-gehlee-vehl/seh-reht-nayk edj so-baht rehg-geh-lee-vehl aysh vo-cho-rah-vol/seh-reht-nayk edj so-baht tehl-yehsh ehl-lah-tahsh-shol.*

**136** How much is it per night?
Mennyibe kerül egy éjjelre?
*mehnn-yee-beh keh-rewl edj ay-yehl-reh*

**137** Is breakfast included?
Az árban a reggeli is benne van?
*oz ahr-bon o rehg-geh-li ish behn-neh von*

**138** May I see the room?
Megnézhetem a szobát?
*mehg-nayz-hehtehm o so-baht*

**139** Do you have any cheaper rooms?
Van olcsóbb szobájuk?
*von ol-chawbb so-bah-yook*

**140** I would like to take the room.
Szeretném kivenni a szobát.
*seh-reht-naym ki-vehn-ni o so-baht*

**141** I would like to stay for . . . nights.
Szeretnék . . . éjjelt maradni.
*seh-reht-nayk . . . ay-yehlt mo-rod-ni*

**142** The shower/light/tap doesn't work.
A zuhany/villany/csap nem működik.
*o zoo-honn-y/veel-lonn-y/chop nem meew-kuh-dik*

### 143 At what time/where is breakfast served?
Hány órakor/hol lehet reggelizni?
*hahnn-y aw-rokor/hol leh-eht rehg-geh-leez-ni*

### 144 What time do I have to check-out?
Hány órakor kell átadnom a szobát?
*hahnn-y aw-ro-kor kehll aht-od-nom o so-baht*

### 145 Can I have the key to room no . . ?
Megkaphatnám a . . . -os számu szoba kulcsát.
*meg-kop-hot-nahm o . . . -osh sah-moo so-bah kool-chaht*

### 146 My room number is . . .
A szobaszámom . . .
*o so-bo-sah-mom . . .*

### 147 Do you accept travellers' cheques/Eurocheques/credit cards?
Elfogadnak Traveller's csekket/Euro-csekket/hitelkártyát?
*el-fo-god-nok travellers chehk-keht/euro-chehk-keht/hee-tehl-kahrt-yaht*

### 148 May I have the bill please?
Megkaphatnám a számlát?
*meg-kop-hot-nahm o sahm-laht*

### 149 Excuse me, I think there is a mistake in this bill.
Elnézést kérek, de azt hiszem hiba van a számlában.
*ehl-nay-zay-sht kay-rehk, deh ozt hee-sehm hee-bo von o sahm-lah-bon*

## Youth Hostels

### 150 How much is a dormitory bed per night?
Mennyibe kerül a hálóteremben egy ágy egy éjjelre?
*mehnn-yee-beh keh-rewr o hah-law-teh-rehm-behn edj ahdj ehdj ay-yehl-reh*

### 151 I am/am not an HI member.
HI tag vagyok/Nem vagyok HI tag.
*HI tog vo-djok/nem vo-djok HI tog.*

### 152 May I use my own sleeping bag?
Használhatom a saját hálózsákomat?
*hos-nahl-ho-tom o sho-yaht hah-law-zhah-ko-mot*

### 153 What time do you lock the doors at night?
Hány órakor zárják be a kaput éjjelre?
*hahnn-y aw-rokor zahr-yahk beh o ko-poot ay-yehl-reh*

## Camping

### 154 May I camp here for the night/two nights?
Campingezhetünk itt egy éjjelre/két éjjelre?
*com-pin-gehz-heh-tuhnk itt edj ay-yehl-reh/kayt ay-yehl-reh*

### 155 Where can I pitch my tent?
Hol verhetem fel a sátramat?
*hol vehr-heh-tehm fehl o saht-ro-mot*

156 How much does it cost for one night/week?
Mennyibe kerül egy éjjelre/egy hétre?
*mehnn-yee-beh keh-rewr edj ay-yehl-reh/edj hayt-reh*

157 Where can we park our caravan?
Hol állíthatjuk le a lakókocsinkat?
*hol ahl-leet-hot-yook leh o lo-kaw-ko-cheen-kot*

158 Where are the washing facilities?
Hol van a mosakodási lehetőség?
*hol von o mo-sho-ko-dah-shi leh-heh-tur-shayg*

159 Is there a restaurant/supermarket/swimming pool on site/nearby?
Van étterem/szupermarket/uszoda a területen/környéken?
*von ayt-teh-rehm/soo-pehr-mor-keht/oo-sodo o teh-rew-leh-tehn/kuhr-nn-yay-kehn*

160 Do you have a safety deposit box?
Van önöknek értékmegőrzőjük?
*von uh-nuhk-nehk ayr-tayk-meg-ur-zur-yewk*

## EATING AND DRINKING

### Cafés and Bars

161 I would like a cup of/two cups of/another coffee/tea.
Szeretnék kérni egy csésze/két csésze/mégegy kávét/teát.
*seh-reht-nayk kayr-ni edj chay-seh/kayt chay-seh/mayg-edj kah-vayt/teh-aht*

162 With milk/sugar. Without milk/sugar.
Tejjel/Cukorral. Tej nélkül/Cukor nélkül.
*tehy-yehl/tsoo-kor-rol. tehy nayl-kewl/tsoo-kor nayl-kewl.*

163 I would like a bottle/glass/two glasses of mineral water/red wine/white wine, please.
Szeretnék kérni egy üveg/egy pohár/két pohár ásvány vizet/vörös bort/fehér bort.
*seh-reht-nayk kayr-ni edj ew-vehg/edj po-hahr/kayt po-hahr ahsh-vahnn-y vee-zeht/vuh-ruhsh bort/feh-hayr bort.*

164 I would like a beer/two beers, please.
Szeretnék kérni egy sört/két sört.
*seh-reht-nayk kayr-ni edj sh-uhrt/kayt sh-uhrt*

165 May I have some ice?
Kaphatok jeget?
*kop-ho-tok yeh-geht*

166 Do you have any matches/cigarettes/cigars?
Van gyufája/cigarettája/szivarja?
*von djoo-fah-yo/tsee-go-reht-tahyo/see-vor-yo*

### Restaurants

167 Can you recommend a good/inexpensive restaurant in this area?
Tud egy jó/olcsó éttermet

ajánlani ezen a környéken?
*tood edj yaw/ol-chaw ayt-tehr-meht o-yahn-loni eh-zehn o kuhr-nn-yay-kehn*

168 I would like a table for . . . people.
Szeretnék egy asztalt . . . főre.
*seh-reht-nayk edj os-tolt . . . fur-reh*

169 Do you have a non-smoking area?
Van itt nem dohányzó rész?
*von itt nem do-hahnn-yzaw rays*

170 Waiter/Waitress!
Pincér/Pincérnő!
*pin-cayr/pin-cayr-nur*

171 Do you have a set menu/children's menu/wine list?
Van komplett menüjük/gyermek menüjük/itallapjuk?
*von komp-lett meh-new-yewk/djehr-mehk meh-new-yewk/ee-tol-lop-yook*

172 Do you have any vegetarian dishes, please?
Van vegetariánus ételük?
*von veh-geh-to-ri-ah-noosh ay-teh-lewk*

173 Are there any local specialities?
Van valamilyen helyi specialitásuk?
*von volo-mee-yehn heh-yi shpe-tsi-o-lee-tah-shook*

174 Are vegetables included?
A zöldségek is benne vannak az árban?

o zuhld-shay-gehk ish behn-neh von-nok oz ahr-bon

175 Could I have it well-cooked/medium/rare please?
Kérhetem a húst jól átsülten/közepesen sülten/angolosan sülten?
*kayr-heh-tehm o hoosht yawl aht-shewl-tehn/kuh-zeh-peh-shehn shewl-tehn/on-golo-shon shewl-tehn*

176 What does this dish consist of?
Miből készült ez az étel?
*mee-bur kay-sewlt ehz oz ay-tehl*

177 I would like the set menu, please.
Szeretném kérni a komplett menüt.
*seh-reht-naym kayr-ni o komp-lett meh-neewt*

178 We have not been served yet.
Még nem szolgáltak ki minket.
*mayg nem sol-gahl-tok kee meen-keht*

179 Excuse me, this is not what I ordered.
Elnézést kérek, de nem ezt rendeltem.
*ehl-nay-zaysht kay-rehk, deh nem ehzt rehn-dehl-tem*

180 May I have some/some more bread/water/coffee/tea?
Kérhetek kenyeret/még kenyeret/vizet/kávét/teát?
*kayr-heh-tehk kehnn-yeh-reht/mayg kehnn-yeh-reht/vee-zeht/kah-vayt/teh-aht?*

H U N G A R I A N

168 ↕ 180

**181 May I have the bill, please?**
Szeretném kérni a számlát.
*seh-reht-naym kayr-ni o sahm-laht*

**182 Does this bill include service?**
A számla a felszolgálási díjat is
tartalmazza?
*o sahm-lah o fehl-sol-gah-lah-shi
dee-yot ish tor-tol-moz-zo*

**183 Do you accept travellers'
cheques (travelers' checks)/
Eurocheques/MasterCard/US
dollars?**
Elfogadnak travellers'csekket/
Euro-csekket/Master Cardot/
Amerikai Dollárt?
*el-fo-god-nok travellers chehk-
keht/euro-chehk-keht/master card-
ot/a-meh-ree-koi dol-lahrt*

**184 Can I have a receipt, please?**
Kérhetek nyugtát erről?
*kayr-heh-tehk nn-yoog-taht ehr-
rurl*

**185 Where is the toilet
(restroom), please?**
Megmondaná hol találom a WC-t?
*mehg-mon-do-nah hol to-lah-lom
o vay-tsayt*

## On the Menu

**186 First courses**
Előételek
*eh-lur-ay-teh-lehk*

**187 Soups**
Levesek
*leh-veh-shehk*

**188 Main courses**
Főételek

*fur-ay-teh-lehk*

**189 Fish dishes**
Halételek
*hol-ay-teh-lehk*

**190 Meat dishes**
Húsételek
*hoosh-ay-teh-lehk*

**191 Vegetarian dishes**
Vegetariánus ételek
*veh-geh-to-ree-ah-noosh ay-teh-
lehk*

**192 Cheese**
Sajtok
*shoy-tok*

**193 Desserts**
Édességek
*ay-dehsh-shay-gehk*

**194 Specialities**
Specialitások
*shpeh-tzi-o-li-tah-shok*

## GETTING AROUND

## Public Transport

**195 Where is the bus stop/coach
station/nearest metro
(subway) station?**
Hol van a buszmegálló/
autóbusz állomás/legközelebbi
metro állomás?
*hol von o boos-mehg-ahl-law/o-
oo-taw-boos ahl-lo-mahsh/leg-
kuh-zeh-lehb-bi meht-raw ahl-lo-
mahsh.*

**196** When is the next/last bus to . . ?
Mikor indul a következő/utolsó
busz . . . -ba/-be?
*mee-kor in-dool o kuh-veht-keh-
zur boos . . . -bo/-beh*

**197** How much is the fare to the
city centre (downtown)/
railway (railroad station/
airport?
Mennyibe kerül a menetjegy a
városközpontba/
vasútállomáshoz/repülőtérre?
*mehnn-yee-beh keh-rewl o meh-
neht-yehdj o vah-rosh-kuhz-pont-
bah/vo-shoot-ahl-lo-mahsh-hoz/
reh-pew-lur-tayr-reh*

**198** Will you tell me when to get
off?
Szólna, mikor kell leszállnom?
*sawl-no mee-kor kehll leh-sahll-
nom*

**199** Does this bus go to . . ?
Ez a busz megy . . . -ba/-be?
*ehz o boos mehdj . . . -bo/-beh*

**200** Which number bus goes to . . ?
Hányas busz megy . . . -ba/-be?
*hahnn-yos boos mehdj . . . -bo/-
beh*

**201** May I have a single (one-
way)/return (round-trip)/day
ticket/book of tickets?
Szeretnék kéni egy egyszeri
utazásra szóló/retúr/napi
jegyet/jegycsomagot.
*seh-reht-nayk kayr-ni edj edj-seh-ree
oo-to-zahsh-ro saw-law/reh-toor/
nopi ye-djeht/yedj-cho-mo-got*

## Taxis

**202** I would like to go to . . .
How much will it cost?
Szeretnék eljutni . . . -ba/-be.
Mibe fog ez kerülni?
*seh-reht-nayk ehl-yoot-ni . . . -bo/-
beh Mee-beh fog ehz keh-rewl-ni*

**203** Please stop here.
Kérem itt álljon meg.
*kay-rehm itt ahll-yon mehg*

**204** I would like to order a taxi
today/tomorrow/at 2pm to
go from . . . to . . .
Szeretnék rendelni egy taxit
mára/holnapra/délután 2 órára
hogy elvigyen . . . -ból/-ből . . .
-ba/-be.
*seh-reht-nayk rehn-dehl-ni ehdj
toxit mah-ro/hol-nop-ro/dayl-oo-
tahn kayt aw-rah-ro hodj ehl-vee-
djehn . . . -bawl/burl . . . -bo/-beh*

## Asking the Way

**205** Excuse me, do you speak
English?
Bocsánat, beszél angolul?
*bo-chah-not, beh-sayl on-go-lool*

**206** Excuse me, is this the right
way to . . ?
Bocsánat, erre kell menni . . . -
ba/-be?
*bo-chah-not, ehr-reh kehll mehn-ni
. . . -bo/-beh*

**HUNGARIAN**

**207**
↕
**218**

207 . . . the cathedral/the tourist
information office/the castle/
the old town
. . . a katedrális/a turista
információs iroda/a kastély/az
óváros
. . . .o ko-tehd-rah-leesh/o too-rish-
to in-for-mah-tsi-awsh ee-ro-do/o
kosh-tay/oz aw-vah-rosh

208 Can you tell me the way to
the railway (railroad station)/
bus station/taxi rank (stand)/
city centre (downtown)/
beach?
Meg tudná mondani hogy jutok
el a vasútállomáshoz/
buszmegállóhoz/taxiállomáshoz/
városközpontba/tengerpartra?
mehg tood-nah mon-doni hodj yoo-tok
ehl o vo-shoot-ahl-lo-mahsh-hoz/boos-
mehg-ahl-law-hoz/toxi-ahl-lo-mahsh-
hoz/vah-rosh-kuhz-pont-bo/tehn-
gehr-port-ra

209 First/second left/right/
straight ahead.
Első/második balra/jobbra/
egyenesen előre.
eehl-sur/mah-sho-dik bol-ro/yobb-
ro/edj-eh-neh-shen eh-lur-re

210 Where is the nearest police
station/post office?
Hol van a legközelebbi
rendőrőrs/postahivatal?
hol von o lehg-kuh-zeh-lehb-bi
rehn-dur-uhrsh/posh-to-hee-vo-tol

211 Is it far?
Messze van?
mehs-seh von

212 Do I need to take a taxi/catch
a bus?
Taxival/Busszal kell mennem?
toxi-vol/boos-sol kehll mehn-nehm

213 Can you point to it on my
map?
Megmutatná ezt a térképen?
mehg-moo-tot-nah ehzt o tayr-
kay-pehn

214 Thank you for your help.
Köszönöm a segítségét.
kuh-suh-nuhm o sheh-geet-shay-
gayt

## SIGHTSEEING

215 Where is the Tourist
Information office?
Hol van a Turista Információs
Iroda?
hol von o too-reesh-to in-for-mah-
tsee-awsh ee-ro-do

216 Where is the cathedral/
church/museum?
Hol van a katedrális/templom/
múzeum?
hol von o ko-tehd-rah-leesh/
tehmp-lom/mooh-zeh-oom

217 How much is the entrance
(admission) charge?
Mennyibe kerül a belépődíj?
mehnn-yee-beh keh-rewl o beh-lay-
pur-deey

218 Is there a discount for children/
students/senior citizens?
Adnak árengedményt
gyermekeknek/
egyetemistáknak/
nyugdíjasoknak?

od-nok ahr-ehn-gehd-maynn-yt
djehr-meh-kehk-nehk/e-djeh-teh-
meesh-tahk-nok/nn-yoog-dee-yo-
shok-nok

**19** **What time does the next guided tour start?**
Mikor indul a következő csoport idegennyelvű vezetővel?
*mee-kor in-dool o kuh-veht-keh-zur cho-port ee-deh-gehn-nn-yel-veew veh-zeh-tur-vehl*

**20** **One/two adults/children, please.**
Egy/Két felnőtt/gyermek jegyet kérek.
*edj/kayt fehl-nurtt/djehr-mehk ye-djeht kay-rehk*

**21** **May I take photographs here?**
Lehet itt fényképezni?
*leh-heht itt faynn-y-kay-pehz-ni*

## ENTERTAINMENT

**22** **Can you recommend a good bar/nightclub?**
Tudna ajánlani egy jó bárt/éjjeli szórakozóhelyet?
*tood-no o-yahn-loni edj yaw bahrt/ay-yeli saw-ro-ko-zaw-heh-yeht*

**23** **Do you know what is on at the cinema (playing at the movies)/theatre at the moment?**
Meg tudná mondani, most mit játszanak a moziban/szinházban?
*mehg tood-nah mon-doni, mosht mit yaht-sonok o mo-zee-bon/seen-hahz-bon*

**224** **I would like to book (purchase) . . . tickets for the matinée/evening performance on Monday.**
Szeretnék . . . jegyet foglalni venni a hétfő délutáni/esti előadásra.
*seh-reht-nayk . . . yeh-djeht fog-lolni o hayt-fur dayl-oo-tah-ni/ehsh-tee eh-lur-o-dahsh-ro*

**225** **What time does the film/performance start?**
Mikor kezdődik a film/az előadás ?
*mee-kor kehz-dur-dik o film/oz eh-lur-o-dahsh*

## MEETING PEOPLE

**226** **Hello/Goodbye.**
Helló/Viszontlátásra
*hehl-law/vee-sont-lah-tahsh-ro*

**227** **Good morning/good afternoon/good evening/goodnight.**
Jó reggelt/jó napot/jó estét/jó éjszakát.
*yaw rehg-gehlt/yaw no-pot/yaw ehsh-tayt/yaw ay-y-so-kaht*

**228** **Pleased to meet you.**
Örülök hogy találkoztunk.
*uh-rew-luhk hodj to-lahl-koz-toonk*

**229** **How are you?**
Hogy van?
*hodj von*

**230** **Fine, thank you. And you?**
Köszönöm, jól. És ön?
*kuh-suh-nuym yawl. aysh uhn*

# MEETING PEOPLE/TRAVELLING WITH CHILDREN

**231** My name is . . .
A nevem . . .
*o neh-vehm . . .*

**232** This is my friend/boyfriend/
girlfriend/husband/wife/
older brother/younger brother/
older sister/younger sister.
Ez a barátom/udvarlóm/barátnőm/
férjem/feleségem/bátyám/öcsém/
nővérem/hugom.
*ehz o bo-rah-tom/ood-vor-lawm/
bo-raht-nurm/fayr-yehm/feh-leh-
shay-gehm/baht-yahm/uh-
chaym/nur-vay-rehm/hoo-gom*

**233** Where are you travelling to?
Hova utazik?
*ho-vo oo-to-zik*

**234** I am going to . . . /we are
going to . . .
Én . . . -ba/-be utazom/Mi . . . -
ba/-be utazunk.
*ayn . . . -bo/-beh oo-to-zom/mee . .
. -bo/-beh oo-to-zoonk*

**235** How long are you travelling
for?
Meddig utazik?
*mehd-deeg oo-to-zik*

**236** Where do you come from?
Honnan jött?
*hon-non yuhtt*

**237** I am from . . ./we are from . . .
Én . . . -ból/-ből jöttem/Mi . . . -
ból/-ből jöttünk.
*ayn . . . -bawl/-burl yuht-tehm/
mee . . . -bawl/-burl yuht-tewnk*

**238** We're on holiday.
Szabadságon vagyunk.
*so-bod-shah-gon vo-djoonk*

**239** This is our first visit here.
Most vagyunk itt először.
*mosht vo-djoonk itt eh-lur-suhr*

**240** Would you like a cigarette?/
May I have a cigarette?
Kér egy cigarettát?/ Kérhetek
egy cigarettát?
*kayr edj tsee-go-reht-taht//kayr-
heh-tehk edj tsee-go-reht-taht*

**241** I am sorry but I do not
understand.
Sajnálom, de nem értem.
*soj-nah-lom, deh nem ayr-tehm*

**242** Please speak slowly.
Kérem, beszéljen lassabban.
*kay-rehm, beh-sayl-yehn losh-
shob-bon*

**243** Do you mind if I smoke?
Zavarja ha dohányzom?
*zo-vor-yo ho do-hahnn-y-zom*

**244** Do you have a light?
Kérhetek tüzet?
*kayr-heh-tehk tew-zeht*

**245** I am waiting for my husband/
wife/boyfriend/girlfriend.
A férjemre/feleségemre/
udvarlómra/barátnőmre várok.
*o fayr-yehm-reh/feh-leh-shay-
gehm-reh/ood-vor-lawm-ro/bo-
raht-nurm-reh vah-rok*

## TRAVELLING WITH CHILDREN

**246** Do you have a high chair/
baby-sitting service/cot?
Van önöknek etetőszékük/
gyermek-vigyázó szolgálatuk/
gyermekágyuk?

*von uh-nuhk-nehk eh-teh-tur-say-
kewk/djehr-mehk-vee-djah-zaw sol-
gah-lo-took/djehr-mehk-ah-djook*

**247** Where is the nursery/
playroom?
Hol van az ovoda/játékszoba?
*hol von oz o-vo-do/yah-tayk-so-bo*

**248** Where can I warm the baby's
bottle?
Hol tudom megmelegíteni a
baby cumis-üvegét?
*hol too-dom mehg-meh-leh-gee-teh-
ni o baby coo-meesh-ew-veh-gayt*

## COMMUNICATIONS

### Post

**249** How much will it cost to send
a letter/postcard/this
package to Britain/Ireland/
America/Canada/Australia/
New Zealand?
Mennyibe kerül egy levél/
képeslap/ez a csomag
Angliába/Irországba/
Amerikába/Kanadába/
Ausztráliába/Új Zélandba?
*mehnn-yee-be keh-rewl edj leh-
vayl/kay-pehsh-lop/ehz o cho-mog
ong-li-ahba/eer-or-sahg-bo/o-meh-
ri-kah-bo/ko-no-dah-bo/oust-rah-
liah-bo/ooy zay-londbo*

**250** I would like one stamp/two
stamps.
Szeretnék egy bélyeget/két
bélyeget.
*seh-reht-nayk edj bay-yeh-geht/
kayt bay-yeh-geht.*

**251** I'd like . . . stamps for
postcards to send abroad,
please.
Külföldre küldendő képeslapra
szeretnék . . . bélyeget kérni.
*kewl-fuhld-reh kewl-dehn-dur kay-
pehsh-lopro seh-reht-nayk . . .
bay-yeh-geht kayr-ni*

### Phones

**252** I would like to make a
telephone call/reverse the
charges (make a collect call)
to . . .
Szeretnék telefonálni/R
beszélgetést kérni . . . -ba/-be.
*sehreht-nayk teh-leh-fo-nahl-ni/
ehrr beh-sayl-geh-taysht kayr-ni . .
. -bo/-beh*

**253** Which coins do I need for the
telephone?
Milyen érmével működik a
telefon?
*mee-yehn ayr-may-vehl meew-
kuh-dik o teh-leh-fon*

**254** The line is engaged (busy).
Foglalt a vonal.
*fog-lolt o vo-nol*

**255** The number is . . .
A szám . . .
*a sahm . . .*

**256** Hello, this is . . .
Halló, itt . . . beszél.
*hol-law, itt . . . beh-sayl*

**257** May I speak to . . ?
Beszélhetnék . . . . . . -val/-vel?
*be-sayl-heht-nayk . . . . -vol/-vehl*

**258** He/She is not in at the moment. Can you call back?
Pillanatnyilag nincs a helyén. Visszaszólna később?
*peel-lo-not-nn-yee-log neench o heh-yayn. vees-so-sawl-no kay-shurbb*

## MONEY

**259** I would like to change these travellers' cheques (travelers' checks)/this currency/this Eurocheque.
Szeretném beváltani ezeket a Travellers csekkeket/ezt a valutát/ezt az Euro csekket.
*seh-reht-naym beh-vahl-toni eh-zeh keht o travellers chehk-keh-keht/ehzt o vo-loo-taht/ehzt oz euro chehk-keht*

**260** How much commission do you charge? (What is the service charge?)
Mennyit számolnak fel jutalékként?
*mehnn-yeet sah-mol-nok fehl yoo-to-layk-kaynt*

**261** Can I obtain money with my MasterCard?
Válthatok ki pénzt a MasterCard-ommal?
*vahlt-ho-tok ki paynzt o mastercard-om-mol*

## SHOPPING

### Names of Shops and Departments

**262** Könyvüzlet/Irószerbolt
*kuhnn-yv-ewz-leht/ee-raw-sehr-bolt*
Bookshop/Stationery

**263** Ékszerész/Ajándéküzlet
*ayk-seh-rays/o-jahn-dayk-ewz-leht*
Jeweller's/Gifts

**264** Cipők
*tsee-purk*
Shoes

**265** Vaskereskedés
*vosh-keh-rehsh-keh-daysh*
Hardware

**266** Antikvárium
*on-teek-vah-ree-oom*
Antiques

**267** Férfi/Női Fodrász
*fayr-fi/nur-i fod-rahs*
Hairdressers (men's)/(women's)

**268** Dohányáruda/Dohányüzlet
*do-hahnn-y-ah-roo-do/do-hahnn-y-ewz-leht*
Tobacconist

**269** Pékség/Kenyérüzlet
*payk-shayg/keh-nn-yayr-ewz-leht*
Baker's

**270** Szupermarket
*supermarket*
Supermarket

**271** Ofotért/Fotóüzlet
*o-fo-tayrt/fo-taw-ewz-leht*
Photoshop

**272** Játéküzlet/Játékbolt
*yah-tayk-ewz-leht/yah-tayk-bolt*
Toys

**273** Utazási Iroda/IBUSZ
*oo-to-zah-shi ee-rodo/ee-boos*
Travel Agent

H
U
N
G
A
R
I
A
N

258
↕
273

**274 Illatszerek**
*eel-lot-seh-rehk*
Toiletries

**275 Lemezek**
*leh-meh-zehk*
Records

## In the Shop

**276 What time do the shops open/close?**
Mikor nyitnak/zárnak az üzletek?
*mee-kor n-y-eet-nok/zahr-nok oz ewz-leh-tehk*

**277 Where is the nearest market?**
Hol van a legközelebbi piac?
*hol von o lehg-kuh-zeh-lehb-bi pee-ots*

**278 Can you show me the one in the window/this one?**
Megmutatná nekem az ablakban levőt/ezt?
*mehg-moo-tot-nah neh-kehm oz ob-lok-bon leh-vurt/ehzt*

**279 Can I try this on?**
Felpróbálhatom?
*fehl-praw-bahl-ho-tom*

**280 What size is this?**
Mekkora méret ez?
*mehk-koro may-reht ehz*

**281 This is too large/too small/too expensive.**
Ez túl nagy/túl kicsi/túl drága.
*ehz tool nodj/tool kee-chi/tool drah-go*

**282 Do you have any others?**
Van még más is?
*von mayg máhsh eesh*

**283 My size is . . .**
. . . -os/-es a méretem.
*. . . -osh/-ehsh o may-reh-tehm*

**284 Where is the changing room/childrens/cosmetic/ladieswear/menswear/food department?**
Hol van a próbafülke/a gyermek osztály/a kozmetikai osztály/a nőiruha osztály/a férfiruha orszály/az élemiszer osztály?
*hol von o praw-bo-fewl-keh/o djehr-mehk os-tahy/o koz-meh-tee-koi os-tahy/o nur-y-roo-ho os-tahy/o fayr-fee-roo-ho os-tahy/oz ay-lehl-mee-sehr os-tahy*

**285 I would like . . .**
Szeretnék egy . . . -t.
*seh-reht-nayk edj . . . -t*

**286 I would like a quarter of a kilo/half a kilo/a kilo of bread/butter/cheese/ham/tomatoes.**
Kérek egy negyed kiló/fél kiló/kiló kenyeret/vajat/sajtot/sonkát/paradicsomot.
*kay-rehk edj neh-djehd kee-law/fayl kee-lawo/kee-law keh-nn-yeh-reht/vo-jot/soy-tot/son-kaht/poro-dee-cho-mot*

**287 How much is this?**
Ez mennyibe kerül?
*ehz mehnn-yee-beh keh-rewl*

**288 I'll take this one, thank you.**
Ezt megveszem, köszönöm.
*ehzt mehg-veh-sehm, kuh-suh-nuhm*

**289** Do you have a carrier (shopping) bag?

Kérhetek egy nylonzacskót?

*kayr-heh-tehk edj nehy-lon-zoch-kawt*

**290** Do you have anything cheaper/larger/smaller/of better quality?

Van önnek olcsóbb/nagyobb méretű/kisebb méretű/jobb minőségű áruja?

*von uhn-nehk ol-chawbb/nod-jobb may-reh-teew/kee-shehbb may-reh-teew/yobb mee-nur-shay-geew ah-roo-yo*

**291** I would like a film for this camera.

Ehhez a fényképezőgéphez szeretnék filmet venni.

*eh-hehz o faynn-y-kay-peh-zur-gayp-hehz seh-reht-nayk feel-meht vehn-ni*

**292** I would like some batteries, the same size as this old one.

Ugyanolyan méretű elemet szeretnék venni, mint ez a régi.

*oodjon-ol-yon may-reh-teew eh-leh-meht seh-reht-nayk vehn-ni, meent ehz o ray-gi*

**293** Would you mind wrapping this for me, please?

Becsomagolná nekem ezt, kérem?

*beh-cho-mogol-nah neh-kehm ehzt, kay-rehm*

**294** Sorry, but you seem to have given me the wrong change.

Elnézést kérek, de azt hiszem rosszul adott vissza.

*ehl-nay-zaysht kay-rehk, deh ozt hee-sehm ros-sool o-dott vees-so*

### Car Hire (Rental)

**295** I have ordered (rented) a car in the name of . . .

Egy autót béreltem . . . néven.

*ejd o-oo-tawt bay-rehl-tehm . . . nay-vehn*

**296** How much does it cost to hire (rent) a car for one day/two days/one week?

Mennyibe kerül egy autó bérlése egy napra/két napra/egy hétre?

*mehnn-yee-beh keh-rewl edj o-oo-taw bayr-lay-sheh edj nop-ro/kayt nop-ro/edj hayt-reh*

**297** Is the tank already full of petrol (gas)?

Az autó fel van már tankolva?

*oz o-oo-taw fehl von mahr ton-kol-vo*

**298** Is insurance and tax included? How much is the deposit?

A biztosítás és az adó is az árban benne van? Mennyi letétet kérnek?

*o beez-to-shee-tahsh ays oz o-daw eesh oz ahr-bon behn-neh von? mehnn-yee leh-tay-teht kayr-nehk*

**299** By what time must I return the car?

Mikorra kell visszahoznom az autót?

*mee-kor-rah kehll vees-so-hoz-nom
oz o-oo-tawt*

**300** I would like a small/family
car with a radio/cassette player.
Szeretnék egy kisméretű/családi
autót rádióval/magnóval.
*seh-reht-nayk edj keesh-may-reh-
teew o-oo-tawt rah-dee-aw-vol/
mog-naw-vol*

## Asking the Way

**301** Excuse me, can you help me
please?
Bocsánatot kérek, segítene
nekem?
*bo-chah-no-tot kay-rehk, sheh-gee-
teh-neh neh-kehm*

**302** How do I reach the
motorway/main road?
Hogy jutok el az autópályára/a
főútvonalra?
*hodj yoo-tok ehl oz o-oo-taw-pah-
yah-ro/o fur-oot-vo-nol-ro?*

**303** I think I have taken the
wrong turning.
Azt hiszem rossz helyen
fordultam be.
*ozt hee-sehm ross heh-yehn for-
dool-tom beh*

**304** I am looking for this address.
Ezt a címet keresem.
*ehzt o cee-meht keh-reh-shem*

**305** I am looking for the . . . hotel.
A . . . szállót keresem.
*o . . . sahl-lawt keh-reh-shem*

**306** How far is it to . . . from
here?

Milyen messze van a . . . innen?
*mee-yehn mehs seh von o . . . in-
nehn*

**307** Carry straight on for . . .
kilometres.
Menjen egyenesen . . . kilométert.
*mehn-yehn eh-djeh-neh-shehn . . .
kee-lo-may-tehrt*

**308** Take the next turning on the
right/left.
Forduljon be a következő
sarkon jobbra/balra.
*ford-ool-jon beh o kuh-veht-keh-
zur shor-kon yobb-ro/bol-ro*

**309** Turn right/left at the next
crossroads/traffic lights.
Forduljon jobbra/balra a
következő útkereszteződésnél/
közlekedési lámpánál.
*for-dool-yon yobb-ro/bol-ro o kuh-
veht-keh-zur ooht-keh-rehs-teh-
zur-daysh-nayl/kuhz-leh-keh-day-
shi lahm-pah-nahl*

**310** You are going in the wrong
direction.
Ön rossz fele megy.
*uhn ross feh-leh mehdj*

## Parking

**311** How long can I park here?
Meddig parkolhatok itt?
*mehd-dig por-kol-ho-tok itt*

**312** Is there a car park near here?
Van itt a közelben egy parkoló?
*von itt o kuh-zehl-behn edj por-ko-
law*

# MOTORING

**HUNGARIAN**

↑
328

**313** At what time does this car
park close?
Mikor zár be ez a parkoló?
*mee-kor zahr beh ehz o por-ko-law*

## Signs and Notices

**314** Egyirányú utca
*edj-ee-rahnn-y-ooh oot-tzo*
One way

**315** Behajtani tilos
*be-hoj-toni tee-losh*
No entry.

**316** Parkolni tilos.
*por-kol-ni tee-losh*
No parking

**317** Útelterelés
*oot-ehl-teh-reh-laysh*
Detour (diversion)

**318** Állj
*ahllj*
Stop.

**319** Elsőbbségadás kötelező
*ehl-shurbb-shayg-o-dahsh kuh-teh-leh-zur*
Give way (yield).

**320** Csúszós út
*choo-sawsh oot*
Slippery road

**321** Előzni tilos
*eh-lurz-ni tee-losh*
No overtaking.

## At the Filling Station

**322** Unleaded (lead-free)/
Standard/Premium
Ólommentes benzin/

Normálbenzin/Szuperbenzin
*aw-lom-mehn-tehsh behn-zeen/
normahl-behn-zeen/soo-pehr-behn-zeen*

**323** Fill the tank please.
Kérem töltse tele a tankot.
*kay-rehm tuhlt-sheh teh-leh o ton-kot*

**324** Do you have a road map of
this area?
Van önnek erről a környékről
autótérképe?
*von uhn-nehk ehr-rurl o kuhr-nn-y-ayk-rurl o-oo-taw-tayr-kay-peh*

**325** How much is the car-wash?
Mennyibe kerül az autómosás?
*mehnn-yee-beh keh-rewl oz o-oo-taw-mo-shah-sh*

## Breakdowns

**326** I've had a breakdown at . . .
Meghibásodott az autónk . . . -
nál/-nél.
*mehg-hee-bah-sho-dott oz o-oo-tawnk . . . -nahl/-nayl*

**327** I am on the road from . . . to . . .
A . . . -tól . . . -ig vezető úton
vagyok.
*o . . . -tawl . . . -ig veh-zeh-tur ooh-ton vod-jok*

**328** I can't move the car. Can you
send a tow-truck?
Lerobbant az autóm. Tudna
küldeni egy autómentőt?
*leh-rob-bont oz o-oo-tawm. tood-no kewl-deh-ni edj o-oo-taw-mehn-turt*

# MOTORING

**329** I have a flat tyre.
Defektet kaptam.
*deh-fehk-teht kop-tom*

**330** The windscreen (windshield) has smashed/cracked.
A szélvédő széttörött/megrepedt.
*o sayl-vay-dur sayt-tuh-ruhtt/ mehg-reh-pehdt*

**331** There is something wrong with the engine/brakes/ lights/steering/gearbox/ clutch/exhaust.
Valami baj van a motorral/ fékekkel/lámpákkal/ kormánnyal/sebességváltóval/ kipuffogó csővel.
*vo-lomi boy von o motor-rol/fay- kehk-kehl/lahm-pahk-kol/kor- mahnn-y-ol/sheh-behsh-shayg- vahl-taw-vol/kee-poof-fo-gaw chur-vehl*

**332** It's overheating.
A kocsi túlmelegszik.
*o ko-chi tool-meh-lehg-sik*

**333** It won't start.
Az autó nem indul be.
*oz o-oo-taw nem in-dool beh*

**334** Where can I get it repaired?
Hol tudom megjavíttatni?
*hol too-dom mehg-yo-veet-tot-ni*

**335** Can you take me there?
El tudna vinni engem odáig?
*el tood-no veen-ni ehn-gehm o- dah-eeg*

**336** Will it take long to fix?
Sokáig tart míg megjavítják ?
*sho-kah-ig tort meeg mehg-yo- veet-jahk*

**337** How much will it cost?
Mennyibe fog kerülni?
*mehnn-yee-beh fog keh-rewl-ni*

## Accidents

**338** Can you help me? There has been an accident.
Tudna segíteni? Baleset történt.
*tood-no sheh-gee-teh-ni? bol-eh- sheht tuhr-taynt*

**339** Please call the police/an ambulance.
Kérem hívja a rendőrséget/ mentőket.
*kay-rehm heev-yo o rehn-dur- shay-geht/mehn-tur-keht*

**340** Is anyone hurt?
Megsebesült valaki?
*meg-she-beh-shewlt vo-loki*

## Traffic Offences

**341** I'm sorry, I didn't see the sign.
Bocsánatot kérek, de nem láttam a táblát.
*bo-chah-notot kay-rehk, deh nem laht-tom o tahb-laht*

**342** Must I pay a fine? How much?
Kell büntetés fizetnem? Mennyit?
*kehll bewn-teh-taysht fee-zeht- nehm? mehnn-yeet*

**343** Show me your documents.
Mutassa az okmányait.
*moo-tosh-sho oz ok-mah-nn-y-oit*

HUNGARIAN

↕
343

171

## HEALTH

### At the Pharmacy

**344** Do you have anything for a stomachache/headache/sore throat/toothache?
Tudna adni valamit gyomorfájásra/fejfájásra/torokfájásra/fogfájásra?
*tood-no odni vo-lo-meet djo-mor-fah-yahsh-ro/fehy-fah-yahsh-ro/torok-fah-yah-shro/fog-fah-yash-ro*

**345** I need something for diarrhoea (diarrhea)/consti ation/a cold/a cough/insect bites/sunburn/travel (motion) sickness.
Kérek valamit hasmenésre/székrekedésre/megfázásra/köhögés ellen/rovarcsípésre/leégés ellen/utazás közbeni hányinger ellen
*kay-rehk vo-lo-mit hosh-meh-naysh-reh/sayk-reh-keh-daysh-reh/meg-fah-zahsh-ro/kuh-huh-gays el-lehn/ro-vor-chee-paysh-reh/le-ay-gaysh el-lehn/oo-to-zahsh kuhz-beh-ni hahnn-y-in-gehr el-lehn*

**346** How much/how many do I take?
Mennyit/hány darabot kell bevennem?
*mehnn-yeet/hahnn-y do-ro-bot kehll beh-vehn-nehm*

**347** How often do I take it/them?
Milyen gyakran kell ezt/ezeket bevennem?
*mee-yehn djok-ron kehll ehzt/eh-zeh-keht beh-vehn-nehm*

**348** How much does it cost?
Mennyibe kerül?
*mehnn-yee-beh keh-ruhl*

**349** Can you recommend a good doctor/dentist?
Tud ajánlani egy jó doktort/fogorvost?
*tood o-yahn-loni edj jaw dok-tort/fog-or-vosht*

**350** Is it suitable for children?
Gyermekeknek is való?
*djer-meh-kehk-nehk ish volaw*

### Doctor

**351** I have a pain here/in my arm/leg/chest/stomach.
Fájdalmat érzek itt/a karomban/a lábamban/a mellkasomban/a gyomromban.
*fahy-dolmot ayr-zehk itt/o ko-rom-bon/o lah-bom-bon/a mehll-ko-shom-bon/a djom-rom-bon*

**352** Please call a doctor, this is an emergency.
Kérem azonnal hívjon orvost, sürgősségi esetről van szó.
*kay-rehm o-zon-nol heev-yon or-vosht, shewr-gur-sh-shay-gi eh-shet-rurl von saw*

**353** I would like to make an appointment to see a doctor.
Szeretnék bejelentkezni az orvoshoz.
*seh-reht-nayk beh-yeh-lehnt-kehz-ni oz or-vosh-hoz*

354 **I am diabetic/pregnant.**
Cukorbeteg/terhes vagyok.
*tsoo-kor-beh-tehg/tehr-hesh vod-yok*

355 **I need a prescription for . . .**
Egy receptre van szükségem . . .
-ra/-re.
*edj reh-tzehpt-reh von sewk-shay-gehm . . . -ro/-reh*

356 **Can you give me something to ease the pain?**
Tudna valami fájdalomcsillapítót adni?
*tood-no vo-lo-mee fahy-do-lom-chil-lo-pee-taw odni*

357 **I am allergic to penicillin. He/she is allergic to pencillin.**
Allergiás vagyok a penicillinre.
Ő allergiás a penicillinre.
*ol-lehr-gee-ahsh vod-yok o peh-ni-tzi-lin-reh. Ur ol-lehr-gee-ahsh o peh-ni-tzi-lin-reh.*

358 **Does this hurt?**
Ez fáj?
*ehz fahy*

359 **You must go to hospital. He/she must go to hospital.**
Önnek kórházba kell mennie.
Neki kórházba kell mennie.
*Uhn-nehk kawr-hahz-bo kehll mehn-ni-eh. Neh-ki kawr-hahz-bo kehll mehn-ni-eh.*

360 **Take these once/twice/three times a day.**
Ezt naponta egyszer/kétszer/háromszor kell bevenni.
*ehzt no-pon-to edj-sehr/kayt-sehr/hah-rom-sor kehll beh-ven-ni*

361 **I am taking this medication. He is/she is taking this medication.**
Én ezt a gyógyszert szedem.
Ő ezt a gyógyszert szedi.
*ayn ehzt o djawdj-sehrt seh-dehm. Ur ehzt o djawdj-sehrt seh-dee*

362 **I have medical insurance.**
Van betegbiztosításom.
*von beh-tehg-beez-to-shee-tah-shom*

## Dentists

363 **I have toothache.**
Fáj a fogam.
*fahy o fo-gom*

364 **My filling has come out.**
Kiesett a tömés a fogamból.
*kee-eh-shehtt o toh-maysh o fo-gom-bawl*

365 **I do/do not want to have an injection first.**
Először kérek/nem kérek injekciót.
*eh-lur-suhr kay-rehk/nem kay-rehk ee-nyehk-tzee-awt*

## EMERGENCIES

366 **Help!**
Segítség!
*sheh-geet-shayg*

367 **Call an ambulance/a doctor/the police!**
Hívja azonnal a mentőket/az orvost/a rendőrséget!
*heev-jo ozon-nol o mehn-tur-keht/oz or-vosht/o rehn-dur-shay-geht*

**368** I have had my travellers' cheques (travelers' checks)/ credit cards/purse/handbag/ rucksack (knapsack)/ luggage/wallet stolen.

Ellopták a Travellers csekkjeimet/a hitelkártyáimat/a pénztárcámat/a táskámat/a hátizsákomat/a poggyászomat/ az irattárcámat.

*el-lop-tahk o travellers chehk-ye- hee-meht/o hee-tehl-kahrt-yah-ee- mot/o paynz-tahr-tzah-mot/o tahsh-kah-mot/o hah-tee-zhah-ko- mot/o podj-djah-so-mot/oz ee-rot- tahr-tzah-mot.*

**369** Can you help me, I have lost my daughter/son?

Tudna segíteni, nem találom a lányomat/fiamat?

*tood-no sheh-gee-teh-ni, nem to-lah- lom o lah-nn-y-omot/fee-o-mot*

**370** Please go away/leave me alone.

Kérem menjen innen/hagyjon békében.

*kay-rehm mehn-yehn in-nehn/ hod-jon bay-kay-behn*

**371** Fire!

Tűz van!

*teewz von*

**372** I want to contact the British/ American/Canadian/Irish/ Australian/New Zealand/ South African consulate.

Fel akarom hívni a Brit/ Amerikai/Kanadai/ír/ Ausztráliai/Új Zélandi/Dél Afrikai konzulátust.

*fehl o-korom heev-ni o brit/o-meh- ree-koi/ko-nodoi/eer/o-oost-rah- lee-o-i/ooy zay-lon-di/dayl of-ree- koi kon-zoo-lah-toosht*

# Introduction

Italian, of all the 'Romance' languages the closest to the original Latin, is spoken throughout the Italian peninsula and surrounding islands, and in the southern cantons of Switzerland. Local dialects vary greatly from standard Italian, which is to be expected in a country that consisted of a large number of small independent states for most of its history, but the pure form of the language, derived from the dialect of Tuscany, is understood and spoken everywhere. English is spoken wherever tourists congregate in numbers, but away from those areas you will have to speak Italian. However, it is not the most difficult of languages to pick up, especially because its spelling is entirely regular, with no unexpected quirks of pronunciation, and accented characters are few.

ITALIAN

## Addresses for travel and tourist information

**UK:** *Italian State Tourist Board*, 1 Princes St, London W1R 8AY; tel: (0171) 408 1254.

**USA:** *Italian Government Travel Office (ENIT)*, 630 Fifth Ave (Suite 1565), Rockefeller Center, New York, NY 10111; tel: (212) 245-4822/2324.

ITALIAN

01
↕
13

## ESSENTIALS

### Alphabet

The letters J (i lungo), K (cappa), W (vu doppia), X (ics) and Y (ipsilon) are used only to spell foreign words and names.

| | |
|---|---|
| A | B |
| *a* | *bee* |
| C | D |
| *chi* | *dee* |
| E | F |
| *eyy* | *effe* |
| G | H |
| *gee* | *acca* |
| I | L |
| *ee* | *elle* |
| M | N |
| *emme* | *enne* |
| O | P |
| *o* | *pea* |
| Q | R |
| *ku* | *erre* |
| S | T |
| *esse* | *tee* |
| U | V |
| *oo* | *voo* |
| Z | |
| *zeta* | |

### Basic Words and Phrases

¹ Yes No
Sì No
*See* *Noh*

² Please Thank you

Per favore Grazie
*Perr fahvawreh Grahtsyeh*

³ That's O.K. Perhaps
Va bene Forse
*Vah behneh Forrseh*

⁴ To From
A da
*ah dah*

⁵ Here There
Qui là
*Kwee lah*

⁶ None Also
Nessuno Anche
*Nessoonaw Ahnkeh*

⁷ How When
Come quando
*Cawme kwahndaw*

⁸ What Why
che perché
*keh perrkeh*

⁹ I don't understand.
Non capisco.
*Nawn kahpeescaw*

¹⁰ I don't speak Italian.
Non parlo italiano.
*Nawn parrlaw itahlyahnaw*

¹¹ Do you speak English?
Parla inglese?
*Parrla eenglehzeh?*

¹² Can you please write it down?
Potrebbe scriverlo, per favore?
*Pawtrebbeh screevehrrlaw, perr fahvawreh?*

¹³ Can you please speak more slowly?

Potrebbe parlare più
lentamente, per favore?
*Pawtrebbeh pahrrlahrreh pyoo
lehntahmehnteh, perr fahvawreh?*

**14 How much does it/this cost?**
Quant'è/quanto costa?
*Kwahntèh/kwahntah kawstah?*

## Days

**15 Monday**  **Tuesday**
Lunedì  Martedì
*Loonehdee*  *Marrtehdee*

**16 Wednesday**  **Thursday**
Mercoledì  Giovedì
*Merrcawlehdee*  *Jawvehdee*

**17 Friday**  **Saturday**
Venerdì  Sabato
*Venerrdee*  *Sàbahtaw*

**18 Sunday**  **Morning**
Domenica  Mattino
*Dawméhneeca*  *Mahtteenaw*

**19 Afternoon**  **Evening**
Pomeriggio  Sera
*Pawmehreedjaw*  *Sehra*

**20 Night**  **Week**
Notte  Settimana
*Notteh*  *Setteemahna*

**21 Yesterday**  **Tomorrow**
Ieri  Domani
*Yeree*  *Dawmahnee*

## Numbers

**22 Zero**  **One**
Zero  Uno
*Tsehraw*  *Oonaw*

**23 Two**  **Three**

Due  Tre
*Dweh*  *Treh*

**24 Four**  **Five**
Quattro  Cinque
*Kwahttraw*  *Cheenkweh*

**25 Six**  **Seven**
Sey  Sette
*Say*  *Setteh*

**26 Eight**  **Nine**
Otto  Nove
*Ottaw*  *Noveh*

**27 Ten**  **Eleven**
Dieci  Undici
*Dyehchee*  *Oondeechee*

**28 Twelve**  **Thirteen**
Dodici  Tredici
*Dawdeechee*  *Tréhdeechee*

**29 Fourteen**  **Fifteen**
Quattordici  Quindici
*Kwahttòrrdeechee*  *Kweendeechee*

**30 Sixteen**  **Seventeen**
Sedici  Diciassette
*Sédeechee*  *Deechassetteh*

**31 Eighteen**  **Nineteen**
Diciotto  Diciannove
*Deechottaw*  *Deechannoveh*

**32 Twenty**  **Twenty-one**
Venti  Ventuno
*Ventee*  *Ventoonaw*

**33 Twenty-two**  **Thirty**
Ventidue  Trenta
*Venteedweh*  *Trenta*

**34 Forty**  **Fifty**
Quaranta  Cinquanta
*Kwahrahnta*  *Cheenkwahnta*

ITALIAN

14
↕
34

177

**35 Sixty**
Sessanta
*Sessahnta*

**Seventy**
Settanta
*Settahnta*

**36 Eighty**
Ottanta
*Ottahnta*

**Ninety**
Novanta
*Novahnta*

**37 One hundred**
Cento
*Chentaw*

**Five hundred**
Cinquecento
*Cheenkwechentaw*

**38 One thousand**
Mille
*Meelleh*

**One million**
Un milione
*Oon meellyawneh*

## Time

**39 9.00**
Nove
*Noveh*

**40 9.05**
Nove e cinque
*Noveh eh cheenkweh*

**41 9.10**
Nove e dieci
*Noveh eh dyehchee*

**42 9.15**
Nove e quindici
*oveh eh kweendechee*

**43 9.20**
Nove e venti
*Noveh eh ventee*

**44 9.25**
Nove e venticinque
*Noveh eh venteecheenkweh*

**45 9.30**
Nove e trenta
*Noveh eh trenta*

**46 9.35**
Nove e trentacinque
*Noveh eh trentacheenkweh*

**47 9.40**
Nove e quaranta
*Noveh eh kwahranta*

**48 9.45**
Nove e quarantacinque
*Noveh eh kwahrantacheenkweh*

**49 9.50**
Nove e cinquanta
*Noveh eh cheenkwahnta*

**50 9.55**
Nove e cinquantacinque
*Noveh eh cheenkwahntacheenkweh*

**51 12.00/Midday/Midnight**
Dodici/Mezzogiorno/
mezzanotte
*Dohdychee/metsawjorrnaw/
metsanotteh*

**52 What time is it?**
Che ore sono?
*Keh awreh sawnaw?*

**53 It is . . .**
Sono le . . .
*Sawnaw leh . . .*

## ARRIVING AND DEPARTING

## Airport

**54 Excuse me, where is the
check-in desk for . . . airline?**
Mi scusi, dov'è il banco
accettazioni per la linea aerea . . ?
*Mee scoozee, dawvèh eel bahnkaw
ahchettatsyawnee perr lah
leenayah ah-aerrhayah . . ?*

55 **What is the boarding gate/ time for my flight?**
Qual'è il cancello di imbarco/ orario del mio volo?
*Kwaalèh eel kahnchehlaw dee ihmbahrcaw/awrahreeaw deel meeoh vawloh?*

56 **How long is the delay likely to be?**
Qual'è il ritardo previsto?
*Kwaalhè eel rreehtahrdaw prehveestaw?*

57 **Where is the duty-free shop?**
Dov'è il duty-free?
*Dawvèh eel duty-free?*

58 **Which way is the baggage reclaim?**
Dove si trova il recupero bagagli?
*Dawveh see trawvah eel rehkupehrraw bahgahlyee?*

59 **Where can I get the bus to the city centre?**
Dove posso prendere l'autobus per il centro?
*Dawveh pawssaw prendereh lahutobhuss perr eel chentraw?*

## Train Station

60 **Where is the ticket office/ information desk?**
Dov'è la biglietteria/l'ufficio informazioni?
*Dawvèh lah beelyetteryha/ looffeechaw eenformahtseeawnee?*

61 **Which platform does the train to . . . depart from?**
Da quale marciapiede parte il treno per . . ?

*Dah kwahleh marchyahpyedeh parteh eel trehnaw perr . . ?*

62 **Where is platform . . ?**
Dov'è il marciapiede . . ?
*Dawvèh eel marchyahpyedeh . . ?*

63 **When is the next train to . . ?**
A che ora arriva il prossimo treno per . . ?
*Ah keh awrah arreevah eel prosseemaw trehnaw perr . . ?*

64 **Is there a later train to . . ?**
C'è un altro treno per . . ?
*Chèh oon ahltraw trehnaw perr . . ?*

## Port

65 **How do I get to the port?**
Come arrivo al porto?
*Cawmeh arrevaw ahl pawrrtaw?*

66 **When is the next sailing to . . ?**
Quand'è la prossma partenza per . . ?
*Kwandèh lah prawssema parrtentsa perr . . ?*

67 **Can I catch an earlier ferry with this ticket?**
Posso prendere un traghetto che parta prima con questo biglietto?
*Pawssaw prendereh oon trahgettaw keh pahrrtah preemah kawn kwestaw beelyettaw?*

## Notices and Signs

68 **Carrozza rinfreschi**
*Carrotsa reenfreskee*
Buffet (Dining) Car

I
T
A
L
I
A
N

55
↑
68

179

**ITALIAN**

**69
↕
91**

69 **Autobus**
*Ahootawboos*
Bus

70 **Acqua potabile/non potabile**
*Aqua pawtahbeeleh/non pawtahbeeleh*
Drinking/Non-drinking water

71 **Entrata**
*Entrahta*
Entrance

72 **Uscita**
*Oosheeta*
Exit

73 **Informazioni**
*Eenformahtsyawnee*
Information

74 **Bagaglio depositato**
*Bahgalyaw depawseetahtaw*
Left Luggage (Baggage Claim)

75 **Armadietti per bagagli**
*Armahdyettee perr baghgalee*
Luggage Lockers

76 **Ufficio postale**
*Ooffeechaw pawstahleh*
Post Office

77 **Marciapiede**
*Marchyahpyedeh*
Platform

78 **Stazione ferroviaria**
*Stahtsyawneh ferrawvyarya*
Railway (Railroad) Station

79 **Aeroporto**
*Ahaerrhawpawrrtaw*
Airport

80 **Porto**
*Pawrrtaw*
Port

81 **Ristorante**
*Reestawrahnteh*
Restaurant

82 **Per fumatori/non fumatori**
*Perr foomahtawree/non foomahtawree*
Smoking/Non-Smoking

83 **Telefono**
*Telèfawnaw*
Telephone

84 **Biglietteria**
*Beelyetterya*
Ticket Office

85 **Banco accettazioni**
*Bahnkaw ahchettahtsyawnee*
Check-in Desk

86 **Orario**
*Awraryaw*
Timetable (Schedule)

87 **Tolette**
*Tawletteh*
Toilets (Restrooms)

88 **Signori**
*Seenyawree*
Gentlemen

89 **Signore**
*Seenyawreh*
Ladies'

90 **Tram**
*Trahm*
Tram (Streetcar)

91 **Metropolitana**
*Metrawpawleetahna*
Underground (Subway)

**92 Sala d'attesa**
*Sahla dahttehsa*
Waiting Room

## Buying a Ticket

**93 I would like a first-class/
second-class single (one-
way)/return (round-trip)
ticket to . . .**
Vorrei un biglietto di sola
andata/andata e ritorno di
prima classe/di seconda classe
per . . .
*Vawrray oon beelyettaw dee
sawlah ahndahta/ahndahta eh
reetawrnaw dee preema classeh/
dee seconda classeh perr . . .*

**94 Is my rail pass valid on this
train/ferry/bus?**
Il mio abbonamento è valido su
questo treno/traghetto/
autobus?
*Eel meeoh abhawnahmentaw èh
vahleedhaw soo kwestaw
trehnaw/trahgehtaw/
ahootawboos?*

**95 I would like an
aisle/window seat.**
Vorrei un posto vicino al
corridoio/al finestrino.
*Vawrray oon pawstaw
veecheenaw ahl correedoyaw/ahl
feenestreenaw.*

**96 No smoking/smoking,
please.**
Per favore nello
scompartimento per fumatori/
non fumatori.

*Perr fahvawreh nehllo
scomparteementaw peer
foomahtawree /non foomahtawree.*

**97 We would like to sit
together.**
Vorremmo sedere accanto.
*Vawrremmaw sehdehreh
ahckahntaw.*

**98 I would like to make a seat
reservation.**
Vorrei prenotare un posto.
*Vawrray prehnawtahrreh oon
pawstaw.*

**99 I would like to reserve a
couchette/sleeper for one
person/two people/for my
family.**
Vorrei prenotare una cuccetta/
una cabina per una persona/due
persone/per la mia famiglia.
*Vawrray prehnawtareh oona
coocchetta/oona cahbeena perr
oona perrsawna/dweh
perrsawneh/perr lah myah
fahmeelya.*

**100 I would like to reserve a
cabin.**
Vorrei prenotare una cabina.
*Vawrray prehnawtahrreh oonah
kahbeenah.*

## Timetables (Schedules)

**101 Arrivare**
*Arreevahreh*
Arrive

**102 Ferma a**
*Ferma ah*
Calls (Stops) at

I
T
A
L
I
A
N

92
↑
102

**ITALIAN**

**103 Servizio d'approvvigionamento**
*Serveetsyaw dahpprawvveejawnahmentaw*
Catering Service

**104 Cambiare a**
*Cahmbyareh ah*
Change at

**105 Coincidenza**
*Coincheedentsa*
Connection

**106 Giornaliero**
*Jawrnahlyeraw*
Daily

**107 Ogni quaranta minuti**
*Awnee kwahrahnta meenootee*
Every 40 Minutes

**108 Prima classe**
*Preema classeh*
First Class

**109 Ogni ora**
*Awnee awra*
Hourly

**110 Si raccomanda la prenotazione dei posti**
*See rahcawmahnda la prehnawtatsyawneh day pawstee*
Seat reservations are recommended

**111 Seconda classe**
*Secawnda classeh*
Second Class

**112 Supplemento esigibile**
*Soopplehmentaw eseejeebeeleh*
Supplement Payable

**113 Via**
*Veeha*
Via

## Luggage

**114 How much will it cost to send (ship) my luggage in advance?**
Quanto costa la spedizione anticipata del mio bagaglio?
*Kwahntaw cawstah la spehdeetsyawneh ahnteecheepahta del myaw bahgalyaw?*

**115 Where is the left luggage (baggage claim) office?**
Dov'è il deposito bagagli?
*Dawvèh eel dehpawseetaw bahgahlee?*

**116 What time do you open/close?**
A che ora aprite/chiudete?
*Ah keh awra ahpreeteh/kewdehteh?*

**117 Where are the luggage trolleys (carts)?**
Dove sono i carrelli portabagagli?
*Dawveh sawnaw ee carrellee porrtahbahgalee?*

**118 Where are the lockers?**
Dove sono gli armadietti?
*Dawveh sawnaw lyee ahrmahdyettee?*

**119 I have lost my locker key.**
Ho perso la chiave del mio armadietto.
*Aw perrsaw lah kyahveh del myaw armahdyettaw.*

## On Board

**120 Is this seat taken?**
È libero questo posto?
*Èh leebehraw kwestaw pawstaw?*

**121 Excuse me, you are sitting in my reserved seat.**
Scusi, Lei siede nel mio posto riservato.
*Scoozee, Lay syedeh nel myaw pawstaw reeservahtaw.*

**122 Which station is this?**
Che stazione è?
*Keh stahtsyawneh èh?*

**123 What time is this train/bus/ ferry/flight due to arrive/ depart?**
A che ora è previsto l'arrivo/ partenza di questo treno/ autobus/volo?
*Ah keh awrah èh prehveestaw lahrreevaw/pahrrtehntsah dee kwestaw trehnaw/ ahootawboos/ vawlaw?*

**124 Will you wake me just before we arrive?**
Mi sveglia poco prima dell'arrivo?
*Mee svelyah pawcaw preema dellarreevaw?*

## Customs and Passports

**125 Passaporti per favore!**
*Passaporrtee perr fahvawreh!*
Passports, please!

**126 I have nothing/wine/spirits (alcohol)/tobacco to declare.**
Non ho nulla da dichiarare/ho vino/alcolici/tabacco da dichiarare.
*Non aw noollah dah deekyarareh/ aw veenaw/ahlcoleechee/ tahbahckaw dah deekyarareh.*

**127 I shall be staying for . . . days/weeks/months.**
Mi tratterrò per . . . giorni/ settimane/mesi.
*Mee trahtterraw perr . . . jawrnee/ setteemahneh/mehzee.*

## AT THE TOURIST OFFICE

**128 Do you have a map of the town/area?**
Ha una mappa della città/della zona?
*Ah oona mahppa della cheettàh/ della zawna?*

**129 Can I reserve accommodation here?**
Posso prenotare qui l'alloggio?
*Pawssaw prenotahre kwee lallodjaw?*

**130 Do you have a list of accommodation?**
Ha un elenco di alloggi?
*Ah oon ehlehnkaw dee ahlawdjee?*

## ACCOMMODATION

## Hotels

**131 I have a reservation in the name of . . .**
Ho una prenotazione per . . .
*Aw oona prehnawtahtsyawneh perr . . .*

ITALIAN

120 ↕ 131

# ACCOMMODATION

132 I wrote to/faxed/telephoned you last month/last week in . . .
Vi ho scritto/inviato un fax/ telefonato il mese scorso/la settimana scorsa a . . .
*Vee haw skreehtaw/eenveeahtaw oon fax/tehlehfonahtaw eel mehseh skawrsaw/lah sehteemahnah skawrsah ah . . .*

133 Do you have any rooms free?
Avete camere libere?
*Ahvehteh kahmehreh leebehreh?*

134 I would like to reserve a single/double room with/ without bath/shower.
Vorrei prenotare una camera singola/matrimoniale con/senza bagno/doccia.
*Vawrray prehnawtahreh oona cahmehra seengawlah/ mahtreemawnyahleh con/sentsa bahnyaw/ occha*

135 I would like bed and breakfast/(room and) half board/(room and) full board.
Vorrei una camera con colazione/con mezza pensione/ pensione completa.
*Vawrray oona cahmehra con cawlahtsyawneh/con metsa pensyawneh/pensyawneh complehta.*

136 How much is it per night?
Quant'è per notte?
*Kwahntèh perr notteh?*

137 Is breakfast included?
È compresa la colazione?
*Èh comprehsa lah cawlatsyawneh?*

138 May I see the room?
Posso vedere la camera?
*Pawssaw vehdehreh lah cahmehra?*

139 Do you have any cheaper rooms?
Ha delle camere più economiche?
*Ah delleh cahmehreh pyoo ehcawnohmikeh?*

140 I would like to take the room
Vorrei la camera.
*Vawrray lah cahmehra.*

141 I would like to stay for . . . nights.
Vorrei alloggiare per . . . notti.
*Vawrray allawdjahreh perr . . . nottee.*

142 The shower/light/tap doesn't work.
La doccia/luce/rubinetto non funziona.
*Lah dawcheeah/loocheh/ roobeenehttaw nawn foontsyawnah.*

143 At what time/where is breakfast served?
A che ora/dove viene servita la colazione?
*Ah keh awra/dawveh vyeneh serrveeta lah cawlahtsyawneh?*

144 What time do I have to check-out?
A che ora devo lasciare libera la camera?
*Ah keh awra dehvaw lahshareh leebehra lah cahmehra?*

145 Can I have the key to room no . . ?
Posso avere la chiave della camera numero . . ?

*Payssaw ahvehreh lah keeyahveh dehlah noohmehraw . . ?*

**146** My room number is . . .
La mia camera ha il numero . . .
*Lah myah cahmehra ah eel noomehraw . . .*

**147** Do you accept travellers' cheques/Eurocheques/credit cards?
Accettate assegni turistici/euroassegni/carte di credito?
*Achetahteh asehnyee tooreesteechee/ehooraw-ahsehnyee/kahrrteh dee krehdeehtaw?*

**148** May I have the bill please?
Mi dà il conto per favore?
*Mee dah eel cawntaw perr fahvawreh?*

**149** Excuse me, I think there is a mistake in this bill.
Mi scusi, credo ci sia un errore nel conto.
*Mee scozee, kredaw chee syah oon errawreh nel cawntaw.*

## Youth Hostels

**150** How much is a dormitory bed per night?
Quant'è un letto in dormitorio per notte?
*Kwahntèh oon lettaw een dormeetawryaw perr notteh?*

**151** I am/am not an HI member.
Sono/non sono membro dell'Associazione Internazionale Ostelli della Gioventù.
*Sawnaw/non sawnaw membraw dell Assawchahtsyawne*

*Eenterrnahtsyawnahleh ostelee della Jovehntoo.*

**152** May I use my own sleeping bag?
Posso usare il mio sacco a pelo?
*Pawssaw oozahreh eel myaw saccaw ah pehlaw?*

**153** What time do you lock the doors at night?
A che ora chiudete le porta la notte?
*Ah keh awra kewdehte leh porrteh lah notteh?*

## Camping

**154** May I camp here for the night/two nights?
Posso accamparmi qui per la notte/due notti?
*Pawssaw accahmparmee kwee perr lah notteh/dweh nottee?*

**155** Where can I pitch my tent?
Dove posso piantare la tenda?
*Dawveh pawssaw pyahntareh lah tenda?*

**156** How much does it cost for one night/week?
Qual'è la tariffa per una notte/una settimana?
*Kwalèh lah tahreeffa perr oona notteh/oona setteemahna?*

**157** Where can we park our caravan?
Dove possiamo parcheggiare la roulotte?
*Dawveh pawseeyahmaw pahrkehdjyahreh lah roolhawt?*

ITALIAN

146
↕
157

I
T
A
L
I
A
N

**158**
↑
**168**

**158** Where are the washing facilities?
Dove sono le lavanderie?
*Dawveh sawnaw leh lavahndehryeh?*

**159** Is there a restaurant/supermarket/swimming pool on site/nearby?
C'è un ristorante/un supermercato/una piscina al campeggio/nelle vicinanze?
*Chèh oon reestawrahnteh/oon sooperrmerrcahtaw/oona peesheena ahl cahmpedjaw/nelleh veecheenahntseh?*

**160** Do you have a safety deposit box?
Ha una cassaforte?
*Ah oona cassahforrteh?*

## EATING AND DRINKING

### Cafés and Bars

**161** I would like a cup of/two cups of/another coffee/tea.
Vorrei una tazza di/due tazze di/un altro caffè/tè.
*Vawrray oona tatsa dee/dweh tatseh dee/oon ahltraw caffèh/teh.*

**162** With/without milk/sugar.
Con/senza latte/zucchero.
*Con/sentsa latteh/tsoockehraw.*

**163** I would like a bottle/glass/two glasses of mineral water/red wine/white wine, please.
Per cortesia, vorrei una bottiglia/un bicchiere/due bicchieri d'acqua minerale/vino rosso/vino bianco.

*Peer corrtehzya, vawrray oona botteelya/oon beeckyereh/dweh beeckyeree daqua meenehrahleh/veenaw rawssaw/veenaw byahncaw.*

**164** I would like a beer/two beers, please.
Per cortesia, vorrei una birra, due birre.
*Perr corrteshzya, vawrray oona beerra, dweh beerreh.*

**165** May I have some ice?
Può darmi del ghiaccio?
*Poohòh darrmee del ghyacchaw?*

**166** Do you have any matches/cigarettes/cigars?
Vendete fiammiferi, sigarette/sigari?
*Vendehteh fyammeefehree, seegahretteh, séegaree?*

### Restaurants

**167** Can you recommend a good/inexpensive restaurant in this area?
Può raccomandarmi un buon ristorante/un ristorante economico in questa zona?
*Poohòh raccomahndarmee oon boohòn reestawrahnteh/oon reestawrahnteh ehcawnawmeecaw een kwesta zawna?*

**168** I would like a table for . . . people.
Vorrei un tavolo per . . . persone.
*Vawrray oon tahvawlaw perr . . . perrsawneh.*

**169** Do you have a non-smoking area?
Avete un'area non fumatori?
*Ahvehteh oonahrreyah nawn foomahttawree?*

**170** Waiter/Waitress!
Cameriere/cameriera!
*Cahmehryerel/cahmehryera!*

**171** Do you have a set menu/children's menu/wine list?
Ha un menù fisso/un menù per bambini/una lista dei vini?
*Ah oon mehnoo feessaw/oon mehnoo perr bambeenee/oona leesta day veenee?*

**172** Do you have any vegetarian dishes, please?
Per favore, ha dei piatti vegetariani?
*Perr fahvawreh, ah day pyattee vehgehtahryanee?*

**173** Are there any local specialities?
Avete qualche specialità locale?
*Ahvehteh kwalkeh spehchiahleehtah lawkahleh?*

**174** Are vegetables included?
Sono incluse anche le verdure?
*Sawnaw eenclooseh ahnkeh leh vehrdooreh?*

**175** Could I have it well-cooked/medium/rare please?
Potrei averlo ben cotto/mediamente cotto/poco cotto, per favore?
*Pawtray ahvehrlaw behn cawtaw/mehdeeyahmehnteh cawtaw/*

*pawcaw cawtaw perr fahvawreh?*

**176** What does this dish consist of?
Quali sono gli ingredienti di questo piatto?
*Kwahlee sawnaw lee eengrehdyehntee dee kwestaw pyattaw?*

**177** I would like the set menu, please.
Vorrei il menù fisso.
*Vawrray eel mehnoo feessaw.*

**178** We have not been served yet.
Non ci hanno ancora serviti.
*Non chee annaw ahncawra serrveetee.*

**179** Excuse me, this is not what I ordered.
Mi scusi, questo non è quello che ho ordinato.
*Mee scozee, kwehstaw nawn eh kwellaw keh haw awrdeenahtaw.*

**180** May I have some/some more bread/water/coffee/tea?
Può darmi del/dell'altro pane/caffè/tè?
*Puoh darrmee del/dellahltraw pahneh/caffèh/tèh?*

**181** May I have the bill, please?
Mi dà il conto, per favore?
*Mee dah eel cawntaw, perr fahvawreh?*

**182** Does this bill include service?
Il conto include il servizio?
*Eel cawntaw eencloodeh eel serrveetsyaw?*

<sup>183</sup> **Do you accept travellers' cheques (travelers' checks)/Eurocheques/MasterCard/US dollars?**
Accettate assegni turistici/euroassegni/MasterCard/dollari USA?
*Acchettahte assenee tooreesteechee/ehoorawassenee/MasterCard/dollahree OO EZ AY?*

<sup>184</sup> **Can I have a receipt, please?**
Potrei avere la ricetta, per favore?
*Pawtray ahvehreh lah reechettah, perr fahvawreh?*

<sup>185</sup> **Where is the toilet (restroom), please?**
Dov'è la toletta, per cortesia?
*Dawvèh lah tawletta, perr corrtehzya?*

## On the Menu

<sup>186</sup> **First courses**
Primi piatti
*Preemee pyattee*

<sup>187</sup> **Soups**
Zuppe
*Zooppeh*

<sup>188</sup> **Main courses**
Piatti principali
*Pyattee preencheepahlee*

<sup>189</sup> **Fish dishes**
Piatti di pesce
*Pyattee dee pesheh*

<sup>190</sup> **Meat dishes**
Piatti di carne
*Pyattee dee kahrneh*

<sup>191</sup> **Vegetarian dishes**
Piatti vegetariani
*Pyattee vehjehtaryanee*

<sup>192</sup> **Cheese**
Formaggio
*Fawrmahdyiaw*

<sup>193</sup> **Desserts**
Dessert
*Dehssehrt*

<sup>194</sup> **Specialities**
Specialità
*Spehcheeyahleehtàh*

## GETTING AROUND

### Public Transport

<sup>195</sup> **Where is the bus stop/coach station/nearest metro (subway) station?**
Dov'è la fermata degli autobus/la stazione delle corriere/la più vicina stazione della metropolitana?
*Dawvèh lah ferrmahta delee ahootawboos/lah stahtsyawneh delleh corryereh/lah pyoo veecheena stahtsyawneh della metropawleetahna?*

<sup>196</sup> **When is the next/last bus to . . ?**
A che ora è il prossimo/l'ultimo autobus per . . ?
*Ah keh awra èh eel prawssemaw/loolteemaw ahootawboos perr . . ?*

<sup>197</sup> **How much is the fare to the city centre (downtown)/railway (railroad) station/airport?**

Qual'è la tariffa per il centro
città/la stazione ferroviaria/
l'aeroporto?
*Kwahlèh lah tahreeffa perr eel
chentraw cheettàh/lah
stahtsyawne ferrawvyarya/
l'aheraoporrtaw?*

## 198 Will you tell me when to get off?
Può dirmi quando devo
scendere?
*Poohòh deerrmee kwahndaw
dehvaw shendehreh?*

## 199 Does this bus go to . . ?
Quest'autobus va a . . ?
*Kwest ahootawboos vah ah . . ?*

## 200 Which number bus goes to . . ?
Qual'è il numero dell'autobus
per . . ?
*Kwahlèh eel noomehraw dell
ahootawboos perr . . ?*

## 201 May I have a single (one-way)/return (round-trip)/day ticket/book of tickets?
Vorrei un biglietto di sola
andata/di andata e ritorno
valido per un giorno/un
blocchetto di biglietti.
*Vawrray oon beelyettaw dee sawla
ahndahta/dee ahndahta eh
reetorrnaw vahleedaw perr oon
jawrrnaw/oon blawckettaw dee
beelyettee.*

## Taxis

## 202 I would like to go to . . . How much will it cost?
Vorrei andare a . . . , quant'è?

*Vawrray ahnahre ah . . .
kwahntèh?*

## 203 Please stop here.
Fermi qui, per cortesia.
*Ferrmee koohee perr corrtehzya.*

## 204 I would like to order a taxi today/tomorrow/at 2pm to go from . . . to . . .
Vorrei prenotare un tassì per
oggi/per domani/per le
quattordici che mi porti
da . . . a . . .
*Vawrray prehnawtahreh oon
tassee perr odjee/perrdawmahnee/
perr leh kwahttorrdeechee keh mee
porrtee
dah . . . ah . . .*

## Asking the Way

## 205 Excuse me, do you speak English?
Mi scusi, parla inglese?
*Mee scoozee, parrla eenglehzeh?*

## 206 Excuse me, is this the right way to . . ?
Mi scusi, è questa la strada per . .
*Mee scoozee, eh kwehstah lah
strahda perr . . ?*

## 207 . . . the cathedral/the tourist information office/the castle/the old town.
. . . la cattedrale/l'ufficio
informazioni turistiche/il
castello/la città vecchia.
*. . . lah kahttehdrahleh/
looffeechaw eenforrmahtsyawnee
tooreesteekeh/eel kahstehllaw/lah
cheettàh vehkyah.*

I
T
A
L
I
A
N

208
↑
218

**208** Can you tell me the way to the railway (railroad) station/bus station/taxi rank (stand)/city centre (downtown)/beach?
Sa indicarmmi la strada per andare alla stazione ferroviaria/alla stazione degli autobus/al posteggio di auto pubbliche/al centro città/alla spiaggia?
*Sah eendeecarrmee lah strahda perr ahndare ahlla stahtsyaweneh ferrawvyarya/ahlla stahtsyaweneh delee ahootawboos/ahl pawstedjaw dee ahootaw poobbleekeh/ahl chentraw cheettàh/ahlla spyadjya?*

**209** First/second left/right/straight ahead.
Prenda la prossima/la seconda a sinistra/a destra/Vada sempre diritto.
*Prehnda lah prawsseema/lah secawnda ah seeneestra/ah destra/vahda sempreh deereettaw.*

**210** Where is the nearest police station/post office?
Dov'è la più vicino posto di polizia/ufficcio postale?
*Dawvèh eel pyoo veecheenaw pawstaw dee pawleetsya/ooffechaw pawstahle?*

**211** Is it far?
È lontano
*Èh lawntahnaw?*

**212** Do I need to take a taxi/catch a bus?
Devo prendere un tassì/l'autobus?
*Dehvaw prendehreh oon tassee/lahootawboos?*

**213** Can you point to it on my map?
Può indicarmelo sulla mappa?
*Poohòh eendeecarrmehlaw soolla mappa?*

**214** Thank you for your help.
Grazie dell'aiuto.
*Grahtsyeh dell ahyootaw.*

## SIGHTSEEING

**215** Where is the Tourist Information office?
Dov'è l'Ufficio informazioni turistiche?
*Dawvèh l'ooffeechaw eenforrmahtsyawnee tooreesteekeh?*

**216** Where is the cathedral/church/museum?
Dov'è la cattedrale/la chiesa/il museo?
*Dawvèh lah cattehdrahleh/lah kyehza/eel moozehaw?*

**217** How much is the entrance (admission) charge?
Qual'è la tariffa d'ingresso?
*Kwahlèh lah tahreeffa deengressaw?*

**218** Is there a reduction for children/students/senior citizens?
I bambini/gli studenti/i pensionati hanno diritto a una riduzione?
*Ee bahmbeenee/lee stoodentee/ee pensyawnahtee annaw deereettaw ah oona reedootsyawneh?*

**219** **What time does the next guided tour start?**
A che ora ha inizio la prossima visita guidata?
*Ah keh awra ah eeneetsyaw lah prosseemah veeseeta goohedahta?*

**220** **One/two adults/children, please.**
Un adulto/due adulti/due bambini, per favore
*Oon ahdooltaw/dweh ahdooltee/dweh bahmbeenee, perr fahvawreh*

**221** **May I take photographs here?**
Posso fare fotografie qui?
*Payssaw fahreh fotografyeh kwee?*

## ENTERTAINMENT

**222** **Can you recommend a good bar/nightclub?**
Può raccomandarmi un buon bar/locale notturno?
*Poohòh rahccawmahdarrmee oon bwòn barr/lawcahleh nawttoorrnaw?*

**223** **Do you know what is on at the cinema (playing at the movies)/theatre at the moment?**
Conosce il programma del cinema/teatro?
*Cawnawsheh eel prawgramma del ceenema/tehatraw?*

**224** **I would like to book (purchase) . . . tickets for the matinee/evening performance on Monday.**
Vorrei prenotare . . . posti per la matinée/lo spettacolo serale di lunedì.
*Vawrray prehnawtahre . . . pawstee perr lah mateenéh/law spettahcawlaw sehrahleh dee loonehdee.*

**225** **What time does the film/performance start?**
A che ora incomincia il film/lo spettacolo?
*Ah keh awra eencawmeencha eel film/law spettahcawlaw?*

## MEETING PEOPLE

**226** **Hello/Goodbye.**
Salve/arrivederci
*Sahlveh/arreevehderrchee*

**227** **Good morning/good afternoon/good evening/goodnight.**
Buon giorno/buon pomeriggio/buona sera/buona notte.
*Booawn geeyawrnaw/booawn pawmehreehdjaw/booawnah sehrah/booawnah nawtteh.*

**228** **Pleased to meet you.**
Piacere
*Pyahchehreh*

**229** **How are you?**
Come sta?
*Cawmeh stah?*

**230** **Fine, thank you. And you?**
Bene, grazie. E lei?
*Behneh grahtsyeh. Eh ley?*

**231** **My name is . . .**
Mi chiamo . . .
*Mee kyahmaw . . .*

I
T
A
L
I
A
N

219
↑
231

**ITALIAN**

232 **This is my friend/
boyfriend/girlfriend/
husband/wife/brother/
sister.**
Le presento il mio amico/il mio
ragazzo/la mia ragazza/mio
marito/mia moglie/mio fratello/
mia sorella.
*Leh prehsentaw eel myaw
ahmeecaw/eel myaw rahgatsaw/
lah myah rahgatsa/myaw
mahreetaw/myah mawlyeh/
myaw frahtèllaw/myah sawrella.*

233 **Where are you travelling to?**
Dov'è diretto?
*Dawvèh deerettaw?*

234 **I am/we are going to . . .**
Vado/andiamo a . . .
*Vahdaw/ahndyahmaw ah . . .*

235 **How long are you travelling
for?**
Per quanto tempo sarà in
viaggio?
*Perr kwahntaw tempaw sahràh
een veehadjaw?*

236 **Where do you come from?**
Da dove viene?
*Dah dawveh vyehneh?*

237 **I am/we are from . . .**
Vengo/veniamo da . . .
*Vehngaw/vehnyahmaw dah . . .*

238 **We're on holiday.**
Siamo in vacanza.
*Seeyahmaw een vahkahntsah.*

239 **This is our first visit here.**
Questa è la nostra prima visita
qui.

*Kwehstah eh lah nawstrah
preemah veeseetah kwee.*

240 **Would you like/May I have a
cigarette?**
Vuole una sigaretta?/Potrebbe
darmi una sigaretta?
*Voohòleh oona seegahretta?/
Pawtrebbeh darrmee oona
seegahretta?*

241 **I am sorry but I do not
understand.**
Mi scusi, non capisco.
*Mee scoozee, non cahpeescaw.*

242 **Please speak slowly.**
La prego di parlare lentamente.
*Lah prehgaw dee parrlahreh
lentahmenteh.*

243 **Do you mind if I smoke?**
Le spiace se fumo?
*Leh speehacheh seh foomaw?*

244 **Do you have a light?**
Mi fa accendere?
*Me fah acchendereh?*

245 **I am waiting for my
husband/wife/boyfriend/
girlfriend.**
Sto aspettando mio marito/
moglie/fidanzato/fidanzata.
*Staw ahspehtahndaw meeaw
mahreetaw/mawlyeh/
feedahntsahtaw/feedahntsahtah.*

## TRAVELLING WITH CHILDREN

246 **Do you have a high chair/
baby-sitting service/cot?**
Ha un seggiolone/dei baby-
sitter/un lettino?

192

*Ah oon sedjawlawneh/day baby-sitter/oon letteenaw?*

²⁴⁷ **Where is the nursery/playroom?**
Dov'è la camera dei bambini/la stanza dei giochi?
*Dawvèh lah cahmera day bahmbeenee/las stantsa day jawkee?*

²⁴⁸ **Where can I warm the baby's bottle?**
Dove posso riscaldare il biberon?
*Dawveh pawssaw reescahldareh eel beebehròn?*

## COMMUNICATIONS

### Post

²⁴⁹ **How much will it cost to send a letter/postcard/this package to Britain/Ireland/America/Canada/Australia/New Zealand?**
Qual'è la tariffa per l'invio di una lettera/cartolina postale/di questo pacco in Gran Bretagna/Irlanda/America/Canada/Australia/Nuova Zelanda?
*Kwahlèh lah tahreeffa perr l'eenvyaw dee oona lettehra/carrtawleena pawstahle/dee kwehstaw pahccaw een Grahn Brehtanya/Eerrlahnda/Ahmehreeca/Cahnada/Ahoostrahlia/Noohawva Tsehlahnda?*

²⁵⁰ **I would like one stamp/two stamps.**

Vorrei un francobollo/due francobolli.
*Vawrray oon frahncawbawllaw/dweh francawbawllee.*

²⁵¹ **I'd like . . . stamps for postcards to send abroad, please.**
Vorrei . . . dei francobolli per delle cartoline da inviare all'estero, per favore.
*Vawrray . . . dey frahnkawbawlee perr dehleh kahrtawleeneh dah eenveeyahreh ahlehstehraw, perr fahvawreh.*

### Phones

²⁵² **I would like to make a telephone call/reverse the charges to (make a collect call to) . . .**
Vorrei fare una telefonata/a carico del destinatario a . . .
*(Vawrray fahreh oona telefawnahta/ah càhreecaw del desteenahtahryaw ah . . .*

²⁵³ **Which coins do I need for the telephone?**
Che monete devo usare con quest'apparecchio?
*Keh mawnehteh dehvaw oozahreh con kwestaw apparèckyaw?*

²⁵⁴ **The line is engaged (busy).**
La linea è occupata.
*Lah leeneha èh occoopahta.*

²⁵⁵ **The number is . . .**
Il numero è . . .
*Eel noomehraw èh . . .*

[256] Hello, this is . . .
Pronto, sono . . .
*Prawntaw, sawnaw . . .*

[257] May I speak to . . ?
Potrei parlare con . . . ?
*Pawtray pahrlahreh kon . . ?*

[258] He/She is not in at the
moment. Can you call back?
Ora non c'è. Può richiamare?
*Awrrah nawn cheh. Poohòh
reekyahmahreh?*

## MONEY

[259] I would like to change these
travellers' che ues (travelers'
checks)/this currency/this
Eurocheque.
Vorrei cambiare questi assegni
turistici/questa valuta/questo
euroassegno.
*Vawrray cahmbyahreh kwestee
assenee tooreesteechee/kwesta
vahloota/kwestaw
ehoorawassenyaw.*

[260] How much commission do
you charge (What is the
service charge)?
Qual'è la vostraprovvigione?
*Kwalèh lah vostra
prawvveejawneh?*

[261] Can I obtain money with my
MasterCard?
Posso incassare contanti con il
Mastercard?
*Pawssaw eencassahreh
cawntahntee con eel Mastercard?*

## SHOPPING

## Names of Shops and
Departments

[262] Libreria/Cartoleria
*Leebrehreeyah/Kahrtawlehreeyah*
Bookshop/Stationery

[263] Gioielleria/Articoli da regalo
*Djaweeyehlehreeyah/Ahrteekawlee
dah rehgahlaw*
Jeweller's/Gifts

[264] Scarpe
*Skahrpeh*
Shoes

[265] Ferramenta
*Fehrrahmehntah*
Hardware

[266] Antiquario
*Ahnteehkwahryaw*
Antiques

[267] Parrucchiere (per uomini)/
(per donne)
*Pahrrookyehreh (perr ooawmeenee)
(perr dawneh)*
Hairdressers (men's)/(women's)

[268] Tabaccaio
*Tahbahkaiyaw*
Tobacconist

[269] Panificio
*Pahneefeechyaw*
Baker's

[270] Supermercato
*Soopehrmehrkahtaw*
Supermarket

**271 Fotografo**
*Fotografaw*
Photoshop

**272 Giocattoli**
*Djawkahttawlee*
Toys

**273 Agenzia di viaggi**
*Ahjehntsyah dee veeyahdjee*
Travel Agent

**274 Articoli da toletta**
*Ahrteekawlee dah tawlettah*
Toiletries

**275 Dischi**
*Deeskee*
Records

## In the Shop

**276 What time do the shops open/close?**
A che ora aprono/chiudono i negozi?
*Ah keh awra àhprawnaw/ kewdawnaw ee nehgotsee?*

**277 Where is the nearest market?**
Dov'è il mercato più vicino?
*Dawvèh eel mehrkahtaw pyoo veecheehnaw?*

**278 Can you show me the one in the window/this one?**
Può mostrarmi quello in vetrina/questo?
*Poohòh mawstrahrmee kwehllaw een vehtreenah/kwehstaw?*

**279 Can I try this on?**
Posso provarlo?
*Pawssaw prawvarrlaw?*

**280 What size is this?**
Di che misura è?
*Dee keh meezoora eh?*

**281 This is too large/too small/ too expensive.**
Questo è troppo grande/troppo piccolo/troppo caro.
*Kwestaw eh trawpaw grahndeh/ trawpaw peekawlaw/trawpaw kahraw.*

**282 Do you have any others?**
Ne avete degli altri?
*Neh ahvehteh delyee ahltree?*

**283 My size is . . .**
La mia taglia è . . .
*Lah meeyah tahlyah eh . . .*

**284 Where is the changing room/ childrens/cosmetic/ ladieswear/menswear/food department?**
Dov'è lo spogliatoio/il reparto bambini/cosmetici/ abbigliamento femminile/ abbigliamento maschile/ alimentari?
*Dawvèh law spawlyahtoyaw/eel rehparrtaw bahmbeenee/ cosmeteechee abbeelyahmentaw femmeeneeleh/ abbeelyahmentaw maskeeleh/ahleemehntahree?*

**285 I would like . . .**
Vorrei . . .
*Vawrray . . .*

**286** I would like a quarter of a kilo/half a kilo/a kilo of bread/butter/cheese/ham/tomatoes.

Vorrei due etti e mezzo/mezzo chilo/un chilo di pane/burro/formaggio/prosciutto/pomodori.

*Vawrray dweh ehttee eh metsaw/metsaw keelaw/oon keelaw dee pahneh/boorraw/formmahdjaw/prawshoottaw/pawmawodoree.*

**287** How much is this?

Quant'è?

*Kuahntèh?*

**288** I'll take this one, thank you.

Prenderò questo, grazie.

*Prehndehròh kwestaw, grahtsyeh.*

**289** Do you have a carrier (shopping) bag?

Ha un sacchetto di plastica?

*Ah oon sahckettaw dee plahsteeca?*

**290** Do you have anything cheaper/larger/smaller/of better quality?

Ha un articolo meno caro/più grande/più piccolo/di migliore qualità?

*Ah oon arrteecawlaw mehnaw cahraw/pyoo grahndeh/pyoo peeckawlaw/dee meelyaworeh kwahleetàh?*

**291** I would like a film for this camera.

Vorrei una pellicola per questa macchina fotografica.

*Vawrray oona pelleecawla perr kwesta màckeena fawtawgràhfeeca.*

**292** I would like some batteries, the same size as this old one.

Vorrei delle pile della stessa grandezza di quella vecchia.

*Vawrray delleh peeleh della stehssah grahndetsa dee kwella veckya.*

**293** Would you mind wrapping this for me, please?

Le dispiacerebbe impacchettarmele?

*Leh deespyahcherebbeh eempahckett-arrmehleh?*

**294** Sorry, but you seem to have given me the wrong change.

Scusi, si è sbagliato nel darmi il resto se non erro.

*Scoozee, se eh sbahlyahtaw nel darrmee eel restaw seh non erraw.*

## MOTORING

### Car Hire (Rental)

**295** I have ordered (rented) a car in the name of . . .

Ho ordinato una vettura per . . .

*Aw ordreenahtaw oona vettoora perr . . .*

**296** How much does it cost to hire (rent) a car for one day/two days/one week?

Quant'è il nolo di una vettura per un giorno/due giorni/una settimana?

*Kwahntèh eel nawlaw dee oona vettoora perr oon jornnaw/dweh joornee/oona setteemahna?*

**297** Is the tank already full of petrol (gas)?
Il serbatoio è pieno di benzina?
*Eel serbahtoyaw èh pyehnaw dee bentseena?*

**298** Is insurance and tax included? How much is the deposit?
L'assicurazione e l'imposta sono comprese? Quant'è la caparra?
*Lasseecoorahtsyawne eh leempawsta sawnaw cawmprehseh? Kwahnteh lah cahparra?*

**299** By what time must I return the car?
A che ora devo ritornare la vettura?
*Ah keh awra devaw reetorrnahreh lah vettoora?*

**300** I would like a small/family car with a radio/cassette player.
Vorrei una piccola vettura/una familiare con radio/mangianastri.
*Vawrray oona peeccawla vettoora/ oona fahmeelyareh con rahdyaw/ mahnjanastree.*

## Asking the Way

**301** Excuse me, can you help me please?
Mi scusi, può aiutarmi per favore?
*Mee scoozee, poohòh ahyiootahrmee, perr fahvawreh?*

**302** How do I reach the motorway/main road?
Come si arriva all'autostrada/

strada principale?
*Cawmeh see ahrreevah alahootawstrahdah/strahdah preencheepahleh?*

**303** I think I have taken the wrong turning.
Penso di aver preso la svolta sbagliata.
*Pehnsaw dee avehr prehsaw lah svawltah sbahlyahtah.*

**304** I am looking for this address.
Sto cercando questo indirizzo.
*Staw cherkahndaw kwestaw eendeereetsaw.*

**305** I am looking for the . . . hotel.
Sto cercando l'hotel . . .
*Staw cherkahndaw lotehl . . .*

**306** How far is it to . . . from here?
Quanto dista . . . da qui?
*Kwantaw deestah . . . dah kwee?*

**307** Carry straight on for . . . kilometres.
Vada dritto per . . . chilometri.
*Vahdah dreetaw perr . . . .keehlawmehtree.*

**308** Take the next turning on the right/left.
Prenda la prossima svolta a destra/sinistra.
*Prehndah lah prawseehmah svawltah ah dehstrah/seeneestrah.*

**309** Turn right/left at the next crossroads/traffic lights.
Giri a destra/sinistra al prossimo incrocio/semaforo.
*Djyree ah dehstrah/seeneestrah ahl prawseemaw eencrawchyaw/ sehmahfawraw.*

ITALIAN

297
↑
309

³¹⁰ **You are going in the wrong direction.**
Sta andando nella direzione sbagliata.
*Stah ahndahndaw nehllah deerehtsyawoneh sbahlyahtah.*

## Parking

³¹¹ **How long can I park here?**
Per quanto tempo posso parcheggiare qui?
*Pehr kwantaw tehmpaw payssaw pahrkehdjahreh kwee?*

³¹² **Is there a car park near here?**
C'è un parcheggio da queste parti?
*Cheh oon pahrkehdjaw dah kwesteh pahrtee?*

³¹³ **At what time does this car park close?**
A che ora chiude il parcheggio?
*Ah keh awrah keeyoodeh eel pahrkehdjaw?*

## Signs and Notices

³¹⁴ **Senso unico.**
*Sehnsaw ooneekaw.*
One way.

³¹⁵ **Divieto di accesso.**
*Deeveeyehtaw dee ahchehssaw.*
No entry.

³¹⁶ **Divieto di sosta.**
*Deeveeyehtaw dee sawstah.*
No parking.

³¹⁷ **Deviazione**
*Dehveeyahtsyawneh.*
Detour (diversion

³¹⁸ **Stop.**
*Stop.*
Stop.

³¹⁹ **Dare precedenza.**
*Dahreh prehchehdehntsah.*
Give way (yield).

³²⁰ **Strada sdrucciolevole.**
*Strahdah sdroocheeyawlehvawleh.*
Slippery road.

³²¹ **Divieto di sorpasso.**
*Deeveeyehtaw dee sawrpahssaw.*
No overtaking.

## At the Filling Station

³²² **Unleaded (lead-free)/ Standard/Premium**
Carburante senza piombo/ normale/super
*Kahrboorahnteh sehntsah peeyawmbaw/nawrmahleh/soopehrr*

³²³ **Fill the tank please.**
Il pieno, per favore.
*Eel peeyehnaw perr fahvawreh.*

³²⁴ **Do you have a road map of this area?**
Avete una carta stradale di quest'area?
*Ahvehteh oonah kahrtah strahdahleh dee kwestahreyah?*

³²⁵ **How much is the car-wash?**
Quanto costa l'autolavaggio?
*Kwahntaw kawstah lahootawlahvahdjyoh.*

## Breakdowns

³²⁶ **I've had a breakdown at . . .**
Ho avuto un guasto a . . .

*Haw ahvootaw oon gwastaw*
*ah . . .*

**327** I am on the road from . . . to . . .
Sono sulla stra a da . . . a . . .
*Sawnaw soollah strahdah*
*dah . . . ah . . .*

**328** I can't move the car. Can you send a tow-truck?
Non posso spostare l'auto.
Potrebbe mandare un carro
attrezzi?
*Nawn pawssaw spawstahreh*
*lahootaw. Pawtrebbeh*
*mahndahreh oon kahrraw*
*ahtretzee?*

**329** I have a flat tyre.
Ho una ruota a terra.
*Haw oonah rooawtah ah tehrrah.*

**330** The windscreen (windshield) has smashed/cracked.
Il parabrezza si è sfondato/
incrinato.
*Eel pahrahbretzah see eh*
*sfawndahtaw/eenkreenahtaw.*

**331** There is something wrong with the engine/brakes/ lights/steering/gearbox/ clutch/exhaust.
C'è qualcosa che non va con il
motore/i freni/le luci/lo sterzo/
il cambio/la frizione/lo scarico.
*Cheh kwahlkawsah keh nawn vah*
*kawn eel mawtawreh/ee frehnee/*
*leh loochee/law stehrtsaw/eel*
*kahmbeeyaw/lah freetsyawneh/*
*law skahreenkaw.*

**332** It's overheating.
E' surriscaldato.

*Eh soorreeskahldhataw.*

**333** It won't start.
Non parte.
*Nawn pahrteh.*

**334** Where can I get it repaired?
Dove posso ripararla?
*Dawveh pawssaw reepahrarlah?*

**335** Can you take me there?
Mi ci potrebbe accompagnare?
*Mee chee pawtrebbeh*
*ahkawmpahnyareh?*

**336** Will it take long to fix?
Ci vorrà molto tempo per
ripararla?
*Chee vawrràh mawltaw*
*tehmpaw perr reepahrahrlah?*

**337** How much will it cost?
Quanto mi costerà?
*Kwantaw mee kawstehràh?*

## Accidents

**338** Can you help me? There has been an accident.
Potrebbe aiutarmi? C'è stato un
incidente.
*Pawtrebbeh ahyiootahrmee? Cheh*
*stahtaw oon eencheedehnteh.*

**339** Please call the police/an ambulance.
Per favore, chiami la polizia/
un'ambulanza.
*Perr fahvawreh keeyahmee lah*
*pawleetseeyah/oonamboolahntsah.*

**340** Is anyone hurt?
Ci sono feriti?
*Chee sawnaw fehreetee?*

I
T
A
L
I
A
N

327
↕
340

## Traffic Offences

### 341 I'm sorry, I didn't see the sign.
Mi scusi, non ho visto il cartello.
*Mee scoozee, nawn haw veestaw eel kahrtehllaw.*

### 342 Must I pay a fine? How much?
Devo pagare una multa? Quant'è?
*Dehvaw pahgareh oonah mooltah? Kwantèh?*

### 343 Show me your documents.
Mi mostri i documenti.
*Mee mawstree ee dawcoomehntee.*

## HEALTH

## Pharmacy

### 344 Do you have anything for a stomachache/headache/sore throat/toothache?
Ha un preparato per il mal di stomaco/mal di testa/mal di gola/mal di denti?
*Ah oon prehpahrahtaw perr eel mahl dee stohmahcaw/mahl dee testa/mahl dee gawla/mahl dee dehntee?*

### 345 I need something for diarrhoea (diarrhea)/constipation/a cold/a cough/insect bites/sunburn/travel (motion) sickness.
Ho bisogno di un rimedio per la diarrea/la stitichezza/il raffreddore/la tosse/le punture di insetti/l'eritema solare/il mal di viaggio.
*Aw beesawnyaw dee oon reemehdyaw perr lah dyahrreha/lah steeteeketsa/eel rahffredawreh/lah tawsseh/leh poontooreh dee eensehttee/lehreetehma sawlahreh/eel mahl dee vyahdjaw.*

### 346 How much/how many do I take?
Quanto/quanti ne devo prendere?
*Kwahntaw/kwahntee neh dehvaw préndehreh?*

### 347 How often do I take it/them?
Ogni quanto devo prenderlo/prenderli?
*Awnee kwahntaw dehvaw prenderrlaw/prenderrlee?*

### 348 How much does it cost?
Quanto costa?
*Kwahntaw cawsta?*

### 349 Can you recommend a good doctor/dentist?
Può raccomandarmi un buon medico/dentista?
*Poohò rhaccawmahndarrmee oon boohòn méhdeecaw/denteesta?*

### 350 Is it suitable for children?
È adatto per i bambini?
*Èh ahdahttaw perr ee bahmbeenee?*

## Doctor

### 351 I have a pain here/in my arm/leg/chest/stomach.

Ho un dolore qui/nel braccio/nella gamba/nel petto/nello stamco.
*Aw oon dawlawreh kwee/nel bracchaw/nella gahmba/nel pettaw/nellaw stohmahcaw.*

**352** Please call a doctor, this is an emergency.
La prego di chiamare un medico. È un'emergenza.
*Lah prehgaw dee kyahmahreh oon mèdeecaw. Èh oonemerrgentsa.*

**353** I would like to make an appointment to see a doctor.
Vorrei prendere un appuntamento con un medico.
*Vawrray prendehre oon ahppoontahmentaw con oon mèdeecaw.*

**354** I am diabetic/pregnant.
Sono diabetica/incinta.
*Sawnaw dyahbèhteeca/eencheenta.*

**355** I need a prescription for . . .
Ho bisogno di una ricetta per . . .
*Aw beesohnyaw dee oona reechetta perr . . .*

**356** Can you give me something to ease the pain.
Può prescrivermi qualcosa che allevii il dolore?
*Poohòh prehscreevermee kwahlcawsa keh allevee eel dawlawreh?*

**357** I am/he is/she is allergic to penicillin.
Sono/egli è/ella è allergico (masc.)/allergica (fem.) alla penicillina.

*Sawnaw/ehlyee eh/ehlah eh allehrjeekaw/allehrjeekah ahlah pehneecheeleenah.*

**358** Does this hurt?
Questo fa male?
*Kwestaw fah mahleh?*

**359** You must/he must/she must go to hospital.
Lei deve/egli deve/ella deve andare in ospedale.
*Ley dehveh/ehlyee dehveh/ehlah dehveh ahndahreh een awspehdahleh.*

**360** Take these once/twice/three times a day.
Prenda queste una volta/due volte/tre volte al giorno.
*Prehndah kwesteh oonah vawltah/dooweh vawlteh/treh vawlteh ahl djeeyawrnaw.*

**361** I am/he is/she is taking this medication.
Sto/egli sta/ella sta prendendo questa medicina.
*Staw/ehlyee stah/ehlah stah prehndehndaw kwestah mehdeecheenah.*

**362** I have medical insurance.
Ho un'assicurazione medica.
*Haw oonahseekoorahtsyawneh mehdeekah.*

## Dentist

**363** I have toothache.
Ho mal di denti.
*Aw mahl dee dentee.*

**364** My filling has come out.
È uscita l'otturazione.
*Èh oosheeta lawttoorahtsyawneh.*

**365** I do/do not want to have an injection first.
Voglio/non voglio l'anestetico.
*Vawlyaw/non vawlyaw lahnestehteecaw.*

## EMERGENCIES

**366** Help!
Aiuto!
*Ahyootaw!*

**367** Call an ambulance/a doctor/the police!
Chiamate un'ambulanza/un medico/la polizia!
*Kyahmahteh oon ahmboolahntsa/oon mehdeecaw/la pawleetsya!*

**368** I have had my travellers' cheques (travelers' checks)/credit cards/purse/handbag/rucksack (knapsack)/luggage/wallet stolen.
Mi hanno rubato gli assegni turistici/le carte di credito/il borsellino/la borsetta/lo zaino/il bagaglio/il portafoglio.
*Mee annaw roobahtaw lee assenee tooreesteechee/leh carrteh dee crédeetaw/eel borrsellenaw/lah borrsetta/law tsaheenaw/eel bahgalyaw/eel porrtafawlyaw.*

**369** Can you help me, I have lost my daughter/son?
Può aiutarmi? Ho perduto mia figlia/mio figlio.
*Poohòh ahyootarrmee? Aw perrdootaw myah feelya/myaw feelyaw.*

**370** Please go away/leave me alone.
Se ne vada/mi lasci in pace!
*Seh neh vahda/me lahshee een pahcheh!*

**371** Fire!
Al fuoco!
*Ahl fooawcaw!*

**372** I want to contact the British/American/Canadian/Irish/Australian/New Zealand/South African consulate.
Voglio contattare il consolato britannico/americano/canadese/irlandese/australiano/neozelandese/sudafricano.
*Vawlyaw kawntattahreh eel kawnsawlahtaw breetahnneekaw/ahmehreekahnaw/kahnahdehseh/eerlahndehseh/ahoostrahleeyahnaw/nehawzehlahndehseh/soodahfrikahnaw.*

# Introduction

The official language of Poland, Polish is a Slavic tongue and therefore related to Russian, Czech and many other Eastern European languages. English is spoken to some extent in larger cities, particularly by younger people, though older inhabitants are more likely to speak German or French as a second language. Russian is understood but unpopular.

POLISH

## Addresses for travel and tourist information

**UK:** *Orbis (Polish National Tourist Office)*, 246 King St, London W6 0RF; tel: (0181) 741 5541.
**USA:** *Orbis (Polish National Tourist Office)*, 500 Fifth Ave, New York, NY 10110; tel: (212) 867-5011.

## ESSENTIALS

### Alphabet

| | |
|---|---|
| A | B |
| *ah* | *bey* |
| C | D |
| *tsey* | *dey* |
| E | F |
| *ey* | *ef* |
| G | H |
| *gye* | *hah* |
| I | J |
| *ea* | *yot* |
| K | L |
| *kah* | *el* |
| M | N |
| *em* | *en* |
| O | P |
| *oh* | *pey* |
| Q | R |
| *koo* | *air* |
| S | T |
| *es* | *tey* |
| U | V |
| *oo* | *fow* |
| W | X |
| *voo* | *iks* |
| Y | Z |
| *eegrec* | *zeł* |

### Basic Words and Phrases

**1**
| **Yes** | **No** |
|---|---|
| Tak | nie |
| *Tak* | *nye* |

**2**
| **Please** | **Thank you** |
|---|---|
| Proszę | Dziękuję |
| *Proshem* | *Jenkooyem* |

**3**
| **That's O.K.** | **Perhaps** |
|---|---|
| To jest O.K. | Może |
| *Toe yest O.K.* | *Mozhe* |

**4**
| **To** | **From** |
|---|---|
| Do | Z |
| *Doe* | *Z* |

**5**
| **Here** | **There** |
|---|---|
| Tu | Tam |
| *Too* | *Tam* |

**6**
| **None** | **Also** |
|---|---|
| Nic | Także |
| *Neets* | *Takzhe* |

**7**
| **How** | **When** |
|---|---|
| Jak | Kiedy |
| *Yak* | *Kyedy* |

**8**
| **What** | **Why** |
|---|---|
| Co | Dlaczego |
| *Tso* | *Dlachego* |

**9 I don't understand.**
Nie rozumiem
*Nye rhozoomyem*

**10 I don't speak Polish.**
Nie mówię po polsku.
*Nye movyem po polsku.*

**11 Do you speak English?**
Czy pan (pani) mówi po angielsku?

*Chi pan (pani) movee po*
*angielskoo?*

12 **Can you please write it**
**down?**
Proszę napisać.
*Proshem napisach.*

13 **Can you please speak more**
**slowly?**
Proszę mówić wolniej.
*Proshem moveech volnyey.*

14 **ow much does it/this cost?**
Ile to kosztuje?
*Eele to koshtooye?*

## Days

15 **Monday**          **Tuesday**
Poniedziałek     Wtorek
*Poniejawek*      *Vtorek*

16 **Wednesday**      **Thursday**
Środa            Czwartek
*Shroda*         *Chvartek*

17 **Friday**         **Saturday**
Piątek           Sobota
*Pyontek*        *Sobota*

18 **Sunday**         **Morning**
Niedziela        Rano
*Niejela*        *Rano*

19 **Afternoon**      **Evening**
Po południu      Wieczór
*Po powoodnyoo*  *Vyechoor*

20 **Night**          **Week**
Noc              Tydzień
*Nots*           *Tyjen*

21 **Yesterday**      **Tomorrow**
Wczoraj          Jutro
*Vchoray*        *Yootro*

## Numbers

22 **Zero**           **One**
Zero             Jeden
*Zero*           *Yeden*

23 **Two**            **Three**
Dwa              Trzy
*Dva*            *Tshee*

24 **Four**           **Five**
Cztery           Pięć
*Chteree*        *Pyench*

25 **Six**            **Seven**
Sześć            Siedem
*Sheshch*        *Siedem*

26 **Eight**          **Nine**
Osiem            Dziewięć
*Oshem*          *Dzieviench*

27 **Ten**            **Eleven**
Dziesięć         Jedenaście
*Jeshench*       *Yedenashchiem*

28 **Twelve**         **Thirteen**
Dwanaście        Trzynaście
*Dvanashchiem*   *Tsheenashchiem*

29 **Fourteen**       **Fifteen**
Czternaście      Piętnaście
*Chternashchiem* *Pyentnashchiem*

30 **Sixteen**        **Seventeen**
Szesnaście       Siedemnaście
*Shesnasschiem*  *Shiedemnashchiem*

31 **Eighteen**       **Nineteen**
Osiemnaście      Dziewiętnaście
*Oshemnashchiem* *Jevietnashchiem*

P
O
L
I
S
H

12
↑
31

205

**32** **Twenty** **Twenty-one**
Dwadzieścia Dwadzieścia jeden
*Dvajeshshchia* *Dvajeshchia yeden*

**33** **Twenty-two** **Thirty**
Dwadzieścia dwa Trzydzieści
*Dvajeshchia dva* *Tsheejeshchee*

**34** **Forty** **Fifty**
Czterdzieści Pięćdziesiąt
*Chterjeshchee* *Pyenjeshiont*

**35** **Sixty** **Seventy**
Sześćdziesiąt Siedemdziesiąt
*Sheshjeshiont* *Shiedemjesiont*

**36** **Eighty** **Ninety**
Osiemdziesiąt Dziewięćdziesiąt
*Osiemjeshiont* *Jevienjeshiont*

**37** **One hundred** **Five hundred**
Sto Pięćset
*Sto* *Pyenchset*

**38** **One thousand** **One million**
Tysiąc Milion
*Tyshionc* *Million*

## Time

**39** **9.00**
Dziewiąta
*Jevionta*

**40** **9.05**
Dziewiąta pięć
*Jevionta pyench*

**41** **9.10**
Dziewiąta dziesięć
*Jevionta jeshench*

**42** **9.15**
Dziewiąta piętnaście
*Jevionta pyentnashchiem*

**43** **9.20**
Dziewiąta dwadzieścia
*Jevionta dvajeshchia*

**44** **9.25**
Dziewiąta dwadzieścia pięć
*Jevionta dvajeshchia piench*

**45** **9.30**
Dziewiąta trzydzieści
*Jevionta tsheejeshchee*

**46** **9.35**
Dziewiąta trzydzieści pięć
*Jevionta tsheejeshchee pyench.*

**47** **9.40**
Dziewiąta czterdzieści
*Jevionta chterjeshchee*

**48** **9.45**
Dziewiąta czterdzieści pięć
*Jevionta chterjeshchee pyench.*

**49** **9.50**
Dziewiąta pięćdziesiąt
*Jevionta pyenjeshiont*

**50** **9.55**
Dziewiąta pięćdziesiąt pięć
*Jevionta pyenjeshiont pyench*

**51** **12.00/Midday/Midnight**
Dwunasta/Południe/Północ
*Dvoonasta/Powoodnye/Poownots*

**52** **What time is it?**
Która godzina?
*Ktoora gojeena?*

**53** **It is . . .**
Jest . . .
*Yest . . .*

## ARRIVING AND DEPARTING

### Airport

**54** Excuse me, where is the
check-in desk for . . . airline?
Przepraszam, gdzie jest
stanowisko linii . . ?
*Psheyprasham, gje yest stanovizko
leenyi . . ?*

**55** What is the boarding gate/
time for my flight?
Gdzie jest wyjście na/O której
jest . . . mój lot?
*Gje yest veeyshche na/o kłoorey
yest . . . mooy lot?*

**56** How long is the delay likely
to be?
Jakie będzie opóźnienie?
*Yakhe benjeh opoozhnyenye?*

**57** Where is the duty-free shop?
Gdzie jest sklep wolno-cłowy
*Gje yest sklep volnoh-tzlovy?*

**58** Which way is the baggage
reclaim?
Gdzie jest odbiór bagażu?
*Gje yest odbyoor bagazhoo?*

**59** Where can I get the bus to
the city centre?
Gdzie jest autobus do centrum?
*Gje yest owtohbus do tzentrum?*

### Train Station

**60** Where is the ticket office/
information desk?
Gdzie jest kasa/informacja?

*Gje yest kasa/informatsya?*

**61** Which platform does the
train to . . . depart from?
Z którego peronu odchodzi
pociąg do . . ?
*Z ktoorego peronu odhojee
pochiong do . . ?*

**62** Where is platform . . ?
Gdzie jest peron . . ?
*Gje yest peron . . ?*

**63** When is the next train to . . ?
Kiedy odchodzi następny
pociąg do . . ?
*Kyedy odhojee nastempny pociong
do . . ?*

**64** Is there a later train to . . ?
Czy jest późniejszy pociąg do . . ?
*Chi yest poozhnieyshee pociong
do . . ?*

### Port

**65** How do I get to the port?
Jak się dostać do portu?
*Yak siem dostach doh portoo?*

**66** When is the next sailing
to . . ?
Kiedy odchodzi następny prom
do . . ?
*Kyedy odhojee nastempny prom
doh . . ?*

**67** Can I catch an earlier ferry
with this ticket?
Czy ten bilet jest ważny na
wcześniejszy prom?
*Chi ten beelet yest vazhnee na
wchesnyeyshi prom?*

P
O
L
I
S
H

54
↑
67

207

# ARRIVING AND DEPARTING

## Notices and Signs

**68** **Wagon restauracyjny**
*Vagon restauratsiny*
Buffet (Dining) Car

**69** **Autobus**
*Owtoboos*
Bus

**70** **Woda pitna/nie do picia**
*Voda pitna/nye do pitcha*
Drinking/Non-drinking water

**71** **Wejście**
*Veishchye*
Entrance

**72** **Wyjście**
*Veeyshchye*
Exit

**73** **Informacja**
*Informatsya*
Information

**74** **Przechowalnia bagażu**
*Pshehovalnya bagazhoo*
Left Luggage (Baggage Claim)

**75** **Schowki na bagaż**
*S'hovky na bagazh*
Luggage Lockers

**76** **Poczta**
*Pochta*
Post Office

**77** **Peron**
*Peron*
Platform

**78** **Dworzec kolejowy**
*Dvozhets koleyovy*
Railway (Railroad) Station

**79** **Port lotniczy**
*Port lotneechi*
Airport

**80** **Port**
*Port*
Port

**81** **Restauracja**
*Restauratsya*
Restaurant

**82** **Dla palących/niepalących**
*Dla palontsyh/nyepalontsych*
Smoking/Non-Smoking

**83** **Telefon**
*Telefon*
Telephone

**84** **Kasa biletowa**
*Kasa biletova*
Ticket Office

**85** **Odprawa**
*Odprava*
Check-in Desk

**86** **Rozkład jazdy**
*Rozkwad yazdy*
Timetable (Schedule)

**87** **Toalety**
*Toalety*
Toilets (Restrooms)

**88** **Mężczyźni**
*Menzhtchyzni*
Gentlemen

**89** **Dla kobiet**
*Dla kobyet*
Ladies'

**90 Tramwaj**
*Tramvay*
Tram (Streetcar)

**91 Metro**
*Metro*
Underground (Subway)

**92 Poczekalnia**
*Potchekalnya*
Waiting room

## Buying a Ticket

**93 I would like a first-class/
second-class single (one-
way)/return (round-trip)
ticket to . . .**
Proszę o bilet pierwszej klasy/
drugiej klasy w jedną stronę/
powrotny do . . .
*Proshe o bilet pyervshey/droogyey
klasy v yednom strone/powrotny
doh . . .*

**94 Is my rail pass valid on this
train/ferry/bus?**
Czy ten bilet ważny jest na ten
pociąg/prom/autobus?
*Chi ten beelet yest vazhnee nah ten
pochong/prom/owtohbus?*

**95 I would like an aisle/window
seat.**
Proszę o miejsce przy przejściu/
oknie.
*Proshe o mieystse pshee
psheyshchu/oknye.*

**96 No smoking/smoking, please.**
Palenie wzbronione/
dozwolone.

*Palenye vzbronione/dozvolone.*

**97 We would like to sit
together.**
Chcemy siedzieć razem.
*Htsemy shiejech razem.*

**98 I would like to make a seat
reservation.**
Chcę zamówić miejscówkę
*Htsem zahmooveech myeys-
tsoovkeh.*

**99 I would like to reserve a
couchette/sleeper for one
person/two people/for my
family.**
Chcę zarezerwować kuszetkę/
miejsce sypialne dla jednej
osoby/dwóch osób/rodziny.
*Hcem zarezervoovach kooshetkem/
mieystse sipyalne dla yedney
osoby/dvooh osoob/rojiny.*

**100 I would like to reserve a
cabin.**
Chcę zamówić kabinę.
*Htsem zahmooveech cabin-eh.*

## Timetables (Schedules)

**101 Przyjazd**
*Pshiyazd*
Arrive

**102 Zatrzymuje się w**
*Zatzhimuye shiem v*
Calls (Stops) at

**103 Usługi gastronomiczne**
*Uswoogy gastronomichne*
Catering Service

POLISH

90
↑
103

209

**104** Przesiadka w
*Psheshadka v*
Change at

**105** Połączenie
*Powonchenye*
Connection

**106** Codziennie
*Tsojennye*
Daily

**107** Co 40 minut
*Tso 40 minut*
Every 40 inutes

**108** Pierwsza klasa
*Pyerosha klasa*
First-class

**109** Co godzinę
*Tso gojinem*
Hourly

**110** Zaleca się rezerwację miejsc
*Zaletsa shiem rezerwatsye mieysts*
Seat reservations are
recommended

**111** Druga klasa
*Drooga klasa*
Second-class

**112** Dodatkowa opłata
*Dodatkova opwata*
Supplement Payable

**113** Przez
*Pshez*
Via

## Luggage

**114** How much will it cost to send
(ship) my luggage in
advance?
Ile kosztuje nadanie rzeczy na
bagaż?
*Eele koshtooye nadanye zhechi na
bagazh?*

**115** Where is the left luggage
(baggage claim) office?
Gdzie jest przechowalnia bagażu?
*Gje jest pshehovalnya bagazhoo?*

**116** What time do you open/
close?
O której otwieracie/zamykacie?
*O ktoorey otvyerachie/
zamykachie?*

**117** Where are the luggage
trolleys (carts)?
Gdzie są wózki bagażowe?
*Gje som voozky bagazhove?*

**118** Where are the lockers?
Gdzie są schowki?
*Gje som s-hovkee?*

**119** I have lost my locker key.
Zgubiłem klucz do schowka.
*Zgoobiwem klooch do s'hovka.*

## On Board

**120** Is this seat taken?
Czy to miejsce jest wolne?
*Chi to mieystse yest volne?*

**121** Excuse me, you are sitting in
my reserved seat.
Przepraszam, to jest moje

zarezerwowane miejsce.
*Psheprasham, toe yest moye
zarezervovane mieystse.*

**122 Which station is this?**
Jaka to stacja?
*Yaka to statsya?*

**123 What time is this train/bus/
ferry/flight due to arrive/
depart?**
O której przyjeżdża/odjeżdża
pociąg/autobus/prom? (O
której jest przylot/odlot?)
*O ktoorey pshiezdzha/odyezdzha
pochong/owtohbus/prom? (O
ktoorey yest pshillot/odlot?)*

**124 Will you wake me just before
we arrive?**
Proszę mnie zbudzić przed
przyjazdem.
*Proshem mnye zbujeech pshed
pshyiazdem.*

## Customs and Passports

**125 Proszę o paszporty!**
*Proshem o pashporty!*
Passports, please!

**126 I have nothing/wine/spirits
(alcohol)/tobacco to declare.**
Nie mam do zgłoszenia
niczego/wina/alkoholu/tytoniu.
*Nye mam doe zgwoshenya
nichego/vina/alkoholu/titonyoo.*

**127 I shall be staying for . . .
days/weeks/months.**
Będę tu . . . dni/tygodni/
miesięcy.

*Bendem too . . . dnee/tygodnee/
miesyentsy.*

**128 Do you have a map of the
town/area?**
Czy macie plan miasta/rejonu?
*Chi matsie plan miasta/reyonoo?*

**129 Can I reserve accommodation
here?**
Czy mogę tutaj zarezerwować
zakwaterowanie?
*Chi mogem tutay zarezervovach
zakvaterovanye?*

**130 Do you have a list of
accommodation?**
Gdzie można się zatrzymać?
*Gje mozhna sheh zahtcheemach?*

## ACCOMMODATION

### Hotels

**131 I have a reservation in the
name of . . .**
Mam rezerwację na
nazwisko . . .
*Mam rezervatsyem na nazvisko . . .*

**132 I wrote to/faxed/telephoned
you last month/last week in . . .**
Pisałem(am)/faxowałem(am)/
telefonowałem(am) w zeszłym
miesiącu/zeszłego tygodnia/w . . .
*Peesawem(am)/faxovawem(am)/
telefonovavem(am) v zeshweem
myeshontzoo/zeshwego teegodnya/
v . . .*

P
O
L
I
S
H

122
↕
132

211

**133** Do you have any rooms free?
Czy są wolne pokoje?
*Chi som wolneh pokoye?*

**134** I would like to reserve a single/double room with/without bath/shower.
Chcę zarezerwować pokój pojedynczy/podwójny, z łazienką/prysznicem, bez łazienki/prysznicu.
*Htsem zarezervoovach pokooy poyedynchy/podvooyny, z wazienkom/pryshnitsem/bez wazienki/pryshnicoo.*

**135** I would like bed and breakfast/(room and) half board/(room and) full board.
Chcę pokój ze śniadaniem/z dwoma posiłkami/z pełnym wyżywieniem.
*Hcem pokooy ze sniadanyem/z dvoma poshiwkamy/z pewnym vizhivyenyem.*

**136** How much is it per night?
Ile kosztuje jedna noc?
*Eele koshtooye yedna nots?*

**137** Is breakfast included?
Czy jest w to wliczone śniadanie?
*Chi yest v to vlichoney shniadanye?*

**138** May I see the room?
Czy mogę zobaczyć ten pokój?
*Chi mogem zobachich ten pokooy?*

**139** Do you have any cheaper rooms?
Czy macie tańsze pokoje?
*Chi machie tanishe pokoje?*

**140** I would like to take the room
Wezmę ten pokój.
*Vezmem ten pokooy.*

**141** I would like to stay for . . . nights.
Chcę się zatrzymać na . . . nocy.
*Htsem shiem zatzhimach na . . . notsy.*

**142** The shower/light/tap doesn't work.
Prysznic/światło/kran nie działa.
*Prishnitz/shvyatwo/kran nye dzhawa.*

**143** At what time/where is breakfast served?
O której godzinie/gdzie jest śniadanie?
*O ktoorey gojeenye/gje yest shnyadanye?*

**144** What time do I have to check-out?
O której godzinie mam opróżnić pokój?
*O ktoorey gojeenye mam oproozhnich pokooy?*

**145** Can I have the key to room no . . ?
Proszę o klucz do pokoju numer . . .
*Proshem o klooch doh pokoyoo noomer . . .*

**146** My room number is . . .
Numer mojego pokoju jest . . .

*Noomer moyego pokoyoo yest . . .*

**147 Do you accept travellers' cheques/Eurocheques/credit cards?**
Czy przyjmujecie czeki podróżne/Euroczeki/karty kredytowe?
*Chi pshiymuyecheh chekee podroozhne/Eurochekee/karti kreditoveh?*

**148 May I have the bill please.**
Proszę o rachunek.
*Proshem o rahoonek.*

**149 Excuse me, I think there is a mistake in this bill.**
Przepraszam, wydaje mi się, że jest pomyłka w rachunku.
*Psheprasham, veedayeh me sheh, zhe yest pomiwka w rahoonkoo.*

## Youth Hostels

**150 How much is a dormitory bed per night?**
Ile kosztuje łóżko we wspólnej sypialni, na jedną noc?
*Eele koshtooye woozhko ve vspoolney sypyalnee, na yednom nots?*

**151 I am/am not an HI member.**
Należę/nie należę do HI.
*Nalezhem/nye nalezhem do hah, ea.*

**152 May I use my own sleeping bag?**
Czy mogę używać własny śpiwór?

*Chi mogem uzhivach vwasny shpivoor?*

**153 What time do you lock the doors at night?**
O której zamykacie drzwi na noc?
*O ktoorey zamykatsye djvee na nots?*

## Camping

**154 May I camp here for the night/two nights?**
Czy mogę się tu kampingować przez jedną noc/dwie noce?
*Chi mogem too kampingovach pshes jednom nots/dvye notse?*

**155 Where can I pitch my tent?**
Gdzie mogę rozbić namiot?
*Gje mogem rozbich namyot?*

**156 How much does it cost for one night/week?**
Ile wynosi opłata za jedną noc/za tydzień?
*Eele vynoshi opwata za yednom nots/za tyjyen?*

**157 Where can we park our caravan?**
Gdzie możemy postawić przyczepę?
*Gje mozhemi postaveech pshichepeh?*

**158 Where are the washing facilities?**
Gdzie można się umyć?
*Gje mozhna shiem oomych?*

POLISH

147 ↕ 158

213

159 Is there a restaurant/
supermarket/swimming pool
on site/nearby?
Czy jest na miejscu/w pobliżu
restauracja/supersam/basen
kąpielowy?
*Chi yest na mieystsu/v poblizhoo
restauratsya/supersam/basen
kompielovy?*

160 Do you have a safety deposit
box?
Czy jest tu sejf?
*Chi yest too seyf?*

## EATING AND DRINKING

### Cafés and Bars

161 I would like a cup of/two
cups of/another coffee/tea.
Proszę o jedną/dwie/jeszcze
jedną kawę/herbatę.
*Proshem o yednom/dvye/yeshche
yednom kavem/herbatem.*

162 With/without milk/sugar.
Z mlekiem/bez mleka/z
cukrem/bez cukru.
*Z mlekyem/bez mleka/z tsukrem/
bez tsookroo.*

163 I would like a bottle/glass/
two glasses of mineral water/
red wine/white wine, please.
Proszę o butelkę/szklankę/dwie
szklanki wody mineralnej/
czerwonego wina/białego wina.
*Proshem o bootelkem/shklankem/
dvye shklankee vody mineralney/
chervonego vina/biawego vina.*

164 I would like a beer/two
beers, please.
Proszę o piwo/dwa piwa.
*Proshem o pivo/dva piva.*

165 May I have some ice?
Proszę o lód.
*Proshem o lood.*

166 Do you have any matches/
cigarettes/cigars?
Czy są zapałki/papierosy/
cygara?
*Chi som zapawki/papyerosy/
tsygara?*

### Restaurants

167 Can you recommend a good/
inexpensive restaurant in this
area?
Czy możecie mi polecić dobrą/
niedrogą restaurację w pobliżu?
*Chi mozheche me polechich
dobrom/nyedrogom restauratsye v
poblizhoo?*

168 I would like a table for . . .
people.
Proszę o stolik dla . . . osób.
*Proshem o stolik dla . . . osoob.*

169 Do you have a non-smoking
area?
Czy są miejsca dla niepalących?
*Chi som myeystsa dla
nyepalontzeeh?*

170 Waiter/Waitress!
Kelner/Kelnerka!
*Kelner/Kelnerka!*

**171** Do you have a set menu/
children's menu/wine list?
Czy mogę prosić o zestaw potraw/
menu dla dzieci/listę win?
*Chi mo em proshich o zestav
potrav/menu dla jechee/listem vin?*

**172** Do you have any vegetarian
dishes, please?
Czy są dania jarskie?
*Chi som danya yarskye?*

**173** Are there any local
specialities?
Czy są jakieś specjalności lokalne?
*Chi som jakyesh
spetzyahlnoshchee lokalneh?*

**174** Are vegetables included?
Czy to razem z jarzynami?
*Chi toh razem z yazhinyamee?*

**175** Could I have it well-cooked/
medium/rare please?
Poproszę wysmażone dobrze/
średnio/czerwone.
*Poproshem vysmazhoneh dobzeh/
shrednyo/chervoneh.*

**176** What does this dish consist of?
Co to za potrawa?
*Tso toe za potrava?*

**177** I would like the set menu,
please.
Proszę o zestaw potraw.
*Proshem o zestav potrav.*

**178** We have not been served yet.
Nie obsłużono nas jeszcze.
*Nye obswoozhono nas yeshche.*

**179** Excuse me, this is not what I
ordered.

Przeparaszam, nie to
zamówiłem(am).
*Psheprasham, nye to
zamooviwem(am).*

**180** May I have some bread/
water/coffee/tea?
May I have some more
bread/water/coffee/tea?
Proszę o chleb/wodę/kawę/
herbatę?
Proszę o więcej chleba/wody/
kawy/herbaty?
*Proshem o hleb/vodem/kavem/
herbatem?*
*Proshem o vyentzey hleba/vodee/
kavee/herbatee?*

**181** May I have the bill, please?
Proszę o rachunek.
*Proshem o rahoonek.*

**182** Does this bill include service?
Czy jest w to wliczona obsługa?
*Chi yest v toe vlichona obswooga?*

**183** Do you accept travellers'
cheques (travelers' checks)/
Eurocheques/MasterCard/US
dollars?
Czy przyjmujecie czeki
podróżne/Euroczeki/
MasterCard/dolary USA?
*Chi pshiymooyechie cheky
podroozhne/Eurocheky/
MasterCard/ dolary USA?*

**184** Can I have a receipt, please?
Pokwitowanie poproszę
*Pokveetovanye poproshem.*

**185** Where is the toilet
(restroom), please?
Gdzie jest toaleta?
*Gje yest toaleta?*

## On the Menu

**186** First courses
Pierwsze dania
*Pyerwshe danya*

**187** Soups
Zupy
*Zoopi*

**188** Main courses
Główne dania
*Gwoowneh danyah*

**189** Fish dishes
Dania rybne
*Danya ribneh*

**190** Meat dishes
Dania mięsne
*Danya myensneh*

**191** Vegetarian dishes
Dania jarskie
*Danya yarskye*

**192** Cheese
Ser
*Ser*

**193** Desserts
Desery
*Desseree*

**194** Specialities
Specjalności
*Specyalnoshchee*

## GETTING AROUND

### Public Transport

**195** Where is the bus stop/coach
station/nearest metro
(subway) station?
Gdzie jest przystanek
autobusowy/dworzec
autobusowy/najbliższa stacja
metra?
*Gje yest pshystanek autoboosovy/
dworzec autobusowy/najblizhsha
statsya metra?*

**196** When is the next/last bus
to . . ?
Kiedy odchodzi następny/
ostatni autobus do . . ?
*Kyedy odhojee ostatnee autoboos
doh . . ?*

**197** How much is the fare to the
city centre (downtown)/
railway (railroad) station/
airport?
Ile kosztuje przejazd do
centrum/na dworzec kolejowy/
na lotnisko?
*Eele koshtooye psheyazd do
centroom/na dvozhets koleyovy/
na lotnisko?*

**198** Will you tell me when to get
off?
Proszę mi powiedzieć kiedy
mam wysiąść.
*Proshem mi povyejech kyedy mam
vyshonshch.*

P
O
L
I
S
H

185
↑
198

**199** Does this bus go to . . ?
Czy ten autobus jedzie
do . . ?
*Chi ten autoboos yejee doh . . ?*

**200** Which number bus goes
to . . ?
Który numer jedzie do . . ?
*Ktoory numer yedzhye doh . . ?*

**201** May I have a single (one-
way)/return (round-trip)/day
ticket/book of tickets?
Proszę o bilet w jedną stronę/
powrotny/całodzienny/karnet
biletowy?
*Proshem o bilet v yednom
stronem/povrotny/tzawojennee/
karnet biletovy?*

## Taxis

**202** I would like to go to . . .
How much will it cost?
Chcę jechać do . . . , ile to
będzie kosztować?
*Htsem yehach doh . . . , ile toe
benjey koshtovach?*

**203** Please stop here.
Proszę się tu zatrzymać.
*Proshem shiem too zatzhimach.*

**204** I would like to order a taxi
today/tomorrow/at 2pm to
go from . . . to . . .
Chę zamówić taksówkę na
dzisiaj/jutro/na drugą po
południu, na przejazd z . . .
do . . .
*Htsem zamoovich taxoovkem na*

jishyay/na yootro/na droogom po
powoodnyoo, na psheyazd z . . .
doh . . .

## Asking the Way

**205** Excuse me, do you speak
English?
Przepraszam, czy mówi Pan/
Pani (*woman*) po angielsku?
*Psheprasham, chi moovi pan/
panee po angyelskoo?*

**206** Excuse me, is this the right
way to . . ?
Przepraszam, czy to jest droga
do . . ?
*Psheprasham, chi to yest drogah
doh . . ?*

**207** . . . the cathedral/the tourist
information office/the castle/
the old town
. . . katedry/biura turystycznego/
zamku/starego miasta
*katedree/byura tooristichnego/
zamkoo/stahrego myasta*

**208** Can you tell me the way to
the railway (railroad) station/
bus station/taxi rank (stand)/
city centre (downtown)/
beach?
Jak dojść do dworca
kolejowego/autobusowego/
postoju taksówek/centrum/na
plażę?
*Yak doyshch do dwortsa
koleyovego/autoboosovego/
postoyoo taxoovek/centroom/na
plazhem?*

**209** First/second left/right/
straight ahead.
Pierwsza/druga w lewo/w
prawo/prosto.
*Pyervsha/drooga v levo/v pravo/
prosto.*

**210** Where is the nearest police
station/post office?
Gdzie jest najbliższy posterunek
policji/poczta?
*Gje yest nayblizhshy posteroonek
politsyee/pochta?*

**211** Is it far?
Czy to daleko?
*Chi to daleko?*

**212** Do I need to take a taxi/
catch a bus?
Czy muszę wziąć taksówkę/
jechać autobusem?
*Chi mooshem wzionshch
taksoovkem/jehach autoboosem?*

**213** Can you point to it on my
map?
Czy może mi Pan/Pani (woman)
pokazać na mapie?
*Chi mozhe mi pan/pany pokazach
na mapye?*

**214** Thank you for your help.
Dziękuję za pomoc.
*Jenkooyem za pomots.*

## SIGHTSEEING

**215** Where is the Tourist
Information office?
Gdzie jest Informacja
Turystyczna?

*Gje yest informatsya tooristichna?*

**216** Where is the cathedral/
church/museum?
Gdzie jest katedra/kościół/
muzeum?
*Gje yest katedra/koshchoow/
mooseum?*

**217** How much is the entrance
(admission) charge?
Ile wynosi opłata za wstęp?
*Eele vynoshee opwata za vstemp?*

**218** Is there a reduction for
children/students/senior
citizens?
Czy jest zniżka dla dzieci/
studentów/emerytów?
*Chi yest znizhka dla jechee/
studentoof/emeritoof?*

**219** What time does the next
guided tour start?
O której zaczyna się następny
obchód z przewodnikiem?
*O ktoorey zachina shiem
nastempny obhood z
pshevodnikyem?*

**220** One/two adults/children,
please.
Jeden/dwa bilety dla
dorosłych/dzieci.
*Yeden/dva bilety dla doroswyh/
jechee.*

**221** May I take photographs
here?
Czy można tu fotografować?
*Chi mozhna tu fotografovach?*

## ENTERTAINMENT

**222 Can you recommend a good bar/nightclub?**
Czy możecie mi polecić dobry bar/nocny lokal?
*Chi mozhechie me polechich dobry bar/notsny lokal?*

**223 Do you know what is on at the cinema (playing at the movies)/theatre at the moment?**
Co grają teraz w kinach/teatrach?
*Tso grayom teraz w kinakh/teatrakh?*

**224 I would like to book (purchase) . . . tickets for the matinee/evening performance on Monday**
Chcę zamówić . . . biletów na popołudniowe/wieczorne przedstawienie, w poniedziałek.
*Khtsem zamoovich . . . biletoov na popowoodnyove/vyechorney pshedsytavyenye, v ponyedzyawek.*

**225 What time does the film/performance start?**
O której zaczyna się spektakl?
*O ktoorey zachina shiem spektakl?*

## MEETING PEOPLE

**226 Hello/Goodbye.**
Hallo/Do widzenia.
*Hallo/Do vidzenia.*

**227 Good morning/good afternoon/good evening/goodnight.**
Dzień dobry/dzień dobry/dobry wieczór/dobranoc
*Djen dobri/ djen dobri/dobri vyechoor/dohbranotz*

**228 Pleased to meet you.**
Miło mi poznać.
*Miwo me poznach.*

**229 How are you?**
Jak się Pan (Pani) ma?
*Yak shem Pan (Panee) mah?*

**230 Fine, thank you. And you?**
Bardzo dobrze, dziękuję. A Pan(Pani)?
*Bardzho dobrzhe, djenkooye. Ah Pan (Panee)?*

**231 My name is . . .**
Nazywam się . . .
*Nazyvam shiem . . .*

**232 This is my friend/boyfriend/girlfriend/husband/wife/brother/sister.**
To mój przyjaciel/moja sympatia/moja sympatia/mój mąż/moja żona/mój brat/moja siostra.
*Toe mooy psheyatsyel/moya psheyatsyoowka/moya simpatya/mooy monj/moya zhona/moy brat/moya syostra.*

**233 Where are you travelling to?**
Gdzie jedziesz?
*Gje yejesh?*

**234 I am/we are going to . . .**
Jadę/jedziemy do . . .
*Yadem/yejemy doh . . .*

P
O
L
I
S
H

222
↕
234

**235** How long are you travelling for?

Na jak długo jesteś w podróży?

*Na yak dwoogo yestesh v odroozhee?*

**236** Where do you come from?

Skąd jesteś?

*Skond yestesh?*

**237** I am/we are from . . .

Jestem/jesteśmy z . . .

*Yestem/yesteshme z . . .*

**238** We're on holiday.

Jesteśmy na wakacjach.

*Yesteshme na vakatzyah.*

**239** This is our first visit here.

To jest nasz pierwszy pobyt.

*To yest nash pyerwshee pobeet.*

**240** Would you like/May I have a cigarette?

Czy chcesz/Czy mogę prosić o papierosa?

*Chi khcesh/Chi mogem proshich o papyerosa?*

**241** I am sorry but I do not understand.

Przykro mi, ale nie rozumiem.

*Pshikro me, aly nye rozoomiem.*

**242** Please speak slowly.

Proszę mówić powoli.

*Proshem moovich povolee.*

**243** Do you mind if I smoke?

Czy mogę zapalić?

*Chi mogem zapalich?*

**244** Do you have a light?

Czy mogę prosić o ogień?

*Chi mogem prosheech o ogien?*

**245** I am waiting for my husband/ wife/boyfriend/girlfriend.

Czekam na mego męża/moją żonę/mego chłopca/moją dziewczynę.

*Chekam na megoh menzha/ moyom zhoneh/megoh hwoptza/ moyom dzhevchinee.*

## TRAVELLING WITH CHILDREN

**246** Do you have a high chair/ baby-sitting service/cot?

Czy macie krzesło dla dziecka/ usługi czuwania nad dzieckiem/ łóżeczko dziecinne?

*Chi matsye ksheswo dla jetska/ uswoogi choovanya nad jetskiem/ woozhechko jechinney?*

**247** Where is the nursery/ playroom?

Gdzie jest pokój dziecinny/ pokój zabaw dla dzieci?

*Gje yest pokooy jechinny/pokooy zabav dla jechee?*

**248** Where can I warm the baby's bottle?

Gdzie mogę zagrzać butelkę dla dziecka?

*Gje mogem zagzhach bootelkem dla jetska?*

## COMMUNICATIONS

### Post

**249** How much will it cost to send a letter/postcard/this

package to Britain/Ireland/
America/Canada/Australia/
New Zealand?
Ile kosztuje wysyłka listu/
pocztówki/tej paczki do Anglii/
Irlandii/Ameryki/Kanady/
Australii/Nowej Zelandii?
*Eele koshtooye vysywka listoo/
poochtoovky/tey pachki do
Anglee/Yrlandee/Amerykee/
Kanady/Australee/Novey
Zelandee?*

**250** I would like one stamp/two
stamps.
Proszę o jeden znaczek/dwa
znaczki.
*Proshem o yeden znachek/dva
znachkee.*

**251** I'd like . . . stamps for
postcards to send abroad,
please.
Proszę o . . . znaczków na karty
pocztowe na zagranicę.
*Proshem o . . . znachkoov na
kartee pochtove na zagranitzheh.*

## Phones

**252** I would like to make a
telephone call/reverse the
charges to (make a collect call
to) . . .
Chcę zadzwonić/na koszt
abonenta do . . .
*Ktsem zadzvonich/na kosht
abonenta, doh . . .*

**253** Which coins do I need for the
telephone?

Jakie muszę mieć monety do
tego telefonu?
*Yakye mushem miech monety doh
tego telephonoo?*

**254** The line is engaged (busy).
Linia jest zajęta.
*Linya yest zayenta.*

**255** The number is . . .
Numer jest . . .
*Noomer yest . . .*

**256** Hello, this is . . ?
Halo, tu mówi . . .
*Hello, tu moovee . . .*

**257** May I speak to . . ?
Czy mogę mówić z . . .
*Chi mogem mooveech z . . .*

**258** He/She is not in at the
moment. Can you call back?
Jego/jej niema w tej chwili.
Proszę zadzwonić jeszcze raz.
*Yego/yey nyema v tey hveelee.
Proshem zadhzvoneech yeshche
raz.*

## MONEY

**259** I would like to change these
travellers' cheques (travelers'
checks)/this currency/this
Eurocheque.
Chcę wymienić te czeki
podróżne/tą walutę/ten
Euroczek.
*Khcem vymienich te chekee
podroozhne/tom valootem/ten
Eurochek.*

**260** How much commission do you charge (What is the service charge)?
Ile liczycie za wymianę?
*Eele lichytsye za vymianem?*

**261** Can I obtain money with my MasterCard?
Czy mogę dostać pieniądze na MasterCard?
*Chi mogem dostach pyenyondze na MasterCard?*

## SHOPPING

## Names of shops and Departments

**262** Księgarnia/Materiały papiernicze
*Kshengarnya/materyawee papyerneecheh*
Bookshop/Stationery

**263** Jubiler/Upominki
*Yoobiler/Oopominkee*
Jeweller's/Gifts

**264** Sklep z obuwiem
*Sklep z oboovyem*
Shoes

**265** Artykuły gospodarstwa domowego
*Artikoowe gospodarstva domovego*
Hardware

**266** Antykwariat
*Anticvaryat*
Antiques

**267** Fryzjer (męski)/(damski)
*Frizyer (menskee)/(damskee*

Hairdressers (men's)/(women's

**268** Kiosk z papierosami
*Kiosk z papyerohsammy*
Tobacconist

**269** Piekarnia
*Pyekarnya*
Baker's

**270** Supermarket
*Soopermarkyet*
Supermarket

**271** Foto Optyk
*Photo-optic*
Photoshop

**272** Zabawki
*Zabavkee*
Toys

**273** Biuro podróży
*Bureau podroozhi*
Travel Agent

**274** Perfumeria/Drogeria
*Perfoomerya/Drogerya*
Toiletries

**275** Sklep muzyczny
*Sklep moozichnee*
Records

## In the Shop

**276** What time do the shops open/close?
O której otwierają/zamykają sklepy?
*O ktoorey otvyerayom/ zamykayom sklepy?*

**277** Where is the nearest market?
Gdzie jest najbliższy targ?

*Gje yest nayblizhshi targ?*

**278 Can you show me the one in the window/this one?**
Proszę pokazać mi ten z wystawy/ten.
*Proshem pokazach me ten z vistavee/ten.*

**279 Can I try this on?**
Czy mogę to przymierzyć?
*Chi mogem to pshimiezhich?*

**280 What size is this?**
Jaki to rozmiar?
*Yakee toe rozmyar?*

**281 This is too large/too small/too expensive.**
To jest za duże/za małe/za drogie.
*Toh yest za doozhe/za mawe/za drogye.*

**282 Do you have any others?**
Czy są inne?
*Chi som inneh?*

**283 My size is . . .**
Noszę numer . . . .
*Noshem noomer . . .*

**284 Where is the changing room/childrens/cosmetic/ladieswear/menswear/food department?**
Gdzie jest szatnia/ubrania dla dzieci/kosmetyki/ubrania damskie/ubrania męskie/żywność?
*Gje yest shatnia/ubrania dla jechee/kosmetyki/ubrania damskiey/ubrania menskiey/zhyvnoshch?*

**285 I would like . . .**
Chciałbym (chciałabym)
*Htzchawbim (htzchawabim) . . .*

**286 I would like a quarter of a kilo/half a kilo/a kilo of bread/butter/cheese/ham/tomatoes.**
Proszę o ćwierć kilo/pół kilo/kilo chleba/masła/sera/szynki/pomidorów.
*Proshem o chvyerch kilo/poow kilo/kilo hleba/maswa/sera/shinky/pomidoroov.*

**287 How much is this?**
Ile to kosztuje?
*Eele toe koshtooye?*

**288 I'll take this one, thank you.**
Poproszę ten. Dziękuję.
*Poproshem ten. Dzhenkooyeh.*

**289 Do you have a carrier (shopping) bag?**
Czy mogę prosić o torbę?
*Chi mogem proshich o torbem?*

**290 Do you have anything cheaper/larger/smaller/of better quality?**
Czy macie coś tańszego/większego/mniejszego/w lepszej jakości?
*Chi machye tsosh tanshego/vienkshego/mneyshego/v lepshey yakoshchee?*

**291 I would like a film for this camera.**
Potrzebuję film do aparatu.
*Potshebooyem film doe aparatoo.*

P O L I S H

278 ↕ 291

292 I would like some batteries, the same size as this old one.
Potrzebuję baterie, takie same jak te stare.
*Potshebooyem baterye, takye same yak te starey.*

293 Would you mind wrapping this for me, please?
Proszę mi to zapakować.
*Proshem me toe zapakovac.*

294 Sorry, but you seem to have given me the wrong change.
Przepraszam, ale źle mi Pan wydał.
*Psheprasham, aley zlye me Pan vydaw.*

## MOTORING

### Car Hire (Rental

295 I have ordered (rented) a car in the name of . .
Zamówiłem samochód na nazwisko . . .
*Zamooviwem samohood na nazvisko . . .*

296 How much does it cost to hire (rent) a car for one day/two days/one week?
Ile kosztuje wynajęcie samochodu na jeden dzień/dwa dni/tydzień?
*Eele koshtooye vynayenchye samohodoo na yeden jen/dva dnyee/tyjen?*

297 Is the tank already full of petrol (gas)?
Czy zbiornik jest pełny?
*Chi zbyornik yest pewny?*

298 Is insurance and tax included? How much is the deposit?
Czy to obejmuje ubezpieczenie i podatek? Ile wynosi depozyt?
*Chi toe obeymooye ubezpyechenye ee podatek? Eele koshtooye depozyt?*

299 By what time must I return the car?
Do której godziny mam zwrócić samochód?
*Doe ktoorey gojeeny mam zvroochich samohood?*

300 I would like a small/family car with a radio/cassette player.
Chcę mały/większy samochód z radiem/magnetofonem kasetowym.
*Ktsem mawy/vienkshy samohood z radyem/magnetophonem kasetovym.*

### Asking the Way

301 Excuse me, can you help me please?
Przepraszam, czy może mi Pan(Pani) pomoc?
*Psheprasham, chi mozeh me Pan(Pani) pomotz?*

**302** How do I reach the
motorway/main road?
Którędy do autostrady/głównej
drogi?
*toorendy do autostrady/
gwoovney drogi?*

**303** I think I have taken the
wrong turning.
Chyba źle skręciłem(am)
*Heeba zhle skrencheewem(am).*

**304** I am looking for this address.
Szukam tego adresu.
*Shookam tego adresoo.*

**305** I am looking for the . . . hotel.
Szukam hotelu . . .
*Shookam hoteloo . . .*

**306** How far is it to . . .
from here?
Jak daleko stąd do . . .
*Yak dalekoh stond doh . . .*

**307** Carry straight on for . . .
kilometres.
. . . kilometrów prostą drogą.
*. . . kilomtroov prostom drogom.*

**308** Take the next turning on the
right/left.
Następna przecznica w prawo/
w lewo
*Nastempna pshechneetzha v
pravo/v levo*

**309** Turn right/left at the next
crossroads/traffic lights.
Trzeba skręcić w prawo/w lewo
na następnym skrzyżowaniu/
przy następnych światłach

*Tcheba skrenchich v pravo/v levo
na nastempneem
sksheezhovanyoo/pshee
nastempneeh shvyatwah.*

**310** You are going in the wrong
direction.
Pan(Pani) jedzie w złym
kierunku.
*Pan(Pani) yedzhe v zweem
kyeroonkoo.*

## Parking

**311** How long can I park here?
Jak długo można tu parkować?
*Yak dwoogo mozhna tu
parkovach?*

**312** Is there a car park near here?
Czy jest parking w pobliżu?
*Chi yest parking v pobleezhoo?*

**313** At what time does this car
park close?
O której zamyka się parking?
*O ktoorey zameeka shem parking?*

## Signs and Notices

**314** Jeden kierunek
*Yeden kyeroonek*
One way

**315** Zakaz wjazdu
*Zakaz vyazdoo*
No entry

**316** Nie parkować
*Nye parkovach*
No parking

P O L I S H

302
↕
316

# MOTORING

**317 Objazd**
*Obyahzd*
Detour (diversion)

**318 Stop**
*Stop*
Stop

**319 Pierwszeństwo ruchu**
*Pyervshenstvo roohoo*
Give way (yield)

**320 Śliska nawierzchnia**
*Shleeska navyerzhnya*
Slippery road

**321 Zakaz wymijania**
*Zakaz vimeeyanya*
No overtaking

## At the Filling Station

**322 Unleaded (lead-free)/
Standard/Premium**
Bez-ołowiowa (bez ołowiu)/
Normalna/wysoko oktanowa
*Bez-owoviova(bez owovyou)/
Normalna/visokoh oktanova*

**323 Fill the tank please.**
Do pełna, poproszę.
*Do pewna, poproshem.*

**324 Do you have a road map of
this area?**
Czy jest mapa drogowa tej
okolicy?
*Chi yest mapa drogova tey
okolitzee?*

**325 How much is the car-wash?**
Ile kosztuje auto-myjnia?
*Eele koshtooye awtoh-meeynya?*

## Breakdowns

**326 I've had a breakdown at . . .**
Samochód mi się zepsuł na . . .
*Samohood me shem zepsoow
na . . .*

**327 I am on the road from . . .
to . . .**
Jestem w drodze z . . .
do . . .
*Yestem v drodzhe z . . .
doh . . .*

**328 I can't move the car. Can
you send a tow-truck?**
Nie mogę ruszyć samochodu.
Proszę przysłać pomoc
drogową
*Nye mogem rooshich samohodoo.
Proshem pshiswach pomotz
drogovom.*

**329 I have a flat tyre.**
Mam płaską oponę.
*Mam pwaskom oponeh*

**330 The windscreen (windshield)
has smashed/cracked.**
Szyba się stłukła/pękła.
*Sheba shem stwookwah/penkhwa.*

**331 There is something wrong
with the engine/brakes/
lights/steering/gearbox/
clutch/exhaust.**
Mam problem z silnikiem/
hamulcami/światłami/układem
kierowniczym/skrzynią
biegów/sprzęgłem/tłumikiem.
*Mam problem z shilneekyem/
hamooltzame/shvyatwamee/*

226

ookwadem kyerovneechem/
skhshinyom byegoow/
spshengwem/twoomikyem.

**332** **It's overheating.**
Przegrzewa się.
*Pshegzheva sheh.*

**333** **It won't start.**
Nie chce ruszyć.
*Nye htse rooshich.*

**334** **Where can I get it repaired?**
Gdzie mogę naprawić?
*Gje mogem napraveech?*

**335** **Can you take me there?**
Czy może mnie Pan(Pani) tam
zaprowadzić?
*Chi mozhe mnye Pan(Pani) tam
zaprovadzheech?*

**336** **Will it take long to fix?**
Jak długo potrwa naprawa?
*Yak dwoogoh potrva naprava?*

**337** **How much will it cost?**
Ile będzie kosztowało?
*Eele bendzhe koshtovawoh?*

## Accidents

**338** **Can you help me? There has
been an accident.**
Proszę mi pomoc. Chodzi o
wypadek.
*Proshem mi pomotz. Hodzhi o
vipadek.*

**339** **Please call the police/an
ambulance.**
Proszę zawezwać policję/
pogotowie.

Proshem zavezvach policyem/
pogotohvye.

**340** **Is anyone hurt?**
Czy ktoś jest ranny?
*Chi ktosh yest rannee?*

## Traffic Offences

**341** **I'm sorry, I didn't see the
sign.**
Przepraszam, nie widziałem(am)
znaku.
*Psheprasham, nye
vidzhyawem(am) znakoo.*

**342** **Must I pay a fine? How
much?**
Czy muszę zapłacić mandat?
Ile?
*Chi mushem zapwacheech
mandat? Eele?*

**343** **Show me your documents.**
Dokumenty poproszę.
*Dokumenti poproshem.*

## HEALTH

### Pharmacy

**344** **Do you have anything for a
stomachache/headache/sore
throat/toothache?**
Czy jest coś na ból żołądka/ból
głowy/ból gardła/ból zęba?
*Chi yest tzosh na bool zholondka/
bool gwovy/bool gardwa/bool
zemba?*

332
↑
344

**POLISH**

345
↑
357

345 I need something for
diarrhoea (diarrhea)/
constipation/a cold/a cough/
insect bites/sunburn/travel
(motion) sickness.
Potrzebuję czegoś na biegunkę/
zaparcie/przeziębienie/kaszel/
ukąszenie owada/opaleniznę/
morską chorobę.
*Potshebooyem tsosh na
biegoonkem/zaparchee/
pshezyembyenye/kashel/
ukonshenye ovada/opaleniznem/
morskom horobem.*

346 How much/how many do I
take?
Ile mam zażyć?
*Eele mam zazhych?*

347 How often do I take it/them?
Jak często mam to brać?
*Yak chensto mam toe brach?*

348 How much does it cost?
Ile to kosztuje?
*Eele toe koshtooye?*

349 Can you recommend a good
doctor/dentist?
Czy możecie mi polecić
dobrego lekarza/dentystę?
*Chi mozhetsye me polechich
dobrego lekaja/dentystem?*

350 Is it suitable for children?
Czy nadaje się dla dzieci?
*Chi nadaye shye dla jechee?*

## Doctor

351 I have a pain here/in my
arm/leg/chest/stomach.
Boli mnie tu/w ramieniu/
nodze/piersiach/żołądku.
*Bolee mnye too/v ramyenew/
nodzey/piershiah/zhowondkoo.*

352 Please call a doctor, this is an
emergency.
Proszę wezwać lekarza, to jest
nagły wypadek.
*Proshem wezwoch lekazha, toe yest
nagwy vypadek.*

353 I would like to make an
appointment to see a doctor.
Chcę zamówić wizytę lekarską.
*Khcem zamoovich vizytem
lekarskom.*

354 I am diabetic/pregnant.
Jestem cukrzykiem/w ciąży.
*Yestem tsukshykiem/v tsionjy.*

355 I need a prescription for . . .
Potrzebuję receptę na . . .
*Potshebooyem retseptem na . . .*

356 Can you give me something
to ease the pain?
Czy może mi Pan/Pani (woman)
dać jakiś środek
przeciwbólowy?
*Chi mozhe me Pan/Pany dach
yakish shrodek pshechivboolovy?*

357 I am/he is/she is allergic to
penicillin.
Ja jestem/on jest/ona jest
uczulony/a na penicylinę.

Ya yestem/on yest/ona yest
uchoolonee/a na penitzileenem.

**358 Does this hurt?**
Czy to boli?
*Chi to bolee?*

**359 You must/he must/she must
go to hospital.**
Pan(Pani)/on/ona musi pójść do
szpitala.
*Pan(Pani)/on/ona mooshe
pooyshch doh shpitalah.*

**360 Take these once/twice /three
times a day.**
Proszę zażywać to raz/dwa/
trzy razy dziennie.
*Proshem zazhivach toh raz/dwa/
tshee razee djenye.*

**361 I am/he is/she is taking this
medication.**
Ja zażywam/on zażywa/ona
zażywa to lekarstwo.
*Ya zazheevam/on zazheeva/ona
zazheeva toh lekarstvoh.*

**362 I have medical insurance.**
Mam ubezpieczenie lekarskie.
*Mam oobezpyechenye lekarskye.*

## Dentist

**363 I have toothache.**
Boli mnie ząb.
*Boly mnie zomb.*

**364 My filling has come out.**
Wyleciała mi plomba.
*Vyletsyawa me plomba.*

**365 I do/do not want to have an
injection first.**
Proszę najpierw o zastrzyk/nie
chcę zastrzyku.
*Proshem naipyero o zastsheek/nye
khcem zastsheekoo.*

## EMERGENCIES

**366 Help!**
Pomocy!
*Pomotsy!*

**367 Call an ambulance/a doctor/
the police!**
Prosze wezwać karetkę
pogotowia/lekarza/policję!
*Proshem zavezwach karetkem
pogotovya/lekazha/politsyem!*

**368 I have had my travellers'
cheques (travelers' checks)/
credit cards/purse/handbag/
rucksack (knapsack)/
luggage/wallet stolen.**
Skradziono mi czeki podróżne/
karty kredytowe/portmonetkę/
torebkę/plecak/bagaż/portfel.
*Skrajono me chekee podroozhne/
karty kreditovey/pormonetkem/
torebkem/pletsak/bagazh/portfel.*

**369 Can you help me, I have lost
my daughter/son?**
Czy może mi Pan (Pani) pomóc,
Zgubiłam córkę/syna?
*Chi mozheh me Pan (Panee),
Zgoobiwam tsoorkem/syna?*

**370** Please go away/leave me alone.
Proszę odejść/zostawić mnie w spokoju.
*Proshem odeyshch/zostavich mnye v spokoyoo.*

**371** Fire!
Pożar!
*Pozhar!*

**372** I want to contact the British/American/Canadian/Irish/Australian/New Zealand/ South African consulate.
Chcę się skontaktować z konsulatem brytyjskim/amerykańskim/kanadyjskim/irlandzkim/australijskim/nowo-zelandzkim/RPA.
*Htsem shem skontaktovach z konsulatem britiyskeem/americanskeem/canadeeyskeem/irlandzkhim/awstraleeyskim/novo-zelandzhkhim/er-pe-ah.*

# Introduction

Portuguese is spoken throughout Portugal. In tourist areas a certain amount of English is spoken. Portuguese is a descendant of Latin, like Italian, Spanish and French, and a knowledge of any of these other languages will help you to understand a lot of written Portuguese. Spoken Portuguese, however, can be quite difficult for a beginner to comprehend and to speak, and you may need to ask to have things written down for you more often than in other Western European countries. If you have to resort to speaking a second language, try English or even French rather than Spanish.

Written prices can be misunderstood, particularly by North American visitors, unless you realise that $ stands for escudo, the Portuguese unit of currency; the sign is put where the decimal point would normally be, so that e.g. 200$50 would mean 200 escudos and 50 centavos (a centavo is one-hundredth of an escudo).

**PORTUGUESE**

## Addresses for travel and tourist information

**UK:** *Portuguese National Tourist Office*, 22/25A Sackville St, London W1X 1DE; tel: (0171) 494 1441.

**USA:** *Portuguese National Tourist Office*, 590 Fifth Ave (4th Floor), New York, NY 10036-4704; tel: (212) 3544403.

# ESSENTIALS

## ESSENTIALS

### Alphabet

| | |
|---|---|
| A *ah* | B *bay* |
| C *say* | D *day* |
| E *e* | F *efi* |
| G *jay* | H *agah* |
| I *ee* | J *jota* |
| K *kahpa* | L *eli* |
| M *emi* | N *eni* |
| O *o* | P *pay* |
| Q *kay* | R *erre* |
| S *esi* | T *tay* |
| U *oo* | V *vay* |
| W *vay dooplo* | X *sheesh* |
| Y *eepselohn* | Z *zay* |

### Basic Words and Phrases

**1** 
**Yes** Sim *seem*  
**No** Não *nown*

**2** 
**Please** Por favor *poor favohr*  
**Thank you** Obrigado/a *ohbreegahdoo/a*

**3** 
**That's O.K.** Está bem *istah bayng*  
**Perhaps** Talvez *tahlvaysh*

**4** 
**To** Para *para*  
**From** De *di*

**5** 
**Here** Aqui *akee*  
**There** Ali *alee*

**6** 
**None** Nenhum (a) *nenyoom (a)*  
**Also** Também *tangbayng*

**7** 
**How** Como *kohmoo*  
**When** Quando *kwahndoo*

**8** 
**What** O que *oo ki*  
**Why** Porquê *poorkay*

**9** 
**I don't understand.** Não entendo *nown ayngtayngdoo*

**10** 
**I don't speak Portuguese.** Não sei falar [nome da linguagem] *nown say falahr . . .*

**11** 
**Do you speak English?** Fala Inglês? *fahla eenglaysh?*

**12** 
**Can you please write it down?** Por favor, pode escrever isso? *poor favohr pohd ishkrivayr eessoo?*

232

**13 Can you please speak more slowly?**
Por favor, pode falar mais devagar?
*poor favohr, pohd falahr myish devagahr?*

**14 How much does it/this cost?**
Quanto custa isto?
*kwantoo kooshta ishtoo?*

## Days

**15 Monday** **Tuesday**
Segunda-feira Terça-feira
*sigoongda-fayra tayrsa-fayra*

**16 Wednesday** **Thursday**
Quarta-feira Quinta-feira
*kwahrta-fayra keengta-fayra*

**17 Friday** **Saturday**
Sexta-feira Sábado
*sayshta-fayra sahbadoo*

**18 Sunday** **Morning**
Domingo Manhã
*doomeengoo manyang*

**19 Afternoon** **Evening**
Tarde Noite
*tahrd noyt*

**20 Night** **Week**
Noite Semana
*noyt simana*

**21 Yesterday** **Tomorrow**
Ontem Amanhã
*ohngtayng ahmanyang*

## Numbers

**22 Zero** **One**
Zero Um
*zeroo oong*

**23 Two** **Three**
Dois Três
*doysh traysh*

**24 Four** **Five**
Quatro Cinco
*kwahtroo seengkoo*

**25 Six** **Seven**
Seis Sete
*saysh set*

**26 Eight** **Nine**
Oito Nove
*oytoo nov*

**27 Ten** **Eleven**
Dez Onze
*desh ohngz*

**28 Twelve** **Thirteen**
Doze Treze
*dohz trayz*

**29 Fourteen** **Fifteen**
Catorze Quinze
*katohrz keengz*

**30 Sixteen** **Seventeen**
Dezasseis Dezassete
*dizasaysh dizaset*

**31 Eighteen** **Nineteen**
Dezoito Dezanove
*dizoytoo dizanov*

**32 Twenty** **Twenty-one**
Vinte Vinte e um
*veengt veengt ee oong*

P
O
R
T
U
G
U
E
S
E

13
↑
32

233

**PORTUGUESE**

33 ↑ 54

33 **Twenty-two** **Thirty**
Vinte e dois Trinta
*veengt ee doysh treengta*

34 **Forty** **Fifty**
Quarenta Cinquenta
*kwarayngta seengkwayngta*

35 **Sixty** **Seventy**
Sessenta Setenta
*sisayngta sitayngta*

36 **Eighty** **Ninety**
Oitenta Noventa
*oytayngta noovayngta*

37 **One hundred** **Five hundred**
Cem Quinhentos
*sayng keenyengtoos*

38 **One thousand** **One million**
Mil Um milhão
*meel oong meelyowng*

## Time

39 **9.00**
Nove horas
*nov orash*

40 **9.05**
Nove e cinco
*nov ee seengkoo*

41 **9.10**
Nove e dez
*nov ee desh*

42 **9.15**
Nove e um quarto
*nov ee oong kwahrtoo*

43 **9.20**
Nove e vinte
*nov ee veengt*

44 **9.25**
Nove e vinte e cinco
*nov ee veengt ee seengkoo*

45 **9.30**
Nove e meia
*nov ee maya*

46 **9.35**
Nove e trinta e cinco
*nov ee treengta ee seengkoo*

47 **9.40**
Nove e quarenta
*nov ee kwarayngta*

48 **9.45**
Nove e quarenta e cinco
*nov ee kwarayngta ee seengkoo*

49 **9.50**
Nove e cinquenta
*nov ee seengkwayngta*

50 **9.55**
Nove e cinquenta e cinco
*nov ee seengkwaynta ee seengkoo*

51 **12.00/Midday/Midnight**
Doze horas/Meio dia/Meia noite
*dohzi orash/mayoo-deea/maya-noyt*

52 **What time is it?**
Que horas são?
*ki orash sowng?*

53 **It is . . .**
É/São . . .
*eh/sowng . . .*

## ARRIVING AND DEPARTING

### Airport

54 **Excuse me, where is the check-in desk for . . . airline?**

Desculpe, onde é o balcão de check-in da . . . (companhia aérea)?
*dishkoolp, ohngdee eh oo bahlkowngdi check-een da . . .*

### 55 What is the boarding gate/time for my flight?
Qual é a porta/hora para o meu voo?
*kwal e a porta/ora para oo mayo vo'oo*

### 56 How long is the delay likely to be?
De quanto será o atraso?
*di kwanto sirah oo atrahzoo*

### 57 Where is the duty-free shop?
Onde é a loja duty-free?
*ohngdee eh a lohzha duty-free?*

### 58 Which way is the baggage reclaim?
Onde é a recolha de bagagem?
*ohngdee eh a rrecohlya di bagahzhayng*

### 59 Where can I get the bus to the city centre?
Onde posso tomar o autocarro para o centro da cidade?
*ohngd possoo toomahr oo owtohkahrroo para o sayngtroo da seedahdi*

## Train Station

### 60 Where is the ticket office/information desk?
Onde é a bilheteira/o balcão de informações?
*ohngdee eh a beelyaytayra/oo*

*bahlkowng di eenfoormasoyesh*

### 61 Which platform does the train to . . . depart from?
De que linha parte o comboio para . . .
*di ke leenya pahrt oo kohmboyoo para . . .*

### 62 Where is platform . . ?
Onde é a linha . . ?
*ohngdee eh a leenya . . .*

### 63 When is the next train to . . ?
Quando é o próximo combóio para . . ?
*kwandoo eh oo prohseemoo kohngboyo para . . .*

### 64 Is there a later train to . . ?
Há um combóio mais tarde para . . ?
*ah oong kohngboyo myish tahrd para . . .*

## Port

### 65 How do I get to the port?
Como posso ir para o porto?
*kohmoo possoo eer para oo pohrto*

### 66 When is the next sailing to . . ?
Quando é o próximo barco para . . ?
*kwandoo eh oo prohseemoo bahrkoo para . . ?*

### 67 Can I catch an earlier ferry with this ticket?
Posso apanhar um barco mais cedo com este bilhete?
*possoo apanyahr oong bahrkoo myish saidoo kohm ayste beelyait?*

P
O
R
T
U
G
U
E
S
E

55
↑
67

# ARRIVING AND DEPARTING

## Notices and Signs

**68 Carruagem-Restaurante**
*karrooahzhayng rishtowrahnt*
Buffet (Dining) Car

**69 Autocarro**
*owtokahrroo*
Bus

**70 Água potável /não potável**
*ahgwa pootahvel/nown pootahvel*
Drinking/Non-drinking water

**71 Entrada**
*entrahda*
Entrance

**72 Saída**
*saihda*
Exit

**73 Informações**
*eemfoormasoyesh*
Information

**74 Recolha de Bagagem**
*rrecohliya do bagahzhayng*
Left Luggage (Baggage Claim)

**75 Cacifos de bagagem**
*kaseefoosh di bagahzhayng*
Luggage Lockers

**76 Correio**
*koorrayoo*
Post Office

**77 Linha**
*leenya*
Platform

**78 Estação de Caminho de Ferro**
*ishtasowng di kamihnyo di fehrroo*
Railway (Railroad) tation

**79 Aeroporto**
*aehrohportoo*
Airport

**80 Porto**
*porto*
Port

**81 Restaurante**
*ristowrangt*
Restaurant

**82 Fumadores/Não fumadores**
*foomadohrsh/nown-foomadohrsh*
Smoking/Non-Smoking

**83 Telefone**
*tilifohne*
Telephone

**84 Bilheteira**
*beelyaytayra*
Ticket Office

**85 Balcão de check-in**
*bahlkowng di check-een*
Check-in Desk

**86 Horário**
*orahreoo*
Timetable (Schedule)

**87 Lavabos**
*lavahboosh*
Toilets (Restrooms)

**88 Homens/Cavalheiros**
*omayngsh/kavalyayroosh*
Gentlemen

**89 Senhoras**
*sinyohrash*
Ladies'

**90 Carro eléctrico**
*kahrroo elehtreekoo*

Tram (Streetcar)

**91 Metropolitano**
*metropooleetahnoo*
Underground (Subway)

**92 Sala de espera**
*sahla di ishpehra*
Waiting-Room

## Buying a Ticket

**93 I would like a first-class/ second-class single (one-way)/return (round-trip) ticket to . . .**
Queria um bilhete de primeira classe/segunda classe/simples/ida e volta para . . .
*kireea oong beelyayt di preemayra/sigoonda klahs/seemplish/eeda ee vohlta para . . .*

**94 Is my rail pass valid on this train/ferry/bus?**
A minha assinatura é válida para este combóio/barco/autocarro?
*a meenya aseenatoora eh vahleeda para eshte lohmboyoo/bahrkoo/owtohkahrroo?*

**95 I would like an aisle/window seat.**
Queria um lugar no corredor/na janela.
*kireea oong loogahr noo korridohr/na zhanehla*

**96 No smoking/smoking, please.**
Por favor, fumador/não fumador
*poor favohr, foomadohr/nown foomadohr*

**97 We would like to sit together.**
Queríamos lugares juntos
*kireeamoosh loogahrsh zhoongtoosh*

**98 I would like to make a seat reservation.**
Queria marcar um lugar
*kireea marcahr oong loogahr*

**99 I would like to reserve a couchette/sleeper for one person/two people/for my family.**
Queria marcar uma couchette/cama para uma pessoa/duas pessoas/para a minha família.
*kireea marcahr ooma koooshet/kama para ooma pesoha/dooash pesohash/para a meenya fameehleea*

**100 I would like to reserve a cabin.**
Queria marcar uma cabina.
*kireea markahr ooma kahbeena*

## Timetables (Schedules)

**101 Chegada**
*shigahda*
Arrive

**102 Com paragem em . . .**
*kohng parahzhayng ayng*
Calls (Stops) at

**103 Serviço de Restaurante**
*serveehsoo di rishtowrangt*
Catering Service

P
O
R
T
U
G
U
E
S
E

91
↑
103

237

**P O R T U G U E S E**

**104 ↓ 120**

104 **Mudar em . . .**
*Moodahr ayng . . .*
Change at . . .

105 **Ligação**
*leegasowng*
Connection

106 **Todos os dias**
*tohdoosh oosh deeash*
Daily

107 **De 40 em 40 minutos**
*di kwarayngta ayng kwarayngta meenootoosh*
Every 40 Minutes

108 **Primeira Classe**
*preemayra klahs*
First-Class

109 **De hora a hora**
*di ora a ora*
Hourly

110 **Recomenda-se marcação de lugares**
*rrikoomaynda-si markasowng si loogahrsh*
Seat reservations are recommended

111 **Segunda classe**
*sigoonda klahs*
Second-class

112 **Suplemento Pagável**
*sooplimayngtoo pagahvel*
Supplement Payable

113 **Via**
*veeah*
Via

## Luggage

114 **How much will it cost to send (ship) my luggage in advance?**
Quanto custa mandar a minha bagagem primeiro?
*kwantoo kooshta mandahr a meenya bagahzhayng preemayuroo?*

115 **Where is the left luggage (baggage claim) office?**
Onde é o escritório de recolha de bagagem?
*ohngdee eh oo ishkreetohreeoo di rricohliyadi bagahzhayng*

116 **What time do you open/close?**
A que horas abre/fecha?
*a ke orash ahbre/fesha*

117 **Where are the luggage trolleys (carts)?**
Onde estão os carrinhos (trolleys)
*ohngdee ishtowng oos karreenyoosh (trolleysh)*

118 **Where are the lockers?**
Onde são os cacifos?
*ohngd sowng oos kaseefoosh?*

119 **I have lost my locker key.**
Perdi a chave do meu cacifo.
*Perdee a shahve doo mayo kaseefoo*

## On Board

120 **Is this seat taken?**
Este lugar está ocupado?
*aysht loogahr istah ohkoopahdoo?*

**121** Excuse me, you are sitting in my reserved seat.
Desculpe, está sentado no meu lugar marcado.
*dishkoolp, istah sayntahdoo noo mayo loogahr markahdoo*

**122** Which station is this?
Que estação é esta?
*ki ishtasowng eh ehshta?*

**123** What time is this train/bus/ferry/flight due to arrive/depart?
A que horas deve chegar/partir este combóio/autocarro/barco/voo?
*a ke orash dehv shigahr/parteer aysht kohngboyoo/owtohkahrro/bahrkoo/vo'oo*

**124** Will you wake me just before we arrive?
Acorda-me antes de chegarmos?
*akohrda-mi antishdi shegahrmoosh?*

## Customs and Passports

**125** Os passaportes, por favor!
*oosh pahsaportsh poor favohr!*
Passports, please!

**126** I have nothing to declare.I have wine/spirits (alcohol)/tobacco to declare.
Não tenho nada a declarar. Tenho/vinho/bebidas alcoólicas/tabaco a declarar.
*nown taynyoo nahda a deklarahr. Taynyoo nahda/veenyo/bibeedash ahlcohleecash/tabahkoo a deklarahr*

**127** I shall be staying for . . . days/weeks/months.
Vou ficar durante . . . dias/semanas/meses.
*voh feecahr doorangt . . . deeash/simahnash/mehzesh*

## AT THE TOURIST OFFICE

**128** Do you have a map of the town/area?
Tem um mapa da cidade/zona?
*tayng oong mahpa da seedahde/zohna?*

**129** Can I reserve accommodation here?
Posso fazer marcação de alojamento aqui?
*possoo fazayr markasowng de aloozhamaynтoo akee?*

**130** Do you have a list of accommodation?
Tem uma lista de alojamentos?
*tayng ooma leeshta di aloozhamaynтoosh?*

## ACCOMMODATION

### Hotels

**131** I have a reservation in the name of . . .
Tenho uma marcação em nome de . . .
*taynyo ooma markasowng ayng nohmi di . . .*

**132** I wrote to/faxed/telephoned you last month/last week in . . .
Escrevi/mandei um fax/telefonei no mês passado/na semana passada . . .
*ishkrevee/manday oong fahks/tilifoonay noo mays pasahdoo/na simahna pasahda . . .*

**133** Do you have any rooms free?
Tem quartos vagos?
*tayng kwahrtoosh vahgoosh?*

**134** I would like to reserve a single/double room with/without bath/shower.
Queria marcar um quarto para uma pessoa/para duas pessoas com/sem banho/chuveiro
*kireea marcahr oong kwahrtoo para ooma pesoha/ para dooash pesoash*

**135** I would like bed and breakfast/(room and) half board/(room and) full board.
Queria cama e pequeno almoço/meia pensão/pensão completa
*kireea kam ee pikayno ahlmohso/ maya pengsowng/pengsowng komplehta*

**136** How much is it per night?
Quanto custa por noite?
*kwantoo koosta poor noyt?*

**137** Is breakfast included?
O pequeno almoço está incluído?
*oo pikaynoo ahlmohsoo istah eenklooeedoo?*

**138** May I see the room?
Posso ver o quarto?
*possoo vayr oo kwartoo?*

**139** Do you have any cheaper rooms?
Tem quartos mais baratos?
*tayng kwartoosh myish barahtoosh?*

**140** I would like to take the room.
Queria ficar com o quarto.
*kireea feecahr kohm oo kwartoo*

**141** I would like to stay for . . . nights.
Queria ficar por . . . noites.
*kireea ficahr poor . . . noytish*

**142** The shower/light/tap doesn't work.
O chuveiro/a luz/a torneira não funciona.
*oo shoovayroo/er loosh/er toornayra nown foongsyona.*

**143** At what time/where is breakfast served?
A que horas/onde é servido o pequeno almoço?
*er ke orash eh sirveedo oo pikaynoo ahlmossoo?*

**144** What time do I have to check-out?
A que horas tenho de deixar o quarto?
*a ke orash taynyo di dayshahr oo kwahrto?*

**145** Can I have the key to room no . . ?
Pode-me dar a chave do quarto número . . ?

*pohdi-mi dahr er shahv doo
kwahrtoo noomiroo . . ?*

**146 My room number is . . .**
O número do meu quarto é . . .
*oo noomiroo doo mayo kwahrto
eh . . .*

**147 Do you accept travellers'
cheques/Eurocheques/credit
cards?**
Aceita cheques de viagem/
Eurocheques/cartões de crédito?
*asayta shehkiesh di veeahzhayng/
ayoorosheksh/kartoyesh di
kredeetoo*

**148 May I have the bill please?**
Pode-me dar a conta, por favor?
*pohd-mi dahr er kohngta, poor
favohr?*

**149 Excuse me, I think there is a
mistake in this bill.**
Desculpe, acho que há um erro
nesta conta.
*dishkoolp, ahshoo ke ah oong
ayrroo na kohngta*

## Youth Hostels

**150 How much is a dormitory bed
per night?**
Quanto é uma cama num
dormitório por noite?
*kwantoo eh ooma kama noong
dormeetohreeoo poor noyt?*

**151 I am/am not an HI member.**
Sou/não sou membro do HI
*soh/nown soh mayngbroo doo
agah ee*

**152 May I use my own sleeping
bag?**
Posso usar o meu saco de
dormir?
*possoo oozahr oo mayu sahkoo di
dormeer?*

**153 What time do you lock the
doors at night?**
A que horas fecham as portas à
noite?
*er ki orash fayshowm as pportash
ah noyt?*

## Camping

**154 May I camp here for the
night/two nights?**
Posso acampar aqui esta noite/
por duas noites?
*posso akampahr akee eshta noyt/
poor dooash noytsh?*

**155 Where can I pitch my tent?**
Onde posso armar a minha
tenda?
*ohngd possoo ahrmahr er meenya
tayngda?*

**156 How much does it cost for
one night/week?**
Quanto custa por uma noite/
uma semana?
*kwantoo kooshta poor ooma noyt/
ooma simana?*

**157 Where can we park our
caravan?**
Onde podemos estacionar a
nossa roulotte?
*ohngd podaymosh ishtaseeoonahr
er nossa roolohte?*

P
O
R
T
U
G
U
E
S
E

146
↑
157

**241**

**158** Where are the washing facilities?
Onde são as casas de banho?
*ohngd sowng ash kahzash di banyoo?*

**159** Is there a restaurant/supermarket/swimming pool on site/nearby?
Há aqui/perto um restaurante/supermercado/uma piscina?
*ah akee pehrtoo oong ristowrangt/soopermercahdoo/ooma peeshseena?*

**160** Do you have a safety deposit box?
Tem cofre para guardar valores?
*tayng kohfr para gwardahr valohrsh?*

## EATING AND DRINKING

### Cafés and Bars

**161** I would like a cup of/two cups of/another coffee/tea.
Queria uma chávena de/duas chávenas de/outro café/chá.
*kireea ooma shahvna di/dooash shahvnash di ohtroo kafeh/shah*

**162** With/without milk/sugar.
Com/sem leite/açúcar
*kohng/sayng layt/asookar*

**163** I would like a bottle/glass/two glasses of mineral water/red wine/white wine, please.
Queria uma garrafa/um copo/dois copos/ de água mineral/vinho tinto/vinho branco, por favor
*kireea ooma garrahfa/oong kohpoo/doysh kopoosh/ di ahgwa meenirahl/veenyo teengto/ veenyo brahngkoo poor favohr*

**164** I would like a beer/two beers, please.
Queria uma cerveja/duas cervejas, por favor.
*kireea ooma servayzha/dooash servaizhash, poor favohr.*

**165** May I have some ice?
Pode-me dar gelo?
*pohd-mi dahr zhayloo?*

**166** Do you have any matches/cigarettes/cigars?
Tem fósforos/cigarros/charutos?
*tayng fohshfooroosh/seegahrroosh/sharootoosh?*

### Restaurants

**167** Can you recommend a good/inexpensive restaurant in this area?
Pode recomendar um restaurante bom/económico nesta área?
*pohd rrikoomayndahr oong ristowrangt bohm/eekinohmeekoo nehshta ahreea?*

**168** I would like a table for . . . people.
Queria uma mesa para . . . pessoas.
*kireea ooma mehza para . . . pesoash.*

**169 Do you have a non-smoking area?**
Tem uma área de não fumadores?
*tayng ooma ahreea di nown foomadohrsh?*

**170 Waiter/Waitress!**
Faz favor!
*fash favohr!*

**171 Do you have a set menu/ children's menu/wine list?**
Tem uma ementa turística/ ementa para crianças/carta de vinhos?
*tayng oom eemaynta tooreeshteeca/ para kreeangsash/ kahrta di veenyoosh?*

**172 Do you have any vegetarian dishes, please?**
Tem pratos vegetarianos, por favor?
*tayng prahtoosh vezhetareeahnoosh, poor favohr?*

**173 Are there any local specialities?**
Há algumas especialidades locais?
*ah ahlgoomash ishpiseealeedahdsh lookeyish?*

**174 Are vegetables included?**
Os legumes estão incluídos?
*oosh ligoomish ishtowng eenklooihdoosh?*

**175 Could I have it well-cooked/ medium/rare please?**
Posso escolher bem passado/ médio/mal passado, por favor?

**176 What does this dish consist of?**
De que consiste este prato?
*di ki konseesht aysht prahtoo?*

**177 I would like the set menu, please.**
Queria a ementa turística, por favor
*kireea er eemengta toorihshteeca, poor favohr*

**178 We have not been served yet.**
Ainda não fomos servidos.
*aeehnda nown fohmoosh serveedosh.*

**179 Excuse me, this is not what I ordered.**
Desculpe, não foi isto que encomendei.
*dishkoolp, nown fohee eeshtoo ki inkoomaynday*

**180 May I have some/some more bread/water/coffee/tea?**
Pode-me dar pão/mais pão/ água/café/chá?
*pohde-mi dahr myish powng/ ahgwa/cafeh/shah*

**181 May I have the bill, please?**
Pode-me dar a conta, por favor?
*pohd-mi dahr er kohngta, poor favohr?*

**182 Does this bill include service?**
A conta inclui serviço?
*er kohngta eengklooee sirveesso?*

possoo ishkoolyer bayng pasahdoo/mahl pasahdoo, poor favohr?

**PORTUGUESE**

**169 ↑ 182**

243

**183** Do you accept travellers'
cheques (travelers' checks)/
Eurocheques/MasterCard/US
dollars?
Aceita cheques de viagem/
Eurocheques/MasterCard/
Dólares americanos?
*asayta shehkish di veeahzhayng/
ayoorohsheksh/mahshtehrkahrd/
dohlarsh amireekahnoosh*

**184** Can I have a receipt, please?
Pode-me dar um recibo, por
favor?
*pohd-mi dahr oong rriseeboo, poor
favohr?*

**185** Where is the toilet
(restroom), please?
Por favor, onde são os lavabos?
*poor favohr, ohngdee sowng oos
lavahboosh?*

## On the Menu

**186** First courses
Entradas
*intrahdash*

**187** Soups
Sopas
*sohpash*

**188** Main courses
Pratos principais
*prahtoosh preengseepaheesh*

**189** Fish dishes
Pratos de peixe
*prahtoosh di paysh*

**190** Meat dishes
Pratos de carne
*prahtoosh di kahrni*

**191** Vegetarian dishes
Pratos vegetarianos
*prahtoosh vizhitareeanoosh*

**192** Cheese
Queijo
*kayzhoo*

**193** Desserts
Sobremesas
*sohbrimehzash*

**194** Specialities
Especialidades
*ishpiseealeedahdsh*

## GETTING AROUND

### Public Transport

**195** Where is the bus stop/coach
station/nearest metro
(subway) station?
Onde é a paragem do autocarro/
garagem das camionetas/a
estação de metro mais próxima?
*âgdee eh er parahzhayng doo
owtohkahrroo/garahzhayng das
kameeonehtash/er ishtasowng di
mehtroo myish prohseema?*

**196** When is the next/last bus
to . . ?
Quando sai o próximo/último
autocarro para . . ?
*kwandoo sahee oo prohseemoo/
owtohkahrroo para . . ?*

**197** How much is the fare to the
city centre (downtown)/
railway (railroad) station/
airport?

P
O
R
T
U
G
U
E
S
E

183
↑
197

244

Quanto é o bilhete para o centro da cidade/estação de caminho de ferro/ aeroporto?
*ântoo eh oo beelyayte para oo sengtroo da seedahdi/ishtasowng di kaminyoo di fehrroo/ aehrohportoo*

**198** Will you tell me when to get off?
Diz-me quando devo sair?
*deesh-mi kwandoo dehvoo saeehr?*

**199** Does this bus go to . . ?
Este autocarro vai para . . ?
*aysht owtohkahrroo va'ee para . . ?*

**200** Which number bus goes to . . ?
Qual é o número do autocarro que vai para . . ?
*kwal eh oo noomiroo doo owtohkahrroo ki va'ee para . . ?*

**201** May I have a single (one-way)/return (round-trip)/day ticket/book of tickets?
Pode-me dar um bilhete simples/ida e volta/diário/ caderneta de bilhetes?
*Pohd-mi dahr oong beelyayt seemplish/eeda ee vohlta/ deeahreeoo/kadirnayta di beelyaytsh?*

## Taxis

**202** I would like to go to . . .
How much will it cost?
Queria ir para . . .
Quanto custa?
*kireea eer para . . . kwongtoo kooshta?*

**203** Please stop here.
Pare aqui, por favor.
*pahr akee, poor favohr*

**204** I would like to order a taxi today/tomorrow/at 2pm to go from . . . to . . .
Queria um táxi para hoje/ amanhã/ às duas da tarde para ir de . . . para . . .
*kireea oong tahksee para ohzhay/ ahmanyang/ahsh dooash da tahrd para eer de . . . para . . .*

## Asking the Way

**205** Excuse me, do you speak English?
Desculpe, fala Inglês?
*dishkoolp, fahla eenglays?*

**206** Excuse me, is this the right way to . . ?
Desculpe é este o caminho certo para . . ?
*dishkoolp, eh aysht oo kameenyo sehrtoo para . . ?*

**207** . . . the cathedral/the tourist information office/the castle/ the old town
. . . a catedral/os serviços de informações turísticas (o turismo)/o castelo/a cidade velha
*. . . er katidrahl/ oos sirveessoos de eemfoormasoyesh tooreehshteekash (oo tooreesmoo)/ oo kastehloo/ er seedahd vehlya.*

**208** Can you tell me the way to
the railway (railroad) station/
bus station/taxi rank (stand)/
city centre (downtown)/
beach?
Pode-me indicar o caminho para
a estação de caminho de ferro/a
estação de autocarros/a
paragem de táxis/o centro da
cidade/a praia?
*podd-mi eendeecahr oo kameenyoo
para er ishtasowng de kameenyo
do fehrro/er ishtasowng di
owtohkahrrosh/er parahzhayng de
tahkseesh/oo sayntroo da seedahd/
er prahya?*

**209** First/second left/right/
straight ahead.
Primeira/segunda à esquerda/à
direita/sempre em frente
*premayra/sigoonda ah ishkehrda/
ah deerayta/sayngpri ayng
frayNti*

**210** Where is the nearest police
station/post office?
Onde é o posto da polícia/o
correio mais próximo?
*ohngdee eh oo pohshtoo da
pooleesseea/ oo koorrayoo myish
prohseemoo?*

**211** Is it far?
É longe?
*eh lohnzhi?*

**212** Do I need to take a taxi/catch
a bus?
Preciso de apanhar um táxi/um
autocarro?
*preseezoo di apanyahr oong
tahksee/oong owtohkahrroo*

**213** Can you point to it on my
map?
Pode indicá-lo no meu mapa?
*pohd eendeecahloo noo mayo
mahpa?*

**214** Thank you for your help.
Obrigado pela sua ajuda.
*ohbreegahdoo pehla sooa azhooda*

## SIGHTSEEING

**215** Where is the Tourist
Information office?
Onde é o Turismo?
*ohngdee eh oo tooreeshmoo?*

**216** Where is the cathedral/
church/museum?
Onde é a catedral/igreja/museu?
*ohngdee eh er katidrahl/
eegrayzha/moosayo*

**217** How much is the entrance
(admission) charge?
Qual é o preço da entrada?
*kwal eh oo preso do ayntrahda?*

**218** Is there a discount for
children/students/senior
citizens?
Há desconto para crianças/
estudantes/pessoas da terceira
idade?
*ah dishkohngtoo para
kreeangsash/ishtoodangtish/
pisoahsh da tersayra eedahd?*

**219** What time does the next
guided tour start?

A que horas começa a próxima
visita guiada?
*er ki orash koomehsa er prohseema
veezeeta gueeahda?*

**220** One/two adults/children,
please.
Um/dois adultos, uma/duas
cria ças, por favor.
*oong/doysh adooltoosh, ooma/
dooash kreeangsash poor favohr.*

**221** May I take photographs
here?
Posso tirar fotografias aqui?
*possoo teerahr footoografeeash
akee?*

## ENTERTAINMENT

**222** Can you recommend a good
bar/nightclub?
Pode recomendar um bom bar/
clube nocturno?
*pohd rrikoomayngdahr oong bohm
bahre/kloob nohtoornoo*

**223** Do you know what is on at
the cinema (playing at the
movies)/theatre at the
moment?
Sabe o que vai no cinema/teatro
de momento?
*sahb oo ke va'ee noo seenayma/
teeahtroo do momayngtoo?*

**224** I would like to book
(purchase) . . . tickets for the
matinee/evening
performance on Monday.

Queria comprar . . . bilhetes
para a sessão da tarde/noite,
segunda-feira.
*kireea komprahr . . . beelyaytsh
para er sessowngda tahrd/noyt,
sigoonda-fayra*

**225** What time does the film/
performance start?
A que horas começa o filme/a
sessão?
*er ki orash koomehsa oo film/er
sesowng?*

## MEETING PEOPLE

**226** Hello/Goodbye.
Olá/Adeus
*ohlah/adayoosh*

**227** Good morning/good
afternoon/good evening/
goodnight.
Bom dia/boa tarde/boa noite/
boa noite
*bohm deea/boha tahrd/boha noyt*

**228** Pleased to meet you.
Muito prazer
*muhingtoo prazayr*

**229** How are you?
Como está?
*kohmoo istah?*

**230** Fine, thank you. And you?
Bem obrigado. E você?
*bayng ohbreegahdoo. ee vohsay?*

**231** My name is . . .
Chamo-me . . .
*shamoo-mi . . .*

247

**232** This is my friend/boyfriend/
girlfriend/husband/wife/
brother/sister.
Este é o meu/minha amigo/
amiga/namorado/namorada/
marido/mulher/irmão/irmã
*aysht e oo mayoo/meenya
amighoo/amigha/namoorahdoo/
namoorahda/mareedoo/moolyer/
eermowng/eermang*

**233** Where are you travelling to?
Para onde vai viajar?
*para ohngdee va'ee veeazhahr?*

**234** I am/we are going to . . .
Vou/vamos para . . .
*voh/vamoosh para . . .*

**235** How long are you travelling
for?
Vai para muito longe?
*va'ee para muhingtoo lohngzhe?*

**236** Where do you come from?
De onde vem?
*di ohngd vayng?*

**237** I am/we are from . . .
Sou/somos de . . .
*soh/sohmoosh di . . .*

**238** We're on holiday.
Estamos em férias.
*ishtahmoos ayng fehreeas*

**239** This is our first visit here.
Esta é a nossa primeira visita
aqui
*ehshta e er nossa*

**240** Would you like/May I have a
cigarette?
Quer um cigarro/posso fumar?

*ker oong seegahrro/possoo
foomahr?*

**241** I am sorry but I do not
understand.
Desculpe mas não entendo.
*dishkoolp maysh nown
ayngtayngdoo*

**242** Please speak slowly.
Por favor, fale devagar.
*poor favohr fahl divagahr*

**243** Do you mind if I smoke?
Importa-se se eu fumar?
*eemporta-si see ayoo foomahr?*

**244** Do you have a light?
Tem lume?
*tayng loome?*

**245** I am waiting for my husband/
wife/boyfriend/girlfriend.
Estou à espera do meu/minha
marido/mulher/namorado/
namorada.
*ishtoh ah ishpehra doo mayoo/
meenyia mareedoo/moolyer/
namoorahdoo/namoorahda*

## TRAVELLING WITH CHILDREN

**246** Do you have a high chair/
baby-sitting service/cot?
Tem uma cadeira alta/serviço
de baby-sitting/cama de bébé?
*tayng ooma kadayra ahlta/
sirveessoo di baby sitting/kama di
behbeh?*

**247** Where is the nursery/
playroom?
Onde é a creche/infantário?

*ohngd e er kresh/eengfantahreeoo*

248 **Where can I warm the baby's bottle?**
Onde posso aquecer o biberon do bébé?
*ohngd possoo akesayr oo beeberohng doo behbeh?*

## COMMUNICATIONS

### Post

249 **How much will it cost to send a letter/postcard/this package to Britain/Ireland/America/Canada/Australia/New Zealand?**
Quanto custa mandar uma carta/postal/este pacote para Grã-Bretanha/Irlanda/América/Canadá/Austrália/Nova Zelândia?
*kwantoo kooshta mandahr ooma kahrta/pooshtahl/esht pakoht para grang-britanya/ eerlangda/ amehreeka/kanadah/owstrahleea/ nohva zelangdeea?*

250 **I would like one stamp/two stamps.**
Queria um selo/dois selos.
*kireea oong saylo/doysh sayllosh*

251 **I'd like . . . stamps for postcards to send abroad, please.**
Queria . . . selos para postais para o estrangeiro, por favor.
*kireea . . . sayloosh para pooshtiysh para o ishtrangzhayroo, poor favohr.*

### Phones

252 **I would like to make a telephone call/reverse the charges to (make a collect call to) . . .**
Queria fazer uma chamada/a pagar por quem recebe
*kireea fazayr ooma shamahda/er pagahr poor kayng ressebe*

253 **Which coins do I need for the telephone?**
Que moedas preciso para telefonar?
*ki mwedash preseezoo para tilifoonahr?*

254 **The line is engaged (busy).**
A linha está impedida.
*a leenya istah eempideeda*

255 **The number is . . .**
O número é . . .
*oo noomiroo e . . .*

256 **Hello, this is . . .**
Está, aqui fala . . .
*ishtah, akee fahla . . .*

257 **May I speak to . . ?**
Posso falar com . . ?
*possoo falahr kom . . .*

258 **He/She is not in at the moment. Can you call back?**
Não está neste momento. Pode tornar a chamar?
*nown ishtah nayshte moomayntoo. pohd toornahr a shamahr?*

## MONEY

**259** I would like to change these travellers' cheques (travelers' checks)/this currency/this Eurocheque.
Queria trocar estes cheques de viagem/estas divisas/este Eurocheque.
*kireea trookahr aystsh shehkish di veeazhayng/ehshtash deeveezash/ayst ayroshek*

**260** How much commission do you charge? (What is the service charge?)
Que comissão cobra?
*ke coomeessowng kohbra?*

**261** Can I obtain money with my MasterCard?
Posso levantar dinheiro com o meu MasterCard?
*possoo levangtahr deenyayroo kohm oo mayo mahstercahrd*

## SHOPPING

### Names of Shops and Departments

**262** Livraria/Papelaria
*leevrareea/papilareea*
Bookshop/Stationery

**263** Joalharia/Presentes
*zhooalyareea/prizayntsh*
Jeweller's/Gifts

**264** Sapatos
*sapahtoosh*
Shoes

**265** Ferragens
*ferrahzhayngsh*
Hardware

**266** Antiguidades
*anteegweedadish*
Antiques

**267** Cabeleireiro (de homens)/(de senhoras)
*kabilayrayroo (di ohmayns)/(di sinyorash)*
Hairdressers (men's)/(women's)

**268** Tabacaria
*tabakareea*
Tobacconist

**269** Padaria
*padareea*
Baker's

**270** Supermercado
*soopermercahdoo*
Supermarket

**271** Fotografia
*footoografeea*
Photoshop

**272** Brinquedos
*breengkehdoosh*
Toys

**273** Agente de Viagens
*azhayngt di veeahzhayngsh*
Travel Agent

**274** Perfumarias
*pirfoomareeash*
Toiletries

**275** Discos
*deeshkoosh*
Records

## In the Shop

**276** What time do the shops open/close?
A que horas abrem/fecham as lojas?
*a kee orah abrayng/fayshown ash lohzhash*

**277** Where is the nearest market?
Onde é o mercado mais próximo?
*ohngdee eh oo mercahdoo myish prohseemoo?*

**278** Can you show me the one in the window/this one?
Pode mostrar-me aquele na janela/este
*pohd mooshtrahr-mi akehle na zhanehla/aysht*

**279** Can I try this on?
Posso provar este?
*possoo proovahr aysht?*

**280** What size is this?
Que tamanho (número) é este?
*ki tamanyo (noomiroo) eh ayst?*

**281** This is too large/too small/ too expensive.
Este é muito grande/muito pequeno/muito caro.
*aysht eh muingtoo grangdi/ muingtoo pikaynoo/muingtoo kahroo*

**282** Do you have any others?
Tem outros
*tayng ohtroosh*

**283** My size is . . .
O meu tamanho (número) é . . .
*oo mayo tamanyo (noomiroo) eh . . .*

**284** Where is the changing room/ childrens/cosmetic/ ladieswear/menswear/food department?
Onde é o gabinete de prova/ secção infantil/cosmética/roupa de senhora/roupa de homem/ secção de alimentos?
*ohngdee eh oo gabeeneht di prohva/sehksowng eengfangteel/ koosmehteeca/rohpa di sinyora/ rohpa di omayng/seksowng di aleemayngtoosh*

**285** I would like . . .
Queria . . .
*kireea . . .*

**286** I would like a quarter of a kilo/half a kilo/a kilo of bread/ butter/cheese/ham/ tomatoes.
Queria duzentos e cinquenta gramas/meio quilo/um quilo de pão/manteiga/queijo/ fiambre/ tomate.
*kireea doozayntoosh ee seengkwayngta gramash/mayoo keeloo/ oong keeloo di powng/ mangtayga/kayzhoo/feeangbri/ toomaht*

**287** How much is this?
Quanto custa isto?
*kwantoo kooshta eeshtoo?*

**288** I'll take this one, thank you.
Levo este, obrigado
*lehvoo aysht, ohbreegahdoo*

**289** Do you have a carrier (shopping) bag?
Tem um saco de plástico com pegas?
*tayng oong sahkoo di plahshteekoo kohng pehgash.*

**290** Do you have anything cheaper/larger/smaller/of better quality?
Tem alguma coisa mais barata/maior/mais pequena/de melhor qualidade?
*tayngahlgooma kohyza myish barahta/mahyohr/myish peekayna/do melior kwaleedahd?*

**291** I would like a film for this camera.
Queria um rolo para esta máquina.
*kireea oongrohloo para ehshta mahkeena*

**292** I would like some batteries, the same size as this old one.
Queria umas pilhas do mesmo tamanho que esta.
*kireea oomash peelyash doo maysmoo tamahnyo ki ehshta.*

**293** Would you mind wrapping this for me, please?
Importa-se de me embrulhar isto, por favor?
*eemporta-si di mi aymbroolyahr eeshtoo, poor favohr?*

**294** Sorry, but you seem to have given me the wrong change.
Desculpe mas parece que me deu o troco errado.

*dishkoolp maysh parehse ki mi dayoo oo trohcoo eerrahdoo*

## MOTORING

### Car Hire (Rental)

**295** I have ordered (rented) a car in the name of . . .
Reservei um carro em nome de . . .
*rrizervay oongkahrrooay nohmdi*

**296** How much does it cost to hire (rent) a car for one day/two days/one week?
Quanto custa alugar um carro por um dia/dois dias/uma semana?
*kwantoo kooshta aloogahr oong kahrroo poor oong deea/doysh deeash/ooma simahna?*

**297** Is the tank already full of petrol (gas)?
O depósito já está cheio de gasolina?
*oo depohzeetoo zhah ishtah shayoo di gazooleena?*

**298** Is insurance and tax included? How much is the deposit?
O seguro e o imposto estão incluídos? Quanto é o depósito
*oosigooro ee oo eempohshtoo ishtowng eenklooeehdoosh? kwantoo eh oo depohzeetoo?*

**299** By what time must I return the car?

252

A que horas devo devolver o carro?
*a ki orash devoo divolvehr oo kahrroo?*

**300** I would like a small/family car with a radio/cassette player.
Queria um carro pequeno/familiar com rádio/leitor de cassettes.
*kireea oong kahrroo pikayni/fameeleeahr kohng rahdeeoo/laytohr do casehtsh*

## Asking the Way

**301** Excuse me, can you help me please?
Desculpe, pode dar-me uma ajuda?
*dishkoolp, pohd dahr-mi ooma azhooda?*

**302** How do I reach the motorway/main road?
Como vou para a autoestrada/estrada principal?
*kohngoo voh para a owtoishtrahda/ishtrahda preengseepahl?*

**303** I think I have taken the wrong turning.
Acho que virei no sítio errado.
*ahshoo ki veeray noo seeteeoo irradoo*

**304** I am looking for this address.
Estou à procura desta morada.
*ishtoh ah prohkoora deshta moorahda.*

**305** I am looking for the . . . hotel.
Estou à procura do hotel . . .
*ishtou ah prokoora doo otel . . .*

**306** How far is it to . . . from here?
A que distância daqui fica . . .
*a ki deeshtangseea dakee feeka . . .*

**307** Carry straight on for . . . kilometres.
Continui a direito por . . . quilómetros.
*kongteenooee a deeraytoo poor . . . keelohmetrosh*

**308** Take the next turning on the right/left.
Vire na próxima à direita/esquerda.
*veer na prohseema ah deerayta/ishkayrda*

**309** Turn right/left at the next crossroads/traffic lights.
Vire à direita/esquerda no próximo cruzamento/semáforo.
*veer ah deerayta/ishkayrda noo prohseemoo kroozamengtoo/simahfooroo*

**310** You are going in the wrong direction.
Vai na direcção errada.
*va'ee na deeresowng irrahda*

## Parking

**311** How long can I park here?
Por quanto tempo posso estacionar aqui?
*poor kwantoo taympoo possoo ishtaseeoonahr akee?*

312 **Is there a car park near here?**
Há um parque de
estacionamento aqui perto?
*ah oong pahrki di
ishtaseeoonamayngtoo akee
pehrtoo?*

313 **At what time does this car
park close?**
A que horas fecha este parque
de estacionamento?
*a ki orash faysha aysht pahrk di
ishtaseeoonamayngtoo?*

## Signs and Notices

314 **Via única**
*veea oohneeka*
One way.

315 **Entrada proibida**
*ayntrahda proeebeeda*
No entry.

316 **Estacionamento proibido**
*ishtaseeoonamayngto proeebeedoo*
No parking.

317 **Desvio**
*dishveeoo*
Detour (diversion)

318 **Stop (paragem)**
*stop (parahzhayng)*
Stop.

319 **Dê passagem**
*deh passahzhayng*
Give way (yield).

320 **Estrada escorregadia**
*ishtrahda iskorregadeea*
Slippery road.

321 **Ultrapassagem proibida**
*ultrapassahzhayng proeebeeda*
No overtaking.

## At the Filling Station

322 **Unleaded (lead-free)/
Standard/Premium**
Sem chumbo/Normal/Super
*sayng shoongboo/normahl/sooper*

323 **Fill the tank please.**
Encha o depósito por favor.
*ayngsha oo depohzeetoo poor
favohr*

324 **Do you have a road map of
this area?**
Tem um mapa das estradas
desta zona?
*tayng oong mahpa dash ishtradash
dehshya zona?*

325 **How much is the car-wash?**
Quanto é a lavagem do carro?
*kwanto eh a lavazhayng doo
kahrroo*

## Breakdowns

326 **I've had a breakdown at . . .**
Tive uma avaria em . . .
*teev ooma avareea ayng . . .*

327 **I am on the road from . . .
to . . .**
Estou na estrada de . . .
para . . .
*ishtoh na ishtrahda di . . .
para . . .*

328 **I can't move the car. Can you
send a tow-truck?**

254

Não posso mover o carro. Pode
mandar um reboque?
*nown possoo moovehr oo kahrroo.*
*pohd mandahr oong ribok*

329 I have a flat tyre.
Tenho um pneu furado.
*tayngoo oong pnayoo foorahdoo*

330 The windscreen (windshield)
has smashed/cracked.
O pára-brisas estilhaçou-se/
rachou.
*oo pahra-breezash isteelyasoh-si/
rrashoh.*

331 There is something wrong
with the engine/brakes/
lights/steering/gearbox/
clutch/exhaust.
Qualquer coisa está mal com o
motor/os travões/os faróis/o
volante/a caixa de velocidades/ a
embraiagem/ o tubo de escape.
*kwalkehr kohiza ishtah mahl
kohng oo mootohr/oosh
travoyesh/oosh faroysh/oo
voolangt/a kaisha dash
vilooseedahdish/a
aymbriyahzhayng*

332 It's overheating.
Está a aquecer demais.
*istah a akehser demaish*

333 It won't start.
Não arranca
*nown arrangka*

334 Where can I get it repaired?
Onde posso mandá-lo arranjar?
*ohngd possoo mandahloo
arrangzhahr?*

335 Can you take me there?
Pode-me levar lá?
*pohdmi livahr lah?*

336 Will it take long to fix?
Leva muito tempo a arranjar?
*lehva muingtoo tayngpoo a
arrangzhahr?*

337 How much will it cost?
Quanto vai custar?
*kwantoo va'ee kooshtahr?*

## Accidents

338 Can you help me? There has
been an accident.
Pode-me ajudar? Houve um
acidente.
*pohdmi azhoodahr? ohv oong
aseedayngt*

339 Please call the police/an
ambulance.
Por favor chame a polícia/uma
ambulância.
*poor favohr, shahm a pooleesya/
ooma angboolansya*

340 Is anyone hurt?
Há alguém ferido?
*ah ahlguayng fereedoo?*

## Traffic Offences

341 I'm sorry, I didn't see the
sign.
Desculpe, não vi o sinal.
*dishkoolp nown vee oo seenahl*

329
↑
341

**342** Must I pay a fine? How much?
Tenho de pagar uma multa? De quanto?
*taynyoo di pagahr ooma moolta? di kwantoo?*

**343** Show me your documents.
Mostre-me os seus documentos.
*mohshtrimi oosh sayosh dokoomayngtoosh*

## HEALTH

### Pharmacy

**344** Do you have anything for a stomachache/headache/sore throat/toothache?
Tem qualquer coisa para dores de estômago/dores de cabeça/ dores de garganta/ dores de dentes?
*tayng kwalkehr kohiza para dohrish di ishtohmago/dohrish di kabehsa/ dorish do gargangta/ dorish di dengtish?*

**345** I need something for diarrhoea (diarrhea)/ constipation/a cold/a cough/ insect bites/sunburn/travel (motion) sickness.
Preciso de alguma coisa contra diarreia/prisão de ventre/ uma constipação/ tosse/picadas de insectos/queimaduras do sol/ enzhoo.
*preseezoo di ahlgooma kohiza kongtra deearraya/preezowng di ventre/ooma konshteepasowng/*

*tohs/peekahdash do eensetoosh/ kaymadoorash doo sohl/ingzho'oo*

**346** How much/how many do I take?
Quanto/quantos devo tomar?
*kwantoo/kwantoosh dayvoo toomahr?*

**347** How often do I take it/them?
Quantas vezes devo tomar isto?
*kwantash vehzesh dayvoo toomahr ishto?*

**348** How much does it cost?
Quanto custa?
*kwantoo kooshta?*

**349** Can you recommend a good doctor/dentist?
Pode recomendar um bom médico/dentista?
*pohd rrikoomayngdahr oong bohm mehdeekoo/dayngteeshta?*

**350** Is it suitable for children?
É bom para crianças?
*eh bohm para kreeansash?*

### Doctor

**351** I have a pain here/in my arm/ leg/chest/stomach.
Tenho uma dor aqui/no braço/ na perna/no peito/no estômago.
*taynyoo ooma dohr akee noo brahsoo/na perna/noo ishtohmagoo.*

**352** Please call a doctor, this is an emergency.

Por favor, chame um médico.
É uma emergência.
*poor favohr sahmi oong
mehdeekoo. eh ooma
imerzhayngseea.*

**353** I would like to make an
appointment to see a doctor.
Queria marcar uma consulta
para um médico.
*kireea markahr ooma kongsoolta
para oong mehdeekoo.*

**354** I am diabetic/pregnant.
Sou diabético(a)/estou grávida.
*soh deeabehteekoo (a)/ishtoh
grahveeda*

**355** I need a prescription for . . .
Preciso de uma receita para . . .
*priseezoo di ooma rresayta para . . .*

**356** Can you give me something
to ease the pain?
Pode-me dar alguma coisa para
as dores?
*pod-mi dahr ahlgwma kohiza para
as dohrish?*

**357** I am/he is/she is allergic to
penicillin.
Sou/ele é/ela é/ alérgico/
alérgica à penicilina.
*soh/ili eh/ ehla eh/alehrzheekoo/
alehrzheeka ah peneeseeleena*

**358** Does this hurt?
Isso faz doer?
*eesso fahsh dooayr?*

**359** You must/he must/she must
go to hospital.
Você deve/ele deve/ele deve ir
para o hospital.

*dev/dev/dev eer para oo
ohspeetahl*

**360** Take these once/twice /three
times a day.
Tome isto uma vez/duas vezes/
três vezes ao dia.
*tohmi ishtoo ooma vays/dooash
vayzish/traysh vayzish ow deea*

**361** I am/he is/she is taking this
medication.
Estou/ele está/ela está a tomar
este medicamento.
*ishtoh/ishtah a toomahr aysht
medeekamayngtoo*

**362** I have medical insurance.
Tenho seguro médico.
*taynyo sigooroo mehdeekoo*

## Dentist

**363** I have toothache.
Tenho uma dor de dente.
*taynyo ooma dohr do daynteesh*

**364** My filling has come out.
O meu chumbo caiu.
*oo mayo shoongboo kaeehoo*

**365** I do/do not want to have an
injection first.
Quero/não quero levar uma
injecç#ao primeiro.
*kehroo/nown kehroo levahr ooma
eenzhehsowng preemayroo.*

## EMERGENCIES

**366** Help!
Socorro!
*sookohrroo!*

P
O
R
T
U
G
U
E
S
E

353
↕
366

**367 Call an ambulance/a doctor/
the police!**
Chame uma ambulância/um
médico/a polícia!
*shami ooma angboolangsya/oong
medeekoo/ a pooleesseeya*

**368 I have had my travellers'
cheques (travelers' checks)/
credit cards/purse/handbag/
rucksack (knapsack)/
luggage/wallet stolen.**
Roubaram-me os meus cheques
de viagem/cartões de crédito/a
minha bolsa/ mala de mão/a
minha mochila/bagagem/
carteira.
*rrohbahrowm~-mi oosh mayos
shehkish di veeahzhayng/
kartoyesh di kredeetoo/ a meenya
bohlsa/mahla di mowng/a
meenya moosheela/bagahzhayng/
kartayra*

**369 Can you help me, I have lost
my daughter/son?**
Pode ajudar-me? Perdi a minha
filha/o meu filho.

*pohdee azhoodahr-mi? perdee a
meenya feelya/oo mayo feelyoo*

**370 Please go away/leave me
alone.**
Por favor, vá-se embora/deixe-
me em paz.
*poor favohr, vah-see ayngbohra/
daysh-mi ayng pahsh*

**371 Fire!**
Fogo!
*fohgoo!*

**372 I want to contact the British
American/Canadian/Irish/
Australian/New Zealand/
South African consulate.**
Quero contactar o consulado
Britânico/Americano/
Canadiano/Irlandês/
Australiano/da Nova Zelândia/
Sul Africano.
*keroo kohntaktahr oo
konsoolahdoo breetahngeekoo/
amireekanoo/kanadeeanoo/
eerlahngdays/ owshtraleeanoo/da
nohva zeelangdeea/sool afreekano*

P O R T U G U E S E

367
↓
372

258

# Introduction

Alone among the languages of Eastern Europe, Romanian is a Romance tongue, descended from Latin and therefore a distant cousin of French, Italian, Spanish and Portuguese. This is of more than academic interest, since many words in written Romanian can easily be understood, at least in basic meaning, by someone with a knowledge of one of these other languages. Spoken Romanian is reminiscent of French, which is the most likely second language you will encounter, at least among older and better-educated Romanians. In some regions of the country Hungarian or German will be understood; English is spoken to a limited degree, in the most tourist-oriented parts of the country.

**R**
**O**
**M**
**A**
**N**
**I**
**A**
**N**

## Addresses for travel and tourist information

**UK:** *Romanian National Tourist Office*, 83A Marylebone High St, London W1M 3DE; tel: (0171) 224 3692.
**USA:** *Romanian National Tourist Office*, 573 Third Ave, New York, NY 10016; tel: (212 697-6971.

## ESSENTIALS

### Alphabet

| | |
|---|---|
| A | B |
| *Ah* | *Beh* |
| C | D |
| *Cheh* | *Deh* |
| E | F |
| *Eh* | *Eff* |
| G | H |
| *Djeh* | *Hash* |
| I | J |
| *Ee* | *Zheu* |
| K | L |
| *Kah* | *Ell* |
| M | N |
| *Em* | *En* |
| O | P |
| *Oh* | *Peh* |
| Q | R |
| *Kew* | *Airr* |
| S | T |
| *Ess* | *Teh* |
| U | V |
| *Oo* | *Veh* |
| W | X |
| *Dooblooveh* | *Ecks* |
| Y | Z |
| *Ee-grek* | *Zed* |

### Basic Words and Phrases

**1** Yes | No
Da | Nu
*Dah* | *Noo*

**2** Please | Thank you
Te rog | Mulţumesc
*Teh rohg* | *Multzumesc*

**3** That's O.K. | Perhaps
E în regulă | Poate
*Eh an rehgoolah* | *Pwahteh*

**4** To | From
La | De la
*Lah* | *Deh lah*

**5** Here | There
Aici | Acolo
*Aich* | *Acohlo*

**6** None | Also
Nici unul/una | De asemenea
*Neech oonool/oona* | *Deh asehmehneya*

**7** How | When
Cum? | Când?
*Coom* | *Cund*

**8** What | Why
Ce? | De ce?
*Cheh* | *Deh cheh*

**9** I don't understand.
Nu înţeleg.
*Noo antzeleg*

**10** I don't speak Romanian.
Nu vorbesc româneşte.
*Noo vorbesc romaneshteh*

**11** Do you speak English?
Vorbiţi englezeşte?
*Vorbeetz englezeshteh?*

**12** Can you please write it down?
Scrieţi vă rog.
*Screeyetz vah rohg*

R
O
M
A
N
I
A
N

01
↕
12

3 **Can you please speak more slowly?**
Vorbiți mai rar vă rog.
*Vorbeetz my rar vah rohg.*

4 **How much does it/this cost?**
Cît costă?
*Kewt costa?*

## Days

15 **Monday** **Tuesday**
Luni Marți
*Loony* *Martz*

16 **Wednesday** **Thursday**
Miercuri Joi
*Me-aircooree* *Zhoy*

17 **Friday** **Saturday**
Vineri. Sâmbătă.
*Vinairee* *Sumbahtah*

18 **Sunday** **Morning**
Duminică. Dimineața.
*Doomeeneeka* *Deemeeneyatza*

19 **Afternoon** **Evening**
După amiază. Seară
*Dupah amiazah.* *Sara*

20 **Night** **Week**
Noapte Săptămână.
*Nwapteh* *Saptamerna.*

21 **Yesterday** **Tomorrow**
Ieri Mâine
*Eeyairee* *Meu-eeneh*

## Numbers

22 **Zero** **One**
Zero Unu.
*Zehro* *Oonoo*

23 **Two** **Three**
Doi Trei.
*Doy* *Tray*

24 **Four** **Five**
Patru. Cinci.
*Patroo* *Chinch*

25 **Six** **Seven**
Șase. Șapte.
*Shaseh* *Shapteh*

26 **Eight** **Nine**
Opt. Nouă.
*Opt* *Nower*

27 **Ten** **Eleven**
Zece Unsprezece.
*Zecheh* *Oonsprezecheh*

28 **Twelve** **Thirteen**
Doisprezece Treisprezece
*Doysprezecheh* *Traysprezecheh*

29 **Fourteen** **Fifteen**
Paisprezece. Cincisprezece.
*Pie-sprezecheh* *Cheenchsprezecheh*

30 **Sixteen** **Seventeen**
Șaisprezece Șaptesprezece
*Shy-sprezecheh* *Shaptesprezecheh*

31 **Eighteen** **Nineteen**
Optsprezece Nouăsprezece
*Optsprezecheh* *Nowahsprezecheh.*

32 **Twenty** **Twenty-one**
Douăzeci. Douăzeci și unu.
*Douahzech.* *Duoahzech she oonoo.*

33 **Twenty-two** **Thirty**
Douăzeci și doi. Treizeci.
*Douahzech she doy* *Trayzech*

**ROMANIAN**

13 ↕ 33

261

**34** **Forty**
Patruzeci.
*Patroozech.*

**Fifty**
Cincizeci.
*Cheench-zech*

**35** **Sixty**
Şaizeci.
*Shy-zech*

**Seventy**
Şaptezeci.
*Shaptezech*

**36** **Eighty**
Optzeci.
*Optzech*

**Ninety**
Nouăzeci.
*Nowahzech*

**37** **One hundred**
O sută
*Oh sooter*

**Five hundred**
Cinci sute
*Chinch sooteh*

**38** **One thousand**
O mie
*Oh meeyeh*

**One million**
Un milion
*Oon milion*

## Time

**39** **9.00**
Nouă.
*Nowa*

**40** **9.05**
Nouă şi cinci.
*Nowa she chinch*

**41** **9.10**
Nouă şi zece.
*Nowa she zecheh*

**42** **9.15**
Nouă şi un sfert.
*Nowa she oon sfehrt*

**43** **9.20**
Nouă şi douăzeci.
*Nowa she dowazech*

**44** **9.25**
Nouă şi douăzeci şi cinci.
*Nowa she dowazech she chinch*

**45** **9.30**
Nouă şi jumătate.
*Nowa she zhoomahtateh*

**46** **9.35**
Zece fără douăzeci şi cinci.
*Zecheh fahrah dowazech she chinch*

**47** **9.40**
Zece fără douăzeci.
*Zecheh fahrah dowazech*

**48** **9.45**
Zece fără un sfert.
*Zecheh fahrah oon sfehrt*

**49** **9.50**
Zece fără zece.
*Zecheh fahrah zecheh*

**50** **9.55**
Zece fără cinci.
*Zecheh fahrah chinch*

**51** **12.00/Midday/Midnight**
Douăsprezece/Amiază/Miezul nopţii.
*Dowasprezecheh/Amiazah/Meeyehzool noptz*

**52** **What time is it?**
Cât este ceasul?
*Cut esteh cheyasool?*

**53** **It is . . .**
Este ora . . .
*Esteh ora . . .*

## ARRIVING AND DEPARTING

## Airport

**54** **Excuse me, where is the check-in desk for . . . airline?**

Scuzaţi-mă, unde este ghişeul
liniei aeriene . . ?
*Scoozatz-mah, oondeh esteh gisherl
leeneeyeh aereeyehneh . . ?*

⁵    hat is the boarding gate/
time for my flight?
Care este poarta/ora de
îmbarcare pentru zborul meu?
*Cahreh esteh pwarta/ora deh
umbarcareh pentroo zboroool meu?*

⁶ How long is the delay likely
to be?
Cît de lungă poate fi
întârzierea?
*Cut deh loongah pwateh fee
unterzeeyaireya?*

⁵⁷ Where is the duty-free shop?
Unde este magazinul duty-free?
*Oondeh esteh magazinool duty-
free?*

⁵⁸ Which way is the baggage
reclaim?
De unde se colectează bagajele?
*Deh oondeh seh colectayah-zah
bagazhehleh?*

⁵⁹ Where can I get the bus to
the city centre?
De unde pot lua autobuzul spre
centru?
*Deh oondeh pot lwah autoboozul
spreh chentroo?*

## Train Station

⁶⁰ Where is the ticket office/
information desk?
Unde este ghişeul de bilete/
ghişeul de informaţii?

*Oondeh esteh gisherl deh bileteh/
gisherl deh informatzi?*

⁶¹ Which platform does the
train to . . . depart from?
De la ce peron pleacă trenul
spre . . ?
*Deh la cheh pehron pleyacah
trehnool spreh . . ?*

⁶² Where is platform . . ?
Unde este peronul . . ?
*Oondeh esteh peronool . . ?*

⁶³ When is the next train to . . ?
La ce ora pleacă următorul tren
spre . . ?
*La cheh orah pleyacah
oormahtorool tren spreh . . ?*

⁶⁴ Is there a later train to . . ?
Mai este un alt tren spre . . ?
*My esteh oon alt tren spreh . . ?*

## Port

⁶⁵ How do I get to the port?
Cum ajung în port?
*Coom azhung un port?*

⁶⁶ When is the next sailing
to . . ?
Când este viitoarea cursa
spre . . ?
*Cund esteh veetwareya coorsa
spreh . . ?*

⁶⁷ Can I catch an earlier ferry
with this ticket?
Pot ua cu acest bilet un vas care
pleacă mai devreme?
*Pot ooah coo achest bilet oon vas
cahreh pleyacah my devrehmeh?*

R
O
M
A
N
I
A
N

55
↑
67

# ARRIVING AND DEPARTING

## Notices and Signs

**68** **Bufet/Vagon restaurant.**
*Buffet/Vagon restaurant*
Buffet (Dining) Car

**69** **Autobuz.**
*Autobooz*
Bus

**70** **Apă potabilă/Apă ne potabilă.**
*Apah potabilah/Apah neh potabilah*
Drinking/Non-drinking water

**71** **Intrare**
*Intrareh*
Entrance

**72** **Ieşire**
*Yesheereh*
Exit

**73** **Informaţii**
*Informatzee*
Information

**74** **Birou de bagaje**
*Beero deh bagazheh*
Left Luggage (Baggage Claim)

**75** **Dulăpioare pentru bagaje**
*Doolapeeyowahreh pentroo bagazheh*
Luggage Lockers

**76** **Oficiul poştal**
*Ofeecheeyool poshtal*
Post Office

**77** **Peron**
*Pehron*
Platform

**78** **Gară**
*Garah*
Railway (Railroad) Station

**79** **Aeroport**
*Aeroport*
Airport

**80** **Port**
*Port*
Port

**81** **Restaurant**
*Restaurant*
Restaurant

**82** **Zona pentru fumători/ nefumători**
*Zonah pentroo foomahtoree/ nehfoomahtoree*
Smoking/Non-Smoking

**83** **Telefon**
*Telefon*
Telephone

**84** **Ghişeu de bilete**
*Geesheeyoo deh bileteh*
Ticket Office

**85** **Ghişeu de înregistrare**
*Geesheeyoo deh unredjeestrareh*
Check-in Desk

**86** **Orar**
*Orar*
Timetable (Schedule)

**87** **Toalete**
*Twaleht*
Toilets (Restrooms)

**88** **Bărbaţi**
*Bahrbatz*
Gentlemen

**89 Femei**
*Femay*
Ladies'

**90 Tramvai**
*Tramvye*
Tram (Streetcar)

**91 Metrou**
*Metro*
Underground (Subway)

**92 Sală de aşteptare**
*Salah deh ashteptareh*
Waiting-Room

## Buying a Ticket

**93 I would like a first-class/
second-class single (one-
way)/return (round-trip)
ticket to . . .**
Un bilet de clasa întâi/a doua
dus/dus-întors până la . . . vă
rog.
*Oon bilett deh classa unteuy/ah
dowa dooss/dooss-untors peunah
la . . . vah rohg.*

**94 Is my rail pass valid on this
train/ferry/bus?**
Este permisul meu valabil pe
acest tren/vapor/autobuz?
*Esteh permeesool meh-oo valabil
peh achest tren/vapor/autobooz?*

**95 I would like an aisle/window
seat.**
Un loc pe coridor/lângă
fereastră, vă rog.
*Oon lock peh coridor/lungah
fehreyastra, vah rohg.*

**96 No smoking/smoking, please.**
Pentru nefumători/fumători, vă
rog.
*Pentroo neh foomahtoree/
foomahtoree, vah rohg.*

**97 We would like to sit
together.**
Dorim să stăm împreună.
*Doreem sa stahm umpreyunah.*

**98 I would like to make a seat
reservation.**
Doresc să rezerv un loc.
*Doresc sa rezerv oon lock*

**99 I would like to reserve a
couchette/sleeper for one
person/two people/for my
family.**
Doresc să rezerv o cuşetă/un
pat pentru o persoană/două
persoane/familia mea, la vagonu
de dormit.
*Doresc sah rezerv oh cooshetta/oon
pat pentroo oh persowahnah/
douah persowahneh/familia meya,
la vagonool deh dormeet.*

**100 I would like to reserve a
cabin.**
Doresc să rezerv o cabină.
*Doresc sa rezerv oh cabinah.*

## Timetables (Schedules)

**101 Sosiri**
*Soseeree*
Arrive

**102 Opriri la**
*Opreeree la*
Calls (Stops) at

R
O
M
A
N
I
A
N

89
↑
102

**103 Bufet-Restaurant**
*Boofet-Restaurant*
Catering Service

**104 Schimbați la . . .**
*Skeembatz la*
Change at . . .

**105 Legătură**
*Legahtoora*
Connection

**106 Zilnic**
*Zilnic*
Daily

**107 La fiecare patruzeci de minute**
*La fiehcareh patroozech deh minuteh*
Every 40 Minutes

**108 Clasa întâi**
*Classa untuy*
First-Class

**109 La fiecare oră**
*La fiehcareh orah*
Hourly

**110 Sânt recomandate rezervările**
*Sunt rehcomandateh rezervahrileh*
Seat reservations are recommended

**111 Clasa a doua**
*Classa a doua*
Second-class

**112 De plătit supliment**
*Deh plahtit soopleement*
Supplement Payable

**113 Via/Prin**
*Veeya/Preen*
Via

## Luggage

**114 How much will it cost to send (ship) my luggage in advance?**
Cît mă costă dacă expediez bagajele în avans?
*Cut mah costah dacah expediez bagazhehleh un avans?*

**115 Where is the left luggage (baggage claim) office?**
Unde este biroul de bagaje?
*Oondeh esteh beerol deh bagazheh?*

**116 What time do you open/close?**
La ce ora deschideți/închideți?
*La cheh ora deskidetz/unkidetz?*

**117 Where are the luggage trolleys (carts)?**
Unde sânt cărucioarele de bagaje?
*Oondeh sunt cahroochioahrehleh deh bagazheh?*

**118 Where are the lockers?**
Unde sânt dulăpioarele?
*Oondeh sunt doolapeeyowahreleh?*

**119 I have lost my locker key.**
Am pierdut cheia de la dulăpior
*Am piehrdoot kaya deh la doolapior*

R
O
M
A
N
I
A
N

103
↕
119

## On Board

**120 Is this seat taken?**
Este locul acesta ocupat?
*Esteh locool achesta ocoopat?*

**121 Excuse me, you are sitting in my reserved seat.**
Scuzaţi-mă, dar staţi pe locul meu rezervat.
*Scoozatz-mah, dar statz peh locool meyoo rezervat.*

**122 Which station is this?**
La ce gară ne aflăm?
*La cheh garah neh aflahm?*

**123 What time is this train/bus/ferry/flight due to arrive/depart?**
La ce oră urmează să sosească/să plece/trenul/autobuzul/avionul/acesta?
*La cheh orah oormeyazah sah soseyascah/sah plecheh/trenool/owtoboozool/avionool/achesta?*

**124 Will you wake me just before we arrive?**
Sculaţi-mă vă rog înainte de sosire.
*Sculatz-mah vah rohg unainteh deh soseereh.*

## Customs and Passports

**125 Paşapoartele, vă rog!**
*Pashapoarteleh, vah rohg!*
Passports, please!

**126 I have nothing/wine/spirits (alcohol)/tobacco to declare.**
Nu am nimic/vin/alcool/ţigări/de declarat.
*Noo am neemeek/veen/alcol/tzigahree/deh declarat.*

**127 I shall be staying for . . . days/weeks/months.**
Voi sta . . . zile/săptămâni/luni.
*Voy sta . . . zeeleh/sahptahmuni/loony.*

## AT THE TOURIST OFFICE

**128 Do you have a map of the town/area?**
Aveţi o hartă a oraşului/regiunii?
*Avetz oh hartah a orashoolui/redjeeyoonee?*

**129 Can I reserve accommodation here?**
Pot rezerva aici şederea?
*Pot rezerva aich shehdehreya?*

**130 Do you have a list of accommodation?**
Aveţi o listă cu locuri disponibile?
*Avetz oh listah coo locooree deesponeebeeleh?*

## ACCOMMODATION

## Hotels

**131 I have a reservation in the name of . . .**
Am făcut o rezervare pe numele
. . .
*Am fahcoot oh rezervareh peh numehleh . . .*

R
O
M
A
N
I
A
N

120
↑
131

267

# ACCOMMODATION

**132** I wrote to/faxed/telephoned you last month/last week in . . .
V-am scris/faxat/telefonat/luna/săptămâna trecută . . .
*Vam screece/faxat/telefonat/loona/sahpthmurna trehcootah . . .*

**133** Do you have any rooms free?
Aveţi vreo cameră li eră?
*Avetz vrehoh camerah leebehrah?*

**134** I would like to reserve a single/double room with/without bath/shower.
Doresc să rezerv o cameră cu pat simplu/dublu cu/fără baie/duş.
*Doresc sah rezerv oh cameran coo pat seemploo/doobloo coo/fahrah baieh/doosh.*

**135** I would like bed and breakfast/(room and) half board/(room and) full board.
Doresc o cameră cu micul dejun/semi pensiune/pensiune
*Doresc oh cameran coo meecool dehzhoon/semi pensiuneh/pensiuneh*

**136** How much is it per night?
Cât costă pe noapte?
*Cut costah peh nowapteh?*

**137** Is breakfast included?
Este micul dejun inclus în preţ?
*Esteh meecool dehzhoon incloose un pretz?*

**138** May I see the room?
Pot să văo camera?
*Pot sah vahd camehra?*

**139** Do you have any cheaper rooms?
Aveţi camere mai ieftine?
*Avetz camehreh my yefteeneh?*

**140** I would like to take the room.
Doresc să închiriez o camera.
*Doresc sah uncheeryez o camehrah.*

**141** I would like to stay for . . . nights.
Aş dori să stau . . . nopţi.
*Ash doree sah stau . . . noptz.*

**142** The shower/light/tap doesn't work.
Duşul/lumina/robinetul/este defect.
*Dooshool/loomeenah/robinetool/esteh dehfect.*

**143** At what time/where is breakfast served?
La ce ora/unde se serveşte micul dejun?
*La cheh orah/oondeh seh serveshteh meecool dehzhoon?*

**144** What time do I have to check-out?
La ce oră trebuie să părăsesc camera?
*La cheh orah trebooyeh sah parahsesc camehra?*

**145** Can I have the key to room no . . ?
Daţi-mi vă rog cheia de la camera numărul . . .
*Datz-mee vah rohg kaya deh la camehra noomahrool . . .*

268

**146** My room number is . . .

Numărul camerei mele este . . .

*Noomahrool camehrey mehleh esteh . . .*

**147** Do you accept travellers' cheques/Eurocheques/credit cards?

Acceptaţi cecuri de călătorie/Eurocheques/cărţi de credit?

*Akcheptatz checooree deh cahlahtoreeyah/Eurocheques/cahrtz deh credit?*

**148** May I have the bill please?

Nota de plată vă rog!

*Nohta deh platah vah rohg!*

**149** Excuse me, I think there is a mistake in this bill.

Mă tem că s-a strecurat o eroare în nota de plată.

*Mah tem cah sa strecoorat oh ero-arreh un nota deh platah.*

## Youth Hostels

**150** How much is a dormitory bed per night?

Cât este un pat pe noapte în dormitor?

*Cut esteh oon pat peh nowapteh un dormeetor?*

**151** I am/am not an HI member.

Nu sânt membru HI

*Noo sunt membroo hash ee*

**152** May I use my own sleeping bag?

Pot folosi sacul meu de dormit?

*Pot folosee sacool meyoo deh dormeet?*

**153** What time do you lock the doors at night?

La ce oră se închid porţile?

*La cheh orah seh unkhid portzeeleh?*

## Camping

**154** May I camp here for the night/two nights?

Pot campa aici pentru o noapte/două nopţi?

*Pot campa aich pentroo oh nwapteh/douah noptz?*

**155** Where can I pitch my tent?

Unde pot instala cortul?

*Oondeh pot instahla cortool?*

**156** How much does it cost for one night/week?

Cît costă pe noapte/pe săptămână?

*Cut costah peh nwapteh/peh sahptahmurnah?*

**157** Where can we park our caravan?

Unde putem parca caravana?

*Oondeh pootem parca caravahna?*

**158** Where are the washing facilities?

Unde sânt lavabourile?

*Oondeh sunt lavaboureeleh?*

R
O
M
A
N
I
A
N

146
↑
158

269

**159 Is there a restaurant/
supermarket/swimming pool
on site/nearby?**
Există un restaurant/
supermarket/piscină la faţa
locului/în apropiere?
*Existah oon restaurant/
supermarket/pischeenah la fatza
locoolui/eun apropiereh?*

**160 Do you have a safety deposit
box?**
Unde pot fi păstrate lucrurile de
valoare?
*Oondeh pot fee pahstrateh
loocroorileh deh valwareh?*

## EATING AND DRINKING

### Cafés and Bars

**161 I would like a cup of/two
cups of/another coffee.
I would like a cup of/two
cups of/another tea.**
O cafea/două cafele/altă cafea,
vă rog.
Uh ceai/două ceaiuri/alt ceai,
vă rog.
*Oh cafeya/douah cafehleh/altah
cafeya, vah rohg.
Oon cheai/douah cheaiooree/alt
cheai, vah rohg.*

**162 With/without milk/sugar.**
Cu/fără lapte/zahăr.
*Coo/fahrah lapteh/zahahr.*

**163 I would like a bottle/glass/
two glasses of mineral water/
red wine/white wine, please.**

O sticlă/un pahar/două pahare
cu apă minerală/vin roşu/vin
alb, vă rog.
*O steeclah/oon pahar/dowah
pahareh coo apah minehralah/
veen roshoo/veen alb, vah rohg.*

**164 I would like a beer/two
beers, please.**
O bere/două beri, vă rog.
*O bereh/dowah beree, vah rohg.*

**165 May I have some ice?**
Gheaţă, vă rog
*Gheyatzah, vah rohg*

**166 Do you have any matches/
cigarettes/cigars?**
Aveţi chibrituri/ţigări/ţigări de
foi?
*Avetz keebreetooree/tzigahree/
tzigahree deh foy?*

### Restaurants

**167 Can you recommend a good/
inexpensive restaurant in this
area?**
Îmi puteţi recomanda un
restaurant bun/ieftin în această
zonă?
*Eumi pootetz rehcomanda oon
restaurant boon/yefteen eun
acheyasta zona?*

**168 I would like a table for . . .
people.**
Doresc să rezerv o masă pentru
. . . persoane.
*Doresc sah rezerv oh masah
pentroo . . . perswaneh.*

169 **Do you have a non-smoking area?**
Există un loc pentru nefumători?
*Existah oon loc pentroo nehfumahtoree?*

170 **Waiter/Waitress!**
Chelner/chelneriţă.
*Kelner/Kelnehreetza.*

171 **Do you have a set menu/ children's menu/wine list?**
Aveţi un menu fix/un menu pentru copii/o listă cu vinuri?
*Avetz oon mehnoo fix/oon mehnoo pentroo copii/oh leestah coo veenooree?*

172 **Do you have any vegetarian dishes, please?**
Aveţi mîncăruri pentru vegetarieni?
*Avetz muncahrooree pentroo vegetaryehnee?*

173 **Are there any local specialities?**
Există specialităţi locale?
*Existah spechialitahtz localeh?*

174 **Are vegetables included?**
Sânt legumele incluse în nota de plată?
*Sunt legoomehleh inclooseh eun nota deh platah?*

175 **Could I have it well-cooked/ medium/rare please?**
Doresc carnea bine prajită/nu foarte prajită/în sânge.
*Doresc carneya beeneh prazheetah/ noo fwarteh prazheetah/un sundjeh.*

176 **What does this dish consist of?**
Ce fel de mîncare este asta?
*Cheh fehl deh muncahreh esteh asta?*

177 **I would like the set menu, please.**
Aş dori un menu fix, vă rog.
*Ash doree oon mehnoo fix, vah rohg.*

178 **We have not been served yet.**
N-am fost serviţi încă.
*Nam fost serveetz uncah.*

179 **Excuse me, this is not what I ordered.**
Scuzaţi-mă, n-am comandat aşa ceva.
*Scoozatz-mah, nam comandat asha chehva.*

180 **May I have some/some more bread/water/coffee/tea?**
Pot avea mai multă pâine/apă/ cafea/mai mult ceai?
*Pot aveya my mooltah peu-eeneh/ apah/cafeya/my moolt cheyai?*

181 **May I have the bill, please?**
Nota de plată, vă rog.
*Nota deh platah, vah rohg.*

182 **Does this bill include service?**
E bacşişul inclus în nota de plată?
*Eh bacshishool incloose un nota deh platah?*

R
O
M
A
N
I
A
N

169
↕
182

271

**183** Do you accept travellers'
cheques (travelers' checks)/
Eurocheques/MasterCard/US
dollars?
Acceptaţi ceguri de călătorie/
Eurocheques/MasterCard/
Dolari americani?
*Akcheptatz checooree deh
cahlahtoreeyeh/Eurocheque/
MasterCard/Dolaree
americahnee?*

**184** Can I have a receipt, please?
Pot avea o chitanţă vă rog?
*Pot aveya oh keetantzah va
rohg?*

**185** Where is the toilet
(restroom), please?
Unde este toaleta, vă rog?
*Oondeh esteh twalehta, vah rohg?*

## On the Menu

**186** First courses
Primul fel
*Preemool fel*

**187** Soups
Supe
*Soopeh*

**188** Main courses
Felul principal
*Feloool princheepal*

**189** Fish dishes
Pescărie
*Pescahrieh*

**190** Meat dishes
Mâncăruri cu carne
*Muncahrooree coo carneh*

**191** Vegetarian dishes
Mâncăruri cu legume
*Muncahrooree coo legoomeh*

**192** Cheese
Brânză
*Brunzah*

**193** Desserts
Deserturi
*Dehsertooree*

**194** Specialities
Specialităţi culinare
*Spechialitahtz coolinareh*

## GETTING AROUND

### Public Transport

**195** Where is the bus stop/coach
station/nearest metro
(subway) station?
Unde este staţia de autobuz/
autocar/metrou, cea mai
apropiată?
*Oondeh esteh statzia deh
owtobooz/owtocar/metro, cheya
my apropiatah?*

**196** When is the next/last bus
to . . ?
La ce oră vine următorul/
ultimul autobuz spre . . ?
*La cheh orah veeneh
oormahtorool/oolteemool
owtobooz spreh . . ?*

**197** How much is the fare to the
city centre (downtown)/
railway (railroad) station/
airport?

Cât costă biletul până-n centru/
până la gară/aeroport?
*Cut costah biletool peunahn
chentroo/peunah la garah/
aeroport?*

**198** Will you tell me when to get
off?
Vreți să-mi spuneți când să
cobor?
*Vretz sah-mee spoonetz cund sah
cobor?*

**199** Does this bus go to . . ?
Merge autobuzul ăsta la . . ?
*Mehrdjeh owtoboozool ahsta la . . ?*

**200** Which number bus goes to . . ?
Care autobuz merge la . . ?
*Careh owtobooz mehrdjeh la . . ?*

**201** May I have a single (one-
way)/return (roun -trip)/day
ticket/book of tickets?
Un bilet dus/dus-întors/valabil
24 de ore/un abonament, vă
rog.
*Oon bilet doos/doos-untors/
valabil dwahzech deh oreh/oon
abonament, vah rohg.*

## Taxis

**202** I would like to go to . . . How
much will it cost?
Vreau să merg la . . ? Cât costă
până la . . ?
*Vreyow sah mairg la . . ? Cut
costah pernah la . . ?*

**203** Please stop here.
Opriti aici, vă rog.
*Opreetz ayeechee, vah rohg.*

**204** I would like to order a taxi
today/tomorrow/at 2pm to
go from . . . to . . .
Doresc să comand un taxi azi/
mâine/la ora două după amiază,
care să mă ducă de la . . .
la . . .
*Doresc sah comand oon taxi
ahzee/meu-eeneh/la ora dowa
doopah ameeyazah, careh sah mah
ducah deh la . . . la . . .*

## Asking the Way

**205** Excuse me, do you speak
English?
Scuzați-mă. Vorbiți englezește?
*Scoozatz-mah. Vorbeetz
englehzeshteh?*

**206** Excuse me, is this the right
way to . . ?
Scuzați-mă. Ăsta este drumul
spre . . ?
*Scoozatz-mah. Asta esteh
droomool spreh . . ?*

**207** . . . the cathedral/the tourist
information office/the castle/
the old town
. . . catedrala/oficiul de
informații turistice/castelul/
orașul vechi?
*. . . catedralah/ofeechiool deh
informatzee tooristicheh/castelool/
orashool vehk?*

273

**208** Can you tell me the way to the railway (railroad) station/ bus station/taxi rank (stand)/ city centre (downtown)/ beach?

Vreţi vă rog să-mi spuneţi cum ajung la gară/staţia de autobuz/ staţia de taxiuri/în centru/la plajă?

*Vretz vah rohg sah-mee spoonetz koom azhoong la garah/statzia deh owtobooz/statzia deh taxiooree/un chentroo/la plazhah?*

**209** First/second left/right/ straight ahead.

Prima/a doua la stînga/dreapta/ drept înainte.

*Preema/a dowa la stunga/ dreyapta/drept unainteh.*

**210** Where is the nearest police station/post office?

Unde este postul de poliţie/ oficiul poştal cel mai apropiat?

*Oondeh esteh postool deh politzieh/ofeechiool poshtal chel my apropiat?*

**211** Is it far?

Este departe?

*Esteh dehparteh?*

**212** Do I need to take a taxi/ catch a bus?

Trebuie să iau un taxi/un autobuz?

*Trebooyeh sah eeyow oon taxi/oon owtobooz?*

**213** Can you point to it on my map?

Puteţi să-mi arătaţi pe hartă?

*Pootetz sa-mee arahtatz peh hartah?*

**214** Thank you for your help.

Mulţumesc pentru ajutor.

*Mooltzoomesc pentroo azhootor.*

## SIGHTSEEING

**215** Where is the Tourist Information office?

Unde este Oficiul de Informaţii Turistice?

*Oondeh esteh ofeechiool dee eenformatzee tooristicheh?*

**216** Where is the cathedral/ church/museum?

Unde este catedrala/biserica/ muzeul?

*Oondeh esteh catedrahla/ bisehrica/moozeul?*

**217** How much is the entrance (admission) charge?

Cît costă intrarea?

*Cut costah intrareya?*

**218** Is there a reduction for children/students/senior citizens?

Au copiii/studenţii/bătrânii reducere?

*Ow copeeyee/studentzee/ bahtreunee redoochehreh?*

**219** What time does the next guided tour start?

La ce oră începe următorul tur cu ghizi?

*La cheh orah unchehpeh*
*oormahtorool toor coo gheeze*

**220 One/two adults/children, please.**
Un adult/doi adulți/copii, vă rog
*Oon adoolt/doy adooltz/copeeyee, vah rohg*

**221 May I take photographs here?**
Am voie să fotografiez aici?
*Am voyeh sah fotografiez aich?*

## ENTERTAINMENT

**222 Can you recommend a good bar/nightclub?**
Puteți recomanda un bar/club de noapte bun?
*Pootetz rehcomanda oon bar/club deh nwapteh boon?*

**223 Do you know what is on at the cinema (playing at the movies)/theatre at the moment?**
Știți cumva ce filme rulează/ce piese se joacă în momentul de față?
*Shtitz coomva cheh feelmeh rooleyahza/cheh peeyeseh seh zhowacah un momentool deh fatzah?*

**224 I would like to book (purchase) . . . tickets for the matinée/evening performance on Monday.**
. . . bilete pentru matineul/seara de luni, vă rog.

. . . *bileteh pentroo mateeneyool/ seyara deh loony, vah rohg.*

**225 What time does the film/ performance start?**
La ce oră începe filmul/ spectacolul?
*La cheh orah unchehpeh feelmool/ spectacolool?*

## MEETING PEOPLE

**226 Hello/Goodbye.**
Salut/La revedere.
*Saloot/La revehdereh.*

**227 Good morning/good afternoon/good evening/ goodnight.**
Bună dimineața/Bună ziua/bună seara/noapte bună.
*Boonah deemeenayatz/Boonah zeeyua/boonah seyara/nwapteh boonah.*

**228 Pleased to meet you.**
Încântat de cunoştință.
*Uncuntat deh coonoshteentzah.*

**229 How are you?**
Ce mai faceți?
*Cheh my fachetz?*

**230 Fine, thank you. And you?**
Bine, mulțumesc. Dar dumneavoastră?
*Beeneh, mooltzoomesc. Dar doomneyavowastrah?*

**231 My name is . . .**
Mă numesc . . .
*Mah noomesc . . .*

R
O
M
A
N
I
A
N

220
↕
231

**232** This is my friend/boyfriend/
girlfriend/husband/wife/
brother/sister.
Vă prezint prietenul/prietena/
soţul/soţia/fratele/sora.
*Vah prezint preeyetenool/
preeyetehna/sotzool/sotzia/
fratehleh/sora.*

**233** Where are you travelling to?
Unde călătoriţi?
*Oondeh cahlatoritz?*

**234** I am/we are going to . . .
Călătoresc/călătorim la . . .
*Cahlatoresc/cahlahtoreem la . . .*

**235** How long are you travelling
for?
Cît timp călătoriţi?
*Cut teemp cahlahtoritz?*

**236** Where do you come from?
De unde veniţi?
*Deh oondeh veneetz?*

**237** I am/we are from . . .
Sânt/sântem din . . .
*Sunt/suntem deen . . .*

**238** We're on holiday.
Sântem în vacanţă.
*Suntem un vacantzah.*

**239** This is our first visit here.
Aceasta este prima noastră
vizită aici.
*Acheyasta esteh preema nwastrah
veezeetah aich*

**240** Would you like/May I have a
cigarette?
Doriţi/pot sa iau o ţigară?
*Doritz/pot sa iau oh tzigarah?*

**241** I am sorry but I do not
understand.
Mă scuzaţi dar nu înţeleg.
*Ma scoozatz dar noo untzehleg.*

**242** Please speak slowly.
Vorbiţi mai rar vă rog.
*Vorbeetz my rar vah rohg.*

**243** Do you mind if I smoke?
Pot aprinde o ţigară?
*Pot apreendeh oh tzigarah?*

**244** Do you have a light?
Aveţi un foc?
*Avetz oon fok?*

**245** I am waiting for my husband/
wife/boyfriend/girlfriend.
Îmi aştept soţul/soţia/prietenul/
prietena.
*Eumi ashtept sotzool/sotza/
prietenool/prietehna.*

## TRAVELLING WITH CHILDREN

**246** Do you have a high chair/
baby-sitting service/cot?
Aveţi un scaun pentru copii/un
serviciu baby-sitting/un pătuţ
pentru copii?
*Avetz oon scaun pentroo copee/oon
serveechioo baby-sitting/oon
pahtootz pentroo kopee?*

**247** Where is the nursery/
playroom?
Unde este creşa/camera
copiilor?
*Oondeh esteh cresha/camehra
copeelor?*

**248** Where can I warm the baby's bottle?

Unde pot încălzi biberonul?

*Oondeh pot uncahlzi beebehronool?*

## COMMUNICATIONS

### Post

**249** How much will it cost to send a letter/postcard/this package to Britain/Ireland/America/Canada/Australia/New Zealand?

Cât costă timbrul pentru a expedia o scrisoare/carte poştală/pachetul acesta în Marea Britanie/Irlanda/America/Canada/Australia/Noua Zeelandă?

*Cut costa timbrool pentroo ah expedhia oh scriswareh/karteh poshtala/paketool achesta un Mareya Britanyeh/Irlanda/Amehrica/Canada/Owstralia/Noua Zehlanda?*

**250** I would like one stamp/two stamps.

Un timbru/două timbre, vă rog.

*Oon timbroo/douah timbreh, vah rohg.*

**251** I'd like ... stamps for postcards to send abroad, please.

... timbre pentru cărţi poştale de expediat în străinătate, vă rog.

*... timbreh pentroo cartz poshtaleh deh expediat un strah-eenahtateh, vah rohg.*

### Phones

**252** I would like to make a telephone call/reverse the charges to (make a collect call to) ...

Doresc să telefonez/cu taxă inversă la ...

*Doresc sah telefonez/coo taxah inversah la ...*

**253** Which coins do I need for the telephone?

Cu ce monede funcţionează telefonul?

*Koo cheh monehdeh functzioneyazah telefonool?*

**254** The line is engaged (busy).

Numărul este ocupat.

*Noomahrool esteh ocupat.*

**255** The number is ...

Numărul este ...

*Noomahrool esteh ...*

**256** Hello, this is ...

Alo, ... sânt.

*Alo, ... sunt.*

**257** May I speak to ..?

Pot vorbi vă rog cu ..?

*Pot vorbee vah rohg coo ..?*

**258** He/She is not in at the moment. Can you call back?

El/ea nu este aici pentru moment. Sunaţi vă rog mai târziu.

*Yel/ya noo esteh aich pentroo moment. Soonatz vah rohg my turzioo*

## MONEY/SHOPPING

R
O
M
A
N
I
A
N

259
↕
275

### MONEY

**259** I would like to change these travellers' cheques (travelers' checks)/this currency/this Eurocheque.

Vreau să schimb aceste cecuri de călătorie/aceşti bani/acest Eurocheque.

*Vreyau sa skeemb acheshteh cecooree deh cahlahtoreeyeh/achesht bahnee/achest Eurocheque.*

**260** How much commission do you charge? (What is the service charge?)

Cît este comisionul dumneavoastră?

*Cut esteh comissionool doomneyavwastrah?*

**261** Can I obtain money with my MasterCard?

Pot încasa bani cu MasterCard?

*Pot uncasa bahnee coo MasterCard?*

### SHOPPING

#### Names of Shops and Departments

**262** Librărie/Papetărie
*Leebrahrieh/Papetahrieh*
Bookshop/Stationery

**263** Bijuterii/Cadouri
*Beezhootehrie/Kadooree*
Jeweller's/Gifts

**264** Încălţăminte
*Euncahltzahmeenteh*
Shoes

**265** Ferometal
*Feromehtahl*
Hardware

**266** Antichităţi
*Antikitahtz*
Antiques

**267** Frizer/Coafor
*Freezer/Cwafor*
Hairdressers (men's)/(women's)

**268** Tutungerie
*Tootoondjerie*
Tobacconist

**269** Brutărie
*Brootahrie*
Baker's

**270** Supermarket
*Supermarket*
Supermarket

**271** Magazin fotografic
*Magazeen fotografic*
Photoshop

**272** Jucării
*Zhoocahree*
Toys

**273** Agenţie de voiaj
*Agentzieh de voyazh*
Travel Agent

**274** Drogherie
*Drogherie*
Toiletries

**275** Magazin de discuri
*Magazeen deh deescooree*
Records

## In the Shop

**276** **What time do the shops open/close?**
La ce oră deschid/închid magazinele?
*La cheh ora deskyd/unkyd magazeenehleh?*

**277** **Where is the nearest market?**
Unde este piaţa cea mai apropiată?
*Oondeh esteh piatza cheya my apropiatah?*

**278** **Can you show me the one in the window/this one?**
Puteţi să mi-l/mi-o arătaţi pe cel/cea din vitrină/acesta/aceasta?
*Pootetz sa mee-l/mee-o arahtatz peh chel/cheya deen veetreena/achesta/acheyasta?*

**279** **Can I try this on?**
Pot să-l/s-o încerc?
*Pot sa-l/s-o unchairk?*

**280** **What size is this?**
Ce măsură are?
*Cheh mahsoora areh?*

**281** **This is too large/too small/too expensive.**
E prea mare/prea mic/prea scump.
*Eh preya mareh/preya meek/preya scoomp.*

**282** **Do you have any others?**
Aveţi alţii/altele?
*Avetz altzee/altehleh?*

**283** **My size is . . .**
Măsura mea este . . .
*Mahsoora meya esteh . . .*

**284** **Where is the changing room/childrens/cosmetic/ladieswear/menswear/food department?**
Unde este cabina de probă/raionul de confecţii pentru copii/cosmetice/confecţii pentru femei/bărbaţi/alimentara?
*Oondeh esteh cabina deh prohbah/raionool deh confectzee pentroo copee/cosmeticheh/confectzee pentroo femay/bahrbatz/alimentahra?*

**285** **I would like . . .**
Daţi-mi . . .
*Datz-mee . . .*

**286** **I would like a quarter of a kilo/half a kilo/a kilo of bread/ butter/cheese/ham/tomatoes.**
Daţi-mi un sfert/o jumătate/un kilogram de pâine/unt/brînză/şuncă/roşii.
*Datz-mee oon sfert/oh zhoomahtateh/oon keelogram deh peuineh/oont/breunzah/shooncah/roshee.*

**287** **How much is this?**
Cît costă?
*Cut costah?*

**288** **I'll take this one, thank you.**
Îl iau pe acesta, mulţumesc.
*Eul iau peh achesta, mooltzoomesc.*

ROMANIAN

276
↑
288

279

**289** Do you have a carrier
(shopping) bag?
Aveți o pungă de plastic?
*Avetz oh pungah deh plastic?*

**290** Do you have anything
cheaper/larger/smaller/of
better quality?
Nu aveți nimic mai ieftin/mai
mare/mai mic/de mai bună
calitate?
*Noo avetz neemeek my yefteen/my
mareh/my meek/deh my boonah
calitahteh?*

**291** I would like a film for this
camera.
Dați-mi vă rog un film pentru
acest aparat.
*Datz-mee vah rohg oon feelm
pentroo achest aparat.*

**292** I would like some batteries,
the same size as this old one.
Dați-mi vă rog niște baterii, de
acceeași mărime cu aceasta.
*Datz-mee vah rohg neeshteh
bateree, deh acheeyashi mahrimeh
coo acheyasta.*

**293** Would you mind wrapping
this for me, please?
Vreți vă rog s-o/să-l ambalați?
*Vretz vah rohg so/sahl ambalatz?*

**294** Sorry, but you seem to have
given me the wrong change.
Mă scuzați dar am impresia că
nu mi-ați dat restul corect.
*Mah scoozatz dar am impresia
cah noo mee-atz dat restool correct.*

## MOTORING

### Car Hire (Rental)

**295** I have ordered (rented) a car
in the name of . . .
Am comandat/închiriat un
automobil pe numele . . .
*Am comandat/unkyriat oon
automobeel peh noomehleh . . .*

**296** How much does it cost to
hire (rent) a car for one day/
two days/one week?
Cît costă închirierea unui
automobil pe o zi/două zile/o
săptămână?
*Cut costah unkyriereya oonui
automobeel peh oh zee/dowah
zeeleh/oh saptahmunah?*

**297** Is the tank already full of
petrol (gas)?
I-ați făcut plinul?
*Ee-atz fahcoot pleenool?*

**298** Is insurance and tax
included? How much is the
deposit?
Sânt asigurarea și taxa incluse?
Cât este depozitul?
*Sunt aseegurareya shee taxa
incluseh? Cut esteh dehpositool?*

**299** By what time must I return
the car?
Când trebuie să înapoiez
mașina?
*Cund trebooyeh sah unapoyez
mashina?*

**300** I would like a small/family car with a radio/cassette player.

Vreau o maşină mică/limuzină cu radio/casetofoh.

*Vreyau oh mashinah meecah/ leemoozeenah coo rahdio/ cassetofon.*

## Asking the Way

**301** Excuse me, can you help me please?

Vă rog frumos, puteţi să mă ajutaţi?

*Vah rohg froomos, pootetz sah mah azhootatz?*

**302** How do I reach the motorway/main road?

În ce direcţie este autostrada/ şoseaua naţională?

*Eun cheh directzieh esteh owtostrahda/shoseh-awua natzionalah?*

**303** I think I have taken the wrong turning.

Mă tem că am luat cotitura greşită.

*Mah tem cah am lwat coteetoora greshitah.*

**304** I am looking for this address.

Caut această adresă.

*Caut acheyastah adresah.*

**305** I am looking for the . . . hotel.

Caut hotelul . . .

*Caut hoteloul . . .*

**306** How far is it to . . . from here?

Cât de departe de aici se afla . . ?

*Cut deh dehparteh deh aich seh afla . . ?*

**307** Carry straight on for . . . kilometres.

Continuaţi drept înainte vreo . . . kilometri.

*Continooatz drept unainteh vreh-oh . . . kilometree.*

**308** Take the next turning on the right/left.

Cotiţi prima la dreapta/la stânga.

*Cotitz preema la dreyapta/la stunga.*

**309** Turn right/left at the next crossroads/traffic lights.

Luaţi-o la dreapta/la stânga la prima intersecţie/la primul semafor.

*Lowatz-oh la dreyapta/la stunga la preema eentersectzieh/la preemool sehmafor.*

**310** You are going in the wrong direction.

Circulaţi în direcţie greşită.

*Cheercoolatz un directzieh gresheetah.*

## Parking

**311** How long can I park here?

Cât timp pot parca aici?

*Cut teemp pot parca aich?*

**312** Is there a car park near here?

Este vreun garaj prin apropiere?

*Esteh vreh-oon garahzh preen apropeeyereh?*

R
O
M
A
N
I
A
N

300
↑
312

**313 At what time does this car park close?**
La ce oră se închide garajul?
*La cheh orah seh unkeedeh garazhool?*

## Signs and Notices

**314 Sens unic**
*Sens ooneek*
One way.

**315 Intrarea interzisă**
*Eentrareya eenterzeesah*
No entry.

**316 Staţionarea interzisă**
*Statzionareya eenterzeesah*
No parking.

**317 Deviaţie**
*Deviatzieh*
Detour (diversion)

**318 Stop**
*Stop*
Stop.

**319 Daţi prioritate**
*Datz prioritahteh*
Give way (yield).

**320 Pericol de derapaj**
*Pereecol deh dehrapazh*
Slippery road.

**321 Depăşirea interzisă**
*Dehpahsheereya eenterzeesah*
No overtaking.

## At the Filling Station

**322 Unleaded (lead-free)/ Standard/Premium**
Benzină neetilată/Standard/

Supercarburant
*Benzeena neeteelahtah/Standard/Supercarboorant*

**323 Fill the tank please.**
Faceţi plinul vă rog.
*Fachetz pleenool vah rohg.*

**324 Do you have a road map of this area?**
Aveţi o hartă a regiunii?
*Avetz oh hartah ah redjeeyoonee?*

**325 How much is the car-wash?**
Cât costă spălatul maşinii?
*Cut costah spahlatool mashineei?*

## Breakdowns

**326 I've had a breakdown at . . .**
Sânt în pană la . . .
*Sunt un panah la . . .*

**327 I am on the road from . . . to . . .**
Sânt pe şoseaua de la . . . la . . .
*Sunt pey shosehowua deh la . . . la . . .*

**328 I can't move the car. Can you send a tow-truck?**
Nu pot porni automobilul.
Puteţi trimite o maşină care să mă remorcheze?
*Noo pot pornee owtomobeelool. Pootetz treemeeteh oh mashinah careh sah mah rehmorchezeh?*

**329 I have a flat tyre.**
Am un cauciuc pe geantă.
*Am oon cowoochiook peh djeyantah.*

R O M A N I A N

313 ↑ 329

282

**330** The windscreen (windshield) has smashed/cracked.
Parbrizul este spart/crăpat.
*Parbreezool esteh spart/crahpat.*

**331** There is something wrong with the engine/brakes/lights/steering/gearbox/clutch/exhaust.
Motorul/frânele/farurile/direcţia/cutia de viteze/ambreiajul/eşapamentul nu funcţionează.
*Motorool/fruneleh/farooreeleh/deerectzia/cootia deh veetehzeh/ambreyazhool/eshapamentool noo foonctzioneyazah.*

**332** It's overheating.
Supraîncălzeşte.
*Sooprauncahlzeshteh.*

**333** It won't start.
Nu porneşte.
*Noo porneshteh.*

**334** Where can I get it repaired?
Unde o pot repara?
*Oondeh oh pot rehpara?*

**335** Can you take me there?
Mă puteţi transporta acolo?
*Mah pootetz transporta acolo?*

**336** Will it take long to fix?
Cât timp va dura reparaţia?
*Cut teemp va doora rehparatzia?*

**337** How much will it cost?
Cît costă?
*Cut costah?*

## Accidents

**338** Can you help me? There has been an accident.
Vreţi să mă ajutaţi vă rog? Am avut un accident.
*Vretz sah mah azhootatz vah rohg? Am avoot oon akcheedent.*

**339** Please call the police/an ambulance.
Chemaţi vă rog poliţia/salvarea.
*Kehmatz vah rohg poleetzia/salvareya.*

**340** Is anyone hurt?
Sânt răniţi?
*Sunt rahneetz?*

## Traffic Offences

**341** I'm sorry, I didn't see the sign.
Îmi cer scuze dar n-am văzut semnul.
*Eumi chair scoozeh dar nam vahzoot semnool.*

**342** Must I pay a fine? How much?
Trebuie să plătesc amendă? Cât costă?
*Trebooyeh sah plahtesc amendah? Cut costah?*

**343** Show me your documents.
Arătaţi-mi hărtiile de identitate.
*Arahtatz-mee hahrteeleh deh eedenteetahteh.*

R O M A N I A N

330 ↑ 343

## HEALTH

### Pharmacy

**344 Do you have anything for a stomachache/headache/sore throat/toothache?**
Puteți să-mi dați ceva pentru dureri de stomac/dureri de cap/dureri în gât/dureri de dinți?
*Pootetz sah-mee datz chehva pentroo doorehree deh stomac/doorehree deh cap/doorehree un gut/doorehree deh deentz?*

**345 I need something for diarrhoea (diarrhea)/constipation/a cold/a cough/insect bites/sunburn/travel (motion) sickness.**
Am nevoie de un medicament contra diareei/constipației/răcelii/tusei/mușcăturilor de insecte/arsurilor de soare/răului de călătorie.
*Am nevowyeh deh oon medicament contra deeyareh-ee/consteepatzee-ay/rachehlee/toosay/mooshcatooreelor deh insecteh/arsooreelor deh swahreh/rahwlui deh cahlahtorieh.*

**346 How much/how many do I take?**
Ce cantitate/câte iau?
*Cheh cantitahteh/cuteh yow?*

**347 How often do I take it/them?**
Cât de des iau medicamentul?
*Cut deh des yow medeecamentool?*

**348 How much does it cost?**
Cât costă
*Cut costah*

**349 Can you recommend a good doctor/dentist?**
Puteți să-mi recomandați un doctor/dentist bun?
*Pootetz sah-mee rehcomandatz oon doctor/denteest boon?*

**350 Is it suitable for children?**
Este indicat pentru copii?
*Esteh eendeecat pentroo copee?*

### Doctor

**351 I have a pain here/in my arm/leg/chest/stomach.**
Am o durere aici/în braț/picior/piept/stomac.
*Am oh doorehreh aich/un bratz/peechior/pee-ept/stomac.*

**352 Please call a doctor, this is an emergency.**
Chemați vă rog un doctor de urgență.
*Kehmatz vah rohg oon doctor deh oordjentzah.*

**353 I would like to make an appointment to see a doctor.**
Vreau să văd un doctor.
*Vreh-ow sah vahd oon doctor.*

**354 I am diabetic/pregnant.**
Sânt diabetic/însărcinată.
*Sunt deeyabetic/unsahrcheenatah.*

# HEALTH/EMERGENCIES

355 I need a prescription for . . .
Daţi-mi vă rog o reţetă pentru . . .
*Datz-mee vah rohg oh retzehtah pentroo . . .*

356 Can you give me something to ease the pain?
Puteţi să-mi daţi ceva contra durerilor?
*Pootetz sa-mee datz chehva contra doorehreelor?*

357 I am/he is/she is allergic to penicillin.
Sânt alergic/el este alergic/ea este alergică la penicilină
*Sunt alehrzheek/el esteh alerzheek/eya esteh alerzheekah la peneecheeleenah*

358 Does this hurt?
Doare?
*Dwareh?*

359 You must/he must/she must go to hospital.
Trebuie să mergeţi/el/ea trebuie să meargă la spital.
*Trebweh sah mehrdjetz/el/eya trebooyeh sah meyargah la spital.*

360 Take these once/twice /three times a day.
Luaţi medicamentul o dată/de două ori/de trei ori pe zi.
*Lowatz medeecamentool oh datah/deh dowah oree/deh tray oree peh zee.*

361 I am/he is/she is taking this medication.
Iau/el ia/ea ia acest medicament.
*Yow/el ya/eya ya achest medeecament.*

362 I have medical insurance.
Am asigurare medicală.
*Am aseegoorareh medeecalah.*

## Dentist

363 I have toothache.
Am o durere de dinţi.
*Am oh doorehreh deh deentz.*

364 My filling has come out.
Am pierdut o plombă.
*Am peeyerdoot oh plombah.*

365 I do/do not want to have an injection first.
Vreau/nu vreau un anestetic.
*Vreh-aoo/noo vreh-aoo oon anestetik.*

## EMERGENCIES

366 Help!
Ajutor!
*Azhootor!*

367 Call an ambulance/a doctor/ the police!
Chemaţi salvarea/doctorul/ poliţia.
*Kehmatz salvareya/doctorool/ politzia.*

ROMANIAN

355
↑
367

285

**368** I have had my travellers' cheques (travelers' checks)/ credit cards/purse/handbag/ rucksack (knapsack)/ luggage/wallet stolen.

Mi s-au furat cecurile de călătorie/cărţile de credit/ portmoneul/geanta/rucsacul/ valiza/portofelul.

*Mee saow foorat cecooreeleh deh calatoreeyeh/cartzeeleh deh credit/ portmoneyool/djeyanta/ rooksacool/valeeza/portofelool.*

**369** Can you help me, I have lost my daughter/son?

Vreţi să mă ajutaţi vă rog? Mi-am pierdut fetiţa/băiatul.

*Vretz sah mah azhootatz vah rohg? Mee-am peeyerdoot fetitza/ bye-atool.*

**370** Please go away/leave me alone.

Vă rog plecaţi de aici. Lăsaţi-mă în pace.

*Vah rohg plecatz deh aich. Lasatz-mah un pacheh.*

**371** Fire!

Foc!

*Foc!*

**372** I want to contact the British/ American/Canadian/Irish/ Australian/New Zealand/ South African consulate.

Vreau să contactez consulatul britanic/american/canadian/ irlandez/australian/neo zeelandez/sud african.

*Vreyau sah contactez consoolatool britaneek/americahn/canadiahn/ eerlandez/owstraliahn/neyo zehlandez/sood africahn.*

# Introduction

Castilian Spanish, the official form of the language, is spoken all over Spain. Although some regions have their own official languages (Catalan in Catalonia and the Balearic Islands, Galego in Galicia and Basque in parts of the north-east, all of which are separate languages and not dialects of Spanish), Spanish will be understood everywhere. In the popular tourist areas English is also widely understood by people working in tourist-related trades..

If using a Spanish dictionary, phone directory or other alphabetical listing, remember that words beginning with 'ch' come after all the other 'c's, and words starting with 'll' after all the other 'l's.

## Addresses for travel and tourist information

**UK:** *Spanish National Tourist Office*, 57 St James's St, London SW1A 1LD; tel: (0171) 499 0901.
**USA:** *Spanish National Tourist Office*, 665 Fifth Ave, New York, NY 10022; tel: (212) 759-8822.

## ESSENTIALS

### ALPHABET

| A *a* | B *be* |
|---|---|
| C *ce* | CH *che* |
| D *de* | E *e* |
| F *efey* | G *ge* |
| H *atchey* | I *ee latina* |
| J *hota* | K *ka* |
| L *eley* | LL *elyey* |
| M *emey* | N *eney* |
| Ñ *enyey* | O *o* |
| P *pe* | Q *cu* |
| R *ere* | RR *erre* |
| S *eseh* | T *te* |
| U *oo* | V *ubey* |
| W *ubey doble* | X *ekees* |
| Y *ee greeayga* | Z *theta* |

**S P A N I S H**

**01 ↕ 11**

### Basic Words and Phrases

1. **Yes**
   Si
   *Si*
   **No**
   No
   *noh*

2. **Please**
   Por favor
   *Por fabor*
   **Thank you**
   Gracias
   *Gratheeas*

3. **That's O.K.**
   De acuerdo
   *Dey acwerdo*
   **Perhaps**
   Quizá
   *Keetha*

4. **To**
   a
   *a*
   **From**
   desde/de
   *desdey/dey*

5. **Here**
   Aquí
   *akee*
   **There**
   Allí
   *ayee*

6. **None**
   Ninguno/a
   *Ningoono/a*
   **Also**
   También
   *Tambeeyen*

7. **How?**
   ¿Cómo?
   *como*
   **When?**
   ¿Cuándo?
   *cwandoe*

8. **What?**
   ¿Qué?
   *kay*
   **Why?**
   ¿Por qué?
   *porkay*

9. **I don't understand.**
   No entiendo.
   *Noh enteeyendo.*

10. **I don't speak Spanish.**
    No hablo español.
    *Noh ahblo espanyol.*

11. **Do you speak English?**
    ¿Habla usted inglés?
    *Ahbla oosteth eengless?*

12 **Can you please write it down?**
Lo puede escribir, por favor?
*Lo pwedeh escreebeer, porr abor?*

13 **Can you please speak more slowly?**
Quiere usted hablar más despacio?
*Keyerehh oosteth ablar mas despathio?*

14 **How much does it/this cost?**
Cuánto cuesta?
*Kwanto kwesta?*

## Days

15 **Monday**    **Tuesday**
Lunes    Martes
*Loones*    *Martes*

16 **Wednesday**    **Thursday**
Miércoles    Jueves
*Meeyercoles*    *Hooebes*

17 **Friday**    **Saturday**
Viernes    Sábado
*Beeyernes*    *Sabadoe*

18 **Sunday**    **Morning**
Domingo    Mañana
*Domeengo*    *Manyana*

19 **Afternoon**    **Evening**
Tarde    Noche
*Tardey*    *Nochey*

20 **Night**    **Week**
Noche    Semana
*Nochey*    *Semanna*

21 **Yesterday**    **Tomorrow**
Ayer    Mañana
*Ayer*    *Manyana*

## Numbers

22 **Zero**    **One**
Cero    Uno
*Theroe*    *Oono*

23 **Two**    **Three**
Dos    Tres
*Dos*    *Tres*

24 **Four**    **Five**
Cuatro    Cinco
*Cwatro*    *Thinco*

25 **Six**    **Seven**
Seis    Siete
*Seys*    *Seeyetey*

26 **Eight**    **Nine**
Ocho    Nueve
*Ocho*    *Nwebey*

27 **Ten**    **Eleven**
Diez    Once
*Deeyeth*    *Onthey*

28 **Twelve**    **Thirteen**
Doce    Trece
*Dothey*    *Trethey*

29 **Fourteen**    **Fifteen**
Catorce    Quince
*Catorthey*    *Keeyenthe*

30 **Sixteen**    **Seventeen**
Dieciséis    Diecisiete
*Deeyetheeseys*    *Deeyetheeseeyetey*

31 **Eighteen**    **Nineteen**
Dieciocho    Diecinueve
*Deeyetheoocho*    *Deeyetheenwebey*

32 **Twenty**    **Twenty-one**
Veinte    Veintiuno
*Beintey*    *Beinteoono*

SPANISH

12
↑
↓
32

289

# ESSENTIALS

**S P A N I S H**

**33** **Twenty-two** **Thirty**
Veintidós Treinta
*Beintedos* *Treinta*

**34** **Forty** **Fifty**
Cuarenta Cincuenta
*Cwarenta* *Thincwenta*

**35** **Sixty** **Seventy**
Sesenta Setenta
*Sesenta* *Setenta*

**36** **Eighty** **Ninety**
Ochenta Noventa
*Ochenta* *Nobenta*

**37** **One hundred** **Five hundred**
Cien Quinientos
*Thien* *Keyneeyentos*

**38** **One thousand** **One million**
Mil Un millón
*Mil* *Oon mellion*

## Time

**39** **9.00**
Las nueve
*Nwebey*

**40** **9.05**
Las nueve y cinco
*Nwebey ee thinco*

**41** **9.10**
Las nueve y diez
*Nwebey ee deeyeth*

**42** **9.15**
Las nueve y cuarto
*Nwebey ee quarto*

**43** **9.20**
Las nueve y veinte
*Nwebey ee beinte*

**44** **9.25**
Las nueve y veinticinco
*Nwebey ee beintethinco*

**45** **9.30**
Las nueve y media
*Nwebey ee medeea*

**46** **9.35**
Las diez menos veinticinco
*Deeyeth menos beinteethinco*

**47** **9.40**
Las diez menos veinte
*Deeyeth menos beinte*

**48** **9.45**
Las diez menos cuarto
*Deeyeth menos quarto*

**49** **9.50**
Las diez menos diez
*Deeyeth menos deeyeth*

**50** **9.55**
Las diez menos cinco
*Deeyeth menos thinco*

**51** **12.00/Midday/ Midnight**
Las doce/Mediodía/ Medianoche
*Las dothe/medeeodeea/ medeeanoche*

**52** **What time is it?**
¿Qué hora es?
*¿Kay ora es*

**53** **It is . . .**
Son las . . .
*Son las . . .*

290

## ARRIVING AND DEPARTING

## Airport

**54** Excuse me, where is the check-in desk for . . . airline?
¿Perdone, dónde está la facturación de la línea . . ?
*Perdoneh, dondeh estah el mostrador deh faktoorathion deh la leenya . . ?*

**55** What is the boarding gate/time for my flight?
¿Por qué puerta/a qué hora sale mi vuelo?
*Porr keh pwerta/ah keh ora saleh mee bwehlo?*

**56** How long is the delay likely to be?
¿Cuánto lleva de retraso, aproximadamente?
*Kwanto llieba deh rehtraso, aproksimadamenteh?*

**57** Where is the duty-free shop?
¿Dónde está el duty free?
*Dondeh esta el duty free?*

**58** Which way is the baggage reclaim?
¿Por dónde se va a la recogida de equipajes?
*Porr dondeh seh ba ah rekoheeda deh ekeypahess?*

**59** Where can I get the bus to the city centre?
¿De dónde sale el autobús al centro?
*Deh dondeh saleh el outoboos al thentro?*

## Train Station

**60** Where is the ticket office/information desk?
¿Dónde está la taquilla de billetes/la ventanilla de información?
*¿Donde estaa la taakeellia dey beellietes/la bentaaneellia dey informatheeon?*

**61** Which platform does the train to . . . depart from?
¿De qué andén sale el tren para . . ?
*¿Deke anden sale el tren para . . ?*

**62** Where is platform . . ?
¿Dónde está el andén . . ?
*¿Donde esta el anden . . ?*

**63** When is the next train to . . ?
¿A qué hora sale el próximo tren para . . ?
*¿A key ora sale el proxseemo tren para . . ?*

**64** Is there a later train to . . ?
¿Hay un tren más tarde para . . ?
*¿Eye oon tren mass tarde para . . ?*

## Port

**65** How do I get to the port?
¿Cómo se va al puerto?
*¿Como se ba al pooerto?*

**66** When is the next sailing to . . ?
¿A qué hora zarpa el próximo transbordador para . . ?
*¿A kay ora tharpa el proxeemo transbordador para?*

S P A N I S H

54 ↑ 66

**67** Can I catch an earlier ferry with this ticket?
¿Puedo coger un ferry más temprano con este billete?
*Pwedo coherr oon ferry mas temprano kon esteh billieteh?*

## Notices and Signs

**68** Coche restaurante
*Koche restaoorante*
Buffet (Dining) Car

**69** Autobús
*Awtoeboos*
Bus

**70** Agua potable/Agua no potable
*Agwa potable/agwa no potable*
Drinking/Non-drinking water

**71** Entrada
*Entrada*
Entrance

**72** Salida
*Saleeda*
Exit

**73** Información
*Informatheeon*
Information

**74** Consigna
*Consigna*
Left Luggage (Baggage Claim)

**75** Consigna automática
*Consigna awtomateeka*
Luggage Lockers

**76** Oficina de Correos
*Ofeetheena de korreos*
Post Office

**77** Vía
*Veea*
Platform

**78** Estación de trenes
*Estatheeon de tren*
Railway (Railroad) Station

**79** Aeropuerto
*Aehropwerto*
Airport

**80** Puerto
*Pwerto*
Port

**81** Restaurante
*Restaoorante*
Restaurant

**82** Fumadores/No fumadores
*Foomadoores/no foomadoores*
Smoking/Non-smoking

**83** Teléfono
*Telephono*
Telephone

**84** Taquilla de billetes
*Takeellia de beellietes*
Ticket Office

**85** Facturación
*Faktoorathion*
Check-in Desk

**86** Horario
*Orareeo*
Timetable (Schedule)

**87** Servicios
*Serbeetheeos*
Toilets (Restrooms)

**88** Caballeros
*Kaballieros*

292

Gentlemen

**89 Señoras**
*Senyoras*
Ladies'

**90 Tranvía**
*Tranbeea*
Tram (Streetcar)

**91 Metro**
*Metro*
Underground (Subway)

**92 Sala de espera**
*Sala de espera*
Waiting Room

## Buying a Ticket

**93 I would like a first-class/
second-class single (one-
way)/return (round-trip)
ticket to . . .**
Quisiera un billete de primera
clase/de segunda clase/de ida/
de ida y vuelta a . . .
*Keyseeyera oon beelliete de premera
clase/dey segoonda clase/dey eeda/
dey eeda ee bwelta a . . .*

**94 Is my rail pass valid on this
train?**
Puedo usar mi pase en este
tren/ferry/autobús?
*Pwedo usar mee pasey en esteh
tren/ferry/outoboos?*

**95 I would like an aisle/window
seat.**
Me gustaría un asiento junto al
pasillo/de ventanilla.

*Me goosetareea oon aseeyento
hoontoe al paseellio/de
bentaneellya.*

**96 No smoking/smoking,
please.**
No fumadores/fumadores, por
favor.
*No foomadoores/foomadoores, por
farbor*

**97 We would like to sit
together.**
Nos gustaría sentarnos juntos.
*Nos goosetareea sentarnos
hoontos.*

**98 I would like to make a seat
reservation?**
Quisiera reservar una plaza.
*Keyseeyera rehzerbar oona platha.*

**99 I would like to reserve a
couchette/sleeper for one
person/two people/for my
family.**
Quisiera hacer una reserva en el
coche-literas/coche-camas para
una persona/dos personas/mi
familia.
*Keyseeyera ather oona resserba en
el koche-literas/koche-kama para
oona persawna/dos persawnas/
mee fameleeya.*

**100 I would like to reserve a
cabin.**
Quisiera reservar un
camarote.
*Keyseeyera rehzerbar oon
kamarote.*

# ARRIVING AND DEPARTING

## Timetables (Schedules)

**101** Llegada
*Yeygada*
Arrival

**102** Para en
*Para en*
Calls (stops) at

**103** Servicio de restauración
*Serbeetheeo dey restawratheeon*
Catering Service

**104** Transbordo en
*Transbordoe en*
Change at

**105** Correspondencia
*Correespondenthia*
Connection

**106** Diario
*Deeareeo*
Daily

**107** Cada 40 minutos
*Kada cwarenta menootos*
Every 40 Minutes

**108** Primera clase
*Preemera clase*
First-class

**109** Cada hora
*Kada ora*
Hourly

**110** Se recomienda reservar plaza
*Se rekomeenda reserbar platha*
Seat reservations are
recommended

**111** Segunda clase
*Segoonda clase*
Second-class

**112** Hay que pagar suplemento
*Eye ke pagar sueplemento*
Supplement Payable

**113** Por
*Beea*
Por

## Luggage

**114** How much will it cost to sen
(ship) my luggage in
advance?
¿Cuánto costaría enviar mi
equipaje por adelantado?
*¿Cwantoe costareea enbeear mee
ekeypahe por adelantado?*

**115** here is the left luggage
(baggage claim) office?
¿Dónde está la consigna?
*¿Donde esta la consinya?*

**116** What time do you open/
close?
¿A qué hora abren/cierran?
*¿a kay ora abren/theeyeran?*

**117** Where are the luggage
trolleys (carts)?
¿Dónde están los carretillas para
el equipaje?
*¿Donde estan las karretillias para
el ekeypahe?*

**118** Where are the lockers?
Dónde está la consigna
automática?
*Dondeh esta la konseegna
awtoematika?*

**19 I have lost my locker key.**
He perdido la llave de la
consigna automática.
*Ey perdeedo la lliabe de la consigna
awtoematecar.*

## On Board

**20 Is this seat taken?**
¿Está libre este asiento?
*¿Esta leebre este aseeyento?*

**21 Excuse me, you are sitting in
my reserved seat.**
Perdone, pero se ha sentado en
mi asiento reservado.
*Perdone pero sey a sentado en mee
aseeyento resserbado.*

**22 Which station is this?**
¿Qué estación es esta?
*¿Kay estatheeon es esta?*

**23 What time is this train/bus/
ferry/flight due to arrive/
depart?**
A qué hora sale/llega este tren/
autobús/vuelo?
*Ah keh ora saleh/lliega esteh tren/
outoboos/bwelo?*

**24 Will you wake me just before
we arrive?**
¿Le importaría despertarme un
poco antes de llegar?
*¿Ley inportareea despertarme oon
poco antes de lliegar?*

## Customs and Passports

**25 Los pasaportes, por favor!**
*¡Los pasaportes por farbor!*
Passports, please!

**126 I have nothing to declare. I
have wine/spirits (alcohol)/
tobacco to declare.**
No tengo nada que declarar.
Tengo vino/licores/tabaco que
declarar.
*No tengo nada kay declarar.
Tengo beeno/leekores/tabaco kay
declarar.*

**127 I shall be staying for . . .
days/weeks/months.**
Me quedaré por . . . días/
semanas/meses.
*Mey keydarey por . . . deeas/
semanas/messes.*

## AT THE TOURIST OFFICE

**128 Do you have a map of the
town/area?**
¿Tiene un mapa de la ciudad/de
la zona?
*¿Teeyene oon mapa de la
theeoodath/de la thona?*

**129 Can I reserve
accommodation here?**
¿Puedo reservar alojamiento
aquí?
*¿Pwedo reserbar alohameeyento
akee?*

**130 Do you have a list of
accommodation?**
¿Tiene una lista de hoteles?
*Teeyene oona leesta deh oteles?*

S
P
A
N
I
S
H

119
↑
130

295

## ACCOMMODATION

### Hotels

**131** **I have a reservation in the name of . . .**
Tengo una reserva a nombre de . . .
*Tengo oona resserba a nonbre dey . . .*

**132** **I wrote to/faxed/telephoned you last month/last week in . . .**
El mes pasado/la semana pasada les escribí/envié un fax/llamé por teléfono
*El mes passado/la sehmanna passada les eskreebee/embeeyeh oon faks/lliameh porr tehlehfono.*

**133** **Do you have any rooms free?**
¿Tienen habitaciones?
*Teeyenen abeetathiones?*

**134** **I would like to reserve a single/double room with/without bath/shower.**
Quisiera reservar una habitación individual/doble con/sin baño/ducha.
*keyseeyera resserbar oona abeetatheeon indeebeedooal/doeble con/sin banyo/doocha.*

**135** **I would like bed and breakfast/(room and) half board/(room and) full board.**
Me gustaría cama y desayuno/media pensión/pensión completa.
*Mey goosetareea kama ee desayuno/medeea penseeon/penseeon conpleta.*

**136** **How much is it per night?**
¿Cuánto cuesta por noche?
*¿Cwantoe cwesta por noche?*

**137** **Is breakfast included?**
¿Está el desayuno incluido?
*¿Esta el desayunooh inclueedo?*

**138** **May I see the room?**
¿Puedo ver la habitación?
*¿Pwedo ber la abeetatheeon?*

**139** **Do you have any cheaper rooms?**
¿Tienen habitaciones más baratas?
*¿Teeyenen abeetatheeones mass baratas?*

**140** **I would like to take the room.**
Me gustaría ocupar la habitación.
*Mey goosetareea ocoopar la abeetatheeon.*

**141** **I would like to stay for . . . nights.**
Quisiera quedarme por . . . noches.
*Keyseeyera keydarme por . . . noches.*

**142** **The shower/light/tap doesn't work.**
La ducha/luz/el grifo no funciona.
*La dootcha/looth/el greefoh noh foonthiona.*

**143** At what time/where is breakfast served?
¿A qué hora/dónde se sirve el desayuno?
*¿A kay ora/donde sey seervey el desayoono?*

**144** What time do I have to check-out?
¿A qué hora debo desalojar la habitación?
*¿A kay ora debo desalohar la abeetatheeon?*

**145** Can I have the key to room number?
¿Me quiere dar la llave de la habitación número . . ?
*Meh keyereh dahrr la lliabeh deh la abeetathion noomero . . ?*

**146** My room number is . . .
Mi habitación es el número . . .
*me abeetatheeon es el noomero . . .*

**147** Do you accept travellers' cheques/Eurocheques/credit cards?
¿Aceptan cheques de viaje/Eurocheques/tarjetas de crédito?
*Atheptan tchekes deh biaheh/ehworotchekes/tarhetas deh credeeto?*

**148** May I have the bill please?
¿Por favor me da la cuenta?
*¿Por farbor meh da la cwenta?*

**149** Excuse me, I think there is a mistake in this bill.
Oiga, me parece que la cuenta está mal.

*Oyga, meh parethe keh la kwenta esta mal.*

## Youth Hostels

**150** How much is a dormitory bed per night?
¿Cuánto cuesta una cama por noche?
*¿Cwantoe cwesta oona kama por noche?*

**151** I am/am not an HI member.
Soy/no soy miembro de HI.
*Soy/no soy meeyembro dey hachey ee.*

**152** May I use my own sleeping bag?
¿Puedo utilizar mi propio saco de dormir?
*¿Pwedo ooteeleethar mee propeeo saco de dormeer?*

**153** What time do you lock the doors at night?
¿A qué hora cierran por la noche?
*¿A kay ora theeyerran por la noche?*

## Camping

**154** May I camp here for the night/two nights?
¿Puedo acampar aquí por esta noche/dos noches?
*¿Pwedo acanpar akee por esta noche/dos noches?*

S
P
A
N
I
S
H

143
↑
154

297

155 Where can I pitch my tent?
¿Dónde puedo montar la tienda?
*¿Donde pwedo montar la teeyenda?*

156 How much does it cost for one night/week?
¿Cuánto cuesta por noche/semana?
*¿Cwantoee cwesta por noche/semana?*

157 Where can we park our caravan?
¿Dónde podemos aparcar la caravana?
*Dondeh pohdemos aparkahrr la carabana?*

158 Where are the washing facilities?
¿Dónde están los aseos?
*¿Donde estan los aseos?*

159 Is there a restaurant/supermarket/swimming pool on site/nearby?
¿Hay algún restaurante/supermercado/alguna piscina por aquí/cerca?
*¿Eye algoon restawrante/suepermerkadoe/algoona pistheena por akee/therca?*

160 Do you have a safety deposit box?
¿Tienen cajafuerte?
*¿Teeyenen kahafwerte?*

## EATING AND DRINKING

### Cafés and Bars

161 I would like a cup of/two cups of/another coffee/tea.
Quisiera una taza de/dos tazas de/otra taza de café/té.
*Keyseeyera oona tatha dey/dos tathas/otra tatha dey kafey/te.*

162 With/without milk/sugar.
Con/sin leche/azucar.
*Con/seen leche/athoocar.*

163 I would like a bottle/glass/two glasses of mineral water/red wine/white wine, please.
Quisiera una botella/un vaso/dos vasos de agua mineral/de vino tinto/de vino blanco, por favor.
*Keyseeyera oona botellia/oon baso/dos basos dey agwa meneral/dey beeno tintoe/dey beeno blanco, por farbor.*

164 I would like a beer/two beers, please.
Quisiera una cerveza/dos cervezas, por favor.
*Keyseeyera oona therbeytha/dos therbeythas, por farbor.*

165 May I have some ice?
¿Pueden ponerme hielo?
*¿Pweden ponerme eeyelloe?*

166 Do you have any matches/cigarettes/cigars?
¿Tienen cerillas/cigarrillos/puros?

298

¿Teeyenen thereellias/
theegarrellios/pooros?

## Restaurants

**167 Can you recommend a good/
inexpensive restaurant in this
area?**
¿Puede recomendarme un buen/
restaurante barato en la zona?
¿Pwede recomendarme oon bwen/
restawrante barato en la thona?

**168 I would like a table for . . .
people.**
Quisiera una mesa para . . .
personas.
Keyseeyera oona mesa para . . .
personas.

**169 Do you have a non-smoking
area?**
¿Tiene una zona reservada para
no fumadores?
Teeyene oona thona rehzerbada
para noh foomadores?

**170 Waiter/Waitress!**
¡Camarero/Camarera!
¡Camareroe/camarera!

**171 Do you have a set menu/
children's menu/wine list?**
¿Tienen menú del Día/menú
para niños/ la carta de vinos?
¿Teeyenen menoo del deea/menoo
para neenios/la carta dey beenos?

**172 Do you have any vegetarian
dishes, please?**
¿Dan comidas vegetarianas, por
favor?

¿Dan comeedas behetareanas, por
farbor?

**173 Are there any local
specialities?**
¿Tienen especialidades del
lugar?
¿Teeyenen espethialeedades del
loogar?

**174 Are vegetables included?**
¿Están incluidas las verduras?
¿Estan eenklooeedas las berdooras?

**175 Could I have it well-cooked/
medium/rare please?**
Por favor, la carne bien cocida/
al punto/roja.
Porr fabor, la kahrrne beeyen
kotheeda/al poontoh/roha.

**176 What does this dish consist
of?**
¿Qué contiene este plato?
¿Kay conteeyene este platoe?

**177 I would like the set menu,
please.**
Quisiera el menú del día, por
favor.
Keyseeyera el menoo del deea, por
farbor.

**178 We have not been served yet.**
Todavía no nos han servido.
Toedabeea no nos an serbeedoe.

**179 Excuse me, this is not what I
ordered.**
Perdone, no he pedido esto.
Perdoneh, noh eh pedeedo esto.

<sup>18</sup> **May I have some/some more bread/water/coffee/tea?**
¿Podría traerme/más pan/agua/café/té?
*¿Pordreea trayerme/mass pan/agwa/kafey/te?*

<sup>181</sup> **May I have the bill, please?**
¿Podría traerme la cuenta por favor?
*¿Pordreea trayerme la cwenta por farbor?*

<sup>182</sup> **Does this bill include service?**
¿Está incluido el servicio en la cuenta?
*¿Esta inclueedoe el serbeetheeo en la cwenta?*

<sup>183</sup> **Do you accept travellers' cheques (travelers' checks)/Eurocheques/MasterCard/US dollars?**
¿Aceptan cheques de viaje/Eurocheques/MasterCard/dólares americanos?
*¿Atheptan chekes de beeahe/eurochekes/MasterCard/doelares amereecarnos?*

<sup>184</sup> **Can I have a receipt, please?**
¿Me quiere dar un recibo, por favor?
*¿Meh keyereh dahrr oon resgwardo, porr fabor?*

<sup>185</sup> **Where is the toilet (restroom), please?**
¿Dónde están los servicios, por favor?
*¿Donde estan los serbeetheeos, por farbor?*

## On the Menu

<sup>186</sup> **First courses**
Entradas
*Entradas*

<sup>187</sup> **Soups**
Sopas
*Sohpas*

<sup>188</sup> **Main courses**
Platos principales
*Platos preentheepales*

<sup>189</sup> **Fish dishes**
Pescados
*Peskados*

<sup>190</sup> **Meat dishes**
Carnes
*Kahrrnes*

<sup>191</sup> **Vegetarian dishes**
Platos vegetarianos
*Platos behetaryanos*

<sup>192</sup> **Cheese**
Queso
*Kehso*

<sup>193</sup> **Desserts**
Postres
*Postres*

<sup>194</sup> **Specialities**
Especialidades
*Espetheealeedades*

## GETTING AROUND

## Public Transport

<sup>195</sup> **Where is the bus stop/coach station/nearest metro (subway) station?**

**SPANISH**

180
↕
195

¿Dónde está la parada de autobuses/la estación de autobuses/la estación de metro más cercana?
*¿Donde esta la parrada dey awtoebooses/la estatheeon dey awtoebooses/la estatheeon dey metro mass thercana?*

**196** When is the next/last bus to . . ?
¿A qué hora sale el próximo autobús/el último autobús para . . ?
*¿A kay ora sale el proxseemo awtoeboos/el ultimo awtoeboos para . . ?*

**197** How much is the fare to the city centre (downtown)/railway (railroad) station/airport?
¿Cuánto cuesta el billete hasta el centro/la estación de trenes/el aeropuerto?
*¿Cwantoe cwesta el beelliete asta el thentro/la estatheeon de trenes/el aeropwerto?*

**198** Will you tell me when to get off?
¿Podría decirme cuando tendré que bajar?
*¿Poordreea detheerme cwandoe tendray kay bahar?*

**199** Does this bus go to . . ?
¿Es este el autobús de . . ?
*¿Es este el awtoeboos de . . ?*

**200** Which number bus goes to . . ?
¿Cuál es el número del autobús que va a . . ?
*¿Cwal es el noomero del awtoeboos kay ba a . . ?*

**201** May I have a single (one-way)/return (round-trip)/day ticket/multi-journey ticket?
¿Quisiera un billete de ida/de ida y vuelta/de día/tarjeta
*¿Keyseeyera oon beelliete dey eeda/dey eda ee bwelta/dey dea/tarheyta?*

## Taxis

**202** I would like to go to . . .
How much will it cost?
Quisiera ir a . . . ¿Cuánto me costaría?
*Keyseeyera eer a . . . ¿cwantoe me costarea?*

**203** Please stop here.
Por favor pare aquí.
*Por farbor parey akee.*

**204** I would like to order a taxi today/tomorrow/at 2pm to go from . . . to . . .
Quisiera reservar un taxi para hoy/mañana/a las dos de la tarde para ir de . . . a . . .
*Keyseeyera resserbar oon taxsee para oy/manyana/a las dos de la tarde para eer dey . . . a . . .*

SPANISH

196
↑
204

301

## Asking the Way

**205** Excuse me, do you speak English?
Perdone, ¿habla usted inglés?
*Perdoene, ¿abla oosteth ingles?*

**206** Excuse me, is this the right way to . . ?
Perdone, ¿por aquí se va a . . ?
*Perdoneh, ¿porr akee seh bah ah . . ?*

**207** . . . the cathedral/the tourist information office/the castle/the old town.
. . . la catedral/oficina de turismo/el castillo/el casco antiguo.
*. . . la katehdral/offeetheena deh toorismoe/el kasteellio/el kasko antigwo.*

**208** Can you tell me the way to the railway (railroad) station/bus station/taxi rank (stand)/city centre (downtown)/beach?
¿Puede decirme cómo se va a la estación de trenes/estación de autobuses/parada de taxis/al centro de la ciudad/a la playa?
*¿Pwede detheerme como sey ba a la estatheeon de trenes/estatheeon dey avtoebooses/parada de taxsis/al thentroe de la theeoodath/a la playa?*

**209** First/second left/right/straight ahead.
Primera/segunda a la izquierda/derecha/todo seguido.
*Preemera/segoonda a la eethkeyerda/derecha/toedoe segeedoe.*

**210** Where is the nearest police station/post office?
¿Dónde está la comisaría de policía/la oficina de correos más cercana?
*¿Donde esta la comeesarea dey poleetheea/la ofeetheena dey coreos mass thercarna?*

**211** Is it far?
¿Está lejos?
*¿Esta lehos?*

**212** Do I need to take a taxi/catch a bus?
¿Necesito coger un taxi/un autobús?
*¿Netheeseeto coher oon taxsee/oon aootoeboos?*

**213** Can you point to it on my map?
¿Puede señalármelo en el mapa?
*¿Pwede senyarlarmeloe en el mapa?*

**214** Thank you for your help.
Muchas gracias por su ayuda.
*Moochas gratheeas poor soo ayuda.*

## SIGHTSEEING

**215** Where is the Tourist Information office?
¿Dónde está la oficina de información y turismo?
*¿Donde esta la ofeetheena de informatheeon ee toorismo?*

**216** Where is the cathedral/
church/museum?
¿Dónde está la catedral/la
iglesia/el museo?
*¿Donde esta la catedral/la
igleeseea/el mooseo?*

**217** How much is the entrance
(admission) charge?
¿Cuánto cuesta la entrada?
*¿Cwantoe cwesta la entrada?*

**218** Is there a discount for
children/students/senior
citizens?
¿Tienen descuento los niños/los
estudiantes/los jubilados?
*¿Teeyenen descwento los neenyos/
los estoodeeantes/los hubeelados?*

**219** What time does the next
guided tour start?
¿A qué hora empieza la
siguiente guía?
*¿A kay ora enpeeyetha la
seegeeyente geea?*

**220** One/two adults/children,
please.
Uno/dos adultos/niños, por
favor.
*Oonoh/dos adooltos/neenios
porfarbor.*

**221** May I take photographs
here?
Puedo sacar fotos?
*Pwedo sakar fotos?*

## ENTERTAINMENT

**222** Can you recommend a good
bar/nightclub?
¿Puede recomendarme un bar
bueno/una discoteca buena?
*¿Pwede recomendarme oon bar
bweno/oona discoteca bwena?*

**223** Do you know what is on at
the cinema (playing at the
movies)/theatre at the
moment?
¿Sabe lo que están dando en el
cine/en el teatro en estos
momentos?
*¿Sabe lo key estan dando en el
theenne/en el tayatro en estos
momentos?*

**224** I would like to book
(purchase) . . . tickets for the
matinee/evening
performance on Monday.
Quisiera reservar . . . entradas
para la sesión de tarde/de noche
del lunes.
*Keyseeyera resserbar . . . entradas
para la seseeon dey tarde dey noche
del loones.*

**225** What time does the film/
performance start?
¿A qué hora empieza la sesión/
la función?
*¿A key ora enpeeyetha la seseeon/
la foontheeon?*

S
P
A
N
I
S
H

216
↑
225

303

## MEETING PEOPLE

**226** Hello/Goodbye.
Hola/adiós.
*Ola/adeeos.*

**227** Good morning/good afternoon/good evening/goodnight.
Buenos días/buenas tardes/buenas noches.
*Bwenos dee-ahs/bwenas tarrdess/bwenas notchess.*

**228** Pleased to meet you.
Encantado de conocerle.
*Encantadoe dey conotherle.*

**229** How are you?
¿Cómo está usted?
*¿Como esta oosteth?*

**230** Fine, thank you. And you?
Bien, gracias. Y usted?
*Beeyen, grathias. Ee oosteth?*

**231** My name is . . .
Me llamo . . .
*Meh lliamo . . .*

**232** This is my friend/boyfriend/girlfriend/husband/wife/brother/sister.
Este es mi amigo/novio/novia/marido/esposa/hermano/hermana.
*Este es mee ameego/nobeeo/nobeea/mareedo/esposa/ermano/ermana.*

**233** Where are you travelling to?
¿A dónde viaja?
*¿A donde beeaha?*

**234** I am/we are going to . . .

voy/vamos a . . .
*Boy/bamos a . . .*

**235** How long are you travelling for?
¿Cuánto tiempo van a viajar?
*¿Cwantoe teaempo ban a beahar?*

**236** Where do you come from?
¿De dónde es usted?
*¿Dey donde es oosteth?*

**237** I am/we are from . . .
Soy/somos de . . .
*Soy/somos . . .*

**238** We're on holiday.
Estamos de vacación.
*Estamos deh bakathion.*

**239** This is our first visit here.
Es la primera vez que venimos aquí.
*Es la preemera beth keh benimos akee.*

**240** Would you like/May I have a cigarette?
¿Quiere un cigarrillo/Me da un cigarillo?
*¿Keyerey oon theegarrellio/Mey da oon theegarrillio?*

**241** I am sorry but I do not understand.
Lo siento pero no entiendo.
*Loh siento pero no entiendo.*

**242** Please speak slowly.
Por favor hable despacio.
*Por farbor abley despathio.*

**243** Do you mind if I smoke?
¿Le molesta si fumo?
*¿Ley molesta see foomo?*

S
P
A
N
I
S
H

226
↑
243

304

**244** Do you have a light?

¿Tiene fuego?

*¿Teeyene fwego?*

**245** I am waiting for my husband/ wife/boyfriend/girlfriend.

Estoy esperando a mi marido/ mujer/novio/novia.

*Estoy esperando a mee mareedo/ mooher/nobyoh/nobya.*

## TRAVELLING WITH CHILDREN

**246** Do you have a high chair/ babysitting service/cot?

¿Tienen sillas para bebés/ servicio de kanguro/cuna?

*¿Teeyenen seellias para bebes/ serbeetheeo de cangooro/coona?*

**247** Where is the nursery/ playroom?

¿Dónde está la guardería/el cuarto de niños?

*¿Donde esta la gwardereea/el kwarto de neenyos?*

**248** Where can I warm the baby's bottle?

¿Dónde puedo calentar el biberón?

*¿Donde pwedo calentar el beeberron?*

## COMMUNICATIONS

### Post

**249** How much will it cost to send a letter/postcard/this package to Britain/Ireland/ America/Canada/Australia/ New Zealand?

¿Cuánto cuesta enviar esta carta/postal/paquete a Gran Bretaña/Irlanda/América/ Canadá/Australia/Nueva Zelanda?

*¿Cwantoe cwesta enbeear esta carta/pohstal/pakete a gran bretannia/eerlandda/amereeca/ canada/awstralea/nweyba theylanda?*

**250** I would like one stamp/two stamps.

Quisiera un sello/dos sellos.

*Keyseeyera oon sellio/dos sellios.*

**251** I'd like . . . stamps for postcards to send abroad, please.

Quisiera . . . sellos para postales al extranjero, por favor.

*Keysyera . . . sellios para postales al estranhero, porr favor.*

### Phones

**252** I would like to make a telephone call/reverse the charges to (make a collect call to) . . .

Quisiera llamar por teléfono/ llamar a cobro revertido a . . .

*Keyseeyera lliamar por telephono/ lliamar a cobro reberteto a . . .*

**253** Which coins do I need for the telephone?

¿Qué monedas necesito para el teléfono?

*¿Kay monehdas netheseeto para el telephono?*

²⁵⁴ **The line is engaged (busy).**
La línea está comunicando.
*La leeneea esta comooneecando.*

²⁵⁵ **The number is . . .**
El número es el . . .
*El noomero es el . . .*

²⁵⁶ **Hello, this is . . .**
Hola, habla . . .
*Ola, abla . . .*

²⁵⁷ **May I speak to . . ?**
Puedo hablar con . . ?
*Pwedo ablar kon . . ?*

²⁵⁸ **He/She is not in at the moment. Can you call back?**
No está. ¿Quiere volver a llamar más tarde?
*Noh esta. Keyereh bolber a lliamar mas tarrdeh?*

## MONEY

²⁵⁹ **I would like to change these travellers' cheques (travelers' checks)/this currency/this Eurocheque.**
Quisiera cambiar estos cheques de viaje/dinero/este Eurocheque.
*Keyseeeeyera canbeear estos chekes de beeahe/denero/este eoorocheke.*

²⁶⁰ **How much commission do you charge (What is the service charge)?**
¿Qué comisión recargan?
*¿Kay comeeseeon recargan?*

²⁶¹ **Can I obtain money with my MasterCard?**

¿Puedo sacar dinero con la tarjeta MasterCard?
*¿Pwedo sacar deenero con la tarheta MasterCard?*

## SHOPPING

### Names of Shops and Departments

²⁶² **Librería/Papelería**
*Leebreree-ah/paplehree-ah*
Bookshop/Stationery

²⁶³ **Joyería/Regalos**
*Hoyeree-ah/regalos*
Jeweller's/Gifts

²⁶⁴ **Zapatería**
*Thapatos*
Shoe Shop

²⁶⁵ **Ferretería**
*Ferretehree-ah*
Hardware

²⁶⁶ **Anticuario**
*Antikwaryo*
Antiques

²⁶⁷ **Peluquería (caballeros)/ (damas)**
*Pelookeree-ah (kaballieros)/ (damas)*
Hairdressers (men's)/(women's)

²⁶⁸ **Estanco/Tabaquería**
*Estanko/Tabakeree-ah*
Tobacconist

²⁶⁹ **Panadería**
*Panaderee-ah*
Baker's

SPANISH

254
↓
269

**270 Supermercado**
*Soopermerkado*
Supermarket

**271 Tienda de fotos**
*Teeyenda deh fotos*
Photoshop

**272 Juguetería**
*Hoogetehree-ah*
Toys

**273 Agencia de viajes**
*Ahenthya deh byahes*
Travel Agent

**274 Artículos de tocador**
*Arteekoolos deh tokador*
Toiletries

**275 Discos**
*Deeskos*
Records

## In the Shop

**276 What time do the shops open/close?**
¿A qué hora abren/cierran las tiendas?
*¿A kay ora abren/theeyerran las teeyendas?*

**277 Where is the nearest market?**
Dónde está el mercado más próximo?
*Dondeh kayda el merkado mas proksimo?*

**278 Can you show me the one in the window/this one?**
Quiere enseñarme el del escaparate/este?

**279 Can I try this on?**
¿Puedo probarme esto?
*¿Pwedo probarme esto?*

**280 What size is this?**
¿Qué talla es esta?
*¿Kay tallia es esta?*

**281 This is too large/too small/too expensive.**
Es muy grande/muy pequeño/muy caro.
*Es mooy grandeh/mooy pekenio/mooy karo.*

**282 Do you have any others?**
¿Tienen más?
*¿Teeyenen mas?*

**283 My size is . . .**
Ni número es el . . .
*Mee noomero es el . . .*

**284 Where is the changing room/childrens/cosmetic/ladieswear/menswear/food department?**
¿Dónde están los probadores/niños/perfumería/señoras/caballeros/sección de alimentos?
*¿Donde estan los probadores/neenyos/perfoomereea/senyoras/caballieros/sectheeon dey alimentos?*

**285 I would like . . .**
Me gustaría . . .
*Meh goostaree-ah . . .*

S P A N I S H

270
↑
285

# SHOPPING/MOTORING

**286** I would like a quarter of a kilo/half a kilo/a kilo of bread/ butter/cheese/ham/ tomatoes.
Quisiera un cuarto de kilo/ medio kilo/un kilo de pan/ mantequilla/queso/jamón/ tomates.
*Keyseeyera oon cwarto dey kilo/ medio kilo/oon kilo dey pan/ mantekillia/keso/hamon/tomates.*

**287** How much is this?
¿Cuánto es?
*¿Cwantoe es?*

**288** I'll take this one, thank you.
Me llevo éste.
*Meh llievo esteh.*

**289** Do you have a carrier (shopping) bag?
¿Me da una bolsa por favor?
*¿Meh da oona bolsa por farbor?*

**290** Do you have anything cheaper/larger/smaller/of better quality?
¿Tiene algo más barato/grande/ pequeño/de mejor calidad?
*¿Teeyene algo mass baratto/ grande/pekenio/de mehor caleedath?*

**291** I would like a film for this camera.
Quisiera un rollo para esta cámara.
*Keyseeyera oon rollio para esta camara.*

**292** I would like some batteries, the same size as this old one.
Quisiera pilas, del mismo tamaño que esta vieja.
*Keyseeyera peelas, del mismo tamanio kay esta beeha.*

**293** Would you mind wrapping this for me, please?
¿Le importaría envolvérmelo?
*¿Le inportareea enbolbermelo?*

**294** Sorry, but you seem to have given me the wrong change.
Lo siento, pero no me ha dado la vuelta correcta.
*Lo seeyento, pero no meh a dado la vwelta correcta.*

## MOTORING

### Car Hire (Rental)

**295** I have ordered (rented) a car in the name of . . .
Tengo un coche alquilado a nombre de . . .
*Tengo oon koche alkeyladoe a nombre de . . .*

**296** How much does it cost to hire (rent) a car for one day/ two days/one week?
¿Cuánto cuesta alquilar un coche por un día/dos días/una semana?
*¿Cwantoe cwesta alkeylar oon koche por oon deea/dos deeas/oona semanna?*

**297** Is the tank already full of petrol (gas)?

**286 ↑ 297**

**308**

¿Está el depósito de gasolina lleno?

*¿Esta el deposeytoe de gasoleena llieno?*

**298** Is insurance and tax included? ¿How much is the deposit?

¿Está incluido en el precio los impuestos y el seguro? ¿Cuánto hay que poner de señal?

*¿Esta inclooeedoe en el pretheeo los inpwestoes ee el segooro, cwantoee eye kay poner de senial?*

**299** By what time must I return the car?

¿A qué hora debo entregar el coche?

*¿A kay ora debo entregar el koche?*

**300** I would like a small/family car with a radio/cassette player.

Quisiera un coche pequeño/familiar con radio/casete.

*Keyseeyera oon koche pekenio/familiar con radeeo/caset.*

## Asking the Way

**301** Excuse me, can you help me please?

¿Perdone, me puede ayudar?

*¿Perdoneh, meh pwedeh aiyoodahrr?*

**302** How do I reach the motorway/main road?

¿Por dónde se va a la autopista/carretera principal?

*¿Porr dondeh seh ba a la outopeesta/karretehrra printhipal?*

**303** I think I have taken the wrong turning.

Creo que me he equivocado de camino.

*Kreoh keh meh eh ekeebokado deh kameeno.*

**304** I am looking for this address.

Busco esta dirección.

*Boosko esta deerekthion.*

**305** I am looking for the . . . hotel.

Busco el hotel . . .

*Boosko el ohtel . . .*

**306** How far is it to . . . from here?

¿. . queda muy lejos de aquí?

*¿. . . kayda mooy lehos deh akee?*

**307** Carry straight on for . . . kilometres.

Siga derecho unos . . . kilómetros.

*Seega deretcho oonos . . . keelometros.*

**308** Take the next turning on the right/left.

La próxima a la derecha/izquierda.

*La proksima a la deretcha/eethkyerda.*

**309** Turn right/left at the next crossroads/traffic lights.

Tire a la derecha/izquierda en el próximo cruce/semáforo.

*Teereh a la deretcha/eethkyerda en el proksimo croocheh/sehmaforo.*

**310** You are going in the wrong direction.
No se va por ahí.
*Noh seh ba porr ah-ee.*

## Parking

**311** How long can I park here?
¿Cuanto tiempo puedo aparcar aquí?
*¿Kwanto teeyempo pwedo aparkar akee?*

**312** Is there a car park near here?
¿Hay un aparcamiento cerca de aquí?
*¿Eye oon aparkameeyento therka deh akee?*

**313** At what time does this car park close?
¿ qué hora cierra este aparcamiento?
*¿A keh ora thierra esteh aparkameeyento?*

## Signs and Notices

**314** One way.
Sentido único.
*Senteedo ooneeko.*

**315** No entry.
Prohibido el paso.
*Proeebeedoh el passoh.*

**316** No parking.
Prohibido aparcar.
*Proeebeedo aparcar.*

**317** Detour (diversion)
Desvío
*Desbeeyathion.*

**318** Stop.
Alto
*Alto*

**319** Give way (yield).
Ceda el paso
*Theda el paso*

**320** Slippery road.
Camino resbaladizo.
*Kameeno resbaladeetho.*

**321** No overtaking.
Prohibido adelantar
*Proybeedo adelantar*

## At the Filling Station

**322** Unleaded (lead-free)/ Standard/Premium
Sin plomo/normal/extra
*Seen plohmoh/normall/ekstra*

**323** Fill the tank please.
¿Me llena el tanque, por favor?
*¿Meh lliena el tankeh porr fabor?*

**324** Do you have a road map of this area?
¿Tiene un mapa de carreteras de la zona?
*¿Teeyene oon mapa deh karretehrras deh la thona?*

**325** How much is the car-wash?
¿Cuánto cuesta el lavado?
*¿Kwanto kwesta el labahdo?*

## Breakdowns

**326** I've had a breakdown at . . .
El coche se ha averiado en . . .
*El cotcheh seh ah aberyado en . . .*

**327** I am on the road from . . .
to . . .
Estoy en la carretera de . . .
a . . .
*Estoy en la karretehrra deh . . .
a . . .*

**328** I can't move the car. Can you
send a tow-truck?
El coche no se mueve. ¿Puede
enviar una grúa?
*El cotcheh noh seh mwehbeh.
¿Pwedeh embeeyar oona groo-ah?*

**329** I have a flat tyre.
He tenido un pinchazo.
*Eh tehneedo oom pintchatho.*

**330** The windscreen (windshield)
has smashed/cracked.
El parabrisas se ha hecho trizas/
se ha rajado.
*El parabreesas seh ah etcho
treethas/seh ah rahado.*

**331** There is something wrong
with the engine/brakes/
lights/steering/gearbox/
clutch/exhaust.
El motor/los frenos/las luces/la
dirección/la caja de cambios/el
embrague/el escape no funciona
bien.
*El motor/los frenos/las loothes/la
deerekthion/la caha deh cambyos/
el embrahge/el escape noh
foonthiona bien.*

**332** It's overheating.
Se sobrecalienta
*Seh sobrekalienta.*

**333** It won't start.
No arranca.
*Noh arranka*

**334** Where can I get it
repaired?
¿Dónde lo pueden arreglar?
*¿Dondeh lo pweden arreglar?*

**335** Can you take me there?
¿Me puede llevar allí?
*¿Meh pwedeh lliebar allyee?*

**336** Will it take long to fix?
¿Va a tardar mucho en
arreglarlo?
*¿Ba a tardahrr mootcho en
arreglarlo?*

**337** How much will it cost?
¿Cuanto me va a cobrar?
*¿Kwanto meh ba a kobrar?*

## Accidents

**338** Can you help me? There has
been an accident.
¿Me puede ayudar? Ha habido
un accidente.
*¿Meh pwedeh aiyoodahrr? Ah
ahbeedo oon akthidenteh.*

**339** Please call the police/an
ambulance.
Llame a la policía/ambulancia.
*Lliameh a la poleethee-ah/
amboolanthia*

**340** Is anyone hurt?
¿Se ha lastimado alguién?
*¿Seh ah lasteemado algyen?*

S
P
A
N
I
S
H

327
↕
340

311

## Traffic Offences

**341** **I'm sorry, I didn't see the sign.**
Lo siento, no me fijé en la señal.
*Lo seeyento, noh meh feeheh en el lehtrero.*

**342** **Must I pay a fine? How much?**
¿Tengo que pagar una multa? ¿Cuánto?
*¿Tengo keh pagar oona moolta? ¿Kwanto?*

**343** **Show me your documents.**
Enséñeme sus documentos.
*Ensehniemeh soos dokoomentos.*

## HEALTH

### Pharmacy

**344** **Do you have anything for a stomachache/headache/sore throat/toothache?**
¿Tienen algo para el dolor de estómago/cabeza/garganta/dientes?
*¿Teeyenen algo para el doelor de estoemago/cabeetha/garganta deeyentes?*

**345** **I need something for diarrhoea (diarrhea)/constipation/a cold/a cough/insect bites/sunburn/travel (motion) sickness.**
Necesito algo contra la diarrea/el estreñimiento/el catarro/la tos/las picaduras de insectos/la quemadura del sol/el mareo.
*Netheseeto algo contra la deeareea/el estrenyiemeeyento/el catarro/la tos/las peecadooras de insectos/la khemadoora del sol/el mareo.*

**346** **How much/how many do I take?**
¿Cuánto/cuántas tengo que tomar?
*¿Cwantoe/cwantas tengo kay toemar?*

**347** **How often do I take it/them?**
¿Cada cuánto tiempo tengo que tomarlo/tomarlas?
*¿Cada cwantoe teaenpo tengo kay toemarlo/toemarlas?*

**348** **How much does it cost?**
¿Cuánto cuesta?
*¿Cwantoe cwesta?*

**349** **Can you recommend a good doctor/dentist?**
¿Puede recomendarme un buen médico/dentista?
*¿Pwede recomendarmeh oon bwen meddeeco/denteesta?*

**350** **Is it suitable for children?**
¿Es adecuado para niños?
*¿Es adecwado para neenios?*

### Doctor

**351** **I have a pain here/in my arm/leg/chest/stomach.**
Tengo dolor aquí/en el brazo/la pierna/el pecho/el estómago.
*Tengo oon doelor akee/en el bratho/la peeyerna/el pecho/el estomago.*

# HEALTH

**352** Please call a doctor, this is an emergency.
Por favor, llamen a un médico, es una emergencia.
*Por farbor lliamen a oon meddeeco, es oona emerhentheea.*

**353** I would like to make an appointment to see a doctor.
Quisiera una cita para una consulta.
*Keyseeyera oona thita para oona consoolta.*

**354** I am diabetic/pregnant.
Soy diabético(a)/estoy embarazada.
*Soy deeabetteeko/estoy enbarathada.*

**355** I need a prescription for . . .
Necesito una receta para . . .
*Netheseeto oona rethetta para . . .*

**356** Can you give me something to ease the pain?
¿Puede darme algo para aliviar el dolor?
*¿Pwede darme algo para aleebear el doelor?*

**357** I am/he is/she is allergic to penicillin.
I am/he is/she is allergic to penicillin.
Soy/es alérgico/alérgica a la penicilina.
*Soy alerheeko/alerheeka a la peneetheeleena.*

**358** Does this hurt?
¿Le duele esto?
*¿Leh dweleh esto?*

**359** You must/he must/she must go to hospital.
Usted/él/ella tiene que ir al hospital.
*Oosteth/el/ellia teeyene keh eer al ospeetal.*

**360** Take these once/twice/three times a day.
Tome esto una vez/dos/tres veces al día.
*Tomeh esto oonah beth/dos/tres bethess al dee-ah.*

**361** I am/he is/she is taking this medication.
Estoy/está tomando este medicamento.
*Estoy/esta tomando esteh medeekamento.*

**362** I have medical insurance.
Tengo seguro médico.
*Tengo sehgooro mehdeeko.*

## Dentist

**363** I have toothache.
Tengo dolor de muelas/me duelen las muelas.
*Tengo dolor de mwelas/mey dwelen las mooeylas.*

**364** My filling has come out.
Se me ha caído un empaste.
*Se meh a cayeedo oon enpaste.*

**365** I do/do not want to have an injection first.
Quiero/no quiero que me den una inyección.
*Kiero/no kiero kay meh den oona inyecthion.*

S P A N I S H

352
↑
365

313

## EMERGENCIES

**366** Help!
¡Socorro!
*íSawkoro!*

**367** Call an ambulance/a doctor/
the police!
¡Llame a una ambulancia/un
médico/la policía!
*¡Lliame a oona anboolanthea/oon
meydico/la poletheea!*

**368** I have had my travellers
cheques (traveler's checks)/
credit cards/purse/handbag/
rucksack (knapsack)/
luggage/wallet stolen.
Me han robado los cheques de
viaje/las tarjetas de crédito/el
bolso/la mochila/el equipaje/el
billetero.
*Meh an robadoe los chekes dey
beahe/las tarhetas dey credeeto/el
bolso/la mocheela/el ekeypahe/el
bellietero.*

**369** Can you help me, I have lost
my daughter/son.
¿Puede ayudarme, se ha
extraviado mi hija/mi hijo.
*¿Pwede ajudarme, sey a
extrabeeado mee eekha/mee eekho?*

**370** Please go away/leave me
alone.
Por favor váyase/déjeme en
paz.
*Por farbor bayase/deheme en path.*

**371** Fire!
¡Fuego!
*¡Fwegoh!*

**372** I want to contact the British/
American/Canadian/Irish/
Australian/New Zealand/
South African consulate.
Quisiera llamar al consulado
británico/americano/
canadiense/irlandés/de Nueva
Zelanda/surafricano.
*Keyseeyera lliamar al konsoolado
britaneeko/amehreekano/
kanadeyenseh/eerlandess/deh
nweba theylanda/surafrikano.*

# Introduction

Turkish, brought to the shores of Europe from central-eastern Asia by the invading Ottomans, is unrelated to other European languages; although it contains modern words borrowed from English, the main linguistic influence over the centuries has been Arabic. Turkish uses a roman alphabet, albeit with a large number of accented characters, which was introduced this century as part of the modernising reforms which followed on the fall of the Ottoman Empire.

English, German and French are widely spoken in the cosmopolitan and tourist-frequented areas of Istanbul and the Aegean coast, but elsewhere you will need Turkish phrases.

**T
U
R
K
I
S
H**

### Addresses for travel and tourist information

**UK:** *Turkish Tourist Office*, First Floor, 170/173 Piccadilly, London W1V 9DD; tel: (0171) 734 8681/2.
**USA:** *Turkish Tourist Office*, 821 UN Plaza, New York, NY 10017; tel: (212) 687 2194/6.

# ESSENTIALS

## ESSENTIALS

### Alphabet

The letters Q, W and X are only used in describing foreign words.

| | |
|---|---|
| A | B |
| *ah* | *beh* |
| C | D |
| *jeh* | *deh* |
| E | F |
| *eh* | *feh* |
| G | H |
| *geh* | *heh* |
| I | J |
| *ee* | *zheh* |
| K | L |
| *keh* | *leh* |
| M | N |
| *meh* | *neh* |
| O | P |
| *o* | *peh* |
| Q | R |
| *qu* | *reh* |
| S | T |
| *seh* | *teh* |
| U | V |
| *u* | *veh* |
| W | X |
| *dueblueveh* | *iks* |
| Y | Z |
| *yeh* | *zeh* |

## Basic Words and Phrases

**1**  Yes — No
Evet — Hayır
*Evet* — *Hayer*

**2**  Please — Thank you
Lütfen — Teşekkür ederim
*Luetphen* — *Teshekkuer ederim*

**3**  That's O.K. — Perhaps
Bir şey değil — Belki
*Bir shey de'el* — *Belki*

**4**  To — From
e/a — den/dan
*e/a* — *dan/den*

**5**  Here — There
Burada — Orada
*Burada* — *Orada*

**6**  None — Also
Hiç — de/da
*Hich* — *de/da*

**7**  How — When
Nasıl — Ne zaman
*Nasel* — *Ne zaman*

**8**  What — Why
Ne — Neden
*Ne* — *Neden*

**9**  I don't understand.
Anlamıyorum.
*Anlameyourum.*

**10**  I don't speak Turkish.
Türkçe bilmiyorum.
*Tuerkche bilmiyourum.*

**11**  Do you speak English?
İngilizce biliyor musunuz?
*İnghilizh'dje biliyour musunuz?*

12 **Can you please write it down?**
Lütfen şuraya yazar mısınız?
*Luetfen shuraya yazar me'se'nez?*

13 **Can you please speak more slowly?**
Lütfen biraz daha yavaş konuşur musunuz?
*Luetfen biraz daha yavash konushur musunuz?*

14 **How much does it/this cost?**
O/Bu kaç para?
*O/Bu kach para?*

## Days

15 **Monday**          **Tuesday**
Pazartesi            Salı
*Pazartesi*          *Salae*

16 **Wednesday**       **Thursday**
Çarşamba             Perşembe
*Charshamba*         *Pershembe*

17 **Friday**          **Saturday**
Cuma                 Cumartesi
*Djuma*              *Djumartesi*

18 **Sunday**          **Morning**
Pazar                Sabah
*Pazar*              *Sabah*

19 **Afternoon**       **Evening**
öğleden sonra        Akşam
*Oe'leden sonra*     *Aksham*

20 **Night**           **Week**
Gece                 Hafta
*Ghedje*             *Haphta*

21 **Yesterday**       **Tomorrow**
Dün                  Yarın
*Duen*               *Yaren*

## Numbers

22 **Zero**            **One**
Sıfır                Bir
*Saephaer*           *Beer*

23 **Two**             **Three**
İki                  Üç
*Eki*                *Uech*

24 **Four**            **Five**
Dört                 Beş
*Doert*              *Besh*

25 **Six**             **Seven**
Altı                 Yedi
*Alte*               *Yedi*

26 **Eight**           **Nine**
Sekiz                Dokuz
*Sekiz*              *Dokuz*

27 **Ten**             **Eleven**
On                   On bir
*On*                 *On beer*

28 **Twelve**          **Thirteen**
On iki               On üç
*On eki*             *On uech*

29 **Fourteen**        **Fifteen**
On dört              On beş
*On doert*           *On besh*

30 **Sixteen**         **Seventeen**
On altı              On yedi
*On alte*            *On yedi*

31 **Eighteen**        **Nineteen**
On sekiz             On dokuz
*On sekiz*           *On dokuz*

TURKISH

12 ↑ 31

# ESSENTIALS

| | | | |
|---|---|---|---|
| **32** | **Twenty**<br>Yirmi<br>*Yirmi* | **Twenty-one**<br>Yirmi bir<br>*Yirmi beer* | |

**32 Twenty** **Twenty-one**
Yirmi Yirmi bir
*Yirmi* *Yirmi beer*

**33 Twenty-two** **Thirty**
Yirmi iki Otuz
*Yirmi eki* *Otuz*

**34 Forty** **Fifty**
Kırk Elli
*Kaerk* *Elli*

**35 Sixty** **Seventy**
Altmış Yetmiş
*Altmaesh* *Yetmish*

**36 Eighty** **Ninety**
Seksen Doksan
*Seksen* *Doksan*

**37 One hundred Five hundred**
Yüz Beş yüz
*Yuez* *Besh yuez*

**38 One thousand One million**
Bin Bir milyon
*Been* *Beer million*

## Time

**39 9.00**
Dokuz
*Dokuz*

**40 9.05**
Dokuzu beş geçiyor
*Dokuzu besh gechiyour*

**41 9.10**
Dokuzu on geçiyor
*Dokuzu on gechiyour*

**42 9.15**
Dokuzu onbeş geçiyor
*Dokuzu onbesh gechiyour*

**43 9.20**
Dokuzu yirmi geçiyor
*Dokuzu yirmi gechiyour*

**44 9.25**
Dokuzu yirmibeş geçiyor
*Dokuzu yirmibesh gechiyour*

**45 9.30**
Dokuz buçuk
*Dokuz buchuk*

**46 9.35**
Ona yirmibeş var
*Ona yirmibesh var*

**47 9.40**
Ona yirmi var
*Ona yirmi var*

**48 9.45**
Ona çeyrek var
*Ona cheyrek var*

**49 9.50**
Ona on var
*Ona on var*

**50 9.55**
Ona beş var
*Ona besh var*

**51 12.00/Midday/Midnight**
On iki/öğle üzeri/Gece yarısı
*Oneki/Oe'le uezeri/ghedje yarese*

**52 What time is it?**
Saat kaç?
*Saat kach?*

**53 It is . . .**
Saat . . .
*Saat . . .*

T
U
R
K
I
S
H

32
↑
53

## Airport

**54** **Excuse me, where is the check-in desk for . . . airline?**
Afedersiniz, . . . havayollarının çekin bürosu neresi acaba?
*Afedersiniz, . . . havayollarenen checkin buerosu ne'resi adjaba?*

**55** **What is the boarding gate/ time for my flight?**
Benim uçağımın biniş kapısı neresi/biniş saati kaç acaba?
*Benim ucha'emen binish kapese neresi/binish saati kach adjaba?*

**56** **How long is the delay likely to be?**
Uçağın gecikme süresi ne kadar acaba?
*Ucha'en gedjikme sueresi ne kadar adjaba?*

**57** **Where is the duty-free shop?**
Gümrüksüz mal satış yeri neresi acaba?
*Guemrueksuez mal satesh yeri ne'resi adjaba?*

**58** **Which way is the baggage reclaim?**
Bavulları alma yeri neresi acaba?
*Bavullare alma yeri neresi adjaba?*

**59** **Where can I get the bus to the city centre?**
Kentin merkezine otobüs nereden kalkıyor acaba?
*Kentin merkezine otobues nereden kalkeyor adjaba?*

## Train Station

**60** **Where is the ticket office/ information desk?**
Bilet gişesi nerede?/ Enformasyon masası nerede?
*Bilet gishesi nerede?/Enformasyon masase nerede?*

**61** **Which platform does the train to . . . depart from?**
. . . treni hangi perondan hareket ediyor?
*. . . treni hangi perondan hareket ediyor?*

**62** **Where is platform . . ?**
. . . peronu nerede?
*. . . peronu nerede?*

**63** **When is the next train to . . ?**
. . . treni ne zaman?
*. . . treni ne zaman?*

**64** **Is there a later train to . . ?**
. . . a/e başka tren var mı?
*. . . a/e bashka tren var mae?*

## Port

**65** **How do I get to the port?**
Limana nasıl gidebilirim?
*Leemana nasael gedebilirim?*

**66** **When is the next sailing to . . ?**
Bundan sonraki sefer kaçta?
*Bundan sonraki sepher kachta?*

T
U
R
K
I
S
H

# ARRIVING AND DEPARTING

**67** Can I catch an earlier ferry
with this ticket?
Bu biletle daha erken kalkan
feribota binebilir miyim?
*Bu biletle daha erken kalkan
feribota binebilir miyim?*

## Notices and Signs

**68** Büfe vagonu
*Beufe vagonu*
Buffet (Dining) Car

**69** Otobüs
*Otobeus*
Bus

**70** İçilir/içilmez su
*Echilir/echilmez su*
Drinking/ on-drinking water

**71** Giriş
*Girish*
Entrance

**72** Çıkış
*Chekesh*
Exit

**73** Enformasyon
*Enformasyon*
Information

**74** Emanet
*Emanet*
Left Luggage (Baggage Claim)

**75** Bagaj dolapları
*Bagadj dolaplare*
Luggage Lockers

**76** Postane
*Postane*
Post Office

**77** Peron
*Peron*
Platform

**78** Estasion
*Istasyon*
Railway (Railroad) Station

**79** Havaalanı
*Hava a'lane*
Airport

**80** Liman
*Liman*
Port

**81** Restoran
*Restoran*
Restaurant

**82** Sigara içilir/içilmez
*Sigara echilir/echilmez*
Smoking/Non-Smoking

**83** Telefon
*Telephon*
Telephone

**84** Bilet gişesi
*Beelet ghishese*
Ticket Office

**85** Çekin bürosu
*Checkin buerosu*
Check-in Desk

**86** Tarife
*Tarife*
Timetable (Schedule)

**87** Tuvaletler
*Tuvaletler*
Toilets (Restrooms)

320

**88 Erkekler**
*Erkekler*
Gentlemen

**89 Bayanlar**
*Baianlar*
Ladies'

**90 Tramvay**
*Trumvai*
Tram (Streetcar)

**91 Metro**
*Metro*
Underground (Subway)

**92 Bekleme Odası**
*Bekleme Odase*
Waiting Room

## Buying a Ticket

**93 I would like a first-class/ second-class single (one-way)/return (round-trip) ticket to . . .**
. . . e/a birinci/ikinci mevki sadece gidiş/gidiş geliş bileti istiyorum.
*. . . e/a beerindji/ekindji mevki sadedje ghedish/ghedish ghelis beelete estiyourum.*

**94 Is my rail pass valid on this train?**
Benim tren pasom bu trende/ feribotta/otobüste geçer mi?
*Benim teren pasom bu terende/ feribotta/otobueste gecher mi?*

**95 I would like an aisle/window seat.**

Pencere kenarında/koridor tarafında bir yer istiyorum.
*Pendjere koridoor/kenaraenda tarafaenda beer yer estiyourum.*

**96 No smoking/smoking, please.**
Sigara içilmez/sigara içilir, lütfen
*Sigara icheler/sigara echelmez, leutphen*

**97 We would like to sit together**
Yan yana oturmak istiyoruz.
*Yan yana otoormak estiyouruz*

**98 I would like to make a seat reservation.**
Bir yer ayırtmak istiyorum.
*Bir yer ayertmak istiyourum.*

**99 I would like to reserve a couchette/sleeper for one person/two people/for my family.**
Kuşetlide/yataklıda bir kişilik/ iki kişilik/ailem için yer ayırtmak istiyorum.
*Coushetleede/yataklaeda beer kishelik/eki kishelik yer ayeaertmak estiyourum.*

**100 I would like to reserve a cabin.**
Bir kabin ayırtmak istiyorum.
*Bir kabin ayertmak istiyourum.*

## Timetables (Schedules)

**101 Varış**
*Vareash*
Arrive

T
U
R
K
I
S
H

88
↑
101

**102 . . . da durur**
*. . . da durur*
Calls (Stops) at

**103 Lokanta**
*Lokanta*
Catering Service

**104 . . . da değiştirin**
*. . . da de'shtirin*
Change at

**105 Bağlantı**
*Ba'lantae*
Connection

**106 Günlük**
*Geunleuk*
Daily

**107 Her kırk dakikada bir**
*Haer kerk dakekada beer*
Every 40 Minutes

**108 Birinci mevki**
*Beerindji mevke*
First-class

**109 Saatte bir**
*Sa'atte beer*
Hourly

**110 Yer ayırtılması tavsiye edilir**
*Yer ayertelmase tavsiye edilir*
Seat reservations are recommended

**111 İkinci mevki**
*Ekinci mevki*
Second-class

**112 Ek ücret ödenir**
*Ek eudjret eadenir*
Supplement Payable

**113 Üzerinden**
*euzerinden*
Via

## Luggage

**114 How much will it cost to send (ship) my luggage in advance?**
Bagajımı önceden göndermek kaça mal olur?
*Baghadjaemae eandjeden geandermek kacha mal oleur?*

**115 Where is the left luggage (baggage claim) office?**
Emanet nerede?
*Emanet nerede?*

**116 What time do you open/close?**
Ne zaman açıyorsunuz/kapatıyorsunuz?
*Ne zaman achaeyoursunuz/kapataeyoursunuz?*

**117 Where are the luggage trolleys (carts)?**
Bagaj troleyleri nerede?
*Badghadj troleylere nerede?*

**118 Where are the lockers?**
Kilitli dolaplar nerede acaba?
*Kilitli dolaplar neresi adjaba?*

**119 I have lost my locker key.**
Dolap anahtarımı kaybettim.
*Dolap anahtaraeme kaibettim.*

## On Board

**120 Is this seat taken?**
Bu yer boş mu?
*Bu yer bosh mu?*

**121** Excuse me, you are sitting in my reserved seat.
Pardon, bana ayrılmış yerde oturuyorsunuz.
*Pardon, bana airaelmaesh yerde oturuyoursunuz.*

**122** Which station is this?
Bu hangi istasyon?
*Bu hange istasion?*

**123** What time is this train/bus/ferry/flight due to arrive/depart?
Bu tren/feribot/uçak saat kaçta gelecek/kalkacak?
*Bu teren/feribot/uchak sa't kachta gelecek/kalkadjak?*

**124** Will you wake me just before we arrive?
Varmadan önce beni uyandırır mısınız?
*Varmadan oendje beni uyandaeraer maesaeniz?*

## Customs and Passports

**125** Pasaportlar, lütfen!
*Pasaportlar luetphen!*
Passports, please!

**126** I have nothing/wine/spirits (alcohol)/tobacco to declare.
Gümrüğe tabi (hiçbir eşyam yok)/şarap/içki/tütün var.
*Geumreu'e tabe (hichbir eshiam yok)/sharap/eachki/tuetuen var.*

**127** I shall be staying for . . . days/weeks/months.
. . . gün/hafta/ay kalacağım.
*. . . guen/hafta/ai kaladja'em.*

## AT THE TOURIST OFFICE

**128** Do you have a map of the town/area?
Bu kentin/bölgenin haritası var mı?
*Bu kentin/boelgenin haritasae var mae?*

**129** Can I reserve accommodation here?
Burada kalacak yer ayırtabilir miyim?
*Beurada kaladjak yer ayaertabeler meyem?*

**130** Do you have a list of accommodation?
Kalacak yerlerin bir listesi var mı?
*Kaladjak yerlerin bir listesi var me?*

## ACCOMMODATION

## Hotels

**131** I have a reservation in the name of . . .
. . . adına rezervasyon yaptırmıştım.
*. . . adaena rezervasyon yaptaermaeshtaem.*

T
U
R
K
I
S
H

121
↑
131

323

# ACCOMMODATION

<sup>132</sup> I wrote to/faxed/telephoned you last month/last week in . . .
Geçen ay/geçen hafta size yazmıştım/faks çekmiştim/telefon etmiştim.
*Gechen ay/gechen hafta size yazmeshtem/fax chekmishtim/telephon etmishtim.*

<sup>133</sup> Do you have any rooms free?
Hiç boş odanız var mı?
*Hich bosh odanez var me?*

<sup>134</sup> I would like to reserve a single/double room with/without bath/shower.
Bir/iki kişilik banyolu/banyosuz duşlu/duşsuz oda ayırtmak istiyorum.
*Bir/iki kieshielik banyolu/dushlu banyosuz/dushsuz oda ayaertmak istiyourum.*

<sup>135</sup> I would like bed and breakfast/(room and) half board/(room and) full board.
Sadece kahvaltılı/kahvaltı ve bir öğün yemekli/üç öğün yemekli bir oda istiyorum.
*Sadedje kahvaltaelae/kahvaltae ve beer oe'oen yemekli/euch oe'oen yemekli oda istiyourum.*

<sup>136</sup> How much is it per night?
Gecesi kaça?
*Ghedjesi kacha?*

<sup>137</sup> Is breakfast included?
Kahvaltı dahil mi?
*Kahvaltae dahil me?*

<sup>138</sup> May I see the room?
Odayı görebilir miyim?
*Odayae goerebilir miim?*

<sup>139</sup> Do you have any cheaper rooms?
Daha ucuz odalarınız var mı?
*Daha oodjuz odalaraenaez var me*

<sup>140</sup> I would like to take the room
Odayı tutuyorum.
*Odayae tootooyorum.*

<sup>141</sup> I would like to stay for . . . nights.
. . . gece kalmak istiyorum.
*. . . gedje kalmak istiyourum*

<sup>142</sup> The shower/light/tap doesn't work.
Duş/elektrik/musluk bozuk galiba.
*Dush/electric/musluk bozuk ga'liba.*

<sup>143</sup> At what time/where is breakfast served?
Kahvaltı servisi nerede/ne zaman?
*Kahvaltee servisi nerede/ne zaman?*

<sup>144</sup> What time do I have to check-out?
Saat kaçta ayrılmam lazım?
*Sa'at kachta ayraelmam lazaem?*

<sup>145</sup> Can I have the key to room no . . ?
. . . numaralı odanın anahtarını rica ediyorum.
*. . . numarale odanen anakhtarene ridja ediyourum.*

324

**146** My room number is . . .
Oda numaram . . .
*Oda numaram . . .*

**147** Do you accept travellers'
cheques/Eurocheques/credit
cards?
Seyahat çeki/Euroçek/kredi
kartı kabul ediyor musunuz?
*Seyahat cheki/Eurocheck/kredi
karte kabul ediyor musunu ?*

**148** May I have the bill please?
Hesabı, lütfen
*Hesabee, luetphen.*

**149** Excuse me, I think there is a
mistake in this bill.
Afedersiniz, bu hesapta bir
yanlışlık var galiba.
*Afedersiniz, bu hesapta bir
yanleshlek var ga'liba.*

## Youth Hostels

**150** How much is a dormitory
bed per night?
Bir gecelik yatakhane ücreti ne
kadar?
*Beer ghedjelik yatakhane uedjreti
ne kadar?*

**151** I am/am not an HI member.
Uluslararası Gençlik Hostelleri
Birliği üyesiyim/üyesi değilim.
*Euluslararasae Ghenchlik Hostelleri
Beerli'e ueyesiim/ueyesi deelim.*

**152** May I use my own sleeping
bag?
Kendi uyku tulumumu
kullanabilir miyim?

*Kendi uyku tulumumu kullanabilir
miyim?*

**153** What time do you lock the
doors at night?
Gece kapıları kaçta
kilitliyorsunuz?
*Ghedje kapaelarae kachta
kilitliyoursunuz?*

## Camping

**154** May I camp here for the
night/two nights?
Burada bu gece/iki gece kamp
yapabilir miyim?
*Burada bu ghedje/eki ghedje kamp
yapabilir miyim?*

**155** Where can I pitch my tent?
Çadırımı nereye kurabilirim?
*Chadaeraemae nereye
kurabilirim?*

**156** How much does it cost for
one night/week?
Bir geceliği/bir haftalığı kaça?
*Beer ghedjeli'e/beer haftalae'e
kacha?*

**157** Where can we park our
caravan?
Karavanımızı nereye park
edebiliriz?
*Karava'nemezhe nereye park
edebiliriz?*

**158** Where are the washing
facilities?
Yıkanma yerleri nerede?
*Yaekanma yerleri nerede?*

**159** Is there a restaurant/
supermarket/swimming pool
on site/nearby?
Burada/yakında bir restoran/
çarşı/yüzme havuzu var mı?
*Burada/yakaenda bir restoran,
charshae/yuezme havuzu var
mae?*

**160** Do you have a safety deposit
box?
Kıymetli eşya için kasanız var
mı?
*Kaeymetli eshia eachin kasanaez
var mae?*

## EATING AND DRINKING

### Cafés and Bars

**161** I would like a cup of/two
cups of/another coffee/tea.
Bir fincan/iki fincan/bir fincan
daha kahve/çay istiyorum.
*Beer findjan/eki findjan/beer
findjan daha kahve/chai
istiyourum.*

**162** With/without milk/sugar.
Sütlü/şekerli (with), sütsüz/
şekersiz (without)
*Suetlue/shekerli, suetsuez/
shekersiz.*

**163** I would like a bottle/glass/
two glasses of mineral water/
red wine/white wine, please.
Bir şişe/bardak/iki şişe maden
suyu/kırmızı şarap/beyaz şarap
lütfen.

*Beer shishe/bardak/eki shishe
maden suyu/kaermaezae sharap/
beyaz sharap luethpen.*

**164** I would like a beer/two
beers, please.
Bir bira/iki bira lütfen.
*Beer beera/eki beera luethpen.*

**165** May I have some ice?
Biraz buz alabilir miyim?
*Biraz buz alabilir miyim?*

**166** Do you have any matches/
cigarettes/cigars?
Kibritiniz/sigaranız/puronuz
var mı?
*Kibritiniz/sigaranaez/pueronuz
var m?*

### Restaurants

**167** Can you recommend a good/
inexpensive restaurant in this
area?
Bu bölgede iyi/ucuz bir restoran
tavsiye eder misiniz?
*Bu boelgede eyi/udjuz beer
restoran tavsiye eder misiniz?*

**168** I would like a table for . . .
people.
. . . lik bir masa istiyorum.
*. . . lik beer masa istiyourum.*

**169** Do you have a non-smoking
area?
Sigara içilmeyen bir yeriniz var
mı?
*Sighara ichilmeyen bir yeriniz var
me?*

**170 Waiter/Waitress!**
Garson
*Garson*

**171 Do you have a set menu/
children's menu/wine list?**
Yemek listesi/çocuklar için
yemek listesi/şarap listesi var
mı?
*Yemek listesi/chodjuklar ichin
yemek listesi/sharap listesi var
mae?*

**172 Do you have any vegetarian
dishes, please?**
Etsiz yemekleriniz var mı?
*Etsiz yemekleriniz var mae?*

**173 Are there any local
specialities?**
Bu bölgeye has yemekler var
mı?
*Bu boelgheye has yemekler var me?*

**174 Are vegetables included?**
Garnitür de dahil mi?
*Garnituer de dahil mi?*

**175 Could I have it well-cooked/
medium/rare please?**
İyice kızartılmış/Normal/Az
pişmiş olsun lütfen.
*Iyidje kezartelmesh/Normal/Az
pishmish olsun luetfen.*

**176 What does this dish consist
of?**
Bu yemeğin içinde neler var?
*Bu yeme'en ichinde neler var?*

**177 I would like the set menu,
please.**
Tabldot lütfen.

*Tabldot luetphen.*

**178 We have not been served yet.**
Bize hala servis yapılmadı.
*Bize hala servis yapaelmadae.*

**179 Excuse me, this is not what I
ordered.**
Afedersiniz, benim ısmarladığım
bu değildi.
*Afedersiniz, benim esmarlade'em
bu de'ildi.*

**180 May I have some/some more
bread/water/coffee/tea?**
Biraz/biraz daha ekmek/su/
kahve/çay verir misiniz?
*Beeraz/beeraz daha ekmek/su/
kahve/chai verir misiniz?*

**181 May I have the bill, please?**
Hesap, lütfen?
*Hesap, luetphen?*

**182 Does this bill include service?**
Servis bu hesaba dahil mi?
*Servis bu hesaba dahil mi?*

**183 Do you accept travellers'
cheques (travelers' checks)/
Eurocheques/MasterCard/US
dollars?**
Seyahat çeki/Mastır kart/
Amerikan doları alıyor
musunuz?
*Seyahat cheki/master cart/
american dolarae alaeyour
musunuz?*

**184 Can I have a receipt, please?**
Bir makbuz rica etsem?
*Bir makbuz ridja etsem?*

TURKISH

170
↕
184

327

<sup>185</sup> Where is the toilet
(restroom), please?
Tuvalet nerede acaba?
*Tuvalet nerede adjaba?*

## On the Menu

<sup>186</sup> First courses
Aperitifler
*Aperitifler*

<sup>187</sup> Soups
Çorbalar
*Chorbalar*

<sup>188</sup> Main courses
Ana yemekler
*An'a yemekler*

<sup>189</sup> Fish dishes
Balık yemekleri
*Balek yemekleri*

<sup>190</sup> Meat dishes
Et yemekleri
*Et yemekleri*

<sup>191</sup> Vegetarian dishes
Sebze yemekleri
*Sebze yemekleri*

<sup>192</sup> Cheese
Peynir
*Peynir*

<sup>193</sup> Desserts
Tatlılar
*Tatlelar*

<sup>194</sup> Specialities
Buraya özgü yemekler
*Buraya oezgue yemekler*

## GETTING AROUND

## Public Transport

<sup>195</sup> Where is the bus stop/coach
station/nearest metro
(subway) station?
Otobüs durağı/otobüs
terminali/en yakın metro
istasyonu nerede?
*Otobues dura'ae/otobues
terminali/en yakaen metro
istasionu nerede?*

<sup>196</sup> When is the next/last bus
to . . ?
. . . e/a bundan sonraki otobüs
ne zaman?
*. . . e/a bundan sonrakee otobues
ne zaman?*

<sup>197</sup> How much is the fare to the
city centre (downtown)/
railway (railroad) station/
airport?
Şehir merkezine/tren
istasyonuna/hava alanına bilet
kaça?
*Shehir merkezine/tren istasionuna/
hava alanaena bilet kacha?*

<sup>198</sup> Will you tell me when to get
off?
Ne zaman ineceğimi söyler
misiniz?
*Ne zaman enedje'emi soeyler
misiniz?*

<sup>199</sup> Does this bus go to . . ?
Bu otobüs . . . a/e gidiyor mu?
*Bu otobues . . . a/e gidiyour mu?*

T
U
R
K
I
S
H

185
↕
199

**200** Which number bus goes
to . . ?
. . . ya/ye kaç numaralı
otobüs gidiyor?
*. . . ye/ya kach numaralae
otobues gidiyour?*

**201** May I have a single (one-
way)/return (round-trip)/day
ticket/book of tickets?
Gidiş/gidiş-geliş/günlük/koçan
halinde bilet istiyorum?
*Gidish/gidish-gelish/guenleuk/
kochan halinde bilet istiyourum?*

### Taxis

**202** I would like to go to . . . , how
much will it cost?
. . . a/e gitmek istiyorum, kaç
para tutar?
*. . . a/e ghitmek istiyourum, kach
para tutar?*

**203** Please stop here.
Burada durur musunuz.
*Burada durur musunuz.*

**204** I would like to order a taxi
today/tomorrow/at 2pm to
go from . . . to . . .
Bugün/yarın öğleden sonra saat
2'ye . . . den/dan . . . e/a taksi
ısmarlamak istiyorum.
*Buguen/yaraen oe'leden sonra
sa'at ikiye . . . den/dan . . . e/a taxi
aesmarlamak istiyourum.*

### Asking the Way

**205** Excuse me, do you speak
English?
Afedersiniz, Ingilizce biliyor
musunuz?
*Afedersiniz, engilizdje biliyor
musunuz?*

**206** Excuse me, is this the right
way to . . ?
Afedersiniz, . . .'e/a/ye/ya
buradan mı gidilir?
*Afedersiniz, . . .'e/a/ye/ya
buradan me gidilir?*

**207** . . . the cathedral/the tourist
information office/the castle/
the old town
. . . Katedral/turist
enformasyon bürosu/şato/eski
şehir
*. . . Cathedral/tourist
enformasyon buerosu/shato/eski
shehir*

**208** Can you tell me the way to
the railway station/bus
station/taxi rank (stand)/city
centre (downtown)/beach?
Istasyona/otobüs terminaline/
taksi durağına/şehir merkezine/
plaja nasıl gidilir, söyler misiniz?
*Estasyona/otobues terminaline/
taxi dura'aena/shehir merkezine/
paeladja nasael ghidilir, soeyler
misiniz?*

329

# GETTING AROUND/SIGHTSEEING/ENTERTAINMENT

**209** First/second left/right/
straight ahead.
Birinci/soldan ikinci/sağda/
dosdoğru.
*Beerindji/soldan ekindji/sa'da/
dosdo'ru.*

**210** Where is the nearest police
station/post office?
En yakın polis karakolu/postane
nerede?
*En yakaen polis karakolu/postaine
nerede?*

**211** Is it far?
Uzak mı?
*Uzak mae?*

**212** Do I need to take a taxi/
catch a bus?
Taksiye mi/otobüse mi binmem
gerekli?
*Taxiye me/otobuese me binmem
gherekle?*

**213** Can yo  point to it on my map?
Haritamın üzerinde gösterebilir
misiniz?
*Haritamaen uezerinde goesterebilir
misiniz?*

**214** Thank you for your help.
Yardımınız için teşekkür ederim.
*Yardaemaenaez ichin teshekkuer
ederim.*

## SIGHTSEEING

**215** Where is the Tourist
Information office?
Turist enformasyon bürosu
nerede?

*Tourist enformasion buerosu
nerede?*

**216** Where is the cathedral/
church/museum?
Katedral/Kilise/Müze nerede?
*Catedral/Kilise/Mueze nerede?*

**217** How much is the admission
charge?
Giriş ücreti ne kadar?
*Gherish eudjreti ne kadar?*

**218** Is there a reduction for
children/students/senior
citizens?
Çocuklara/öğrencilere/yaşlılara
indirim var mı?
*Chodjuklara/eurendjilere/
yashlaelara endirim var mae?*

**219** What time does the next
guided tour start?
Bundan sonraki kılavuzlu tur ne
zaman başlıyor?
*Bundan sonraki khaelavuzlu tour
ne zaman bashlaeyour?*

**220** One/two adults/children,
please.
Bir/iki büyük/çocuk, lütfen.
*Beer/eki bueyuek/chodjuk,
luetphen.*

**221** May I take photographs
here?
Burada resim çekebilir miyim?
*Burada resim chekebilir miyim?*

## ENTERTAINMENT

**222** Can you recommend a good
bar/nightclub?

209
↑
222

330

Iyi bir bar/gece kulübü tavsiye edebilir misiniz?
*Eyi bir bar/gedje kuluebue tavsiye edebilir misiniz?*

**223** **Do you know what is on at the cinema (playing at the movies)/theatre at the moment?**
Şu anda sinemada/tiyatroda ne oynuyor?
*Shu anda sinemada/teyatroda ne oynuyor?*

**224** **I would like to book (purchase) . . . tickets for the matinee/evening performance on Monday.**
Pazartesi günü öğle seansı/ akşam için . . . bilet ayırtmak istiyorum.
*Pazartesi guenue oe'le seansae/ aksham ichin . . . bilet ayaertmak istiyourum.*

**225** **What time does the film/ performance start?**
Film/gösteri kaçta başlıyor?
*Film/goesteri kachta bashleyour?*

## MEETING PEOPLE

**226** **Hello/Goodbye.**
Merhaba/Hoşça kal
*Merhaba/hoshcha kal*

**227** **Good morning/good afternoon/good evening/ goodnight.**
Günaydın/merhaba/iyi akşamlar/iyi geceler
*Guenayden/merhaba/iyi akshamlar/iyi gedjeler*

**228** **Pleased to meet you.**
Tanıştığımıza memnun oldum.
*Tanaeshtae'maeza memnun oldum.*

**229** **How are you?**
Nasılsınız?
*Nasaelsaenaez?*

**230** **Fine, thank you. And you?**
Teşekkür ederim, iyiyim. Siz nasılsınız?
*Teshekkuer ederim, iyiyim. Siz naselsenez?*

**231** **My name is . . .**
Adım . . .
*Adaem . . .*

**232** **This is my friend/boyfriend/ girlfriend/husband/wife/ brother/sister.**
Bu benim arkadaşım/erkek arkadaşım/kız arkadaşım/ kocam/karım/erkek kardeşim/ kız kardeşim
*Bu benim arkadashaem/erkek arkadashaem/kaez arkadashaem/ kodjam/karaem/erkek kardeshaem/kaez kardeshaem*

**233** **Where are you travelling to?**
Nereye gidiyorsunuz?
*Nereye ghidiyoursunuz?*

**234** **I am/we are going to . . .**
Ben/biz . . . e/a gidiyoruz.
*Ben/beez . . . e/a ghidiyoruz.*

T
U
R
K
I
S
H

223
↕
234

235 How long are you travelling for?
Kaç günlük bir geziye çıkıyorsunuz?
*Kach guenluek beer gheziye chekeyoursunuz?*

236 Where do you come from?
Neredensiniz?
*Neredensiniz?*

237 I am/we are from . . .
. . . den/dan
*. . . den/dan*

238 We're on holiday.
Tatildeyiz.
*Tatildeyiz.*

239 This is our first visit here.
İlk defa buraya geliyoruz.
*Ilk def'a buraya geliyouruz.*

240 Would you like/May I have a cigarette?
Sigara alır mısınız?/Sigara alabilir miyim?
*Sigara aler mesenez?/Sigara alabilir miyim?*

241 I am sorry, but I do not understand.
Kusura bakmayın, anlamıyorum.
*Kusura bakmayaen, anlameyourum.*

242 Please speak slowly.
Lütfen ağır ağır (tane tane/tek tek) söyleyin.
*Luetphen a'ar a'ar (tane tane/tek tek) soeyleyin.*

243 Do you mind if I smoke?
Sigara içmem sizi rahatsız eder mi?
*Sigara ichmem sizi rahatsaez eder mi?*

244 Do you have a light?
Kibritiniz/çakmağınız var mı?
*Kibritiniz/chakma'anaez var mae?*

245 I am waiting for my husband/wife/boyfriend/girlfriend.
Kocamı/eşimi/erkek arkadaşımı/kız arkadaşımı bekliyorum.
*Kodjame/eshimi/erkek arkadasheme/kez arkadasheme bekliyorum.*

## TRAVELLING WITH CHILDREN

246 Do you have a high chair/baby-sitting service/cot?
Bebek için sandalye/çocuk bakım servisi/karyola var mı?
*Bebek ichin sandalie/chodjuk bakem servisi/kariola var mae?*

247 Where is the nursery/playroom?
Çocuk yuvası/oyun odası nerede?
*Chodjuk yuvase/oyun odase nerede?*

248 Where can I warm the baby's bottle?
Biberonu nerede ısıtabilirim?
*Beeberonu nerede aesetabilirim?*

T
U
R
K
I
S
H

235
↑
248

332

## COMMUNICATIONS

### Post

**249** How much will it cost to send a letter/postcard/this package to Britain/Ireland/America/Canada/Australia/New Zealand?
Ingiltere'ye/Irlanda'ya/Amerika'ya/Kanada'ya/Avustralya'ya/Yeni Zelanda'ya mektup/kartpostal/bu paket kaça gider?
*Inghiltere'ye/Erlanda'ya/Amerika'ya/Kanada'ya/Avustralia'ya/Yeni Zelanda'ya mektup/cartpostal/bu paket kacha geder?*

**250** I would like one stamp/two stamps.
Bir pul/iki pul istiyorum.
*Bir pul/eki pul istiyourum.*

**251** I'd like . . . stamps for postcards to send abroad, please.
Yurt dışına kartpostal göndermek için . . . pul rica ediyorum.
*Yurt deshena kartpostal goendermek ichin . . . pul ridja ediyourum.*

### Phones

**252** I would like to make a telephone call/reverse the charges to (make a collect call to) . . .
Telefon etmek/ telefon etmek istiyorum.
*Telephon etmek/telephon etmek istiyourum.*

**253** Which coins do I need for the telephone?
Telefon için hangi parayı kullanmam lazım?
*Telephon ichin hangi parayae kullanmam lazaem?*

**254** The line is engaged (busy).
Hat meşgul.
*Hat meshgul*

**255** The number is . . .
Numara . . .
*Numara . . .*

**256** Hello, this is . . .
Alo, ben . . .
*Alo, ben . . .*

**257** May I speak to . . ?
. . .'i/ı/yi/yı rica edecektim.
*. . .'i/e/yi/ye ridja ededjektim.*

**258** He/She is not in at the moment. Can you call back?
Kendisi şimdi burada değil. Daha sonra arar mısınız?
*Kendisi shimdi burada de'il. Daha sonra arar mesenez?*

249
↑
258

TURKISH

# MONEY/SHOPPING

## MONEY

**259** I would like to change these travellers' cheques (travelers' checks)/this currency/this Eurocheque.
Bu seyahat çeklerini/bu parayı/bu Euro çeki bozdurmak istiyorum.
*Bu sey'ahat cheklerini/bu paray/bu Euro cheki bozdurmak istiyourum.*

**260** How much commission do you charge (what is the service charge)?
Ne kadar komisyon alıyorsunuz?
*Ne kadar komision alaeyoursunuz?*

**261** Can I obtain money with my MasterCard?
Master Kartla para alabilir miyim?
*Mastaer Cartla para alabilir miyim?*

## SHOPPING

### Names of Shops and Departments

**262** Kitapçı/kırtasiyeci
*Kitapche/kertasiyedji*
Bookshop/Stationery

**263** Mücevheratçı/Hediyelik eşya
*Muedjevheratche/Hediyelik eshya*
Jeweller's/Gifts

**264** Ayakkabılar/ayakkabı
*Ayakka'belar/ayakka'be*
Shoes

**265** Hırdavat
*Herdavat*
Hardware

**266** Antika eşya
*Antika eshya*
Antiques

**267** Erkek berberi/Kadın berberi
*Erkek berberi/Kaden berberi*
Hairdressers (men's)/(women's)

**268** Sigara bayii/tütüncü
*Sighara bayee/tuetuendjue*
Tobacconist

**269** Hamur işleri/Fırın
*Hamur ishleri/Feren*
Baker's

**270** Süpermarket
*Suepermarket*
Supermarket

**271** Fotoğrafçı
*Photo'rafche*
Photoshop

**272** Oyuncaklar
*Oyundjaklar*
Toys

**273** Seyahat Acentası
*Seyahat Adjenta'se*
Travel Agent

**274** Makyaj malzemeleri
*Makiazh maldzemeleri*
Toiletries

TURKISH

↕
274

**275 Plaklar**
*Pilaklar*
Records

## In the Shop

**276 What time do the shops open/close?**
Dükkanlar ne zaman açılır/kapanır?
*Duekkanlar ne zaman a heler/kapanaer?*

**277 Where is the nearest market?**
En yakın alışveriş merkezi/pazar neresi?
*En yaken aleshverish merkedzi/padzar neresi?*

**278 Can you show me the one in the window/this one?**
Vitrindekini/bunu görmek istiyorum.
*Vitrindekini/bunu goermek istiyourum.*

**279 Can I try this on?**
Bunu prova edebilir miyim?
*Bunu prova edebilir miim?*

**280 What size is this?**
Bunun numarası kaç?
*Bunun numarase kach?*

**281 This is too large/too small/too expensive.**
Bu çok büyük/çok küçük/çok pahalı
*Bu chok bueyuek/chok kuechuek/chok paha'le*

**282 Do you have any others?**
Başka çeşitleriniz de var mı?
*Bashka cheshitleriniz de var me?*

**283 My size is . . .**
Benim ölçüm . . .
*Benim oelchuem . . .*

**284 Where is the changing room/childrens/cosmetic/ladieswear/menswear/food department?**
Giyinme odaları/çocuk/kozmetik eşya/bayan giysileri/erkek giysileri/yiyecek bölümü nerede?
*Giyinme odalarae/chodjuk/kozmetik eshia/bayan giysileri/erkek giysileri/yiyedjek boeluemue nerede?*

**285 I would like . . .**
. . . istiyorum/rica edecektim.
*. . . istiyourum/ridja ededjektim.*

**286 I would like a quarter of/half a kilo/a kilo of bread/ butter/cheese/ham/tomatoes.**
İkiyüzelli gram/yarım kilo/bir kilo ekmek/tereyağ/peynir/jambon/domates istiyorum.
*Ekiyuezelli gram/yarem kilo/bir kilo ekmek/tereya' peinir/djambon/domates estiyourum.*

**287 How much is this?**
Kaça?
*Kacha?*

**288 I'll take this one, thank you.**
Bunu alacağım, teşekkür ederim.
*Bunu aladja'em, teshekkuer ederim.*

**289** Do you have a carrier (shopping) bag?
Plastik torbanız var mı?
*Plastic torbanez var me?*

**290** Do you have anything cheaper/larger/smaller/of better quality?
Daha ucuz/büyük/küçük/iyi kalite bir şeyiniz var mı?
*Daha eudjuz/bueyuek/kuechuek/ eyi kalite bir sheyiniz var mi?*

**291** I would like a film for this camera.
Bu makineye bir film istiyorum.
*Bu makineye bir film istiyourum.*

**292** I would like some batteries, the same size as this old one.
Bunlarla aynı büyüklükte yeni pil istiyorum.
*Bunlarla ayne bueyuekluekte peel istiyourum.*

**293** Would you mind wrapping this for me, please?
Lütfen bunu sarar mısınız?
*Luetphen bunu sarar mesenez?*

**294** Sorry, but you seem to have given me the wrong change.
Kusura bakmayın ama paranın üstünü yanlış verdiniz.
*Kusura baknayen ama paranen uestuenue yanlesh verdiniz.*

## MOTORING

### Car Hire (Rental)

**295** I have ordered (rented) a car in the name of . . .
. . . adına araba ısmarladım.
*. . . adaena araba aesmarladaem.*

**296** How much does it cost to hire (rent) a car for one day/ two days/one week?
Bir günlük/iki günlük/bir haftalık araba kiralama ücreti ne kadar?
*Beer guenluek/eki guenluek/beer haftalaek araba kiralama eudjreti ne kadar?*

**297** Is the tank already full of petrol (gas)?
Benzin deposu dolu mu?
*Benzin deposu dolu mu?*

**298** Is insurance and tax included? How much is the deposit?
Sigorta ve vergi dahil mi? Depozit ne kadar?
*Sigorta ve verghi dahil me? Depozit ne kadar?*

**299** By what time must I return the car?
Arabayı ne zamana kadar geri getirmem lazım?
*arabayae ne zamana kadar geri ghetirmem lazaem?*

**300** I would like a small/family car with a radio/cassette player.

336

Radyolu/teypli küçük bir araba/
aile arabası istiyorum.
*Radiolu/teipli kuechuk beer araba/*
*aile arabasae istiyourum.*

## Asking the Way

**301 Excuse me, can you help me
please?**
Afedersiniz, sizden bir ricada
bulunacaktım.
*Afedersiniz, sizden bir ridjada*
*bulunadjaktem.*

**302 How do I reach the
motorway/main road?**
Otobana/ana yola nasıl
çıkabilirim?
*Autoba'na/ana yola nasel*
*chekabilirim?*

**303 I think I have taken the
wrong turning.**
Galiba yanlış yerden/kavşaktan
dönüş yaptım.
*Ga'liba yanlesh yerden/*
*kavshaktan doenuesh yaptem.*

**304 I am looking for this address.**
Şu adresi arıyorum.
*Shu adresi a'reyourum.*

**305 I am looking for the . . . hotel.**
. . . oteli/otelini arıyorum.
*. . . oteli/otelini a'reyourum.*

**306 How far is it to . . . from
here?**
Buradan . . .'e/a/ye/ya mesafe/
uzaklık ne kadar?
*Buradan . . .'e/a/ye/ya mesa'fe/*
*uzhaklek ne kadar?*

**307 Carry straight on for . . .
kilometres.**
Dosdoğru . . . kilometre daha
gidin/sürün.
*Dosdo'ru . . . kilometre daha*
*ghidin/sueruen.*

**308 Take the next turning on the
right/left.**
Bundan sonraki sapaktan/
dönemeçten sağa/sola dönün/
sapın.
*Bundan sonra'ki sapaktan/*
*doenemechten sa'a/sola doenuen/*
*sa'pen.*

**309 Turn right/left at the next
crossroads/traffic lights.**
Bundan sonraki kavşaktan/trafik
ışıklarından sağa/sola sapın.
*Bundan sonra'ki kavshaktan/*
*traffic eshekla'rendan sa'a/sola*
*sapen.*

**310 You are going in the wrong
direction.**
Ters yönde gidiyorsunuz.
*Ters yoende ghidiyoursunuz.*

## Parking

**311 How long can I park here?**
Burada ne kadar süreyle/kaç
saat park edebilirim.
*Burada ne kadar suereyle/kach sa't*
*park edebilirim?*

**312 Is there a car park near here?**
Yakınlarda bir otopark var mı?
*Yakenlarda bir autopark var me?*

### 313 At what time does this car park close?

Bu otopark saat kaçta kapanıyor?

*Bu autopark sa't kachta kapa'neyor?*

## Signs and Notices

### 314 Tek yön

*Tek yoen*

One way

### 315 Girilmez/Girmek yasaktır

*Ghirilmez/Girmek yasakter*

No entry

### 316 Park yapılmaz/Park etmek yasaktır

*Park yapelmaz/Park etmek yasakter*

No parking

### 317 Zorunlu sapış

*Zhorunlu sapesh*

Detour (diversion)

### 318 Dur!

*Dur!*

Stop!

### 319 Yol ver

*Yol ver*

Give way (yield)

### 320 Kaygan yol

*Kayghan yol*

Slippery road

### 321 Sollama yapılmaz.

*Sol'lama yapelmez*

No overtaking

## At the Filling Station

### 322 Unleaded (lead-free)/ Standard/Premium

Kurşunsuz/Normal/Süper

*Kurshunsuz/Normal/Sueper*

### 323 Fill the tank please.

Depoyu doldurun lütfen.

*Depoyu doldurun luetfen.*

### 324 Do you have a road map of this area?

Sizde bu yörenin yol haritası var mı?

*Sizde bu yoerenin yol harita'se var me?*

### 325 How much is the car-wash?

Araba kaça yıkanıyor?

*Araba kacha yeka'neyor?*

## Breakdowns

### 326 I've had a breakdown at . . .

. . .'de/da arabam bozuldu.

*. . .'de/da arabam bozhuldu.*

### 327 I am on the road from . . . to . . .

. . .'den/dan . . .'e/a/ye/ya giden yol üzerindeyim.

*. . .'den/dan . . .'e/a/ye/ya ghiden yol uezerindeyim.*

### 328 I can't move the car. Can you send a tow-truck?

Arabayı çekemiyorum. Bir çekme aracı gönderebilir misiniz?

T
U
R
K
I
S
H

313
↑
328

*Arabaye che'kemiyourum. Bir chekme aradje goenderebilir misiniz?*

**329** I have a flat tyre.
Lastiğim patladı.
*Lasti'im patla'de.*

**330** The windscreen (windshield) has smashed/ cracked.
Ön cam kırıldı/çatladı.
*Oen djam ke'relde/chatla'de.*

**331** There is something wrong with the engine/brakes/ lights/steering/gearbox/ clutch/exhaust.
Motorda/frenlerde/ışıklarda/ direksiyonda/vites kutusunda/ debriyajda/egzosta bir arıza var galiba.
*Motorda/frenlerde/esheklerde/ direxiyonda/vites kutusunda/ debriyazhda/eghzosta bir areza var ga'liba.*

**332** It's overheating.
Motor fazla ısınmış/su kaynatıyor.
*Motor fazla esenmesh/su kayna'teyor.*

**333** It won't start.
Araba çalışmıyor/Marş basmıyor.
*Araba chaleshmeyor/Marsh basmeyor.*

**334** Where can I get it repaired?
Nerede tamir ettirebilirim?
*Ne're'de tamir etti'rebilirim?*

**335** Can you take me there?
Beni oraya götürebilir misiniz?
*Beni oraya goetuerebilir misiniz?*

**336** Will it take long to fix?
Tamiri/takması uzun sürer mi?
*Tamiri/takma'se uzhun suerer mi?*

**337** How much will it cost?
Kaça çıkar/malolur?
*Kacha chekar/malolur?*

## Accidents

**338** Can you help me? There has been an accident.
Bir kaza oldu. Bana yardım edebilir misiniz?
*Bir kazha oldu. Bana yardem e'debilir misiniz?*

**339** Please call the police/an ambulance.
Lütfen polisi/bir ambulans çağırın.
*Luetfen polisi/bir ambulans cha'eren.*

**340** Is anyone hurt?
Yaralı var mı?
*Yara'le var me?*

## Traffic Offences

**341** I'm sorry, I didn't see the sign.
Özür dilerim, işareti görmedim.
*Oezuer dilerim, isha'reti goermedim.*

TURKISH

329
↑
341

**342 Must I pay a fine? How much?**
Para cezası mı ödemem gerekiyor? Kaç para?
*Para djeza'se me oedemem ghe'rekiyor? Kach para?*

**343 Show me your documents.**
Ehliyetinizi/belgelerinizi gösterin.
*Ehliyetinizhi/belghe'lerinizhi goesterin.*

## HEALTH

### Pharmacy

**344 Do you have anything for a stomachache/headache/sore throat/toothache?**
Mide/baş ağrısı/boğaz ağrısı/diş ağrısı için bir ilacınız var mı?
*Mee'de/bash a'raesae/bo'az a'raesae/dish a'raesae ichin bir eladjaenaez var mae?*

**345 I need something for diarrhoea (diarrhea)/constipation/a cold/a cough/insect bites/sunburn/travel (motion) sickness.**
Ishal/kabız/soğuk algınlığı/öksürük/böcek ısırması/güneş yanığı/otobüs tutması için bir şey istiyorum.
*Eshaal/kabaez/so'uk algaenlae'ae/oeksueruek/boedjek aesaermasae/guenesh yanae'ae/otobues tutmasae ichin bir shei estiyourum.*

**346 How much/how many do I take?**
Ne kadar/kaç tane alayım?
*Ne kadar/kach tane alayeem?*

**347 How often do I take it/them?**
Ne kadar aralıklarla alayım?
*Ne kadar aralaeklarla alayeem?*

**348 How much does it cost?**
Kaç para?
*Kach para?*

**349 Can you recommend a good doctor/dentist?**
İyi bir doktor/dişçi tavsiye edebilir misiniz?
*Eyi bir doktor/dishchi tavsiye edebilir misiniz?*

**350 Is it suitable for children?**
Çocuklara uygun mu?
*Chodjuklara uygun mu?*

### Doctor

**351 I have a pain here/in my arm/leg/chest/stomach.**
Şuram/kolum/ayağım/göğsüm/karnım ağırıyor.
*Shuram/kolum/aya'aem/goe'suem/karnaem a'raeyour.*

**352 Please call a doctor, this is an emergency!**
Lütfen doktor çağırın, acil bir vak'a!
*uetphen doktor cha'raen, adjil beer vak'a!*

342
↕
352

**353** I would like to make an
appointment to see a doctor.
Doktoru görmek için randevu
almak istiyorum.
*Doctoru goermek ichin randevu
almak estiyourum.*

**354** I am diabetic/pregnant.
Şeker hastasıyım/hamileyim.
*Sheker hastasaeyaem/hamileyim.*

**355** I need a prescription for . . .
. . . için reçete istiyorum.
*. . . ichin rechete estiyourum.*

**356** Can you give me something
to ease the pain?
Ağrıyı azaltacak bir şey
verebilir misiniz?
*A'raeyae azaltadjak bershey
verebilir misiniz?*

**357** I am/he is/she is allergic to
penicillin.
Benim/onun/onun penisiline
karşı alerjim/alerjisi var.
*Benim/onun/onun penicillin'e
karshe allergim/allergisi var.*

**358** Does this hurt?
Acıtıyor mu?
*Adje'teyor mu?*

**359** You must/he must/she must
go to hospital.
Hastaneye gitmelisiniz/gitmeli.
*Hasta'neye ghitmelisiniz/ghitmeli.*

**360** Take these once/twice /three
times a day.
Bundan günde bir/iki/üç kere
alın.

Bundan guende bir/iki/uech ke're
a'len.

**361** I am/he is/she is taking this
medication.
Ben/o/o bu ilaçları alıyorum/
alıyor.
*Ben/o/o bu ilachla're a'leyourum.*

**362** I have medical insurance.
Sağlık sigortam var.
*Sa'lek sighortam var.*

## Dentist

**363** I have toothache.
Dişim ağrıyor.
*Dishim a'raeyour.*

**364** My filling has come out.
Dolgum düştü.
*Dolgum dueshtue.*

**365** I do/do not want to have an
injection first.
önceden iğne istiyorum/
istemiyorum.
*Oendjeden e'ne estiyourum/
estemiyourum.*

## EMERGENCIES

**366** Help!
İmdat!/Yardım!
*Imdat/Yardaem!*

**367** Call an ambulance/a doctor/
the police!
Ambulans/doktor/polis çağırın!
*Ambulance/doctor/police cha'ren!*

³⁶⁸ I have had my travellers'
cheques (travelers' checks)/
credit cards/purse/handbag/
rucksack (knapsack)/
luggage/wallet stolen.
Seyahat çeklerim/kredi
kartlarım/çantam/el çantam/sırt
çantam/bagajım/cüzdanım
çalındı.
*Sey'ahat cheklerim/credi
cartlarem/chantam/el chantam/
saert chantam/bagadjem/
djuezdanem chalendae.*

³⁶⁹ Can you help me, I have lost
my daughter/son?
Bana yardım eder misiniz,
kızımı/oğlumu kaybettim.
*Bana yardem eder misiniz,
kezeme/o'lumu kaybettim.*

³⁷⁰ Please go away/leave me
alone.

Lütfen gidin/beni yalnız
bırakın.
*Luetphen ghidin/beni yalnaez
baeraken.*

³⁷¹ Fire!
Yangın!
*Yanghen!*

³⁷² I want to contact the British/
American/Canadian/Irish/
Australian/New Zealand/
South African consulate.
İngiliz/Amerikan/Kanada/
İrlanda/Avustralya/Yeni
Zelanda/Güney Afrika
konsolosluğuyla görüşmek
istiyorum.
*Inghilizh/Amerikan/Kanada/
Irlanda/Yeni Zhelanda/Gueney
Afrika konsoloslu'yla goerueshmek
istiyourum.*

TURKISH

368
↕
372

# International Time

Winter time: last weekend in September–last weekend in March.
Summer time: last weekend in March–last weekend in September.

| WINTER: | GMT | GMT + 1 | GMT + 2 | GMT + 3 |
|---|---|---|---|---|
| SUMMER: | GMT + 1 | GMT + 2 | GMT + 3 | GMT + 4 |
| | Canary Isles | Albania | Belarus | Georgia |
| | Faroes | Croatia | Cyprus | Russia |
| | Iceland * | France | Finland | (European) |
| | Ireland ** | Hungary | Latvia | |
| | UK ** | Poland | Moldova | |
| | | Spain | Turkey | |
| | | Austria | Bulgaria | |
| | | Czech Republic | Estonia | |
| | | Germany | Greece | |
| | | Italy | Lithuania | |
| | | Netherlands | Romania | |
| | | Portugal | Ukraine | |
| | | Sweden | | |
| | | Yugoslavia | | |
| | | Belgium | | |
| | | Denmark | | |
| | | Gibraltar | | |
| | | Luxembourg | | |
| | | Norway | | |
| | | Slovakia | | |
| | | Slovenia | | |
| | | Switzerland | | |

\* Summer time ends in October        \*\*GMT all year

| | |
|---|---|
| Midnight depart | = 0000 |
| 1 am | = 0100 |
| 5 am | = 0500 |
| 5.30 am | = 0530 |
| 11 am | = 1100 |
| 12 noon | = 1200 |
| 1 pm | = 1300 |
| 3.45 pm | = 1545 |
| Midnight arrive | = 2400 |

343

# Weather

The weather in Europe is generally mild and pleasant although it varies greatly between the north and the south and between the east and the west. Temperature is also affected by altitude.

Highest = Average highest daily temperature in °C.
Lowest = Average lowest daily temperature in °C.

|  | London | Rome | Stockholm | Budapest |
|---|---|---|---|---|
| **JANUARY** | | | | |
| Highest | 6 | 12 | 2 | 0 |
| Lowest | 1 | 4 | -4 | -5 |
| Rain days | 15 | 8 | 7 | 8 |
| **APRIL** | | | | |
| Highest | 13 | 20 | 17 | 7 |
| Lowest | 4 | 8 | 6 | 0 |
| Rain days | 13 | 6 | 8 | 6 |
| **JULY** | | | | |
| Highest | 22 | 31 | 28 | 21 |
| Lowest | 12 | 18 | 16 | 13 |
| Rain days | 13 | 3 | 7 | 9 |
| **OCTOBER** | | | | |
| Highest | 14 | 23 | 16 | 9 |
| Lowest | 6 | 11 | 7 | 4 |
| Rain days | 16 | 9 | 8 | 9 |

## TEMPERATURE

| °C | °F | | °C | °F |
|---|---|---|---|---|
| -20 | -4 | | 10 | 50 |
| -15 | 5 | | 15 | 59 |
| -10 | 14 | | 20 | 68 |
| -5 | 23 | | 25 | 77 |
| 0 | 32 | | 30 | 86 |
| 5 | 41 | | 35 | 95 |
| | | | 40 | 104 |

**Conversion formulae**

$$°C \times 9 \div 5 + 32 = °F$$
1 Deg. °C = 1.8 Deg. °F
1 Deg. °F = 0.55 Deg. °C

## DISTANCE

| km | miles | km | miles | km | miles |
|---|---|---|---|---|---|
| 1 | 0.62 | 40 | 24.85 | 500 | 310.69 |
| 2 | 1.24 | 50 | 31.07 | 600 | 372.82 |
| 3 | 1.86 | 60 | 37.28 | 700 | 434.96 |
| 4 | 2.49 | 70 | 43.50 | 800 | 497.10 |
| 5 | 3.11 | 80 | 49.71 | 900 | 559.23 |
| 6 | 3.73 | 90 | 55.92 | 1000 | 621.37 |
| 7 | 4.35 | 100 | 62.14 | 1100 | 683.54 |
| 8 | 4.97 | 125 | 77.67 | 1200 | 745.68 |
| 9 | 5.59 | 150 | 93.21 | 1300 | 807.82 |
| 10 | 6.21 | 175 | 108.74 | 1400 | 869.96 |
| 15 | 9.32 | 200 | 124.27 | 1500 | 932.10 |
| 20 | 12.43 | 300 | 186.41 | 2000 | 1242.74 |
| 30 | 18.64 | 400 | 248.45 | 3000 | 1864.11 |

1 Kilometre = 0.6214 Miles
1 Mile = 1.609 Kilometres

## WEIGHT

| Unit | Kilograms | Pounds |
|---|---|---|
| 1 | 0.45 | 2.205 |
| 2 | 0.90 | 4.405 |
| 3 | 1.35 | 6.614 |
| 4 | 1.80 | 8.818 |
| 5 | 2.25 | 11.023 |
| 6 | 2.70 | 13.227 |
| 7 | 3.15 | 15.432 |
| 8 | 3.60 | 17.636 |
| 9 | 4.05 | 19.840 |
| 10 | 4.50 | 22.045 |
| 15 | 6.75 | 33.068 |
| 20 | 9.00 | 44.889 |
| 50 | 22.50 | 110.225 |
| 100 | 45.00 | 220.450 |

1 kilogram (kg) = 1000 grammes (g)
100g = 3.5 oz.
1 oz. = 28.35 g.
1 lb = 453.60 g.

## FLUID MEASURES

| Litres | Imp. gal. | US gal. |
|---|---|---|
| 5 | 1.1 | 1.3 |
| 10 | 2.2 | 2.6 |
| 15 | 3.3 | 3.9 |
| 20 | 4.4 | 5.2 |
| 25 | 5.5 | 6.5 |
| 30 | 6.6 | 7.8 |
| 35 | 7.7 | 9.1 |
| 40 | 8.8 | 10.4 |
| 45 | 9.9 | 11.7 |
| 50 | 11.0 | 13.0 |

1 litre (l) = 0.88 imp. quarts
1 litre (l) = 1.06 US quarts
1 imp. quart = 1.14 l
1 imp. gallon = 4.55 l
1 US quart = 0.95 l
1 US gallon = 3.81 l

# REFERENCE SECTION

## METRES AND FEET

| Unit | Metres | Feet |
|------|--------|------|
| 1 | 0.30 | 3.281 |
| 2 | 0.61 | 6.563 |
| 3 | 0.91 | 9.843 |
| 4 | 1.22 | 13.124 |
| 5 | 1.52 | 16.403 |
| 6 | 1.83 | 19.686 |
| 7 | 2.13 | 22.967 |
| 8 | 2.44 | 26.248 |
| 9 | 2.74 | 29.529 |
| 10 | 3.05 | 32.810 |
| 12 | 3.66 | 39.372 |
| 18 | 5.49 | 59.058 |
| 20 | 6.10 | 65.520 |
| 50 | 15.24 | 164.046 |
| 75 | 22.86 | 246.069 |
| 100 | 30.48 | 328.092 |

## LADIES' CLOTHES SIZES

| UK | France, Italy, Rest of Europe | USA |
|----|-------------------------------|-----|
| 10 | 36, 38, 34 | 8 |
| 12 | 38, 40, 36 | 10 |
| 14 | 40, 42, 38 | 12 |
| 16 | 42, 44, 40 | 14 |
| 18 | 44, 46, 42 | 16 |
| 20 | 46, 48, 44 | 18 |

## MEN'S SUIT SIZES

| UK | Europe | USA |
|----|--------|-----|
| 36 | 46 | 36 |
| 38 | 48 | 38 |
| 40 | 50 | 40 |
| 42 | 52 | 42 |
| 44 | 54 | 44 |
| 46 | 56 | 46 |

## LADIES' SHOE SIZES

| UK | Europe | USA |
|----|--------|-----|
| 3 | 36 | 4.5 |
| 4 | 37 | 5.5 |
| 5 | 38 | 6.5 |
| 6 | 39 | 7.5 |
| 7 | 40 | 8.5 |

## MEN'S SHOE SIZES

| UK | Europe | USA |
|----|--------|-----|
| 6 | 40 | 7 |
| 7 | 41 | 8 |
| 8 | 42 | 9 |
| 9 | 43 | 10 |
| 10 | 44 | 11 |
| 11 | 45 | 12 |

## MEN'S SHIRT SIZES

| UK | Europe | USA |
|------|--------|------|
| 14 | 36 | 14 |
| 15 | 38 | 15 |
| 15.5 | 39 | 15.5 |
| 16 | 41 | 16 |
| 16.5 | 42 | 16.5 |

## INCHES AND CENTIMETRES

| Unit | Inches | Feet | Yards |
|--------|--------|------|-------|
| 1mm | 0.039 | 0.003 | 0.001 |
| 1cm | 0.39 | 0.03 | 0.01 |
| 1metre | 39.40 | 3.28 | 1.09 |

| Unit | mm | cm | metres |
|--------|-------|-------|--------|
| 1 inch | 25.4 | 2.54 | 0.025 |
| 1 foot | 304.8 | 30.48 | 0.304 |
| 1 yard | 914.4 | 91.44 | 0.914 |

To convert cms into inches, multiply by 0.3937
To convert inches into cms, multiply by 2.54